RESPECTABLE CITIZENS: GENDER, FAMILY,
AND UNEMPLOYMENT IN ONTARIO'S GREAT DEPRESSION

High unemployment rates, humiliating relief policy, and the spectre of eviction characterized the experiences of many Ontario families in the Great Depression. *Respectable Citizens* is an examination of the material difficulties and survival strategies of families facing poverty and unemployment as well as an analysis of how collective action and protest redefined the meanings of welfare and citizenship in the 1930s.

Lara Campbell draws on diverse sources including newspapers, family and juvenile court records, premiers' papers, memoirs, and oral histories to uncover the ways in which the material workings of the family and the discursive category of 'respectable' citizenship were invested with gendered obligations and Anglo-British identity. *Respectable Citizens* demonstrates how women and men represented themselves as entitled to make specific claims on the state, shedding new light on the cooperative and conflicting relationships between men and women, parents and children, and citizen and state in 1930s Canada.

LARA CAMPBELL is an assistant professor in the Department of Women's Studies at Simon Fraser University.

STUDIES IN GENDER AND HISTORY

General Editors: Franca Iacovetta and Karen Dubinsky

LARA CAMPBELL

Respectable Citizens

Gender, Family, and Unemployment
in Ontario's Great Depression

UNIVERSITY OF TORONTO PRESS
Toronto Buffalo London

ISNB 978-08020-9974-7 (cloth)
ISBN 978-08020-9669-2 (paper)

Printed on acid-free, 100% post-consumer recycled paper with vegetable-based inks.

Library and Archives Canada Cataloguing in Publication

Campbell, Lara, 1970–
   Respectable citizens: gender, family. and unemployment in Ontario's
   Great Depression / Lara Campbell.

(Studies in gender and history)
Includes bibliographical references and index.
ISBN 978-0-8020-9974-7 (bound).   ISBN 978-0-8020-9669-2 (pbk.)

1. Unemployed – Ontario – Social conditions – 20th century.   2. Women –
Ontario – Social conditions – 20th century.   3. Family – Ontario – Social
conditions – 20th century.   4. Unemployed – Services for – Ontario – History
– 20th century.   5. Ontario – Economic conditions – 1918–1945.   6. Ontario –
Social conditions – 1918–1945.   7. Ontario – History – 1918–1945.   I. Title.
II. Series: Studies in gender and history

HB3717.1929C26 2009   305.9′06940971309043   C2009-903294-5

University of Toronto Press acknowledges the financial assistance to its publishing program of the Canada Council for the Arts and the Ontario Arts Council.

 Canada Council   Conseil des Arts   ONTARIO ARTS COUNCIL
for the Arts   du Canada   CONSEIL DES ARTS DE L'ONTARIO

University of Toronto Press acknowledges the financial support for its
publishing activities of the Government of Canada through the Book
Publishing Industry Development Program (BPIDP)

This book has been published with the help of a grant from the Canadian
Federation for the Humanities and Social Sciences, through the Aid to
Scholarly Publications Program, using funds provided by the Social Sciences
and Humanities Research Council of Canada.

For my grandmothers
Elspeth Hume Siequien (1908–1995)
Agnes Blagrave Campbell (1914–2006)

Contents

Acknowledgments ix

Introduction 3

1 'Giving All the Good in Me to Save My Children': Domestic Labour, Motherhood, and 'Making Do' in Ontario Families 23

2 'If He Is a Man He Becomes Desperate': Unemployed Husbands, Fathers, and Workers 57

3 The Obligations of Family: Parents, Children's Labour, and Youth Culture 84

4 'A Family's Self-Respect and Morale': Negotiating Respectability and Conflict in Home and Family 116

5 Militant Mothers and Loving Fathers: Gender, Family, and Ethnicity in Protest 149

Conclusion: Survival, Citizenship, and State 184

Notes 189

References 249

Index 273

Illustrations follow page 124

Acknowledgments

This book has taken shape over the course of many years, and its present form owes a great deal to the advice, guidance, and support of friends, colleagues, scholars, and archivists. My dissertation supervisor Karen Dubinsky has provided numerous comments and critiques on this book from its inception at Queen's University. Her encouragement, insight, and knowledge of gender history have helped this become a better work. At the University of Toronto Press, Franca Iacovetta has provided helpful feedback and encouragement, while Len Husband has skilfully ushered the manuscript through various stages of the editing process. At the University of Toronto, Sylvia Van Kirk provided feedback on an early version of this project. Archivists at the Archives of Ontario, especially Jack Choules and Judith Emery, have provided an enormous amount of help wading through court files and the vagaries of the Freedom of Information Act. I would also like to thank the staff and archivists at numerous local libraries and archives in Timmins, Thunder Bay, Kirkland Lake, and North Bay, and the staff at the Royal Canadian Legion Library in Ottawa for access to the entire run of the *Legionary* magazine. My high school history teacher Hans Schlechta predicted my career as a historian and encouraged me to ask the 'big questions.' Parts of this material have previously appeared in 'A Barren Cupboard at Home: Ontario Families Confront the Premiers During the Great Depression,' *Ontario since Confederation: A Reader* (Toronto: University of Toronto Press, 2000, 284–306), edited by Edgar-Andre Montigny and Lori Chambers, and in '"We Who Have Wallowed in the Mud of Flanders": First World War Veterans, Unemployment, and the Development of Social Welfare in Canada, 1929–1939,' *Journal of the Canadian Historical Association*, new series, 11 (2000): 125–49. This book has been published with the help of a grant from the Canadian Federation for the Humanities and Social Sciences, through the Aid to Scholarly Publications Program, using funds provided by the Social Sciences and Humanities Research Council of Canada.

I am lucky to have benefited from the kindness and encouragement of friends and family, who have been enthusiastic and supportive about my work, have offered me a place to stay, and have provided much-needed and entertaining distractions. Many thanks to Jo Beaton, Ross Cameron, Craig Campbell, Sasha Colby, Michael Dawson, Dave DeFelice, Joy Frith, Patrizia Gentile, Helen Harrison, James Murton, Catherine Murton Stoehr, Jennifer Marotta, Dev Mekerji, Tamara Myers, Todd McCallum, Susan McGowan, Anne O'Connor, Leslie Paris, Cindy Patton, Joan Sangster, Amy Sproule-Jones, Mary Lynn Stewart, Gilaine Truelove, Paige Raibmon, Joanne Ritcey, Sharon Wall, and Hans and Gerd Wredenhagen. Melissa White made sure my wine glass stayed full and offered comments on various drafts. The two years I spent teaching at Nipissing University in North Bay were more supportive (and colder) than I ever could have imagined. The intellectual generosity and warm friendship of Wayne Borody, Kari Brozowski, Anne Clendenning, Terry Dokis, Steve High, Barbara Lorenzkowski, Françoise Noël, Larry Patriquin, and Michelle Roycroft made my time there a true adventure. Stephen Tomlinson always made me laugh, even when we disagreed. I have been lucky to end up in the Women's Studies Department at Simon Fraser University, where my new colleagues have been both generous and supportive.

I am a better historian, teacher, and writer thanks to the inspiration and support of several people. Since meeting Catherine Gidney in Watson Hall in 1994, she has provided encouragement, love, and support, and her historical rigour and incredible work ethic continue to inspire me. Laura Robinson continues to provide sage advice, challenge me to sharpen my feminist theory, and make me remember that some friendships are meant to last. In Vancouver, Helen Leung's desire to fulfil the requirements of the Kyoto Accord have led to such engaging conversations that I actually enjoy the commute to Burnaby mountain. Karen Ferguson's wise counsel reminds me that life inside academia is negotiable and life outside academia is joyful.

Finally, my family has supported me in numerous ways. My parents, Mel and Marg Campbell, have provided financial support and incredible faith in this project. Eric Wredenhagen has also provided this, along with reading each chapter, providing suggestions, and editing the entire manuscript from beginning to end. His ability to spot problematic gerunds has been indispensable. In the end, this book is dedicated to the lives of my two grandmothers, Elspeth Margaret Hume Siequien (1908–1995) and Agnes Annie Lucinda Blagrave Campbell (1914–2006), both of whom lived through the Great Depression, and both of whom would have been proud to see this project come to fruition.

Vancouver 2008

RESPECTABLE CITIZENS: GENDER, FAMILY,
AND UNEMPLOYMENT IN ONTARIO'S GREAT DEPRESSION

Introduction

You did your best. You didn't dwell on it. You were thankful for what you had.

History books will tell of the hunger marches and strikes, but how will our descendants find out about our everyday lives?[1]

Almost everyone has a story to tell about the Great Depression. When conversing with family friends or grandparents of acquaintances or travelling within Canada, the remark that I was writing about families in the Great Depression elicited memories of unemployment and stories about relief, welfare, and thrift. People's memories, however, are not direct linkages to the past but are framed by experiences and tempered by time and age, and by sadness or pride. Recollections, for example, that times were simpler or easier, communities friendlier, neighbours more cooperative, and individuals more independent, should be understood as the contemporary interpretation of events and experiences that occurred more than seventy years ago.[2] Beyond these images lie the complexities and tensions of family life, the demands on women's domestic labour, the impact of unemployment on culturally defined notions of male pride, and the relationship between citizen and state.

The Great Depression was a devastating national and international economic crisis. Despite previous depressions and recessions, none had such a lasting impact on Canadian political and economic life as the one that occurred between 1929 and 1939.[3] Labour statistics for the 1930s are notoriously unreliable, but historical estimates place unemployment at approximately 30 per cent by 1933, with two million Canadians in receipt of public relief by 1934.[4] Unemployment was regional in nature, both across the country and within the province of Ontario. The prairie provinces were devastated, as plummeting crop prices combined with an extended drought forced many farmers into bankruptcy. Unemployment was highest in areas dominated by industries such as construction or staple exports such as coal, forestry, fishing, and wheat.[5] Yet 'official' unemployment numbers most certainly underestimated the extent of unemployment, given that many women, especially married women, were not counted as unemployed by census takers. For example, Ontario Premier George Henry's attempt to voluntarily register the unemployed in 1931 focused mainly on urban areas, did not survey all municipalities, and did not include women.[6]

The popular image of Ontario as a rich and dominant province hides 'a grimmer side' of poverty and unemployment that existed alongside economic abundance and prosperity for some.[7] Poverty, and the fear of poverty, was of central concern to all but the most well-off Ontario families. Only in-depth local studies will be able to make direct comparisons about the experiences of unemployment or relief between various communities; nevertheless, the Depression was not experienced in the same way everywhere across the province. For example, cities that relied on heavily hit industries such as construction, pulp and paper, steel, and heavy manufacturing were particularly devastated by high unemployment rates.[8] The experience of going on relief in an urban centre was very different from that of a struggling farmer facing low crop prices and high mortgage payments. The expectations and needs of farmers and workers over relief policy could conflict, as when the government provided subsidies for cheap farm labour to farmers who could not otherwise afford to hire help to harvest crops.[9] Despite these differences, there were similarities of experience across the province and across the country, especially since the principle of *less eligibility* shaped relief administration throughout Canada, even though specific local rules differed.[10]

Unemployment did not affect everyone equally. Most of the unemployed and those on relief were unskilled and semi-skilled members of the working class, particularly general labourers or workers in the construction industry.[11] Yet it is important to note two things. First, the 1932 survey of unemployment and relief in Ontario, done by social work professor Harry Cassidy, showed that though those most affected by unemployment were lowest on the socioeconomic scale, most had been employed steadily before the Depression and were permanent residents of the city in which they lived. Second, by 1932, unemployment numbers were so high that joblessness was a threat to 'practically every' working-class family in Ontario.[12] By 1932, Cassidy argued, many of the skilled working class and also the middle class had 'exhausted' their assets, and this brought a 'noticeable' change in relief recipients, many of whom had once lived with some degree of economic security.[13] Moreover, since so many people had experience of unemployment or knowledge of someone who had lost a job, there was a general and overwhelming 'dread' of unemployment. The economic consequences of unemployment and the 'psychological uncertainty' of the era in general touched many families, even as the material effects of unemployment and poverty affected the working class and poor more heavily.[14] This decade, then, is framed by the trauma associated with loss, uncertainty, and fear.

While the nature and effect of the economic crisis varied by region, no area of the country entered the 1930s with a welfare administration capable of handling the increased levels of poverty and unemployment. The federal government, resting on the division of constitutional powers that gave provinces and municipalities responsibility for relief, initiated a series of 'temporary' relief acts. The initial Relief Act of 1930 designated a $20 million cost-sharing grant for unemployment relief projects, $4 million of which was to be spent on direct relief. Ontario also embarked on a number of its own public works projects in the early 1930s, including road construction and additions to the parliament buildings and the Royal Ontario Museum in Toronto.[15] But by 1932 Prime Minister R.B. Bennett, acknowledging the massive costs of funding public works, directed all future money towards the provision of direct relief. Direct relief was administered by the municipalities and was designed around the principle of less eligibility, a rate of support intended to be meagre and humiliating in order to preserve the work ethic. Relief policy, both large-scale public works projects and direct relief, was targeted at male workers and gave preference to married men. Unemployed single women were generally left to the care of private charities, and married women were classified as dependents of men, who were expected to work and apply for their wives' relief. Because both Bennett and Prime Minister Mackenzie King, after him, refused to take full responsibility for unemployment, federal government initiatives were minimal. Both administrations were more preoccupied with balancing the budget and avoiding deficits than undertaking the kind of constitutional reform necessary to adequately address the policy implications of massive, nationwide unemployment. Other federal government initiatives included relief camps for single men, run by the Department of National Defence, back-to-the-land settlements that provided grants and loans to re-establish urban families on farms, and the Farm Employment Plan, which placed mainly men, but also some women, as workers on western farms for the wage of $5 per month.[16]

The Great Depression, however, was more than an economic crisis: high unemployment also had a powerful impact on gender relations.[17] The most riveting images of the Depression revolve around the central figures of unemployed men, particularly men 'riding the rods,' working in relief camps, or queuing for relief. But while male unemployment was certainly high, these iconic images serve to subsume the history of women and to hide the complexities of marital and family life in the Depression. Beyond the dichotomous image of the unemployed man and his suffering wife lies a complex history of family life, revolving around the value of women's domestic labour, the familial conflicts that arose from unemployment or applying for relief, and the gendered obligations of men, women, and children within the family unit.[18]

The political and economic crisis created by the Great Depression was experienced in personal relationships between family members, and it was also expressed through public debates over proper definitions of citizenship. Gendered ideologies of breadwinning and domesticity, of male independence and female dependence, were the underlying tenets of relief provision, and these tenets framed debates surrounding the development and expansion of government-sponsored social welfare. The visible suffering and the seeming crisis of capitalism during the Great Depression were important factors in the transition to a liberal welfare state and increased government intervention in social welfare provision and in the economy. Social unrest and demands – made by individual men and women, communist, and social democratic political organizations, and unemployed unions and veterans' organizations – that the government act to end both unemployment and the humiliating provisions of relief were important elements in this transition. The conflicts and survival strategies of family life were intricately bound with the struggle for economic security, a living wage, and adequate social welfare.

This book revolves around two intertwined themes: a detailed examination of the material difficulties and survival strategies of Ontario families is combined with an analysis of the way that individual protest and collective action helped to redefine the meanings of welfare and citizenship. To explore these themes, this book draws on a number of different sources. The records of social service organizations and government departments and the observations of social workers, judges, and probation officers from family court and criminal court case files provide insight into the way that poverty and unemployment were negotiated by families and by the state. Much information on family survival strategies also comes from newspapers, memoirs, oral histories, and recipes, as well as from novels and plays written in the period. Records of veterans' organizations, in particular the veterans' lobby group of the Royal Canadian Legion (both the Dominion and Ontario Command), hold a wealth of information about the plight of First World War veterans. And finally, the records of the premiers of Ontario, George Henry and Mitchell Hepburn, hold thousands of letters written by Ontario citizens asking for money, demanding unemployment insurance, criticizing state policy, or offering solutions to the economic crisis.[19] Since many of the surviving records are from either urban or southern Ontario, I visited a number of local archives, libraries, and historical societies in northern and rural Ontario. These local institutions hold collections of oral history projects, unpublished books and memoirs, and records of relief organizations. I also interviewed men and women who lived and worked in northern and rural Ontario throughout the 1930s.[20] Such research has broadened the field of reference for this study and suggests ways that future work on the Great Depression might examine the specificities of how regional factors mediated families' and communities' experience of unemployment. Both the material workings of the family and the discursive category of respectable citizenship, which was invested with specific gender obligations and obligations to the state, worked together to help shift definitions of welfare state policy and expectations of family life. Beyond the stock images of the resourceful mother and the defeated father lie relationships, sometimes cooperative and often conflictual, between men and women, parents and children, and citizen and state.

Canadian historiography on the topic of the Great Depression is surprisingly fragmented and incomplete. Much of the richest work done on this decade subsumes the Depression into the topic of the interwar years or into a larger thematic study such as a history of the labour movement, the development of the welfare state, or women's roles in the family or the labour force.[21] There is little historical work on the social history of the Great Depression, particularly on the impact of unemployment on masculinity, family life, and ethnic communities, the history of women's domestic labour, or complex community studies of the intersections of relief, charity, and protest. As Margaret Hobbs points out, many of the best-known social histories and collections of primary documents on the Depression appeared in the late 1960s and early 1970s, reflecting a revival of interest in the topic of unemployment within the newly developing field of social history.[22] Yet, for such an important and dynamic period in Canadian political economic and social history, there are few monographs that specifically address the impact of the Depression.[23]

Recent historical work on the Depression is scattered between the fields of labour, women's, and welfare state history. Labour history has perhaps the richest collection of work that addresses the history of relief camps, radical protest, and union organizing in the 1930s.[24] One of the weakest areas in Depression-era historiography is the history of women and family life. Denyse Baillargeon's analysis of the domestic labour of Montreal working-class housewives is the only published monograph available, and the history of masculinity and fatherhood in this era is even sparser and usually integrated into a larger theme or era.[25] Finally, welfare state literature tends to subsume the Depression years into larger topics such as the history and development of specific social welfare policies or the professionalization of social work.[26] This book, though rooted within Ontario communities, draws from and contributes to several broad bodies of literature and theory on citizenship, welfare policy formation, the construction of 'Britishness' and national identity, social activism, and the relationship between individuals, families, and institutions of state regulation. Much of the theoretical context for interpreting what happened to families, communities, and ideas of gender in this era is rooted in literature on the meaning of citizenship and in research on the development of the post–Second World War liberal welfare state. The way that people understood themselves and their place within the family, the nation, and the economy was connected with their understanding of the mutual obligations of citizen and state. The idea of *social citizenship*, the belief that the state owes its citizens, by virtue of right or entitlement, a comfortable standard of living and protection from unemployment and the ravages of poverty, frames much of the archival evidence from the 1930s, tempering the overdone assertion that this generation was fundamentally independent and unlikely to demand government intervention in social welfare – or was passive and resigned to poverty and suffering.[27] Responses to unemployment ranged broadly, from resigned to radical. This period witnessed a shift from a charity model of welfare provision to one based on an articulation of rights, and it was accompanied by increased government involvement in the economy and social welfare, ultimately making way for postwar welfare expansion. The Second World War is often credited with initiating this shift, yet it was the grassroots pressure placed on the political system during the Great Depression that partly accounts for the development of social policy reform. This shift to the modern liberal welfare state was, however, an ambiguous project fraught with tension and conflict, one that never adequately redistributed wealth nor proved to be a guarantor against poverty. Older notions of the deserving and undeserving poor and the principle of less eligibility were woven into the fabric of the welfare state, as were gendered concepts of the male breadwinner and female homemaker.

It is possible to interpret this movement towards state-sponsored welfare as an attempt by the state to ward off social unrest and challenges to its legitimacy, preserving the values of competitive capitalism and individualism that appeared to be under threat.[28] This interpretation, however, is ultimately too narrow to understand the origins, development, and consequences of welfare state reforms. Clearly, welfare policies were not meant to completely redistribute wealth, nor as historians have shown, was there a linear progression from charity or 'residual' welfare to one of institutional support.[29] But welfare state policies and expansion did challenge the conception of unemployment as the moral failure of the individual worker by admitting structural problems in the capitalist economy and by recognizing a level of state responsibility for the economic welfare of men, women, and children. This transition in policy remained limited, imbricated as it was with tensions between charity and entitlement and conceptions of Britishness, respectability, and the gendered roles of breadwinning and domesticity. Tensions between values of independence and self-sufficiency, on the one hand, and growing claims to rights and entitlement to social welfare, on the other, remained unresolved.

While the history of the welfare state in Canada has been well documented, most historians use a top-down approach to debate the development of policies, institutions, and the origins and objectives of welfare state programs.[30] In recent years, feminist historians have argued that the state regulates gender along with relationships of class and inequality. One theoretical model argues that the welfare state replaced the patriarchal male figure in the private family with dependence on the state, thus promoting female inequality and social and moral control of women's sexuality and labour.[31] Another model posits the development of a two-tiered social welfare state, one in which welfare policies developed along two separate, and gendered, tracks. Policies that rewarded breadwinning, such as workmen's compensation and unemployment insurance, were predicated on upholding men's roles as workers and providers in the labour force, and these were rights or entitlement-based programs. In comparison, programs targeted at women, such as mothers' allowance, were discretionary, needs-based, and concerned with regulating women's moral and sexual propriety.[32] Some feminist historians have also recognized the more ambiguous impact of state welfare on the position of women. Welfare policies are often structured around female dependency and male independence, but they have at times benefited women: by increasing their bargaining power within the family, by giving them a direct relationship with the state, and by providing them with an 'escape route' from complete economic dependence on men.[33] Finally, it is important to remember that welfare state policy regulates both men *and* women by attempting to prescribe the boundaries of gendered behaviour. Early domestic-legal legislation attempted to regulate men's duties of financial support as breadwinners and providers, as well as to limit state expenses for dependent women and children.[34] The state has upheld the notion of the ideal man as a self-supporting provider for his dependent wife and children. For a man to be dependent on social welfare – though not on his wife's labour – was considered shameful and humiliating.[35]

Canadian welfare state history has mainly been written from an institutional perspective, leaving little room for understanding the agency of welfare recipients or to assess their role in policy development. Some work on the depression period addresses the role of popular protest and the agency of welfare recipients. The work of James Struthers on social welfare minimums and of Margaret Little on mothers' allowance both examine the potential for gender and class resistance, while Dominique Marshall, Shirley Tillotson, and Magda Fahrni acknowledge the importance of citizenship ideals and grassroots organization in the formation of the welfare state in the postwar era.[36] While the 1930s were not a productive period for traditional union organizing, they were characterized by political protest ranging from individual letter writing to organized local and national unemployed and relief work strikes. The various forms of political activism in the 1930s, such as writing letters to politicians or participating in relief protests, helped to create a shift in public opinion that cohered around the concept of entitlement to state-sponsored economic security.[37] A historical and theoretical focus on state administration, government bureaucracy, ideology, and policy makers, though crucial to understanding the development of state welfare, is only part of the story. As Cynthia Comacchio points out, historians must 'remember not to give the state a life purely its own by leaving the people out' and pay attention to the way that men, women, and children interacted with welfare policy and providers.[38] The role of popular protest and grassroots social and political activism is one important factor in the development of the Canadian welfare state.

The rights, duties, and obligations of citizenship are closely entwined with the development of welfare state policy. Citizenship stands as a marker of boundaries. Who belongs within the body of a nation? Who has or does not have the right to criticize the government or to make claims for services and protection?[39] By the nineteenth century the liberal ideal of an individual as a 'rights-bearer' dominated the meaning of citizenship: to be fully human was to be able to claim individual rights. T.H. Marshall's model of citizenship development argues that civil citizenship, formed in the eighteenth century, was based on the right to free labour, while in the nineteenth century political citizenship was based on the right to exercise political power and was marked by the gradual extension of suffrage to working-class men, non-property owners, and non-white men.[40] As Nancy Fraser and Linda Gordon have argued, these modes of citizenship are typed male, and based on the right to own property or to work outside of the feudal system of labour. The claim to universal human rights and freedoms and the ability to claim a political relationship with the state were both rooted in the archetypal citizen, who was imagined as male, white, economically independent, and the head of the family unit. Thus, citizenship was fundamentally rooted in the economic discourse of commercial or contractual exchange and linked to the classical liberal rights of freedom of exchange and private property.[41]

Initially, women and non-whites were excluded from the definition of a full citizen, and for some male workers a restricted definition of citizenship could be used to claim rights as workers set apart or above 'non-citizens,' including Aboriginal peoples, immigrants, or 'foreigners.'[42] Women have not, however, been completely excluded in redefining the contours of citizenship. Attempts to claim the rights of citizenship extend back to the work of feminists such as Olympe de Gouges and Mary Wollestonecraft and the suffragists in Great Britain, Europe, and North America. Critics of citizenship discourse have asked whether the very concept itself should be jettisoned because the language of rights and entitlement is so individualistic and exclusionary that it cannot be redefined in a broader, more inclusive way. But a number of feminist scholars have pointed out that the definition of citizenship can be expanded beyond the dichotomous categories of contract or charity, of property or dependence.[43] Women have used 'rights consciousness' to create a common vision and collective identity, and to fight for greater equality.[44] The concept of 'social citizenship,' defined by Marshall as the right to 'a modicum of economic welfare, security, to the right to share in the full social heritage, live the life of a civilized being according to society's prevailing standards,' is visible in women's rhetoric and demands for greater security in the Great Depression, largely through the discourse of maternalism.[45] Women were central participants in developing definitions of a more inclusive type of citizenship and language of rights, in the debates over what humans truly need, and in how those needs should be met. Arising from women's activism in the 1930s was a definition of citizenship embedded in the limiting and gendered categories of contract and duty, yet also premised on the right of women, as wives and mothers, to demand material security, respect, and a voice in political affairs in return for loyalty to the nation. It is in these often-contradictory ways that we see women as wives and mothers and men as fathers, husbands, and workers, actively engaging with and redefining citizenship, duty, and reciprocity in the Depression years.

Since women have historically been excluded from the earliest definitions of citizenship, they have struggled to claim tenuous links to its entitlements, mainly by claiming rights through the duties associated with marriage and motherhood. Women have long engaged with the state, asking for intervention from politicians and social workers and demanding money, help in solving domestic problems, and advice.[46] Thus, the historical picture is not so simple as one of a patriarchal state pressing down on its female victims, a moralistic state regulating private family life, or a capitalist state preserving economic inequality. Ultimately, when women engaged politically with the state by making their demands heard, they were defining themselves as active citizens and members of a broader social and political community. Women most often approached the state on the basis of their maternal status as wives and mothers, demanding employment for their husbands and material aid for their families. Working-class women embraced a material politics of motherhood, emphasizing the economic value of women's domestic labour, the centrality of women to family survival, and the material necessity of adequate relief provision.[47] 'Militant mothering,' as Joan Sangster points out, was a way for radical groups to organize women, though it was not the arena only of the Co-operative Commonwealth Federation and the Communist Party, but also of women's groups such as the Women's Christian Temperance Union, the Women's Institutes, and traditional political parties.[48] While maternalism did not challenge the fundamental inequalities of gender-based hierarchies, it was one way, though limited, to make claims on the state, create room for women's activism, and place the needs of families on the public agenda.

Citizenship was also framed and organized by constructions of ethnicity and by concepts of nationhood. Historical studies of ethnic groups and radical politics have demonstrated that class militancy and ethnic identity were often conflated, placing non–Anglo-Celtic and immigrant men and women in the vanguard of class action. Governments have historically played on this connection as well, by conflating 'red' with 'foreigner' in order to justify police repression and campaigns of state censorship.[49] But reactionary state measures occurred in the 1930s because the state also understood that radical language and actions existed beyond 'foreigners,' immigrants, or Communist Party politics. To contain the activities of radical groups of immigrant labourers was one thing; to contain radicalism once it was being articulated by racial and ethnic 'insiders' was another. By the 1930s the state was increasingly concerned about the radical critiques of capitalism coming from within the 'British' population, considered to be the backbone of morality and civilization. Britishness itself, of course, was not a solid or unified identity, but one that contained divisions among English, Irish, Scottish, and Welsh Anglo-Celtic groups, particularly with regard to cultural background, religion, class, and traditions of political militancy. But these distinctions are blurred somewhat when Britishness is examined in the colonial context of white-settler societies. Within the Canadian nation, Britishness was an invented identity, defined as a broad historical connection to Great Britain and rooted in the belief that those of British 'stock' had built the Canadian nation, settled and civilized the country, and built institutions founded on the principles of British democracy.[50]

Canadian political history on national identity in the interwar years tends to focus on intellectual and policy developments rooted in a political and intellectual culture that increasingly emphasized North American rather than imperial connections.[51] National identity, however, does not only happen from the top down; men and women are formed, and form themselves, into national subjects.[52] For many men and women living in Ontario in the 1930s, Canadian nationality was intimately connected with British traditions, most especially at the popular level. While the Canadian intellectual elite attempted to redefine a particular Canadian identity, for many, claims to Britishness signified loyalty to nation and state, a connection to political tradition, and an organic relationship to neighbour, community, and nation. At the popular level, this nationalism was deeply entwined with older conceptions of identity based on Upper Canadian connections to the Loyalists and with long-standing imperial connections to Great Britain. If not a cohesive national ideology, it was an 'imagined community,' one that blended elements of faith in and loyalty to the British Empire, the Loyalist mythology of heroism and self-sacrifice, and a strong conception of duty and patriotism to the Canadian nation.[53] While a vague concept, Britishness nonetheless captured the place of citizens of Loyalist, Scottish, Irish, and English background – the vast majority of the population in Ontario.[54] Outsiders to this tradition and mythology were labelled *agitators* or *communists*, and it is not surprising that such a high number of deportations occurred during this period of economic dislocation.[55]

By understanding this cultural sense of Britishness, we can take seriously both its radical and its conservative role. National identity was one way for men and women to claim greater rights, blending nationalism with demands based on class or maternalism.[56] A Canadian identity rooted in Britishness marked one a true citizen of Canada, and it was a way for women, single mothers, and the unemployed to make political claims on the state and to place themselves within the national narrative. Citizens were simultaneously constructing themselves in relation to this Anglo-Celtic identity and history, which was used to claim greater social and economic rights, and against the 'other' in the guise of immigrants and agitators, who were seen to be less deserving of those rights and also as responsible for creating poverty and unemployment. Yet those drawing on British rights were adapting the language and, in some cases, the action and organizational techniques of radical ethnic organizations and traditions to make these broader claims to economic justice and security. Britishness combined with Canadian nationhood created a powerful discourse of rights language rooted deeply in the language of citizenship itself.[57]

Finally, it is important to discuss the role of the family courts and social agencies in this study, as the case records generated by the workings of these institutions have become a topic of historical debate.[58] In the late nineteenth century, child and family welfare legislation was employed so that the state could intervene to address the problems of a modern industrial state, such as intemperance, poverty, crime, and poor health.[59] During the early 1920s in Ontario the Drury government amended and created new family welfare legislation intended to regulate social problems. The Deserted Wives' and Children's Maintenance Act allowed certain interested parties to lay charges against husbands and fathers who deserted their families, while the Children of Unmarried Parents Act created a provincial agency where a provincial officer was the 'statutory protector and guardian' to unmarried mothers and their children and acted to force fathers to meet their financial obligations of support.[60] In addition to these provincial statutes, courts also applied sections of the Criminal Code that made it an indictable offence for a man to refuse the 'necessaries' of life to support his wife or children under the age of sixteen or to refuse to look for work if capable of doing so. Police courts could administer family welfare legislation, and they worked in conjunction with the Children's Aid Society to examine cases and to act as probation officers, though in some locations, specialized courts were developed to try cases involving women and children.[61] Some reformers, such as Charlotte Whitton, director of the Canadian Council on Child and Family Welfare, as well as church councils and councils of women, believed that problems of non-support and desertion would benefit from a more 'social approach.' Domestic relations courts, reformers argued, would centralize family welfare cases in a separate system based on social casework methods and allow trained social workers and judges to administer the system.[62] In this vein, successive Ontario governments created unified domestic relations courts – in Toronto in 1929, Ottawa in 1931, and Hamilton in 1936. Exact procedures differed, but in all of these locations, separate courts or divisions administered federal and provincial family welfare legislation. However, even in municipalities where family welfare legislation was administered by magistrates of the police courts, social workers and social reformers were still involved in the court system. Social workers, police, crown attorneys, and school attendance officers worked together to regulate women, children, and families through ongoing supervision. Probation officers in particular appear frequently in family court records, because they unofficially administered cases that never appeared before a judge. They gave advice to men and women on how to be better husbands and wives; wrote up support, separation, and temperance agreements; and occasionally supervised relief payments.[63]

Case files created through the workings of family welfare legislation in the 1930s provide a wealth of information on poor and unemployed families, but the sources are heavily mediated by 'expert' and legal discourse. Looking for the 'truth' in these files is an impossible endeavour, for we only hear the voices of women, children, and families through the judgment and analysis of court officials and social workers and the rhetorical framework of social welfare legislation and relief policy. Case records encapsulate many of the issues surrounding the limitations of historical evidence. They are impressions of working-class family life, made by middle-class 'experts' including judges, social workers, lawyers, and probation officers, and they are rooted in particular understandings of gendered behaviour and moral standards. Similarly, the actions and responses of clients are framed within the discourses offered by the court system: historians do not hear the direct voices of men and women, but voices shaped by the necessary legal language and municipal regulations surrounding eligibility for support and relief. However, it is important to remember that all historical actions are framed by these factors. Memory is conditioned by life experiences and by a desire to frame a life narrative from a series of experiences, while newspapers are not objective 'reports' of the facts, but are conditioned by particular ideologies and interpretations of events.[64] Court records, when read sensitively, offer a glimpse into the way that men and women responded to state interventions and how relief regulations, social welfare policy, and the court system were fundamentally entwined in the period of the Great Depression.

Interpreting case files is difficult. Most scholars have rejected simple social control theories that interpret welfare legislation and family courts as direct state repression of the lives and actions of the working class and poor.[65] Scholars making use of such files have had to grapple with Foucault's work on expert discourse and the organization of knowledge. Such scholars have developed the useful concept of *moral regulation*, which Joan Sangster defines as 'the discursive and political practices whereby some behaviours, ideals and values were marginalized and proscribed while others were legitimized and naturalized.'[66] Indeed, courts intervened in relationships and in families that did not fit the 'modern' values of the era. Marriages were to be gendered yet companionate; children were to be cherished and loved while simultaneously respectful, obedient, and educated; and families were to solve financial problems and interpersonal conflicts independently, quietly, and with dignity. That families so often behaved in messy, argumentative, and noisy ways, refused to follow proper gender roles, and struggled to make ends meet was a frustrating situation for many a minister, judge, or social worker.

Does this mean that institutions only imposed middle-class standards of normality on the marginalized, poor, or working-class families through discursive practices?[67] It does seem evident that the families most likely to come into contact with the family court system were those already on relief, poor, or unemployed. Non-Anglo-Celtic families also appear slightly overrepresented in some of the case files.[68] Nevertheless, for a great many women and families on relief or living in poverty, family welfare legislation offered help in negotiating their survival or ameliorating family conflict. Women could approach judges and probation officers for assistance in forcing reluctant husbands to work for relief or in mediating conflicts over alcohol or the budgeting of relief funds. Courts attempted to track down missing husbands, help deserted women gain access to relief, or aid elderly parents in eliciting economic support from adult children. While acknowledging the relationships of power, coercion, and regulation embedded within such institutions, these files also reflect the various and complex kinds of resistance available to those without institutional power. By attending to such examples of resistance, historians can analyse more than simply the 'social organization of knowledge.'[69] In these files are clients who defied judicial orders, who refused to be labelled promiscuous, lazy, or criminal, and who insisted on collective notions of value, respect, and responsibility. In the variety of ways that individual men, women, and children spoke back to experts, historians can assess, at least partially, the experiences of women and families as they butted up against dominant notions of respectable behaviour and faced material limits placed on their lives by structural inequality. Families could at times 'embrace the regulatory aims' of courts, or they could challenge them, provide an alternative to them, or attempt to manipulate them to get the help they needed from what was, in many cases, the only institution offering financial aid or mediation.[70] These case records reflect the delicate balancing act between the agency of clients and the regulation and intervention of the court system.

This book highlights the complex relationships among the home, workplace, and state and demonstrates that the 'private' and the 'public' were deeply entwined. The material and domestic everyday responsibilities that tied families together, or that maintained the economic dependence of wives on husbands and children on parents, also led men and women to increasingly demand active state involvement in social welfare. The family unit was not simply a conservative institution that deadened class conflict, struggle, and political action. The concerns of parents for feeding, clothing, housing, and educating their children, of men for supporting a wife and children, and of women for nurturing and running a household were not private, individual affairs. Rather, these concerns for the well-being or very survival of the family unit often led to demands for broader political action by the provincial and federal governments, and they were central to the rhetoric of relief protests and politics throughout the 1930s.[71] If we take seriously the argument that power itself is not a static, repressive, one-way thing that some possess and others do not, that there always lies the potential for resistance, then we can identify and analyse the moments when families, as Dominique Marshall so eloquently argues, might find their interests 'temporarily coinciding' with those of the state and thus become instruments of 'social change.'[72] Taking seriously the role that families played in Depression-era politics means rethinking the way welfare state development occurred. Without denying the way in which professionalization, bureaucratization, or expert discourse shaped understandings of need or appropriate responses to such needs, taking families out of this analysis means missing out on an important way in which familial concerns, needs, and deprivations were central to public policy. The way in which mothers and fathers and husbands and wives articulated family needs, as well as duties and responsibilities, was central to the development of the postwar liberal welfare state. Through various kinds of protest and struggle, which were in turn shaped by the rhetoric of gender, race, and class, families participated in a wide-ranging political debate over the role of government in the economy and in the structure of the family.

Chapter Overview

This book combines a detailed examination of the material difficulties and survival strategies faced by families struggling with poverty and unemployment with an analysis of the way that grassroots organization and individual protest helped to redefine the meaning of welfare and citizenship. In assessing the social history of family survival and the details of women's work in the family economy, I piece together the actual techniques employed to survive conditions of inadequate relief and low wages. The way women cooked, cleaned, and shopped, the varied ways that children contributed to the family economy, and men's attempts to find work were all central to family survival. It is in the process of what Michael Gardiner names *everyday life* that we can weave together the connections between a social history of family life with a look at the roles men, women, and children played in what Ann Shola Orloff calls the 'epochal' transition to a modern liberal welfare state.[73] This era is marked by the fluidity between personal and public, and the interconnected interests of the state, the family, and the economy.[74]

It is within the home that the ravages of unemployment were most deeply felt, and Chapters 1 and 2 examine the roles, expectations, duties, and responsibilities of men and women to their families. Unemployment had a devastating effect on women's ability to manage a household and raise a family. Women took pride in their abilities as mothers and as spouses. Unemployment and relief made their duties as a homemaker more onerous. The first chapter explores the way that the Great Depression added to the domestic workload as women attempted to make up for reduced cash with greater domestic services. To fill in the gap, women famously 'made do' in a variety of ways, such as cooking economically, shopping and budgeting carefully, and taking on formal and informal labour to earn money. The labour of these women demonstrates women's work was not 'extra,' but central to family survival, laying bare the myth of the sole male breadwinner. This chapter also examines the particular difficulties faced by women on mothers' allowance in this period, as well as women who acted outside the boundaries of respectable feminine behaviour by working as prostitutes or deserting their families.

Colliding with poverty was the psychological trauma of unemployment. The masculine cultural edict to provide for wives and children – together with the intimate association between masculinity and employment – was severely challenged by economic crisis. However, while the Great Depression disrupted these masculine ideals, it did not ultimately destroy the breadwinner ethos. The second chapter, on husbands and fathers, examines the ways that men attempted to provide for their families while unemployed, the sense of failure or shame that could lead to suicide, breakdowns, or desertion, and the ways that men attempted to maintain their pride, not just as independent workers, but also as loving husbands and caring fathers.

The domestic ethic in men's gender identity was deeply entwined with their status as breadwinners.

The family economy functioned into the twentieth century, despite the countervailing forces of modernity in the form of school attendance regulations and child labour laws. Children's formal and informal labour was crucial to family survival. Chapter 3 explores the contours of children's contributions to the family economy, as well as the particular impact of the Great Depression on youth culture, dating, and marriage. Unemployment framed much of the lives of youth and children in this decade, from difficulty finding employment to delayed marriages. At times the family economy ran efficiently, with young girls helping mothers with child care or housework or boys taking on extra paid labour. Court records, however, reveal the tensions in these arrangements, as mothers and fathers conflicted with the family courts over their children's need to work or the community practice of coal theft to heat homes. Similarly, relief regulations surrounding economic responsibility meant that older children were held responsible for their parents' maintenance. Threats of charges under the Parents' Maintenance Act and the structuring of relief regulations insured that children, rather than the state, were to be held responsible for elderly or incapacitated parents. Ontario's children were intricately bound in the web of family survival.

The fourth chapter, a discussion of the home, weaves together the many threads of gender, unemployment, ethnicity, youth, citizenship, and respectability. Home was a material and physical structure, as well as a metaphor for family survival and security. In brick and mortar, men and women fought evictions or foreclosures. In domestic arrangements and relationships, men, women, and children argued, debated, and called on the state to mediate disputes or provide relief. Here we see many elements of working-class women's ambivalent yet active relationship with the state and its officials. Resentment at the moralistic intrusion of social workers or probation officers was balanced by women's, and occasionally men's, active attempts to seek intervention in disputes with family members. Wives sought help in particular for husbands who spent wages or relief money on alcohol or intervention in cases where men refused to find employment. Ultimately these disputes were ways of forcing the state to take their problems seriously, a dance between acceptance of surveillance and a defiant stance of entitlement. For those even further outside the definition of proper citizenship in Ontario, such as the poor or unemployed, non-British immigrants, francophones, and single mothers, the court system was one place where their concerns could be articulated, but also the point at which officials were more likely to intervene in family life. Of course, assimilation to Canadian middle-class standards of proper moral and gendered behaviour was one of the goals behind state expansion, but clearly these men and women were not passive and defeated. They fought back, wrote letters, and demanded action on behalf of their problems. What historians often define as 'middle-class standards' were not, as Comacchio points out, necessarily unacceptable to working-class families. While there were some differences in family structure and goals, most notably a class-based focus on 'collective survival' over that of middle-class 'self-actualization,' working-class families were deeply concerned with their children's educational and work opportunities and the quality of their relationships with children, parents, and spouses.[75]

The final chapter, on social activism, documents the grassroots organization and individual struggle of the unemployed in protesting against government policy and making claims on the state. Forms of protest were gendered, as was citizenship itself. As wives and mothers or as husbands, fathers, and workers, men and women used the rhetoric of rights and entitlement, family duty, and respectability to frame their protests. Chapter 5 looks at the way that individual citizens and organized groups, through letters of protest and collective action, helped to push against the narrow boundaries of state responsibility for social welfare. Looking closely at the many letters written to Ontario Premiers George Henry and Mitchell Hepburn suggests that the meaning of the word 'political' must be defined to include the actions of those women and men who did not belong to a union or a political party. These letters tell us a great deal about the concerns of working-class and unemployed people in Ontario. While their rhetoric is located in discourse of the work ethic and the family wage, they use the language of rights and entitlement to argue for a greater role for state-sponsored services and welfare. Similarly, the dominance of letter writers of British descent indicates that those citizens outside the dominant ethnic groups in Ontario found it even more difficult to lay direct claim to the social and economic rights of citizenship. While letters are not necessarily direct links to the thoughts of men and women, the demands for state-sponsored welfare cannot be considered false consciousness or simply a cynical manipulation or parroting of what they thought political leaders wanted to hear. Rather, demands, suggestions, or even threats were all expressed within a broad vision of what seemed possible at the time, and they offer a varied set of demands and concerns that articulate an alternative vision of economic and social justice.[76] These letters offer a fascinating glimpse of the rich variety of ideas, complaints, and concerns among those deeply affected by the economic crisis. They reveal little about how politicians understood or judged these fears and demands, for responses tended to be stock in nature, generally thanking the writers for their letter but indicating that little could be done to help them. The collective action of unemployed men and women is also addressed through an examination of the role of veterans' organizations, in particular the Royal Canadian Legion, and the development of relief worker or unemployed unions that used direct action to press for more adequate and humane methods of relief in towns and cities across the province. Thus, this study expands the definition of the political beyond formal political participation to include the organized and individual ways that men and women actively engaged with redefining the terms of social welfare and the state's social and economic responsibility for its citizens.

If, by the end of the decade, few of these demands for social entitlement were met, limited by political expediency, the desire to keep the costs of welfare as privatized as possible, and the onset of war, it is not that the subjects of this study were conservative or resigned. Ontario citizens played an important role in the transition to the postwar liberal welfare state, based on an expansion and implementation of state services that would have been unthinkable even at the beginning of the decade. Studying this transition also recovers the continuities in the importance of domestic labour and the work of children in the family economy well into the twentieth-century consumer era. Local, individual, and community-based activism, culture, and political engagement existed in conjunction with the newly developing strains of mass culture. It is the decade before the onset of the Second World War that so richly illustrates the impact of unemployment on Ontario families, the individual and collective obligations of men, women, and children to family and community, the changing definitions of citizenship, and the public debate over the extent of state responsibility for the economic and social welfare of its citizens.

1 'Giving All the Good in Me to Save My Children': Domestic Labour, Motherhood, and 'Making Do' in Ontario Families

The family economy is crucial to understanding the impact of the Great Depression on women and the family. In the 1930s, as in previous decades, women's contribution to the family economy, in the form of both paid and unpaid labour, was central to the survival of families. Women's labour helped to pay rent, mortgages, or taxes, stretched limited budgets, created nourishing and filling meals, made over second-hand clothes, and preserved food for leaner times. To support their husbands and children, women worked informally or at odd jobs, took in boarders, or found work in the labour force despite the cultural proscription against married women's employment. Women's ability to maintain home and family was a crucial component of female respectability and proper womanhood. Domestic activities such as budgeting, shopping, cooking, and sewing were central to family survival and, though carefully planned, were often difficult on a low income. Finally, this chapter will look at the discrimination that married women faced on taking paid employment during a time of high male unemployment.

As wives and mothers, women believed they had a right to protect and nurture their families. While men were more visibly affected by Depression-related unemployment, unemployment and poverty also moved women to criticize inadequate social welfare measures and welfare benefits. Women generally placed their demands for rights within the context of their relationships to their families and not as independent citizens and workers, but they still demanded entitlement to economic security. In addition to the survival strategies and domestic labour of 'respectable' mothers and wives, this chapter will look at women who lived outside the bounds of culturally prescribed 'proper womanhood,' such as single mothers, women who took money for sex, or women who deserted their families while they looked for work. The boundaries between proper and improper and respectable and disreputable womanhood were fluid and not always clearly drawn.

Making Do: Strategies, Mother-Work, and Domestic Skills

The term *family strategies* is a matter of historiographical debate, though it is generally understood to mean the ways in which the family acts to make decisions involving its survival and upward mobility. Part of the reason for theorizing family strategies is to challenge the 'modernization argument,' which labelled families in the past as victims of economic and political forces, unable to make or carry out decisions for the future.[1]

Debate over the concept of family strategies has important implications in two areas: whether the family can be understood as a cohesive unit acting in the best interests of all of its individual members and whether it is possible to label specific behaviours as deliberate choices. The terminology of family strategies often assumes that the family acts cohesively and in the best interests of all of its members, regardless of structural inequalities between men and women and parents and children.[2] Louise Tilly argues that historians can identify strategies, defined as 'predictable interdependent behaviours in which one outcome is regularly favoured over another,' though we must attend to the conditions of inequality under which they arose.[3] How to understand the functioning of the family economy is caught up in these debates over hierarchy and inequality. Even though historians can demonstrate, for example, that the male breadwinner relied on his wife's domestic labour, it was still possible for him to survive economically without her. A woman was much less likely to survive outside the boundaries of the traditional family because of discrimination in the labour market and cultural proscriptions about women's natural role as wife and mother. While women's domestic labour was a strategic bulwark against even worse privation, this kind of 'strategy' was rooted in women's association with the realm of domestic labour and motherhood. Survival strategies, much like family relationships, were linked to female inequality and dependence and on the generosity and sense of responsibility of the male breadwinner within the capitalist labour market.

In the 1930s the alarmingly high male unemployment rate stripped bare the dependence of families on wage labour and the dependence of women on men for economic survival. The response of most men and women was not, however, to call for the restructuring of society so that people were less dependent on wage labour or to agitate for the increased economic independence of women, but to bolster men's wages, employment rights, and social security within the labour force. In examining the functioning of the family economy and methods of survival in the 1930s, it is crucial to remember that these decisions, actions, and responses were shaped by both the material needs of families and by the constraints and inequalities of gender. The response of women within the family to economic crisis was a complex interplay between gender expectations, labour force constraints, and social conventions around ideas of work, charity, and relief.[4]

While paid labour and the home were neither separate nor dichotomous spheres, the daily maintenance and functioning of the home was considered to be the domain of women.[5] Women were understood to be managers of home and family in addition to any paid work they might undertake, and their skills at budgeting and stretching the male income were tested throughout the Great Depression. Traditional female skills were qualities that women took great pride in, but these domestic skills reinforced the connection of women to the domestic realm. Moreover, these strategies of survival and ways of making do or 'picking up the slack' meant that women had an increased workload at a time when their resources were drastically reduced.[6] Concurrently, the interwar years saw the emergence of new household technology and the evolution of housework into a form of 'household science.' Yet, even in middle-class families, it was often difficult to manage on a male breadwinner wage alone, making new technology unaffordable and making do more important than modernizing the kitchen. Women's work and supplementary income were 'not the preserve of the desperately poor,' but crucial to the functioning of the capitalist economy and the functioning of the home.[7] While the height of women's domestic production was in the nineteenth century, this trend continued into the 1930s and beyond.[8] Rural and urban women, and wives of professionals and of workers, all had a long tradition of earning extra money to supplement or maintain the family income. As Denyse Baillargeon succinctly points out, 'despite a greater dependence on the part of workers' families on wages and on the consumer goods market, the labour of women in the home still comprised a whole host of tasks altogether necessary to support the family.'[9]

Mothers' skills were crucial to survival and highly valued by both husbands and children. While women's domestic work was not remunerated, oral histories and memoirs suggest there was cultural recognition and appreciation for their labour. Adult children most clearly remembered their mothers' skills at budgeting and household management, suggesting that these tasks were of central value and importance to family survival in the Depression years.[10] Mary Cleeson remembered her mother as an 'astute' woman, who 'watched every cent.' Before her father died, in 1934, he proudly claimed that his wife could 'make a dollar do the work of five.'[11] Magne Stortroen, a Norwegian immigrant who worked as a miner in Northern Ontario, acknowledged his wife Elsa's 'spirit, resourcefulness and willingness to work,' crediting her with such 'clever managing' of their home that they could eventually buy a piece of land and build their own home mid-way through the Depression.[12] M.J. Scully claimed his family, who lived in Cobalt, 'survived because of my mother. When ... there was nothing to spend money on, she saved it.'[13]

The women who budgeted, shopped, cooked, and cleaned on limited budgets were revered by husbands and children as 'good women,' who were thrifty, capable, and resourceful. Dorothy Osmars' recollection of her mother in Timmins was of a careful woman who was 'never wasteful' and who successfully managed the family finances and ran the household.[14] Because married women's labour was central to the family economy, children usually had a close relationship with their mothers, based on daily interaction. As a result, children of the interwar era tend to vividly recall their mothers' active domestic role and to respect their skills, their domestic labour, and their talent at cooking meals.[15]

Women's domestic labour comprised a variety of tasks, including managing wages and budgets, feeding and clothing family members, occasionally performing paid labour to supplement the breadwinner wage, and bearing and raising children. All of these elements demonstrate the difficult work that women did on a regular basis for the family, particularly in a time of economic instability and limited resources. But women's domestic labour, while more than a 'labour of love,' also embodied a kind of emotional labour that was understood to be an important component of women's work. It was crucial for women to be 'good managers' in the material world, as Susan Porter Benson discusses in her analysis of working-class marriages, but this feat was not enough. The emotional support and nurturance of children and husbands was central to women's role in the Great Depression, though it is rarely discussed and generally undervalued.[16] Women were expected to help their husbands maintain their sense of pride in the face of unemployment, to keep the family happy and contented, and to stay cheerful regardless of financial problems. Women's columns in news-papers and advice columns in women's magazines celebrated women's emotional labour as central both to female identity and family unity. The women's column in the *Farmer's Advocate* glorified the role of rural women: 'Out of her bag of tricks she will pull a really helpful idea when Himself gets discouraged over low prices or low yields. She is a real Lady of the Lamps; a lamp of hospitality and of genuine cheerful-ness and love of people which sheds light and warmth on the path that is bound to be dark and rough for all of us at times.'[17] Similarly, a col-umn in Kirkland Lake's newspaper, the *Northern News*, when listing the stresses faced by farm families, claimed 'the worst calamity that can befall the establishment is the loss of courage in the head of it. When a man gives up, his wife will lay her head on his shoulder and wait confidently until he has himself in hand again ... [a]ll he was needing was the assurance of her love and reliance on him – then he knew he could conquer.'[18]

The domestic labour of the 1930s' housewife was supposed to em-body emotional support, love, and caretaking. This work was under-stood as particularly important in times of high male unemployment because of fear of the fragmentation of masculinity. Meg Luxton found a similar set of values at play in Flin Flon, Manitoba, where part of women's domestic labour was considered to be creating a nurturing, loving home for hard-working men.[19] When men 'lost hope' in the face of economic ruin or the shame of unemployment, the only thing that stood between familial stability and social disorder was women's abil-ity to soothe, stay strong, and give men hope.

Food

Budgeting for and preparing food was one of the most important jobs for a wife and mother, and it was a domestic role that linked the women of the 1930s to those of the nineteenth century. The kitchen was a place where the domestic economy and the capitalist economy met, where women demonstrated their love for their family in material form. Women carefully and painstakingly worked out their budgets and income. Economical food had to be tasty, filling, and nutritious. Housewives performed 'feats of ingenuity both in buying and prepar-ing food for the table,' in buying cheaper cuts of meat, and in utilizing inexpensive root vegetables such as potatoes, carrots, turnips, and onions. Even limited amounts of food signified survival; it was the 'total absence of all food that was often associated with genuine poverty.'[20] Cooking nutritious meals, wrote one domestic science 'expert' in an advice column, was a skill that women were expected to perfect: 'food is of first importance on the list of necessities ... [g]ood cooking is essential if good meals are to be enjoyed, no matter what materials are used.'[21] Cooking was not just a domestic skill, it was a way to demonstrate a woman's concern for her family and therefore an important component of proper womanhood. As one newspaper explained, women should make home-cooked food 'as tasty and tempting as food that is purchased "ready made." It is within the power of every woman ... to become a competent cook.'[22]

Finding enough food to adequately feed a family was always a central concern for women. For families who were on relief or unemployed, lack of food and proper nutrition could easily lead to illness and malnourishment. Problems related to lack of food therefore frequently appear in family court records, letters to politicians, advice columns, and memoirs. The Bertrand family in Ottawa, whose father was an unemployed labourer on relief, came to the attention of the juvenile court when one son was charged with stealing two sacks of fruit and vegetables, presumably to help provide adequate food for the family. A home visit from the probation officer revealed the mother was in poor health with stomach ulcers. 'Family are on relief and it is very difficult for her to have the proper food,' reported the court worker, who obtained a special relief order for her.[23] Malnutrition was not unknown. When Gerard Paquin of Ottawa was put on probation for theft, court records noted that he lived 'in a very poor home' that was ineligible for relief. His probation officer, Miss Beoard, expressed concern that Paquin suffered from 'painful boils' that were 'due to a faulty diet' and that he was often absent from school because of the lack of clothing and food. His mother contacted the court herself, saying the family was in 'want,' needed help getting relief, and that she 'was afraid that he might be tempted to steal fuel (coal) – to help out.'[24] After twelve-year-old Lester Paulson was arrested and charged with truancy, Dr George A. Campbell reported to his probation officer that he was 'suffering from malnutrition and fatigue. He is seventeen per cent underweight.' His father was an unemployed labourer, and his mother found it difficult to get 'desirable' boarders because, she said, of the poor condition of the home.[25]

In their letters to the premiers asking for help, inadequate food was often a central concern of mothers. Women outlined inadequate food budgets and told stories of families and children who verged on the brink of starvation. Mrs Pat O'Ray wrote to Premier Hepburn that 'there are times when we sit down to our table with nothing save bread and tea and sometimes scarcely a piece for all,' while Mrs Arthur Oddy asked for money because her children only had bread and cocoa to eat.[26] 'People are awaiting the coming winter in despair,' wrote the mothers of Sturgeon Falls, 'for starvation stares them in the face.'[27] Unsurprisingly, families on relief or suffering in the face of unemployment ate a diet heavy in starches and light on meat and protein, and they relied on bread to fill the gap.[28]

Women used their domestic skills in stretching food budgets. They read and shared a variety of ways to save money, stretch food allowances, and cook with relief rations. Recipes relied heavily on relatively inexpensive root vegetables, such as potatoes and cabbage.[29] Cabbage salad mixed with fruits and vegetables, for example, was a popular recipe in the 1930s.[30] Soups and stews were made with bones from scratch, and many recipes emphasized fish, which was often cheaper than meat.[31] One creative housewife made sandwiches filled with ketchup or mustard.[32] Inexpensive cuts of meat such as brisket, pork neck ribs, and liver were used in place of more expensive cuts, and they ensured a meal with at least some protein. Mary Cleeson's mother found a variety of ways to provide meat for her family, using cheap meat cuts and dividing them into smaller portions to help flavour dough and vegetables. Bones were saved for soup, and inexpensive fish like 'fin and haddy' were simmered in milk. A nice cut of roast, fresh fruit, or even celery were considered luxuries.[33]

Recipes that replaced beef with more economical foodstuffs were commonly published in newspapers, such as one for lamb stew, which featured soaking coarse cuts of lamb and bone in cold water with onions, carrots, potatoes, turnips, and cabbage.[34] When eggs were cheaper than meat in 1932, the *Oshawa Daily Times* recommended that women create 'Chilean Style Eggs' with tomatoes, eggs, cheese, dried beef, and bread.[35] Making soups, stews, or casseroles thicker made food portions look more generous and also filled families up faster. Using rhubarb was an inexpensive way to increase the bulk of jams and preserves, and rolled oats thickened recipes more cheaply than flour.[36] Since men often supplemented family meals by hunting, women were at times faced with preparing unusual dishes, for which lessons in family studies could not have prepared them. The *North Bay Nugget* introduced the following recipe for 'Brunswick Squirrel Pie' in 1933, with the following lines: 'Is the man in your family a mighty hunter who sallies forth with a gun and … brings home game in the form of squirrel … [a]nd you wonder how on earth you do cook the things':

Brunswick Squirrel Pie – 3 squirrels, 3 slices salt pork, 2 onions, 4 cups tomatoes, 2 cups corn, 1 cup lima beans, 3–4 potatoes, 2 tsp sugar, 1 tbsp salt, 2 qt boiling water, 4 tbsp butter, 2 tbsp flour. Clean wash and disjoint squirrels. Stand in cold salt water for an hour. Drain. Finely chop salt pork. 1 layer pork, onions, potatoes. 1 layer corn, beans, squirrel. Cover with veggies and pork. Season with pepper and cayenne, pour over boiling water, stew for 3 hours. Add tomatoes, salt, and sugar and cook another hour. Work flour and butter into smooth paste, stir into stew, boil 5 minutes and serve.[37]

The 1930s witnessed a reversal in the trend towards purchasing canned goods, as women attempted to stretch budgets by canning and preserving fruit and vegetables themselves.[38] Large gardens, either private or provided by communities or relief boards, made it possible to grow fruit and vegetables and can them for private use or sell them for extra money. Preserving was labour intensive and dependent on being able to afford fuel for stoves, and it was not practical for those who could not afford to run wood stoves for long periods of time. Rural women with easier access to large amounts of wild berries or land to grow vegetables found it easier to make preserves. Earl Craig of North Bay, who described his mother as 'thrifty and economical,' remembered that she once preserved 165 quarts of strawberries, while a woman from Peterborough recalled that during one year of her husband's unemployment she preserved sixty quarts of tomatoes.[39] Preserving large quantities of food, however, involved intensive domestic labour. Making three or four 'little jars' of strawberry jam, for example, took almost two hours of work. The wood stove had to be lit and carefully maintained at the proper temperature, the fruit washed, hulled, and then boiled with sugar, and the jars sterilized in a pot of boiling water. After the jars were allowed to air dry, the fruit was then sealed and waxed.[40]

Families in some municipalities could not qualify for relief without maintaining a vegetable garden, and relief rates were predicated on an assumption that families would grow a certain quantity of their own food. In North Bay, for example, applicants for relief were asked what size garden they worked and whether they grew vegetables for their own use.[41] Fort William set aside enough land so that by June 1931 there were 169 gardens in four wards of the city, and by June 1933 the number had increased to 650 garden lots;[42] 250 families in North Bay shared seven acres of relief gardens.[43] Private gardens were another way to stretch budgets in the interwar years. Though the process of preserving was generally considered to be a female job, growing food could be either men's or women's work. Men participated in gardening and took pride in their ability to grow food for their families; the garden was therefore a place where gendered roles and expectations could overlap and where men might display their fatherly respectability.[44] An article in *Child and Family Welfare* on running municipal relief and community gardens claimed that gardening was a way to provide 'moral encouragement' to unemployed men, as well as a means of keeping families off relief. In some cases, the author noted, men preferred to work on the garden without the help of women and children.[45] Basil Libby remembered specifically that his father maintained the family vegetable garden, and similarly, Mary Cleeson recalled that her father, while on short time as a CPR machinist, tended a vegetable garden for their family.[46] For many men the ability to garden was a source of pride because it signalled self-sufficiency and survival, even in terrible economic conditions. As John Gore of Cobalt declared, 'I always say to my son, "You have to remember how to grow a potato."'[47] While it clearly contributed to the domestic production of the household, gardening was a job that men could participate in without worry of becoming 'feminized.' Gardening was connected to values of economic independence and manly self-reliance, and a 'stocked larder' was a source of pride for many men.[48]

Because of the material and symbolic importance of food, relief diets became a focal point for protest and reform in the 1930s, and both men and women recognized and rebelled against the poor quality provisions and lack of choice in relief diets and vouchers. Malnourishment and starvation hovered close by for poor families throughout the 1930s, suggesting that bodies must not be dematerialized or seen solely, as Joan Sangster warns, as 'textual renderings.'[49] Basic provisions, whether obtained in kind or through a limited voucher system, were neither nutritionally sound nor adequate, and they were uniformly bland. Like the diets of the poor in general, relief diets relied heavily on carbohydrates and root vegetables, and they lacked protein and calcium. Citrus fruits such as oranges and lemons were considered luxuries by the Ontario government, and they were not provided under direct relief.[50] Relief food was also, as the Ottawa Dietetic Association recognized, monotonous and boring.[51] Though newspapers and advice columns repeatedly suggested ways for mothers to feed their families creatively on low budgets, specialists realized that women's choices were limited. While Dr Harry Cassidy criticized working-class housewives for their lack of knowledge and skill in economizing with rations from Toronto's House of Industry, Mrs Muriel Redmond, acting director of the Toronto Visiting Housewives Association pointed out that many working-class women could not cook economically because of the shortage of fuel and lack of proper equipment, particularly stoves.[52] By 1934 the VHA, a division of the Red Cross that sent dieticians and mothers' helpers into the homes of the poor, claimed that food allowances were nowhere near high enough for housewives to 'stretch.'[53] Some suggestions, such as baking bread, dramatically increased women's workload, while tips such as buying canned goods or food and supplies in bulk saved money in theory – but were too costly for many women to undertake.[54] The Ottawa Dietetic Association claimed that 'in most of cases the women in the house manage on very little, generally speaking they do wonders.'[55]

Lack of proper food was recognized by some medical and welfare authorities to be detrimental to the health of families and children. A 1932 report by Dr A.E. Ranney, medical officer of health for North Bay, claimed that the health repercussions of a diet lacking in proper vitamins included scurvy, rickets, poor bones and teeth, underdevelopment, indigestion, and constipation. Ranney recognized that a housewife often had to 'economize first through her food budget,' that vegetables were luxuries, and that poor diets were linked to 'extensive unemployment.'[56] Studies in Canada and Great Britain also found that those who were unemployed or on relief were more likely to suffer from rickets, defective vision, and cardiovascular problems. The effects of malnutrition were seen most profoundly in maternal and infant mortality rates. While social reformers had long been concerned with lowering these, the overall rate of decline slowed markedly in the Great Depression, only improving in the late 1930s.[57] As Dr Alan Brown reported to the Canadian Medical Association, low-income pregnant mothers did not receive food adequate to maintain their own health, let alone that of the fetus.[58]

The health consequences of poor diets resulting from inadequate relief and high unemployment created a political battleground for politicians, social workers, and physicians from across the political spectrum. Health problems were often long term, as Ranney's list suggested: weakened bones and teeth or subtler problems such as a lack of focus in school or low energy were not given much medical credence by politicians. Opponents of increased food allowances could claim that since no one was literally starving to death families on relief were adequately provided for, and mothers should simply learn to cook more economically and nutritiously. Not everyone was convinced, however. The case of the family of Ambrose Hearn illustrates the impact of inadequate food on relief families. Hearn, who was unemployed and supporting five children, wrote an impassioned letter to Premier Mitchell Hepburn. His family had been surviving on $2 a week in relief money for groceries, and his wife, he claimed, had weakened and died from the resulting poor diet. 'As my wife was a great and motherly woman to our children,' he wrote proudly, 'she was forced to often eat only one meal a day in order to leave a little for the children. This ruined her health ... I am thoroughly convinced that had my wife had proper nourishment ... she would be alive today.'[59] Regardless of the actual medical cause of death, clearly the Hearn family was living under conditions in which no family member was receiving enough nutrition to ensure good health.

Women whose families were on relief cooked with inadequate rations and with food that was of poor nutritional quality. Prior to 1932 in Ontario relief rates were not standardized, and food orders across municipalities varied anywhere from $3.50 to $8.50 a week.[60] In his 1932 report on conditions of unemployment and relief in Ontario, Dr Harry Cassidy, a founding member of the League for Social Reconstruction and professor of social science at the University of Toronto, reported that all municipalities in Ontario, except for Toronto's House of Industry, gave food allowances in the form of grocery orders for staples such as flour, lard, salt, sugar, oats, butter, stewing meat, potatoes, and soap at specified stores. The particular rules varied among municipalities; in Ottawa, for example, food orders could only be claimed at two stores that had agreements with the city; in Windsor, Brantford, and Kitchener arrangements were made with a number of stores for discounts on relief orders.[61] The Campbell Report recommended standardizing relief allowances in Ontario, and in 1933 it was implemented by the Henry government. The committee was chaired by Wallace Campbell, general manager of Ford Canada, and it consisted of six businessmen and one social welfare worker, but no doctors, women, or nutritionists.[62] However, the Campbell Report was commissioned to develop ways to combat relief fraud and to set standardized ceilings for relief rates across Ontario, not as a response to concern over inadequate relief standards. The report set out maximum rates of relief, recommended that municipalities centralize relief administration in public welfare boards and develop standardized forms and procedures of investigation. Because the report did not address the need for a minimum standard of living, relief rates still differed by municipality even after 1932. Municipalities were not required to provide fuel, clothing, or shelter relief. The only universal provision offered was food, and each municipality had the power and authority to decide the type, quantity, and form of relief.[63]

Most contemporary studies of relief and food budgets in the 1930s found that relief provisions could not adequately nourish families. In 1933 in Montreal, for example, 55 per cent of adults and 47 per cent of youths on relief were considered to be undernourished.[64] While the Campbell Report established a maximum food allowance of $5 per week for a family of five, to be increased by 10 per cent in the winter, the Ontario Medical Association reported that the 'bare essentials of health' for a family of five should be set at $6.59 to $7 per week.[65] The Visiting Housewives Association established a minimum for a family of five as $6.75 per week in 1932, and Cassidy noted that it would be impossible to lower food allowances to under $5 a week and still meet basic standards of nutrition.[66] Yet the financial reality in many municipalities was even worse than the $5 weekly maximum suggested by the Campbell Report. In many areas of Ontario, families survived on amounts of money set far below the commonly accepted standards for the bare minimum of heath. In Fort William in 1933 a family of five received $4.45 per week; in Sudbury in 1932 a family of five received $5.35, and Lloyd Dennis and his parents received $3 a week in food relief, which could be spent only on staples at the local general store.[67] Regardless of the municipality, the method of relief distribution, or the cooking skills of mothers, families on relief never received enough to meet basic nutritional standards. To have received adequate supplies would have violated the principle of less eligibility, and it would also have made clear the dietary inadequacies in poor, working-class, and unemployed families in general.

Sewing

While cooking and preparing food was clearly the most essential reproductive labour needed to maintain a family, sewing was another traditionally female skill that women could employ in making cheaper clothes for themselves and their children. Sewing and mending were skills of crucial importance in cash-strapped families, and women could reuse, mend, or take in sewing to earn extra money. In North Bay the newspaper reported a noticeable increase in the purchase of patterns and materials at local stores: 'The general business of depression has caused many housewives to look twice at their purse before making extravagant purchases.' The paper surmised that 'women have apparently found a great deal of pleasure in adopting the art with which their grandmothers were so familiar.'[68] Sewing may have been a pleasurable act for some, but generally it was laborious work. Ellen Stafford's memories of sewing consisted of a litany of never-ending chores: 'Sewing, patching, darning, mending. Handing down, cutting down, and making over. Turning sheets sides to middle. Reversing frayed shirt collars. Ripping seams and remodeling old suits and dresses. Unravelling sweaters and using the wool to knit other sweaters as the children grew. Mending socks, stockings, underthings. Patching worn places, and then patching the patches.'[69]

Women sewed clothing from scratch or made over second-hand clothes received from friends, relatives, or charity. Creative use of materials such as a father's old clothes or worn-out linens resulted in what would have been some interesting and non-standardized clothing.[70] Mrs Edith Grace Taylor used her brother's old Canadian National Railroad uniforms and made them into outfits for her two sons, while another woman remembered her mother sewing children's clothes out of 'beautiful green drapes' and shirts made from old sheets.[71] But clothing was more than just simple material: it reflected one's status within the community as well. To have visibly worn clothes or hand-me-downs could be a source of shame, especially for children. Worn and poor quality clothing was a very public marker of poverty and unemployment. Tips in papers and magazines abounded on how to make homemade clothes look more fashionable. The *North Bay Nugget* reported that women should be careful to avoid the 'home-made look' when sewing children's clothes and that boys were particularly sensitive: 'If they are kidded about home-made clothes, it sears their souls.'[72] Oral histories support this concern over masculinity and pride. None of the housewives interviewed by Denyse Baillargeon sewed clothes for their husbands, even if they sewed them for themselves and their children. Not only were men's garments difficult to sew and fit, men were 'too proud' to wear homemade clothing.[73] When children wore clothes handed down from wealthier families they were, like one young Toronto girl, humiliated when they had to face their benefactors.[74] Yet reminiscences also suggest that shame was balanced by pride in wives' and mothers' ability to create clothing and save money and by their attempts to make clothing attractive and fashionable, though this perspective was generally acquired with the distance of time. Recalled a woman from Sault Ste Marie: 'I remember one [dress] she made for me for a concert ... she took lace off a slip of her own and she sewed it all around the top. The bottom was plain and the little dress was all blue and white from the sugar bag. She made a great big bow from another sugar bag and trimmed it in white. I figure I was the nicest dressed there!'[75]

Informal Paid Labour

Women engaged in a wide variety of income-earning activities after marriage, often at home or in forms of work connected to traditional domestic skills. Informal labour had long been an acceptable way for married women to earn money to supplement men's low or non-existent wages.[76] As Joan Sangster points out, while women and their families termed this informal labour an 'extra' source of income, it was actually central to family survival.[77] Women found a wide range of ways to supplement family incomes, from establishing creative businesses to working in traditionally female-typed jobs. A woman and her two sons started their own home-based knitting business, making yarn on a spinning wheel, carding it by hand, and knitting socks and mittens that they then sold to highway workers.[78] Mrs Rose Jessop had to quit her job as a telephone operator when she married, but when her husband came down with tuberculosis, she worked as a waitress and did occasional sewing work for the public.[79] Many married women who worked outside the home did so in the field of domestic service.[80] Mrs Anne McCormack of Toronto supported herself and her unemployed husband by doing occasional domestic labour after parties and dinners, while Mrs Christien Thatcher kept her family off relief with her dressmaking skills, which, she explained, served to 'tide us over for more than one month when there was no money coming in from anything else.'[81] For many women, however, undertaking informal domestic labour left them vulnerable to extremely low wages, poor working conditions, or even violence. Mrs Clara Jessop, a forty-three-year-old woman from Middlesex County, was hired to do housework for her neighbour Daniel McDonald in September 1938. While she was working, he attempted to sexually assault her and held her captive for four hours. When she refused to comply, he took back the $1 he had paid her for her work, and she escaped, telling her daughter, her husband, and eventually, the police.[82] Child protection legislation, which restricted children's employment, could not protect young women who worked informally at domestic labour. Fourteen-year-old Daniela D'Ambrosio of Sault Ste Marie was employed in the home of Giovanni Bertossi, where she received 10 cents for cleaning his home. She testified in court that while she was working he raped her and threatened to kill her if she reported it.[83]

Women's informal paid labour was often connected to their do-mestic roles, such as cooking, cleaning, or selling produce or other goods. Mrs George Amos ran a part-time bakery and cooking business, maintained a garden from which she sold produce, and worked as a seamstress and a domestic.[84] Mrs Mary Niemczyk, a thirty-year-old mother of two, received her family's apartment for free by doing the cooking and washing for her landlord. Such initiative, however, was not appreciated by her unemployed husband, who lodged a complaint with the family court protesting that she was 'too friendly' with the landlord and that she refused to do his own laundry and cooking.[85] Rural women had a long tradition of selling goods and produce to con-tribute to the family economy. Daily farm production, in which women played a prominent role, was a 'major source of income for farm fam-ilies during the Depression decade,' and the production of homemade cheese 'more than doubled' from 1926 to 1937, a reversal of the previ-ous trend towards factory cheese production.[86] John A. Matheson of Southampton credited his mother's ability to keep the family afloat by raising a cow, geese, hens, and two pigs and by making and selling milk and butter to local families, while Mrs Jane Mill raised chickens and rabbits and kept a large potato garden for food.[87]

Keeping boarders was a popular way to supplement the family in-come and one way that women's domestic labour could be turned into much-needed cash; 19 per cent of Canadian households had lodgers in 1931, while in cities like Toronto the numbers were even higher, at 23.2 per cent. In Baillargeon's study of Montreal housewives, 20 per cent of the women took in lodgers or boarders as an extra source of in-come.[88] Most lodgers were housed in urban households, though ap-proximately one-third of all boarders were located in rural areas in 1931.[89] Taking boarders was not a mark of extreme poverty, but rather a way to stretch a limited budget. Very poor families did not have enough money to invest in the necessary extra space, sheets, and blankets needed to house boarders.[90] Both boarders and their 'hosts' came from a wide range of class and occupational backgrounds, from semi-skilled and working-class families to white-collar and middle-class families. Taking in boarders served a variety of purposes: it could help provide food for poor families, contribute towards rent or mortgage payments, or be an important way for immigrant, working-class, and middle-class families to save for home ownership.[91]

Taking in boarders, whether in a lodging house or a private home, was clearly situated in the realm of women's work, and as Peter Baskerville suggests, historians should understand running boarding-houses as a female-dominated occupation.[92] When Tony Schafer, an immigrant from Austria, was laid off from his job in Hamilton, his wife Mary 'kept the family by doing housework for 25 cents an hour, and by taking in boarders to supplement the eighteen dollars a month in rent.'[93] For the widowed Mrs M. Cook, taking boarders and working as a cook were the only ways to pay rent and doctor's bills after her husband died. 'When the Bread earner [sic] is taken,' she wrote Premier Hepburn, 'it is a hard fight for a woman alone.'[94] Of course, opening up the family home to boarders, who were often unmarried men, created not only work for women, but also a variety of dangers, particularly if the women or their daughters were left at home with them. The presence of boarders could lead to conflict in marriages or leave children or women vulnerable to sexual assault. These kinds of conflicts are not captured in census records on boarding, and they suggest that such commonplace strategies simultaneously contained both economic advantages and potential dangers. After her mother's death in Hamilton in 1931, for example, twelve-year-old Emily Blake moved in with her sister's family and five boarders, where she worked as a babysitter for her nephew. Jack Cranmer, eventually accused of 'unlawful carnal knowledge,' was one of the boarders; he was a cabinetmaker who rented their garage.[95] Women were vulnerable to sexual assault by boarders, who as already pointed out, were often single men. Working behind closed doors in the privacy of the home, and dependent on the income, women might find themselves victims of sexual or physical assault or fighting the expectation that they should trade sex for money.[96] In 1932 Jan Olczak was charged with the indecent assault of Ruth Zaludek. Through an interpreter, Zaludek testified that Olczak was a boarder in her home.

ZALUDEK: He came from upstairs to the kitchen and he say 'Good day misses are you clean the peaches, the peaches is ripe alright' and then I say 'Well it don't make any difference if ripe or not' and he say 'I ask your peaches misses.'
CROWN: What does that mean?

ZALUDEK: That means 'her cunt' in Hungarian, and he say ...
   Mr Zaludek told him we can sleep three together in the bed.

Olczak physically prevented her from leaving the house for almost
three hours. Mrs Zaludek demanded that he leave her alone, asserting
her respectability by telling him: 'Very nice to live with my husband
and family and I do not try to do anything like that, not for any money
or anything at all [sic].'[97] Despite the necessity of taking in boarders, it
is clear that such work placed women, at least occasionally, in precarious situations.

   Keeping a boardinghouse could create difficulties between husbands
and wives, because of the women's intimate knowledge of their male
boarders. Bertha George complained to the family court in July 1934
that her husband Edward, an unemployed veteran and barber, had an
'uncontrollable temper' that was causing 'constant friction' in the home.
The probation officer, Miss Mayhew, noted that they had a male boarder
who helped out around the house and the barbershop, and after interviewing the husband she wrote that he 'resented [his] wife consulting
this man about household affairs instead of him ... [he] would not be
ignored in his own home.'[98] Similarly, Peter Yaroshevsky complained to
the family court that his wife, who kept a roominghouse, was living
with one of the roomers.[99] Despite the conflicts that could ensue, taking
boarders or lodgers was essential to economic survival for many families, and it was a common form of women's labour that contributed
much-needed cash to family resources.[100]

Budgeting

Women struggled and worried over ways to budget, save money, and
maintain their homes through domestic labour and informal paid
labour. But women's work, though it often took place in the context of
the home, was not just a private act. Their skills at budgeting were
subject to criticism by outsiders, welfare officials, or other families.[101]
One woman who identified herself as 'A Worried Housewife' wrote to
the *Farmer's Advocate* in 1931 to ask for advice on how to better manage her income for a family of six on her husband's income of $15 per
week. Lack of money, she said, was causing tension in the home: 'I
have a good man, kind and a good worker, but we do have words over
this, as he works so hard and cannot save anything. I hope someone
can give me some idea how to do better. I certainly do worry myself
almost sick sometimes over it.' The advice columnist, while praising

her hard work and ability, suggested she also grow her own food and send her eldest daughter out to work. This was apparently not good enough, however, for she was also advised to increase her emotional caretaking. 'In addition to managing to daily work,' wrote the columnist, 'you will have to manage also to be happy about it and to take an attitude that will make for encouragement and hope.'[102] Yet the toll of holding together a husband and family, of 'all this sewing on of buttons, swatting of flies, scrimping and saving, turning and making over – doing with and doing without,' was difficult and exhausting. Ultimately, acknowledged one woman, it was the 'lack of money that wears us down in the long run.'[103]

Women's close association with the home was reflected in the way they were addressed as consumers by the government, political parties, and advice columnists. Because they were responsible for domestic-related purchases, women enjoyed a limited amount of power as consumers. However, women's association with consumption could easily devolve into condemnation for spending money foolishly and unwisely or into a thinly disguised critique of feminine 'frivolity.' Joked the *Nugget*, 'ONE [sic] thing the Depression hasn't affected and that's the paint job on the feminine face.'[104] Much of this critique, however, was connected to class status. Middle- and upper-class women were encouraged to spend money on luxuries and were informed that the moral value of thriftiness did not apply to them. Instead, shopping and spending money were ways for women to express their citizenship, which was not surprising, given women's historical association with consumption. This foreshadowed the growing trend to see citizenship articulated in the ability of consumers to more easily purchase wide varieties of consumer goods.[105] 'In the interest of humanity, it simply becomes a duty to buy new clothes,' wrote the *North Bay Nugget*. 'Every woman who can afford to buy a new garment and still decides to wear her old one is helping to keep people out of jobs.'[106] The Ontario legislature discussed the possibility of encouraging women to wear wolf-skins as a way of developing a market for fur. As part of the Bennett government's attempt to end the Depression in 1930 by increasing the consumption of Canadian-made goods, Minister of Trade and Commerce H.H. Stevens developed an advertisement targeted at women, playing on their dependence on the male breadwinner and their fears of losing that crucial income: 'Are you one of those whose lot in life consists in looking after the home? ... It would be a terrible thing, wouldn't it, if next week your house allowance were suddenly to be shut off! Yet that is what might happen if your breadwinner were unexpectedly to lose his business, or his job! Are you doing everything you can do – to spare yourself a misfortune of that kind? ... protect the job of your breadwinner by always giving a Canadian made article preference over one that has been imported.'[107] A later government policy initiative, this time under Prime Minister Mackenzie King, was the Home Improvement Plan, which, based on the recommendations of the National Employment Commission, was an attempt to stimulate the building trades through low-cost loans for home renovations. In government-sponsored advertising, men were addressed as proud homeowners, while women were addressed as consumers, home-makers, and shoppers. Their contribution to ending unemployment and maintaining respectable homes was through redecorating their living rooms and renovating their kitchens.[108]

Women who were single mothers, widowed, or wives of unemployed men often recognized the disjunction between a prescriptive culture that celebrated women's domesticity and maternal and consumer roles and an economy that made it impossible to fulfil those roles. One woman wrote an anonymous letter to *Chatelaine*, pointing out this discrepancy: 'When depression comes, my country rushes to the rescue. But when the SOS goes out, do Canadians say "Mothers and babies first?" Is my name exalted when it appears on the relief list? Hardly.'[109] While women could draw on traditional domestic skills and traditions of making do, these skills of sewing, cooking, and budgeting increased women's workload and did not guarantee family survival. Women were aware that sometimes no matter how creatively they budgeted, they could only stretch relief money or low wages in limited ways. 'I have been fighting vs worry until I feel as if I am going to break down completely,' wrote a woman to Prime Minster Bennett. 'There isn't a thing wasted in my house, and I couldn't get my rent light gas and water [sic] cheaper no matter how I tried.'[110] One rural woman suggested that the 'government should also give every needy mother so much to feed and clothe the children. There are lots in need of this, and it would save a lot of sickness.'[111] After paying for rent and food, this woman, like others, found that little was left for children's other needs such as new shoes, clothing, or textbooks.[112] An overwhelming concern of most mothers was the inability to provide proper clothes and books for their children to attend school, because limited funds always went first to rent. Many children were kept home from school because they had inadequate winter clothing, no shoes, or not enough food to eat.

For example, Juliet Framer of Sudbury was a widow with nine dependent children and an ill brother to support. She received $73 a month for
rent, light, and fuel, but the money was still not enough to provide clothing so that her children could go to school. [113] Similarly, Laurent Martin's
mother kept him home from school because he had no shoes, a particularly significant problem during the winter months in Ottawa. [114]

Women with husbands who refused to register for relief, or who
spent relief money or wages on alcohol, illustrated even more clearly
the problems of female dependence. Women's domestic skills, in these
situations, could do little to help ensure family survival. Claire Dupes,
who worked at Presage's in Ottawa, was the sole support for her husband and two children. But her wages did not go far enough, she told
the family court, because her unemployed husband took the rent money
and used it to buy alcohol. [115] One woman wrote to Prime Minister
Bennett in frustration: 'I just don't know what to do for money the children come to me about everything its the women and the children who
suffer in these terrible times [sic].' [116] Women were held responsible for
family budgeting and household management, even though they could
not make enough money to support a family. Women's labour and
management skills, while often 'unseen and unrecorded,' were therefore crucial to family survival. [117]

Women in the Labour Force

While women's ultimate responsibility was the home, many women
did participate in the paid labour force in the 1930s, and working
women, especially those who were married, became a topic of heated
political debate throughout the decade. Married women workers were
condemned for usurping the role of the male breadwinner or selfishly
working for pin money. [118] At first, data from the 1931 census seem to
indicate that women were relatively unhurt by unemployment in comparison with men. Women's participation in the workforce increased
during the interwar period, from 17.7 per cent of the gainfully employed population in 1921 to 22.9 per cent in 1941. [119] According to the
1931 census, only 8.74 per cent of women who wanted to work were
unemployed, compared with 20.87 per cent of men. [120] These numbers
seem to explain the enormous amount of cultural bitterness over
women perceived to be stealing what were considered to be men's
rightful jobs. As one woman wrote to the editor of the *Evening Examiner*,
it was selfish for married women to take jobs 'when so many families

are out of work.'[121] Some debate has existed over whether the public outcry over women's work was indicative of men attempting to preserve their position in the labour market or whether it reflected a deeper sense of working-class justice and equity over the distribution of paid employment. Alice Kessler-Harris argues that the anger against married women workers was actually a 'shared conception of justice,' part of a working-class value system that wanted jobs to be fairly apportioned among whose who needed them the most.[122] However, as Margaret Hobbs points out, all women, regardless of their economic situation, came under attack as illegitimate workers selfishly working for pin money, and this criticism assumed that men were rightful workers whose masculinity was fundamentally eroded through loss of employment.[123] Criticism over women's labour was wide-ranging and complex, and it came from women as well as men. Some simplistically saw the economic crisis as easily solved by banning all women from the labour market in favour of men who 'rightfully' deserved jobs, while others upheld the breadwinner norm and the family wage. Still others claimed that married women's labour prevented single women from obtaining temporary employment before marriage. An anonymous writer from Toronto wrote to the Department of Labour in 1939 to complain about a company that employed a woman who owned her own home and car and who had a working husband and no children. 'Is this justice?' asked the writer. 'There's no wonder the city's crippled with reliefees. Can't this be rectified?'[124] According to another anonymous writer, 'If the married women worker of Toronto, as a tribute of love and patriotism to our King and Country, would hand over their jobs to relief families ... would not the Gratitude [sic] of discouraged relief recipients be showered upon them?'[125] Unemployed single women also vocally condemned the paid labour of married women. A 'working girl' from Carleton Place asked Hepburn to ban from working all married women whose husbands had jobs. Like Vera Rogers, who complained to Premier Hepburn that married women worked for pin money while she had to support her widowed mother, 'working girl' was the only source of income for her widowed mother, and she was struggling to keep the family out of debt and off relief.[126] These popular criticisms of married women's labour were concerned with economic justice and fair distribution of jobs in a limited market, but at their root was the deeply felt belief in the essential right of men to labour, the value of a family wage, and the gendered ideals of breadwinner and homemaker.

The nature of the debate around working women, especially married women in the paid labour force, was not just a matter of individual complaint or cultural criticism, but part of a public initiative to keep women out of jobs that could be performed by men. The Ontario civil service was under pressure to exclude married women from its payrolls and struggled to purge married women from the service after being lobbied by a number of organizations, including the Legion, some labour unions and women's groups, and various newspapers.[127] Labour Minister N.O. Hipel wrote in 1939: 'So far as the Ontario Government is concerned, all girl employees when marrying are automatically returned from the service. No married women are engaged unless their husbands are totally incapacitated.'[128] The government discovered early in the Great Depression, however, that it was not so easy to remove women from the civil service, because most desperately needed the work. By 1931 the government required that women inform it of their married status, 'as the general tendency at present in public services is not to retain women in the service after they marry.' Some women responded, however, by continuing to work under their maiden names.[129] In 1931 there were 269 married women in the civil service, 120 of whom worked part-time. But when the government investigated these female employees, it discovered that women were working for more than pin money.[130] For example, in the Department of Agriculture, married women workers included a woman who supported her elderly and invalid husband, a woman who supplemented her family income because her husband was a low-paid farmhand, and a woman whose husband was a student. In all departments, investigations revealed married women whose husbands earned low wages or were ill or disabled, or women who were separated, divorced, or had dependents to support.[131]

Politicians' musings aside, the provincial government had no formal or consistent policy on the issue of married working women. Mrs Christina Bunnett of Belleville, who worked at a shirt factory while her husband was unemployed, wrote to Dr Faulkner of the Department of Public Welfare. She expressed concern over the public discourse discouraging married women from working, claiming: 'I don't want charity from any one. I just want to work and feel I've earned what I've got.' Demonstrating that even public officials were confused over the status of working women, Faulkner forwarded her letter to Labour Minister Morrison MacBride and asked his consent for her to continue working; he replied that there were no regulations or 'attempts' to 'prevent any married woman from working.'[132]

Despite figures showing the persistence of female labour force employment in the Depression, women did not 'steal' men's jobs, nor did they enjoy high levels of employment. The labour market was structured so that women were often clustered in sex-typed occupations, which were not hit as hard as male jobs, or in jobs that were unlikely to attract male workers.[133] In fact, 84 per cent of female wage-earners were concentrated in three main occupational groups: service, clerical, and textile work.[134] Women made up 94.8 per cent of stenographers, 96 per cent of housekeepers, and 100 per cent of nurses.[135] Yet the census figures also undercount the extent of women's unemployment, since married women who were laid off or were trying to re-enter the workforce or single women who lived with their parents were generally classified as dependents rather than as unemployed.[136] Census figures also do not capture the devastating effect that Depression conditions had on non-white women, who were pushed into the lowest-paying jobs in domestic service. Dionne Brand estimates that at least 80 per cent of urban black women worked in domestic service because of discrimination in finding factory and clerical jobs. One African-Canadian woman recalled that she was paid $5 a week in old clothes for her labour.[137]

Even minimum wage laws did little to protect women. The two royal commissions established in the 1930s to examine working conditions in the textile and garment industries revealed that minimum wage laws were continually violated. Only seventy minimum wage and factory investigators existed for all of Canada, and employers were legally allowed to designate new workers as inexperienced in order to pay them at lower rates.[138] Since minimum wage legislation only applied to women, it was men who could potentially undercut women's wages. Though women formed 43 per cent of gainfully employed textile workers in 1934, their numbers decreased throughout the 1930s because of employers who hired men at lower wages.[139] It was difficult for the Department of Labour to gather enough evidence to prosecute employers who were accused of firing women and hiring men at lower wages.[140] As A.W. Crawford, chairman of the minimum wage board wrote in February 1937, there was no 'effective means of preventing the replacement of girls by men.' Employers who were 'determined to do away with female help' simply claimed that the work of a man or boy was different from women's work. Crawford argued that the only way to prevent this problem was to implement a minimum wage for men, noting that his inspectors had warned employers against making threats to female employees, but it was almost impossible to secure proper evidence.[141]

Married women mainly took jobs out of economic necessity, and even then rarely saw themselves as breadwinners and providers. Rather, they continued to uphold the ideal of the male breadwinner family and to comment on the impact of unemployment on men's identity.[142] The debate around the disastrous impact of married women's labour force participation was rooted in popular gender ideology rather than economic reality. Most women in the paid labour force were young single women who worked in sex-typed industries.[143] Women rarely displaced male workers in industry or became sole family breadwinners. The moral panic about women working was primarily embedded in concern over the demise of traditional gender roles and, most importantly, in the fear over the erosion of masculinity.

Prostitution

While most women found ways to undertake paid labour that negotiated the fragile boundaries of female respectability, some women acted outside those boundaries. Prostitution was one way that women could supplement a meagre income or inadequate relief. Little historical work has been done on prostitution in twentieth-century Canada; nevertheless, there is some anecdotal evidence of occasional prostitution in the 1930s, and in some oral histories and court records there is evidence of women engaging in prostitution as a means to make money in tight economic times.[144] Much of this work suggests that 'casual' prostitution was not uncommon for poor women and younger girls and was one 'choice' within structural inequalities and limited economic options. Fourteen-year-old Leila Seguin of Ottawa was charged with incorrigibility in March 1938 after her neighbour, Mrs Paquette, witnessed Laura looking inside the coat of an older, drunk man on the street. Paquette confronted her, followed her home, then called the police, who discovered the family was on relief, the father was unemployed, and Leila was not attending school. Neither Leila nor her parents seemed particularly concerned about her admission of taking money for sexual favours, echoing feminist historians' suggestion that the line between sexual exchange and casual prostitution was easily blurred and that most young girls involved in prostitution were paid by other working-class men in their own neighbourhood.[145] Seguin claimed that she had, on several occasions, taken money to 'touch men' and then demanded they pay her $10 not to call the police. She took the money home to her mother and told her how she earned it, and her mother then used it to buy her daughter clothing and food. The judge took a dim view of Seguin's attempts to make money, stating: 'I am rather of the opinion that this child is a neglected child' and that her mother has supported 'certain suggestive methods where she might be able to get money.' The family was then turned over to the Children's Aid Society for on-going supervision.[146] A tradition of sexual barter did exist, one in which girls and young women 'traded' their sexuality for money, goods, or food. These trades were hardly done under equal conditions and were shaped by conditions of coercion, but it is often difficult to tell from court records how much negotiation or coercion actually took place.[147] In the case of twelve-year-old Willa Owen, for example, the relation-ship between Willa, her young friends, and John Pym seemed to move from one of 'barter' to one of sexual coercion. Willa lived with her aunt and uncle in Sault Ste Marie while her father worked outside the city. She, along with three other young girls, cleaned the home of Pym, an engineer for the Canadian Pacific Railroad, who lived nearby. When she was twelve, they had a sexual relationship, which resulted in her pregnancy. In her court statement she claimed that he often invited her and the other girls for supper and to play the piano and that 'he also entertained us by telling dirty jokes.' He gave her a watch, wine, music lessons, and occasionally, small amounts of spending money. 'At first when he wanted to use me I fought with him,' she stated, 'until about a year ago when I found out it was no use.' The three other girls blamed her, claiming that that 'she wasn't smart in her talk or her behaviour.'[148]

For some women, prostitution was evidently one way to either earn a living or to supplement low wages or relief. In 1938 Elizabeth Spiegel was arrested for bringing in 'a few men' to her apartment on Mutual Street in Toronto. 'I was not working and I went out to make a few dollars,' she claimed, noting that she took only men she knew or had been introduced to 'by some other girl.'[149] One court record contains the reference that two 'coloured' prostitutes in Hamilton charged $3, but this reveals little information on how much a woman might expect to earn over the course of a week, a month, or a year.[150]

Some married women found prostitution a viable way to earn extra money, and not all husbands were ignorant of their wives' actions. In the winter of 1931 Mrs Mary Hume was arrested for prostitution, and when the CAS investigated, they found she had a husband and four young children, two of whom were living with relatives and a friend.

When Mrs Hume was interviewed in jail, she admitted that her husband knew of her job, that they had a female boarder 'who was in the racket,' and 'as we were in debt very considerably, my husband suggested that I should go out and do the same thing.' In the three to four months she had been working, Mrs Hume noted, with some pride: 'I have reduced the amount of rent that was owing, which was one hundred dollars, to about fifty-seven dollars and have helped to reduce other debts and keep the house going. My husband has not had steady work for about two years and he wanted a radio and other things for the home and suggested that I go out and get money in this way.' When the CAS intervened by bringing him to court and removing his children to a shelter, he admitted that he had asked his wife to become a prostitute and that she had earned up to $20 a week. He was arrested and jailed.[151]

In the late nineteenth and early twentieth centuries prostitution was labelled primarily as an issue of immorality and vice. Alhough social reformers indicated that poverty or low wages were factors in prostitution, it was overwhelmingly linked to women's 'moral weakness and cupidity.'[152] In the 1930s social workers or courts could understand prostitution as a moral vice but also as a response to or a result of poverty. When George Yaremchuk complained to the York family court that his wife was having sex with another man for money, the probation officer threatened the wife with the removal of her children and instructed the man to apply for relief, as his wages were 'quite inadequate to provide in a proper way for his wife, three children and himself.'[153] While the overwhelming concern with prostitution as the great social evil had diminished by the interwar years, most reformers and social workers still maintained that prostitutes embodied sexual deviance and that such women were in need of 'moral training.'[154] Ultimately, the assessment of how 'free' the women who were engaged in prostitution were is impossible to judge. Low wages, inadequate relief, and abusive relief officers did make prostitution an option that many women would not have otherwise considered, and therefore, it was in some sense compelled by structural gender and economic inequality. The Canadian left had long equated prostitution with capitalist failure, yet they were not immune to viewing it through the lens of morality, often speaking about prostitution in terms of 'degradation' for women.[155] For example, the *Canadian Congress Journal* often pointed out that poverty and inadequate relief could lead to prostitution and ultimately threaten women's morality, dignity, and pride, while the *Canadian Forum* referred to prostitution as a form of 'steady degradation.'[156] Whether this understanding changed in the Depression, as unemployment rates soared, is a question for further study by women's historians.

Single Motherhood

Single motherhood placed women in a difficult economic position. Though divorce was rare in the 1930s, separations, both official and unofficial, were not uncommon, and there were a number of ways that women could find themselves raising children without the support of a male breadwinner. Some women were widowed, others had children outside of marriage, and still others were deserted by their husbands.[157] The Great Depression exposed the phenomenon of temporary desertions, where men left for extended periods of time to look for work, often leaving women unsure as to when, or if, they would return. Depending on the type and length of desertion, options for single mothers were limited. Relief and mothers' allowance were the only types of government aid available to women, and as the Depression pushed wages even lower in typical female fields of domestic service, women found it difficult to make ends meet. Both the East End Day Nursery and the assistant professor of medicine at the Toronto General Hospital wrote to Premier Henry on behalf of single mother Anne Phillips who, only able to get part-time work, often had to do without food. 'Our opinion is that she is suffering from a nervous state due to being in a constant environment of anxiety and worry over the effort to support her children and herself.'[158] For Yvette André, the Depression, widowhood, and a dependent child combined to create severe health problems, leading to a nervous breakdown. When her husband committed suicide after the birth of their son in 1925, she left for Montreal from Glen Robertson in order to learn the hairdressing trade, returning in 1930 to open a beauty parlour. Unfortunately, a fire destroyed her business, and her insurance did not cover most of the costs. The mothers' allowance investigator noted that 'the loss of everything discouraged her very much and her health broke down and she suffered from the nervous shock as well ... I think this is a worthy case in every way.'[159]

One of the few provincial government–sponsored welfare programs for women was the Mothers' Allowance Act, established in 1920 in Ontario. Yet eligibility for mothers' allowance was strictly regulated. For example, until 1953 only women who were British subjects or naturalized citizens were eligible.[160] Until 1935, women with only one child under the age of sixteen were excluded. Furthermore, mothers' allowance policy was built on contradictory ideals. Though rooted in the rhetoric of maternalism, which claimed motherhood as an honourable profession, it was never generous enough to fully support a woman and her children in place of a breadwinner's wage. As a result, women were expected to supplement mothers' allowance through their own labour or that of their older children. Irma Ambrosino, for example, received mothers' allowance for nine years after her husband deserted her and her two children. At the time of her application in 1930, she worked for $10 a week as a hosiery mender at a local factory in Ingersoll and paid board to live with her parents, later establishing her own household by taking in sewing and boarders and growing her own vegetables. Yearly reports indicate her precarious economic position. In March 1937 she wrote to the mothers' allowance board to say the casket company, where she earned 10 cents an hour, was threatening to close and that the allowance was 'not sufficient to run my home and send my children to school on.' She was told that her allowance would be revoked if she moved to look for work, so she stayed in town in hopes that the company would continue to provide her with work.[161] Women were ultimately not free to move to find work; they struggled to find jobs to supplement inadequate allowances and desperately tried to care for young children.

Despite the recognized problem of youth unemployment in the Great Depression, mothers' allowance benefits were calculated with the assumption that children over the age of sixteen would find work and contribute to their mothers' support. Mrs Corinna Ryan, for example, was denied mothers' allowance because she had three children in their twenties who, the Mothers' Allowance Commission informed Ryan, should support her. Yet she pointed out in protest that 'my family hasn't anything for me. as the married ones has all or more than they can do to keep them selves and the single women are unemployed so much that they can scarcely keep them selves [sic].'[162] Children were not unaware of the assumptions encoded in government policies. Mrs Helen Bryan's nineteen-year-old son moved out of her home in frustration after her allowance was cut off. Her son, she wrote, 'thinks I should have help from somewhere else he says as long as he stays home and keeps us no one else will help us [sic]'[163] The high youth unemployment rate seemed to make little difference to mothers' allowance policy and administrators, nor did administrators allow for the possibility of conflictual mother-child relationships. Even in cases where children could find work in the 1930s, it was usually low-paid labour, barely enough to support a family. Mrs Ethel Burley of Bowmanville, a widow with two daughters, was unable to support her family on the combination of her own low wages, mothers' allowance, and her daughter's low-paid job as a domestic servant.[164]

While five Canadian provinces had mothers' allowance legislation during the 1930s, deserted wives were eligible only in British Columbia and Ontario. Women who had been deserted by their husbands faced a difficult time when applying for Ontario mothers' allowance, however, as they had to wait five years after the desertion before they were eligible.[165] If anyone interviewed by the investigators had knowledge of the man's whereabouts, the application was delayed yet again. Mrs Clarence Green of Toronto faced such a situation in 1931, after her husband left to look for work in 1929 and failed to return, leaving her to raise their three children. Laid off in 1931 and facing the prospect of having her children removed for neglect because of her attempt to work, she sold all of her furniture and told Premier Henry, 'I cannot endure this torture and misery much longer.'[166]

Some social workers and investigators recognized that the myriad problems faced by single mothers were linked to lack of money and not to immoral behaviour or laziness, though they stopped short of recommending an end to the moral regulation of recipients. The Baker family of Ottawa, for example, consisted of eight children and a widowed mother who received an allowance of $40 a month. The family first came into the juvenile court system in February 1930 when the young boys were arrested for a variety of petty thefts. During a home visit by juvenile court workers, Mrs Baker was described as 'very discouraged,' and her home as 'not very clean.' She often kept her children home from school for lack of clothes; at various times, her children suffered impetigo and scabies. The minutes of a Children's Aid Society case conference note that social workers agreed that the 'General Problem' was 'Insufficient Income.' By this time, the array of state involvement in Mrs Baker's case was stunning: four social workers from the Children's Aid Society, a Mothers'Allowance investigator, members from the Ottawa Welfare Bureau and the juvenile court, a school nurse, and a member of the United Church. The conference minutes recorded that Mrs Baker was in tax arrears and that she had tried to 'do some painting and decorating' of the home but could not afford to buy supplies. Her mothers' allowance was on the verge of being revoked because she had a four-month-old illegitimate child in a CAS home. The welfare

plan arrived at from the case conference maintained the high level of
state intervention, recommending a camp holiday for her sons, 'per-
suading' her children to help out more, and asking church members to
clean the home and put in fresh curtains. Yet the report did not acknowledge or resolve the initial and fundamental problem identified by social workers: lack of money. The CAS agreed to explain the situation to
the Mothers' Allowance Commission in order to keep her on the allowance and to find help administering it.[167] As with so many women
receiving mothers' allowance, social workers and administrators maintained the discourse of moral administration even in the face of poverty.
If women only tried harder, raised more cooperative children, and
refused to become despondent or lonely, then lack of money need not
lead to poverty.

Like other men and women, women who were deserted, separated,
widowed, or never married used the language of entitlement to claim
the right to mothers' allowance. While the state used mothers' allowance as a form of moral regulation, many female recipients understood
it as a form of entitlement rather than charity and were able to draw on
a number of discourses to legitimate their requests for financial aid.[168]
Charlotte Whitton, of the Canadian Council on Child and Family Welfare,
saw this tendency to claim government aid as a right to be highly problematic. 'There are a great number of people,' Whitton claimed in 1935,
'who do not hesitate to apply for a Mothers' Allowance, which unfortunately is regarded as a pension ... I think there is a real problem of an
increasing tendency to look upon a public grant as a right just by virtue
of widowhood.'[169] Many women attempted to define their needs as
rights that were inextricably tied to the female roles of marriage and
motherhood. 'To raise a future Canadian in the way he should be
raised,' claimed one widow, 'is an important and full time job, enough
responsibility for any woman however strong without the added burden of trying to find a job.'[170] Social welfare was not understood by
these women to be a gift that the state had no obligation to provide.

Women were able to draw on the gendered expectations of womanhood to legitimate their requests, frequently asserting that because they
had fulfilled their proper roles as wives and mothers, they were therefore owed financial support in return.[171] A deserted wife whose remar-
riage disqualified her from a veterans' pension drew on her status as a
mother as well as the language of service and sacrifice used by veterans: 'at the same time after I have struggled to raise my boys up to manhood the Government would expect my boys to step out and do their

share to protect the country would a war break out; that go to show how much respect the Government has for the citizens of the country [sic].'[172] Women claimed that they were deserving mothers who had struggled to raise 'honest and respectable' children and that they de-served the allowance because it 'belongs to my kids.'[173] When allow-ances were cut off, denied, or reduced, women contacted local mothers' allowance boards or the Mothers' Allowance Commission and wrote to provincial politicians in protest. 'Why do innocent children have to suf-fer the loss of a good home,' asked one woman, 'when we are Canadians, and our parents before us.'[174] For women who saw the allowance as a right, the intrusions and judgments of investigators were deeply re-sented. Annie Boucher, a deserted mother of six children in Ottawa, sought the intervention of the family court to fight the local mothers' allowance board. In a home visit, the mothers' allowance investigator reported that the mother was a 'very aggressive type.' In October 1934 Boucher turned to Judge Balharrie to ask for help, writing that the so-cial worker 'has taken too much authority in my home in threatening me' and by unfairly judging her child-raising abilities. She claimed: 'I'm giving all the good in me to save my children and I'm constantly under nervous strain from effects ... is there anything that can be done to get justice from these female social workers, not all of them, mind you, one or two of them.'[175] Similarly, in Prescott, Martina Barton fought with the local mothers' allowance investigator who was attempting to control where she bought her groceries. In July 1932 the investigator reported that Mrs Barton was telling people 'that the check [sic] be-longs to her and that she can do as she likes with it. She stated that I have nothing to say about what she does.'[176] While their protests were not always successful, women were determined to force the state to recognize their concerns and duties as mothers, and they cannot be understood simply as passive or grateful recipients.

Mothers' allowance demonstrates the fluidity between public and pri-vate welfare, Margaret Little argues, because eligibility was dependent on women's moral propriety and respectability, such as proper house-keeping standards and the cleanliness and behaviour of their children. Women were consistently praised for fulfilling the expectations of respectable motherhood, for attempting to remain economically self-sufficient, and for being good mothers and 'excellent homemakers.' Mrs Irene Arthur, for example, was praised by the investigator for her homemaking skills and her 'desire to be independent. She has never received assistance from any outside source and is reluctant to do so now.'[177] Sexual standards were of particular concern to administrators, and many women were cut off from the allowance after being accused of immorality.[178] But even those recipients who were accused of impropriety could draw on the rhetoric of reformers who had originally envisioned the allowance as a payment that recognized 'the reproductive work of women merited some degree of entitlement.'[179] A woman from Longbranch accused of moral impropriety for keeping a male boarder in her home unsuccessfully protested the removal of her allowance by claiming: 'I am a member of the Church of England and a conservative and I am trying to bring my children up right.'[180] In a few cases, being a good mother was enough to maintain the allowance, even in the face of sexual scandal. Mrs Ruth Coulter, who had two children by a man who turned out to be a bigamist, was turned down for mothers' allowance because she was not legally married. She successfully appealed, saying 'I am a Canadian girl born and raised in Toronto and I am a Mother. I think I am deserving of that allowance.'[181] Claiming entitlement based on fulfilling the gendered duties of wife and mother could be a source of power for women, who could use those accomplishments to demand financial aid from the state. As women and mothers, these women believed that they were entitled to economic security for themselves and their children, as did most women who wrote to the premiers asking for help.

Women Deserting Families

Despite a cultural emphasis on respectability, and the traditional roles of childrearing and homemaking, some women lived and acted outside the boundaries of respectable womanhood. Some actions were a deliberate choice within a limited realm of economic opportunity, while others were less a conscious choice than a reaction to overwhelming financial problems. Yet all of these actions indicate attempts by women to take control of their circumstances and their bodies within a restricted realm of options. Women who earned money through prostitution were not the only ones acting outside the boundaries of respectable womanhood, for example. While it was most commonly men who were taken to court for deserting families, there were some cases when women's attempts to find employment left them vulnerable to charges of neglect or desertion, and such women were labelled improper and inadequate mothers. Madeleine Charette was charged by the Children's Aid Society in 1937 with abandoning her seventeen-month-old daughter. Her mother told

Judge McKinley that she went out and left the baby with her, but 'if she works it is all right.' In her testimony, Madeleine claimed: 'I am willing to sign any paper and work in offer that I can help and work for my baby ... I am willing to work at anything.' She was given probation for desertion, and she and her parents and siblings, all unemployed and on relief, were still being monitored by the family court a year later.[182] While men were the ones generally charged with desertion or neglect, they also had greater freedom to move and look for work or to live apart from spouses or children for extended periods without being categorized as neglectful. It was men's responsibility to look for work, and it was women's duty to stay close to children and the home.

In November 1937 Iris Fisher of Prescott was reported to the court by her husband Ron for deserting her family. She left home to find work and sent him a letter saying she was 'going to Montreal to make her own living.'[183] For Francine Brassard finding work and establishing a household away from her husband was her first priority. She attempted to do this in defiance of the interventions by the CAS and the family court system, continually refusing to define her actions as a form of neglect. Three of her children lived in an orphanage, and one lived with an aunt. She refused to take them back until she found employment, claiming that 'I don't want to take custody of the children because I cannot look after them myself; I want to go out and work' and that '[they] come and eat the little bit that I get, and I will be starving.' In addition, she was living with a man who was helping to support her and wanted to remain with him.[184] That desertion was considered an essentially male crime is evident in the lack of tools that courts had at their disposal to prosecute women who deserted their families. Only men, or women who were legally designated as 'heads of families,' for example, could be charged under the Criminal Code with abandoning their children.[185]

While women are often absent from Depression images or discussions of unemployment, their labour was an integral part of the functioning and survival of the family economy. Managing decreased wages, budgeting relief money and rations, or mending second-hand clothes were all examples of the many ways that women helped families to survive during the Depression years. Yet women's close association with the home and with consumerism could leave them vulnerable to criticism. Working-class women and women on relief, for example, were often condemned for their choices in shopping and food preparation, despite the overwhelming evidence that families dealing with unemployment rarely had the resources available to meet basic nutritional standards.

Women who did formally enter the labour force faced low wages and minimal protection, and a cultural and political climate that blamed married women's labour for maintaining the economic crisis. Whether women worked out of economic need, personal fulfilment or independence, or some combination of both, they came under attack for 'stealing' men's jobs regardless of their economic situation. Yet there is little evidence to support the fears that women were replacing men in the paid labour force, and in reality they suffered from unemployment at a greater level than census numbers indicate.

Women who had been deserted or widowed, even if eligible for public welfare such as mothers' allowance, still had to undertake or have their older children find paid employment. Some women found 'respectable,' if low-paying jobs, particularly in domestic service, while for others, unemployment and poverty led to complicated situations involving desertion or prostitution. Motherhood may have been women's most glorified occupation, and some women and social reformers understood it as a profession entailing the right to economic security, but the rhetoric of maternalism never translated into the material welfare that women desperately needed to support either themselves or their families.

2 'If He Is a Man He Becomes Desperate': Unemployed Husbands, Fathers, and Workers

It is images of men and of male unemployment that often frame the popular imagination of the 'dirty thirties': men standing in relief lines or in soup kitchens, men protesting on the streets, and men 'riding the rods' in search of work. But although such images symbolize the general hardship of the era, they hide and subsume gender conflicts, the crucial role of women's domestic labour, and how the changing definitions of manhood shaped the experiences of men over time.[1] Beyond 'reclaiming' a consciously gendered male history, the study of masculinity reveals how ideas about masculinity are deeply embedded in relationships of production and the hierarchies of family life at a given historical moment. What makes men masculine has shifted over time and varied by region and race. The high male unemployment rate of the 1930s did not necessarily lead to a 'crisis' in masculinity, since the definition of what made a man was not stable, but always shifting.[2] Changes in the definition and the meaning of manhood can be profound without being considered an actual crisis: even in times of economic and cultural upheaval, men 'never lost confidence that those with a male body had the right to wield power.'[3] However, for white, heterosexual men, becoming a 'man' had long been associated with the ability to work and to provide for a family. The economic crisis of the 1930s laid bare the unstable association of economic independence and masculinity, and the anxiety contained within that hegemonic definition of manhood.

While recognizing there are competing definitions of masculinity, hegemonic ideas of what makes a man – and also, a woman – are embedded in institutions, state policy, welfare provision, and within the very concept of citizenship itself. Citizenship status delineates who is considered a full member of a national community, whose voices are considered most relevant in a political crisis, and who is allowed to criticize the state or to claim entitlement to state support as the basis of a right.[4] Men, including working-class men, have attempted to 'claim certain kinds of authority through the rights and responsibilities accorded to masculinity,' finding ways to uphold patriarchal privilege while simultaneously promoting economic independence, criticizing government policy, condemning unemployment, and upholding their status as full citizens.[5]

The Great Depression provides an important opportunity to explore how ideals of interwar masculinity were tested and reshaped in Canada during a period of economic crisis, when the links between breadwinning, labour, respectability, and manliness were under deep strain. Through an examination of the connections between masculinity, work, and family, this chapter explores the shame and humiliation many men felt because of their unemployment, as well as the ways in which men struggled to support their families, including everything from odd jobs to theft and relief fraud. The letters written by men to Premiers George Henry and Mitchell Hepburn, and to politicians in the Department of Labour to demand adequate jobs and living wages, are also examined in the context of a common political fear: that unemployed married men would be driven to social unrest because of their inability to provide for their families. Finally, we look at those men who, because of their shame at their inability to find work, deserted their families, leaving wives and children to negotiate for relief benefits or approach the family court system to locate and prosecute their husbands.

Understanding men as gendered beings demonstrates that men were not 'just workers' but were also family men who laboured because of their responsibilities as husbands, fathers, and sons.[6] Men attempted to claim the right to a job in place of charity and to support their families according to the norms of breadwinner status. Unemployment forced men to reconcile the expectations of a man as breadwinner, provider, and producer with the reality of joblessness. Yet while the hegemonic ideals that associated masculinity with labour and employment were tested in the Great Depression, the association of manhood with breadwinning survived the economic crisis, and man as breadwinner was ultimately encoded into the social policies of the developing welfare state.

Men, Work, and Unemployment

The impact of unemployment on men and their families in the Great Depression cannot be considered without an understanding of the connections between manhood, respectability, and labour. With industrial development and increased dependence on waged labour, masculinity was 'organized around' the ability to earn wages, workplace skill, 'domestic patriarchy,' and male workplace solidarity.[7] Labour historians have demonstrated that skill, survival, and mastery of the work process have played crucial roles in the link between manliness and work. The myth of the independent, 'self-made' man, which emerged along with the rise of industrial capitalism, was increasingly tested by the loss of autonomy within twentieth-century mass industrialization.[8] But as unemployment threatened the association between masculinity and work in the 1930s, ideological boundaries surrounding gender roles tightened. The 'economic collapse of the Great Depression,' claims historian Margaret Hobbs, 'placed the boundaries that delineate gender relations under great stress.'[9]

In the 1930s both men and women still linked masculine pride and self-worth to paid labour. Employment was an essential element of manhood and central to being an active and respectable participant in the social and economic order. Mrs Renald Pierini of northern Ontario wrote to her local newspaper, 'My husband is working again and his chest is out two inches more.'[10] Employment was linked both to men's sense of masculinity and gender identity, but also to their position of authority and sense of 'validation' in the family. Unemployment therefore brought more than material insecurity: for men, it struck at the very heart of their status in the family and the community.[11] Since citizenship has been historically equated with independent labour status, unemployed men existed outside the boundaries of respectable manhood and, consequently, of full citizenship.[12] Conversely, being unemployed – or worse, having to accept relief or private charity – was considered shameful and humiliating because it degraded independence and therefore the very 'essence' of manhood.

Numerous historians have traced the evolution of the concept of the breadwinner or family wage as a right embedded in masculinity itself. The normative male breadwinner was a cross-class cultural ideal that encoded a range of values from working-class autonomy to the protection of gender privilege and, by the 1930s, was embraced by social reformers, labour unions, the state, and middle- and working-class men and women. The economic conditions and high unemployment rates of the Great Depression did not displace the hegemonic definition of a proper man as an independent breadwinner.[13]

The letters of unemployed male workers to politicians, along with memoirs, court records, and newspapers, all reflect a deep-seated cultural anxiety as the association between work and masculinity began to unravel. Work, associated with vigour, virility, and independence, was the converse of relief or private charity, considered by many to be shameful and humiliating because it degraded independent manhood. Popular cultural beliefs of unemployment as a failure of public policy and a structural problem of capitalist production coexisted with discourses of joblessness as a moral failure, a result of decadence, easy money, and excessive moral freedom. 'We are bringing a curse on our beloved Canada,' claimed the Peterborough *Examiner* in 1930, 'by the wretched drunk, the terrible amount of cigarette smoking ... people will need to learn to live more simply, and be willing to get down to work.'[14] Lack of initiative, enterprise, and 'pioneer' independence were often blamed for the high numbers of unemployed men and men on relief. Prime Minister Bennett held a similar view, commenting that 'the fibre of some of our people has grown softer and they are not willing to turn in and save themselves.'[15]

Stories and reminiscences of the Great Depression are often framed around men's shame of being unemployed. Relief, or the 'dole,' is remembered as 'mortifying ... to be avoided at all costs,' and fathers in particular were recalled as refusing to accept the degradation and humiliation of charity.[16] One man, for example, recalled seeing his father performing relief work sweeping the streets of Toronto: 'I remember so vividly seeing my father one day with this push broom in the gutter. I ran up yelling to him. He wouldn't answer. Wouldn't even look at me.'[17] One oft-quoted excerpt seems to capture the profound impact of unemployment on male pride, and comes from Barry Broadfoot's *Ten Lost Years*, from a woman who worked in a city relief office: 'I've seen tears in men's eyes,' she told Broadfoot, 'as though they were signing away their manhood, their right to be a husband and sit at the head of the table and carve the roast.'[18] Men's letters to politicians reflect the assumption that accepting relief was considered shameful, though asking the government to provide work was not. 'I haven't asked for any relief of any kind yet,' wrote Russel Morris of Toronto to Premier George

Henry. 'If I had to do that it would break my heart, all I want is some work to make my own Living [sic].'[19]

Those who were unemployed or who lived in constant fear of losing their jobs wrote of the shame, humiliation, and anxiety that infected their lives in the workplace and in the home. Because the stereotype of the lazy, unemployed worker persisted into the 1930s, unemployed men were careful to point out their strong work ethic and willingness to perform any type of labour. 'I am very nearly at the end of my rope,' wrote Herbert T. to Premier Hepburn in 1934, 'and unless something turns up we will be forced to live on the charity of others which would be a terrific blow to my pride as I have made my own way ever since I was fifteen.'[20] Harold Foate informed Hepburn that 'it is not the ambition of any red-blooded human being to spend his best years living on charity.'[21] One man who applied for relief in Timmins was told by the council to remain on relief rather than take bush work, because the money would not be enough to keep his family from suffering. This man, the local paper reported, 'made an impression of evident fairness and manliness,' because he had 'always worked when he could and that he wanted to support his own family. He didn't want to be idle.'[22]

Accepting relief conflicted with ideas of a self-reliant masculinity, and public commentary associated relief with 'feminine weakness' and softness and work with hardness and masculine strength. This association was strengthened by the fact that men on relief had to relinquish items such as liquor permits, telephones, and cars.[23] Members of the community helped the state to regulate the deserving and undeserving, since relief recipients were often the subject of public knowledge and community gossip and judgment. 'Any corner grocery store can furnish good information on how people on relief are living,' reported East York storeowner Frank Hitchings to Premier Hepburn. Hitchings volunteered to report men on relief who bought beer, gasoline, and 'picture show' tickets.[24] Politicians received letters from neighbours naming people who drank, went to the movies, or owned radios, and municipalities debated ways in which to publicly identity those receiving aid. Sudbury Alderman J.D. McInness claimed that he possessed many letters from city residents naming those people who claimed relief when they owned cars and radios, held parties, and made their own beer.[25] This public identification of individuals on relief acted as a work test to dissuade all but the poorest and most desperate from applying for relief. The moral and economic regulation of relief recipients was a state-supported imperative, reflected in media attention paid to 'de-frauders' of the welfare system. It was not uncommon for cities to sym-bolically criminalize relief recipients by registering the unemployed at the local police building or forcing recipients to make an 'oath' of un-employment. But Timmins went even further when, in 1932, the town council voted to publish the names and addresses of all direct relief recipients each month in the newspaper.[26]

In addition to being the subject of public surveillance, relief recipi-ents were scrutinized closely by welfare officials. While relief regula-tions were arbitrary and differed by community, they were generally humiliating. Investigators were known to search cupboards to ensure that recipients were really hungry.[27] Relief visitors in Hamilton were expected to make ongoing inventories of 'every article of clothing owned by each individual,' as well as monitor all family earnings, the general cleanliness of the home, and how the relief vouchers for grocer-ies, fuel, and clothing had been used.[28] A relief officer in Timmins, I.E. Dunn, refused to pay a hospital bill for a man's daughter until he gave up his liquor permit.[29] These investigations of family finances and the workings of the home undermined the fragile sense of independence of many relief recipients.

But relief administration, while a form of financial and moral regula-tion, also served to regulate gender relationships. Where female inves-tigators enforced these restrictive relief rules and regulations, the hier-archical relationship between men and women was inverted. Not only were men treated as supplicants and dependents on the state, but they answered to female relief officers, who were often unmarried women. One sociological survey of American families specifically commented on this 'problem' for men. Because female relief visitors usually dealt directly with housewives to discuss household budgets, unemployed men were seen as losing even more of their masculine self-reliance.[30] Relief administration was not standardized in Ontario, so each munici-pality had a different form of administration. In some locations relief officers and investigators were drawn from the ranks of white-collar unemployed men.[31] In other areas, however, women dominated the ranks of relief visitors. In London, for example, male 'investigators' supervised the work of seven female 'visitors' who had direct contact with relief recipients. Women were also probation officers in the family court system and in agencies such as the Children's Aid Society or private charities. In areas where women were active in relief adminis-tration, problems arose when male recipients protested against being investigated by and held accountable to women. J. Frise complained that relief recipients 'are forced to answer the regulation 137 questions to obtain relief and become the object of curious official investigating old maids.'[32] To temper this gender inversion, in Oshawa, the city council decided that the relief officer, Miss Farncomb, be given a male inspector to work alongside her 'during the period of unemployment.'[33]

The politics of relief administration in the city of Ottawa, however, illustrates the extent to which the profession of social work was feminized in contrast to the 'scientific' administration of unemployment. A 1934 investigation into the administration of relief recognized that female relief workers were considered by unemployed men to be problematic. The report suggested that female case workers be replaced by 'competent male investigators' and that the 'present female staff ... be retained to attend to the investigation of cases where the head of the family is not a man.'[34] While there is no record of whether any women were fired in 1934, Ottawa proceeded down this path in 1936. In response to cuts in federal and provincial funds, the city reorganized the administration and staff of the Public Welfare Department. Until then Ottawa was one of the few municipalities in Ontario to employ trained social workers, mostly women, in relief work. Ottawa fired forty female social workers and replaced them with eleven 'male detectives.' Critics claimed that the social casework approach spent too much time and money on social problems unrelated to unemployment and that relief provision should be focused on collecting economic 'facts' and preventing fraud.[35] This was part of a trend in the 1930s towards what Nancy Christie calls the 'scientific study' of unemployment, which emphasized a supposedly objective form of data collection and which eclipsed the social work view of joblessness in relationship to a broader range of family problems including desertion and illness. Encapsulated in the work of social scientists such as Leonard Marsh, this type of work focused largely on finding solutions to male unemployment.[36] In this vein, in 1935 Public Welfare Minister David Croll established a school for relief inspectors to monitor municipal administration. The school had twenty graduates in its first year; all were white-collar men, and only one had a social work background.[37] These concerns probably shaped the decision by Tisdale County (Timmins) in 1938 that hiring a woman as the local relief inspector was 'unsuitable.' However, after interviewing at least fifteen male candidates, the town council found no one else qualified for the position.[38]

Pride and Entitlement: Fathers and Workers

High and consistent unemployment proved to be traumatic for many men during the 1930s. While cyclical or seasonal periods of unemployment were not new, for many working-class men the extended terms of unemployment in the Great Depression, and the inability of public and private welfare authorities to financially cope with the crisis, created a much more profound challenge to men's material survival and masculinity.[39] Sally Alexander's analysis of Depression-era British memoirs shows that unemployed men felt a powerful sense of 'sexual wrong' due to the loss of work, 'the public exposure of their plight,' and the resulting 'loss of male dignity.'[40] While unemployment had a heavier impact on members of the unskilled and semi-skilled working class, by 1932 the unemployment rate was so high that contemporary observers argued that joblessness was a potential threat to the security of 'practically every' working family in Ontario.[41] Men's responses to unemployment ranged widely: some expressed shock, shame, or fear, others anger and bitterness. Some were resigned to long-term unemployment, while others developed a commitment to socialism, communism, or collective unemployed politics. While responses diverged, employment was no longer a reliable ground for 'measuring masculinity,' and a level of anxiety, fear, and bewilderment ensued.[42] When disrupted, the deep connections between self-respect and work, and independence and the male wage, left many men feeling as if they had lost status as a man, their sense of purpose, or their very desire to live.[43]

Many men verged on a nervous breakdown for fear of losing their jobs, their status as family providers, and for middle-class men especially, loss of face or status in the community. Newspapers expressed concern that even the fear of unemployment could lead to health and mental problems for men. While the *North Bay Nugget* suggested a simple 'warm bath and drink' for worried middle-class men suffering potential 'disease, fatigue, insomnia,' one woman wrote to Premier Hepburn to say that her husband's shock of losing his optometrist business had led to a nervous breakdown and hospitalization. His wife was forced to ask Hepburn for help finding a job, 'in order that I may keep what social standing I have in this community.'[44] A lawyer wrote to Hepburn on behalf of Albert Emard, who, he said, was 'on the verge of a nervous breakdown ... from his apprehension of losing his position as a manager' of the local liquor store in Russell County.[45] And nineteen-year-old George Wilson of Toronto wrote several desperate letters to

Hepburn, trying to find a job before his pregnant wife discovered that he was unemployed. 'She thinks everything is fine as far as I'm concerned and I wouldn't want her to think different.' His debts and the burden of keeping the extent of his problems a secret led to despair and threats of suicide. 'Im [sic] through trying to make a go of life so I've decided to end it all tonight,' wrote Wilson. 'Even now I'm crying. For if you had creditors coming at you in four thousand directions, a wife and baby with no clothes, had to walk the streets all night and then pretend to go to work with nothing to eat and [no] signs of getting anything you would give up too.'[46]

While suicide was a drastic response to the shame of unemployment, media stories of men taking their own lives were frequent in this era. It is difficult for social scientists to assess the extent of unemployment-related suicides or to show causation between the Great Depression and suicide, but suicide rates did increase during the early years of the Depression. The Canadian suicide rate for men ages thirty to thirty-five in 1930, for example, was double the 1924 rate. For men aged forty to forty-nine, the rate was even higher.[47] Work done in the United States on the psychological and sociological reasons for suicide suggests a correlation, though not a simple causal equation, between suicides and unemployment. While employment status is not the only explanatory factor, suicide generally 'declines in periods of prosperity and full employment, and increases during periods of business depression.'[48] In the 1930s the unemployment rates had a stronger effect on the male rather than the female suicide rates, suggesting the powerful connections between masculinity, work, and self-worth.[49] 'In a fit of despondency,' reported the *Porcupine Advance*, thirty-eight-year-old George Cicione, unemployed for several months, took his own life. 'He had always been a good provider,' said his wife of thirteen years, but had grown desperate over his inability to find a job.[50] In unemployed memoirs, several men had pondered killing themselves. One unemployed housepainter, married with six children, wrote, 'I should not drag along and endure helplessly under any circumstances, preferring death in the gutter as a man, though perhaps before that time society may have been pressured to condemn me as something less.'[51] Suicides received a great deal of attention in the media, and even incidents that occurred in the United States often made the front pages of local Canadian newspapers. Certainly, the media, and the readers of such media, made connections between job loss, masculine pride, and suicide, regardless of the complex reasons that may have prompted these men to kill themselves. For example, Norman Wakefield Huston, a twenty-five-year-old truck driver from Englehart, 'despondent apparently over the loss of his job,' shot himself in the head, leaving behind his wife and three small children.[52] Family court records reveal the tensions within an Ottawa family during these years. In March of 1936 Gary Sims, married for six years, unemployed, and with two young children, was convicted of attempted suicide and given one year on probation. He stated that after being laid off he had fallen behind in payments for his stove, clothes, radio, and rent. 'He became discouraged at his inability to find work and his attempted suicide was due to this fact,' stated the report. A home visit by a probation officer revealed, according to a neighbour, that he and his wife 'quarreled constantly' over money.[53]

Most unemployed married men did not have a nervous breakdown or commit suicide. Rather, they attempted to alleviate unemployment by devising creative strategies to support themselves and their families. Men searched constantly for both permanent and odd jobs and tried to find unique ways of contributing to the household. Domestic labour was still considered women's work, however, and there are few references in court records, reminiscences, or oral histories to men doing anything connected with women's work in the domestic sphere such as shopping, cooking, sewing, or even looking after children. Sociological surveys of unemployed men and families in the United States and Great Britain confirm that the gendered division of labour continued during times of male unemployment.[54] Because unemployment was associated with weakness and dependency, most men tried to remain as active as possible. Men hunted, picked, or scavenged food, or did odd jobs.[55] Men who lived in rural areas and in northern Ontario could hunt game or scavenge food to supplement inadequate food supplies. One man in Timmins found a field full of mushrooms on which he managed to feed his family, and he sold the rest.[56] A carpenter in St Thomas sold his clothes because relief payments were not enough to feed his children.[57] Men also went from door to door to find odd jobs, hoping that what they earned would not be discovered and subtracted from relief payments. The Oshawa Daily Times, for example, celebrated the 'cardinal virtues' of initiative and industry of an unemployed mechanic who shovelled coal and worked at odd jobs for the doctor and druggist in order to pay his bills.[58] But unemployment numbers were simply too high for all jobless men to find work this way. In the Timmins area alone approximately one thousand men were looking for work by knocking on doors during the 1935 Christmas season, reinforcing the media's focus on individual tenacity in the face of unemployment.[59]

While politicians or the media might celebrate cases of individual tenacity and, conversely, mourn the loss of rugged individuality, men's survival strategies could encompass a broad range of activities outside of what was considered respectable manhood. Some men, for example, resorted to various kinds of theft to help provide for their families. Leeds and Grenville County's surviving case files show a prevalence of electricity theft in the mid-1930s.[60] Records indicate that most of this theft occurred in the winter months and totaled small amounts of money, suggesting that it was a desperate attempt to provide energy for heating, cooking, or more likely, light for dark winter days and evenings. For example, Norman McAllister stole $8.37 from the Public Utilities Commission in the winter of 1934–35, and Henry Gardiner, an unemployed window cleaner, stole $13.60 of electricity in the winter of 1936 after his meter had been sealed for non-payment.[61] Those who were caught were usually convicted and forced to pay a fine of $2 to $5 and court costs and to make restitution.

Kurt Pelman went even further to obtain money, when in March 1934 he was charged with arson and sentenced to nine months in prison. The fire marshall claimed that Pelman set fire to his home to obtain insurance because 'he is a lazy type of man, and owing to his abhorrence of work, the authorities will not allow him to go on relief.' In his legal statement, Pelman confessed to starting the fire because, he claimed, he 'had a hard time trying to get work,' and both his parents were ill. In court under cross-examination, the initial fire inspector on the scene admitted that Pelman had tearfully confessed that 'they were having a very hard time, that he was unable to get work and asked if his mother would obtain the insurance.'[62]

For some men relief fraud was another way to squeeze money from the welfare system in order to support their families. While it is impossible, due to scattered and incomplete records, to estimate how many men defrauded welfare authorities, it is clear that many found creative ways around restrictive regulations. For some men it was an act of desperation, while for others, a form of protest at the strict regulations and paltry amounts of money given by municipalities. The state seemed unsure of what to do in these situations, in some cases finding a degree of sympathy for unemployed married men. As Eva Garcia's analysis of relief in London, Ontario, indicates, city authorities were reluctant to withdraw relief even in proven cases of fraud. If caught, relief was often temporarily withdrawn as punishment, but soon reinstated if the recipient promised not to do it again.[63] In most surviving records, men received no jail time and were ordered to make restitution or given a suspended sentence. When Timothy Porter was found guilty of fraudulently obtaining relief vouchers for $302.13, for example, he was given a suspended sentence but not ordered to make restitution, as he was still on relief. In some cases, relief fraud was minimal, as in the case of Caleb Johnson, a married labourer who was found guilty of fraudulently obtaining $31.85 in relief vouchers and who was given a suspended sentence and ordered to pay restitution of $11.20.[64]

In some cases men clearly misinformed relief officials of their extra earnings, living arrangements, or the earnings of wives or children, because these forms of extra income were used to claw back relief benefits. In 1935 Henry Brant was found to have defrauded the city of London's relief authorities of $108.84 between February and May 1935. He was convicted and fined $25 but received no jail time. According to welfare investigator Eva Birss, Brant had hidden the income of his daughter Iris, who had worked secretly for nine months. Under cross-examination Birss confirmed that the family was poor and in rent arrears. The fact that Birss judged the home 'clean and well kept' had, ironically, led to the discovery of the fraud: 'I wondered how it could be done on the money we were allowing them.'[65]

While it was common for working-class families to take in boarders for extra money, being discovered with a boarder also meant a certain cut in relief. Women in the Macedonian community in Toronto often had boarders to supplement low relief payments and remembered hiding all evidence of boarders every time a welfare officer was spotted in the neighbourhood.[66] Frank Jedrezejck was charged with relief fraud in 1937 for obtaining $36 in relief and not declaring the $6 a month derived from his boarder. Relief department visitor Marion Johnston reported that Jedrezejck, a thirty-eight-year-old Polish labourer, defended himself by claiming that he did not know 'what type of work his wife did each month.' Regardless, he was the one charged because, as household head, he was responsible for abiding by relief regulations.[67] Informal living arrangements also came under the prosecutorial radar in the 1930s. John Lightman's living arrangements brought him under criminal investigation in 1935, when he was charged, but acquitted, of defrauding relief authorities in Sault Ste Marie. The relief officer testified that Lightman began receiving relief in March 1931 because he claimed he was a married man with a wife and daughter. When his residence was searched by two relief officers and the chief of police on the basis of a complaint, they discovered he was a widower and was living with a woman, Audrey Smith, her teenaged daughter, and her parents. They searched the home and the cupboards and found a variety of groceries stored in the back room. Lightman, a labourer, had only made $150 in casual employment between 1930 and 1935.[68] Lightman and Smith may have doubled up their households in order to survive, or perhaps they were an unmarried couple, desperate to find a way to support themselves and their dependents.

Court records indicate that men, out of desperation and resentment, could occasionally react violently towards relief officials. In 1937 Alex Ainsley was convicted of 'forcibly confining' Mildred Thomas, a London welfare department visitor, who had denied him a fuel order because of concern over 'extravagant' use of fuel by the family. C.C. Carruthers, the defence lawyer, claimed that Ainsley had nine children and a wife who was suffering from 'living in a cold house,' and that the welfare office had delayed his order the last time he had gone in person. In the family's relief file was a letter written by Ainsley's daughter, referring to the family's involvement with the Communist Party, and passed on to the court by an anonymous source. While not addressed in the court proceedings, the letter indicates that the family's political affiliations were being monitored by relief officials.[69] Ainsley ultimately pled guilty and was given a suspended sentence.

Court decisions, like relief rates and regulations, differed across municipalities. Though most cases of relief fraud have not been preserved, it seems that it was rare, though not impossible, for Anglo-Celtic men to receive jail time for relief fraud. Alex Ainsley, the man who held a female relief officer hostage, received only a suspended sentence, while in the many cases of relief fraud in Middlesex County, men who were convicted of fraud were usually given a suspended sentence and a fine rather than jail time. In some cases, however, judges did sentence men to jail time for relief fraud. Mr Cameron appealed his sentence of thirty days in jail for defrauding the Township of East York of $396.02. He had worked while collecting relief and forged relief cheques to pay for his family's rent. His lawyer presented many elements of his client's respectable manhood to the court: he had served three years during the First World War, had helped support his poor parents, and had told his wife that he was earning the extra money by selling radios. The judge told him that he could serve his thirty-day sentence on the jail farm, saying, 'You are in a tough position, one I understand which is quite foreign to you. I do not think ... that there was anything in the nature of criminal intent on your part.'[70]

Yet this measure of sympathy for struggling married men and their families did not usually extend to ethnically or racially marginalized men who broke the law to provide for their wives and children, illustrating the association between manliness, respectability, and ethnicity in interwar Canada. Lester McMahon, for example, a First World War veteran who lived on the Chippewa reserve near London, received four months in jail for assaulting A.D. Moore, the local Indian agent in charge of relief. The McMahon case illustrates the extreme poverty on reserves during the Great Depression, as well as the power and authority enjoyed by Indian agents, who were responsible for administering relief payments.[71] Moore testified that, on 27 January 1936, McMahon came into his office from the waiting room to ask for more relief. 'There was a number of Indians in the waiting room,' Moore testified. 'I didn't pay much attention to them.' When refused further relief, Moore claimed McMahon yelled, 'God damn you, you are going to let my children starve,' then 'struck me on the left cheek,' leaving him with a bloody nose. When cross-examined, Moore said McMahon was refused relief because he had made some extra money in January by digging ditches. Indian agents believed that First Nations peoples did not 'need as much money to survive as their non-aboriginal neighbours,'[72] and Moore's response to questioning about the adequacy of relief on the reserve illustrates this mindset:

Q: [D]o you think 7.00 a month is enough to pay a man who is trying to keep a wife and two children?
A: He has 25 acres. He should be able to grow potatoes and vegetables, keep pigs. All they need to buy is flour.
Q: If they have the money to buy pigs or chickens with in the first place?
A: Yes.

Clearly, McMahon's lack of deference to authority was also a factor in Moore's decision to deny further relief, indicating that resistance to Indian agents' authority would result in punishment. When he was working in the ditch, Moore noted that McMahon was 'very critical of having to work for relief and also of the amount that was paid. I showed him my letter of instructions from Ottawa, even that didn't seem to appease him.' McMahon, along with other men on the reserve, represented a threat to state authority. Local Police Constable Bella reported to the court, 'There is considerable unrest among the Indians on the Reserve and ... it was feared trouble would be had with them ... other Indians have threatened that they were going to "beat up" the Agent if he refused them relief. It is believed that this assault ... was premeditated.'[73]

Those who were not British subjects or who were recent immigrants were also denied the already limited entitlement to relief, since Ontario policy dictated that non-citizens claiming relief could be deported. This policy regulated access to relief, and it also regulated involvement with unemployed protests, which in the 1930s were commonly associated with immigrants. Peter Niemkiewicz, a Polish immigrant who had worked in Canada for twelve years, was sentenced to four months in jail for fraudulently obtaining $25 in grocery relief vouchers in Toronto. On appeal, his lawyer produced evidence that his client had not been represented by counsel. After the judge admonished him for not speaking English properly, Niemkiewicz defended himself, saying, 'Well, I not work very much. I have lots of debts to pay. I have five children; they sleep in one room. I have to buy new mattresses. The doctor them. [sic] I need to get extra money for the children.' The judge dismissed his appeal, saying, 'These are not only offences against the state but against the people.'[74] There is much work yet to be done in assessing the impact of ethnicity on cases of relief fraud, especially given that many men and their families would have risked deportation for becoming dependents on the state.

While it was generally considered humiliating for men to ask for and accept relief or charity, men did not feel that it was shameful to remind the government of its responsibility to help them find work. The demand for jobs, in opposition to charity, was based on a powerful sense of masculine entitlement and enabled a man to claim respectable status and avoid the shame of relief. The state, men declared, had an obligation to help them fulfil their manly duties, as it would 'lift a man up to be given work instead off [sic] charity.'[75] A dichotomy existed in the images and understandings of masculinity in the 1930s: the shamed and humiliated unemployed man coexisted with the image of the proud worker who fought for adequate relief, provision of work, or the rights of workers. Many unemployed men, while noting the humiliation of relief, claimed that their unemployment was 'no fault of their own' and demanded that the government act to create enough jobs to meet the demands of men who saw themselves as 'entitled' and 'deserving'.[76]

This tension also existed in Canadian protest literature of the 1930s. Stock characters in many plays, agitprops, and short stories embodied dichotomous characterizations of the strong and proud worker or the defeated, emasculated man. In Bertram Brookner's *Mrs Hungerfords' Milk*, for example, Joe, a struggling farmer, takes out his frustration with unemployment on his wife and daughter. His failure as a bread-winner results in his emasculation, and he is ultimately feminized as a man who 'flapped his arms,' cried, and submitted to the criticism of a wife who spoke to him 'in a tone you use to a child.' He unsuccessfully tries to reclaim his male pride through anger: 'he wanted to hurt them. He wanted to fill the house again when he came home, the way he used to, instead of sort of sneaking off to bed to be out of their way ... [h]e wanted that feeling of weight in his hands ... they had softened him.'[77] In Frank Love's play *Looking Forward*, two stock male figures appear: Father, who is 'tall, lean and disheartened,' stands in contrast to his daughter's boyfriend Jim, 'young, husky, brimming over with life.' Father is unemployed and resigned to accepting charity. When the bailiff's notice of eviction arrives, he throws up his hands in defeat, but Jim responds by 'talking about revolution and the rights of workers.'[78]

The contrast to the figure of the impotent, defeated man is that of the proud, strong worker. In Mary Quayle Innis' *Staver*, Staver is unemployed, with a wife and child to support. Yet he is not ashamed to ask for the work he needs. Disconcertingly, and proudly, he looks his bene-factors straight in the eye and refuses to accept pity or shame.[79] Much of the power of agitprops and mass recitations came from forceful repetitions of monologues that portrayed the male worker as strong, confident, and powerful through collective protest, resting on a rich labour iconography that associated collective action with masculinity.[80] In Oscar Ryan's *Unity*, for example, the four workers are militant and forceful: they clench their fists, condemn capitalism, Section 98 of the Criminal Code (used to arrest members of organizations advocating the change of government, industry, or the economy by force), and force the 'capitalists' to nervous retreat in the face of their strength.

1ST WORKER: And we're going to put an end,
2ND WORKER: An end,
3RD WORKER: An end,
4TH WORKER: An end,
ALL FOUR: (taking a step forward, while capitalists retreat) An end
    to you.[81]

The contrast between the dignity of work and the humiliation of charity permeated men's critiques of the unemployment situation. Yet part of this willingness to work was based on a system of gendered economic values that held that men should not labour for less than a living wage. Thus, the political and economic issue of unemployment was connected to men's sense of masculine authority and, ultimately, to their status within the family. Many unemployed men argued that unemployment was not their fault and demanded that the state act to create enough jobs for those men who were 'entitled, deserving, and in dire need of work.'[82] Despite the lack of jobs, increased dependence on relatives, charity, or the state, the male breadwinner ideal re-emerged revitalized in the post–Second World War era, demonstrating its resiliency and its ability to draw legitimacy from not just the workplace but from the role of husband and father as well.[83]

This sense of entitlement to work led men to protest poor working conditions and low wages by writing of their grievances to politicians and state officials. But the high unemployment rate and the willingness to work meant that in the fight for a limited number of jobs the unemployed were divided by gender and marital status. A complex hierarchy existed of who was most entitled to jobs, though public consensus gave married men first priority. This consensus was bolstered by the belief that men, unlike women, had a natural right to a position in the paid labour force. Jobs were seen as essential to men for economic reasons, but also to uphold masculine self-worth and to prevent a descent into pauperism, idleness, and despair.[84] Rumours abounded of single women or men getting jobs that should rightly have gone to married men, a common complaint of those writing to politicians and the premier. 'Well now Mr Henry,' complained one man, 'there is a young single man employed steady as time keeper since this Normal School started his Father is a salaried man in the C.N.R. shopes [sic] here and here I am a married man having a hard time to make ends meet.'[85] Married men were the first group to benefit from relief works and job schemes, and the provincial government and municipalities adopted special rules favouring married men for relief work and jobs. H.A. Desjardins, superintendent of the North Bay branch of the Employment Service of Canada, promised to give first priority for jobs to married men, and as early as November 1929, Fort William city council's unemployment committee began discussing employment programs for unemployed married men.[86] In Peterborough married men were given preference for board of works' projects at 40 cents an hour, and some men pretended to be married with children in order to make their case appear more deserving.[87]

On the surface there was a general consensus around the hierarchy of entitlement to jobs. Underneath, this consensus was unstable. Questions raged about the entitlement of widows with children and single men and women with dependents. Was the stability of the social order endangered more by unemployed single men congregating in cities, where they might be persuaded to join the Communist Party or by job-less women who might resort to prostitution to survive?[88] Negotiating these conflicting interests proved to be difficult for the public, the government, relief agencies, and charities. North Bay city council promised to investigate complaints that unmarried men were being given relief work before married men, but Mayor Rowe made it clear that those single men hired 'had been supporting dependents and were justly entitled to consideration.'[89] As F.W. Gibbard wrote in a series of letters to Premier Henry, though he was single, he had a father and sister to support, which he felt made his case more deserving than that of a married man without children. Yet, according to the Department of Public Works, because he lived alone, he was considered 'a single man with no dependents.'[90] Ultimately, public discourse upheld the association between masculinity and work, even though some women, such as single mothers or young women supporting dependent parents, could be an 'exception' to this norm. Women could, in certain specific situations, be considered legitimate workers, but for the most part their gender identity was not constructed in the public discourse as that of worker. The overwhelming preference given to married male breadwinners in the relief system, the lack of state initiative in addressing women's unemployment problems, and the criticisms levelled at women workers all demonstrate that the association between masculinity, jobs, and breadwinning remained powerful throughout the Great Depression.

While men argued for entitlement from the contract- and rights-based position of employment, it is crucial to remember that they spoke of these rights within a familial context. Married men were inextricably linked to the domestic sphere as breadwinners and providers. For a man, the pride in being able to say, 'I have always provided for my family' was a crucial component of proper masculinity and the basis of his ability to demand better working conditions.[91] Men continually referred to their obligations and duties as family providers and to the emotional and psychological trauma of failing in those roles. T.H. Gray wrote to the premier in 1933, 'Whereas I have a right, legal and constitutional, to live; and therefore to work in order to produce the essentials for the preservation and development of that life, and the lives of those legally and morally dependent upon me ... I respectfully request that the Government will give the opportunity to work ... [and] provide fully all that is needed for the support of my wife and child, for whom, and for whose welfare, both the Government and myself are legally and morally responsible.'[92]

By the interwar period the representation of fatherhood had shifted slightly to accommodate the more involved roles expected of men in the ideal companionate family. The 'new fatherhood' articulated by advice columnists and experts encouraged men to become more involved in the daily life of their children, though without challenging the hierarchy of the gendered division of labour or questioning the central importance of male breadwinning.[93] Masculine authority, both in the labour force and in the family, rested on employment status and domestic relationships. Men saw themselves as loving fathers and husbands, suggesting that masculine identity was shaped by the intertwined roles of work and fatherhood. Breadwinning itself came to symbolize the emotional ideals of 'fatherly devotion' and 'paternal protection' as well as material provision.[94] To see their children go hungry was a visible and painful reminder to men of their failure as providers and a challenge to the duties of respectable manhood.

Men were concerned for the health and well-being of their wives and children, feared the separation of their families, and struggled to support wives, children, parents, and siblings. A.E. Owen of Todmorden wrote to Premier Henry that he was sick with anxiety over his low wages, and 'I do not like to let my wife know how much pain I am in and how bad I feel.'[95] D.G. Firth hoped to find a job allowing him to be 'at home nights' because his wife, with six children and a newborn to look after, had suffered a nervous breakdown, while Grant MacMillan was struggling to keep his family together after being unemployed for three years and losing the family home. His wife had threatened to return to the United States and put their children in an infants' home.[96] Like many mothers, fathers were also ashamed of their children's ragged clothing and lack of proper coats or shoes. Family court records are replete with fathers who, along with mothers, were charged with keeping children from school. The father of John and Fred Ryan testified that he kept his children from school because 'they did not have shoes. I want them to go to school, but I certainly would not want to go to school myself with the clothes my children have.'[97] Even in the play *Eight Men*

Speak, which is primarily an indictment of capitalism and the state, Communist Party leader Tim Buck is initially portrayed as a father, eagerly reading a letter from his young daughter while in jail. Missing her, and despondent over the time away from his family, it is her letter and his pride as a father that gives 'fresh incentive' to continue his protest to the minister of justice.[98]

The inability to support their wives and children was, for many men, a catalyst to demand government intervention in the labour market, in terms of demanding employment, adequate relief, or a living wage. A range of workers from urban and rural settings, white-collar and working-class jobs, bitterly complained about the impact of the Depression on their wages, pointing out that survival for their families was growing increasingly difficult. Men consistently pointed out to the government that low wages made it almost impossible to live and that the values of hard work and thriftiness were unlikely to be rewarded in a depressed economy. A truck driver for a company that worked for the Department of Highways complained that his wage of $8 a week was not enough to support his family of three children. His wages were supplemented by relief vouchers for milk and bread.[99] Some men also drew on racist discourses that blamed immigrants and 'foreigners' for devaluing the cost of labour: 'no wonder Anglo Saxon stock in Canada is getting less all the time when in the year 1937 not 1837 people have to work such long hours for such small pay.'[100] Marcus Klee's work on state, capital, and labour in Toronto outlines the complex struggle for a male minimum wage in the context of the practice of paying wages so low that men had to supplement them with relief. In Toronto over 60 per cent of the labour force consisted of men earning less than $12.50 a week, which was the minimum wage board's minimum rate for the survival of a single woman.[101] Cabdrivers at Uptown Cab in Toronto, for example, made only $2 to $3 a week, while a skilled welder at National Electric made only $10 a week.[102] Through the Industrial Standards Act, the Ontario government attempted to persuade businesses to voluntarily submit to industry standards on wages, but the legislation failed due to lack of regulation as well as resistance to raising the male minimum wage high enough to be a 'family wage.'

The financial situation of travelling salesmen provides an example of how the lack of minimum wage legislation contributed to ongoing suffering in the Depression years. Not only was it increasingly difficult to make sales in a depressed economy, but salesmen were required to pay all car, insurance, and gas expenses in advance and then make the money back on commission. As a result many men found themselves heavily in debt because they were never able to fully recover their expenses. George Gilpin of the Commercial Travellers Association wrote to David Croll at least five times complaining about the lack of a minimum wage in his industry, where jobs typically paid only $20 to $25 a week before expenses.[103] Bert Tipping, a salesman from Toronto, also claimed that salesmen 'load the relief rolls,' ultimately contributing to the profits of the businesses that hired them.[104] For example, Charles Reardon was charged in July 1931 with stealing $800 over seven months from his employer, Balfour's Ltd. Wholesale Grocers, where he was employed as a salesman for the Niagara Peninsula. When the judge questioned Balfour on his responsibilities as an employer and on the low wages of his employee, the exploitation of salesmen soon became apparent. Balfour admitted that salesmen needed a car, but the company refused to provide them with one; he did not know 'a fair estimate of mileage costs' for fuel reimbursement, and he had no idea of his employee's gross salary or his rate of commission.[105]

Men, women, local governments, and even some business interests recognized that low wages supplemented by relief were not enough for men to survive on or to support their families. The city of London, for example, passed a resolution that stated that low wages made it impossible for men to support their families and recommended that the government establish a committee to investigate a minimum wage for men.[106] Sometimes businesses saw a male minimum wage as a way to prevent labour unrest, stabilize an industry, and ultimately benefit capital. A.A. Holland, president of the Holland Fuel Company, told Premier Hepburn, 'We cannot blame the men [for striking] because they do not receive enough to buy food and clothing let alone support a family or do more than merely exist.' A fair wage, set through a labour code, he argued, 'will actually benefit the coal dealer by attracting a better class of laborer to this industry and enabling these men, to maintain their self-respect instead of eking out an existence and them having to depend on relief.'[107]

Paradoxically, this commitment of men to the well-being of the family, often celebrated as the very basis of society, could act to undermine the stability of the social order. It was not only the bodies of young, unemployed, and unmarried men who in the 1930s were viewed as a potential threat to the state.[108] Unemployment also threatened the stability of a social order that no longer rewarded married men for fulfilling the expected roles of husband, father, and provider.

Doctors, social scientists, and political observers in Canada, the United States, and Great Britain worried that unemployment could lead to 'violent uncontrollable behaviour,' a loss of faith in the system, and political revolt.[109] Police began warning the public of a crime wave hitting Toronto, claiming 'Unemployed Men Driven to Desperation.'[110] Sam Harris, president of the Navy League, reminded the government that 'you can readily understand a hungry man, especially if he has children, is dangerous. Holdups, robberies, purse-snatchings, porch-climbings and other things, might easily happen.'[111] Claimed British physician Dr Morris Robb, 'Diseases of thought and behaviour are as infectious as influenza ... phantasies of revenge struggle with a sense of impotence.'[112] While it is unclear whether an actual increase in crime occurred in the 1930s, the presence of men in organized protest or in socialist organizations was clearly a matter of concern for governments. Dr J.W. MacMillan, chairman of the Ontario Employment Service, wrote in *Maclean's* that unemployment provoked 'a bitter quality' in unemployed men with families, yet acknowledged that 'he would be less than a man if he did not feel unjustly treated. No wonder that all revolutionist factions have tried to mobilize the unemployed in order to provoke them to revolt.'[113] Mrs Charles Lickman warned Premier Hepburn, 'Millions of men are driven to being red. A man can stand a good deal but when his wife and children suffer if *he is a man* [sic] he becomes desperate.'[114] The status of the male bread-winner and his ability to support a wife and children and to meet the material needs of his family was a crucial element linking masculinity and class action.[115]

Men used their role as father to remind the government that the stability of the state and the security of the family were intricately bound. 'It will be a strong man patriotically who this winter will drown out the cries of his children for bread with the strains of the *Maple Leaf Forever*,' stated one unemployed veteran.[116] Unemployed men drew on images of suffering families, starving children, and broken households. 'We hear our little ones crying for many things that they cannot have under this wave of charity, they do not get enough to eat and they have to starve and suffer these evictions,' claimed a man who had faced several evictions. They 'see the Bailiffs throwing their home on the street their toys and Belongings can you wonder why men are clamering [sic] for a Revolution.'[117] Loss of employment and the consequent shame and humiliation meant that the Canadian state could no longer count on married men to uphold the status quo.

Leaving for Work

Some men, however, neither protested against unemployment nor stayed with their families and diligently looked for work. Both single and married men 'rode the rails,' moving to areas across the province and across the country in hopes of finding employment. Historical accounts of these travels have become a romanticized celebration of the freedom of the road or the drive to organize workers, reminiscences only slightly tempered by the loss of home and family. For Hugh Garner, young and unemployed in the 1930s, life on the road was later recalled as an adventure: 'I don't think I'd have wanted to miss the Great Depression for the world.'[118] Ronald Liversedge's reminiscences of the On-to-Ottawa Trek portray the trekker as 'a collective, surrogate figure for [the] ... hopeless, hungry people who suffered at home.' It was, Liversedge says, an 'epic' protest, covering 'hundreds of miles of majestic terrain.'[119] In Pierre Berton's popular history of the Great Depression, riding the trains was an 'adventure,' particularly for young men. Their action, 'the very fact that they were *moving* helped to temper ... the harshness of those times.'[120] Travelling to find work was understood to be an active and therefore quintessentially male response to unemployment, in contrast to the feminization associated with unemployment and relief. In the reminiscences of life on the road women appear primarily as maternal figures, offering food and comfort. In Barry Broadfoot's collection of oral histories, 'Mother Melville' met unemployed men with stamped envelopes, imploring them to write home to their mothers, while in Calgary, Mrs Collins was famous for feeding transients out of her garage. Liversedge also recalls how the trekkers arrived in Golden, British Columbia, where they were met by 'two or three quiet, smiling women, salting, peppering and tasting' large vats of stew.[121] While it is important not to diminish the important role that women played in alleviating the effects of unemployment, in the symbolism of 'the road,' it is the men who walked, travelled, and organized, and the women who offered support and dealt with the economic consequences of being left behind.

Even in radical political parties the economic consequences of male action and protest on the material position of women and children went largely unacknowledged. Unemployed activism was a higher priority than the individual poverty of women and families. For example, when Ellen Stafford's husband Malcolm was sent to the Soviet Union in 1935 by the Communist Party to study Marxism, she was left without any means of support. While this proved a respite from his abusive domestic behaviour, the party did little to help her financially. As a result, she had to feign desertion both in private, to friends and family, and in public, when she had to claim desertion in front of Calgary city council in order to qualify for relief. 'It ... hurt my feminine pride,' she recalled, 'that I had to allow people to believe I'd been deserted. *Deserted? Me?* [sic].'[122] Similarly, as the National Unemployed Workers' Association prepared for a conference in July 1930, it sent two male members on an organizing drive through southwestern Ontario. George Wanden left his wife and children without economic support, and her letter to him captures her frustration with the Communist Party: 'I don't know what kind of game the Party is playing but I should say damn rotten ... I don't know whether you are so wrapped up in the Party to worry about home ... if they do not pay, try and get a job somewhere else or come back to the children and I shall try to get out steady somewhere.'[123] Travelling, organizing, protesting, and looking for work were all active responses to the Great Depression, but the material reality was that a husband who went off to look for work left women and children without a source of income – and often with few options but to take out an arrest warrant for desertion in order to qualify for relief.

While the problem of desertion certainly existed before the Great Depression, temporary desertions became common, as men left to look for work or because they were too ashamed to stay on relief. Alain Lissoir, for example, a painter by trade, found unemployment in Ottawa too difficult to bear. In a letter to Judge Balharrie, in December 1931, he explained that he left his family because he 'could not stand for it any longer ... I love my family... I am trying to do the best I can for I am not afraid of work.'[124] Jeanne Gagnon told the Ottawa family court that her husband had left her and their two children to find work, that she had no idea where he was, and that 'he was discouraged at having no work.'[125] In the 1930s the relief and family court system in Ontario acted to preserve the male breadwinner family while controlling access to public funds. Women were expected to lay criminal charges against deserting husbands and to provide as much information as possible on their whereabouts before relief was given.[126] Authorities were concerned by the visible problem of desertion. York Township, for example, reported that the numbers of deserted women were increasing in an 'alarming' way. The number was still high even in 1937, despite municipal relief regulations stipulating that deserted wives had to take out an arrest warrant when applying for relief.[127] Similarly, mothers' allowance administrators, despite rules that women had to be deserted for five years before being eligible for relief, saw the number of applications from deserted women increase throughout the 1930s. When legislation was changed in 1935 to reduce the period of desertion from five to three years, strict regulations were used to keep the numbers under control.[128]

Also problematic for those attempting to regulate access to relief was that for many men northern Ontario held out the hope of jobs in primary industry, especially mining and logging, and was therefore the hopeful destination of many who left their families. City authorities in the north struggled with an influx of transient workers and were particularly concerned with 'foreigners' and Communists gaining a foothold in the region's mining industries, which employed men throughout the 1930s.[129] In and around Kirkland Lake in the 1930s, approximately fifteen mines were functioning, employing 4,460 people in 1936.[130] Local newspapers recognized that northern Ontario at least offered the hope of jobs for unemployed men, but argued that in the face of limited jobs, municipalities should show little concern for men coming from elsewhere in the province. In 1932 the town of Kirkland Lake issued a warning that no more jobs were available, and the *Porcupine Advance* argued that Timmins should do the same. 'Southern towns and cities,' argued the paper, 'have been all too ready to try to get rid of their surplus unemployed by telling them things are good in the North.'[131]

The isolation of work in northern lumber or mining camps left women unable to contact men or to claim their income, forcing them to use the family court system to claim desertion or non-support. Frank Ross, a moulder from Guelph, left his wife and eleven children in November 1937 to work in Callander and later in Hamilton. His wife, left to survive on relief, told the court, 'He has gone away to hunt work at different times, whether he was hunting or not I do not know.'[132] When Mary Davis' husband left to find work in Chalk River, she was unable to contact him and had to have him criminally charged in order to qualify for relief.[133] As Dorothy Chunn points out, neither specialized family courts nor police courts were particularly successful in tracing men who deserted or in enforcing support payments. It took a great deal of coordination between municipal officials to track men down, and local authorities were reluctant to spend the necessary funds to locate men, return them to their homes, and then prosecute or jail them.[134]

What many of these case records reveal, other than the cultural strength of the ideal that men should find work at any cost, is the extent of women's and children's dependence. The development of twentieth-century welfare polices such as mothers' allowance in Canada and the United States were predicated not just on regulating women's private and public lives but on regulating men as breadwinners and ensuring that the volume of women dependent on state welfare would be limited. Even advocates of early mothers' allowance were worried that such legislation could 'encourage' men to desert their families and believed that women should first turn to the courts and use the Criminal Code to prosecute male deserters.[135] This fear of the disintegration of the male breadwinner role, combined with the amount of state money that might be needed to support women, explains the long waiting period for deserted wives to receive mothers' allowance and why relief boards required deserted women to initiate legal proceedings against their husbands before they received relief.

Having to accept relief and explain their personal and marital problems to relief investigators and probation officers was a humiliating experience for some women. Emma Partridge encouraged her husband Cecil to remain in New Brunswick and find work despite being left on relief. In a letter to her husband in March 1939, Mrs Partridge asked him to save his money and then send for her and the child, because 'there is two many [sic] people here that know our business and that we owe money to.'[136] An argument over several months of unemployment precipitated Henry Levy's desertion of his wife Frances and their two children. Four days after he took his barber's tools and left to look for work, Mrs Levy contacted the York family court for help, as the relief department had refused to help her. She admitted that she had been so ashamed to tell the relief department that her husband had deserted her that she told them he was sick. To help her get relief the probation officer wrote a letter to the relief department, outlining the problems in her marriage and the desertion of her husband.[137]

The argument that it was a fundamental state responsibility to protect families from economic instability created a powerful demand for increased state involvement in social welfare programs, evidenced by later policy developments such as family allowance, unemployment insurance, and universal old age pensions. As Annalee Golz argues, by the postwar reconstruction period, the state had accepted a moral obligation to protect and ensure the stability and welfare of the Canadian family.[138] This concern over the stability of the family existed not only in the discourse of state officials or policy makers, however. Part of the powerful rhetoric of post–Second World War welfare programs was rooted in the grassroots demands of Depression-era families for their right to economic protection by the state. The overwhelming number of complaints received by politicians at all levels of government from men who were struggling to raise a family on low wages or inadequate relief created a degree of concern among government and business leaders, who recognized the threat to the social stability by men unable to fulfil the role of breadwinner.

The postwar welfare state encoded hierarchies of gender, race, class, and marital status into its terms of provision. The overwhelming public and state support for the association of manhood with breadwinner status was encoded in welfare state policy.[139] The Great Depression first challenged, then solidified the long-standing equation of manhood with full citizenship rights, economic independence, and respectability, and of women with motherhood and dependency. The deeply felt belief in male entitlement to labour helps to partly explain the question of why the economic crisis did not ultimately destroy the male bread-winner ideal and why domesticity emerged as a central organizing principle of the postwar years. Hierarchical gender roles of bread-winner and dependent were rarely challenged in popular discussion or public policy; masculinity drew legitimacy not just from a man's relationship to the workforce, but from his status as a husband and father as well. The crisis of capitalism threatened the hegemonic stability of the association of Anglo-Celtic manhood with breadwinner status and independence, but allowed for unemployed and poor men to play on these assumptions to make increasing demands on the state for intervention in the economy through job creation, social insurance policy, and comprehensive relief payments.

Women's concerns were not completely invisible in the postwar welfare state, but men's domestic concerns as fathers and husbands were embedded in demands for greater social and economic entitlement. The demand for full employment and expanded social welfare achieved political popularity because it was predicated on the importance of men's breadwinner status. Without the emphasis on fatherly domesticity, demands for government intervention would likely not have been so powerful or so popular. After the Depression years, it is not surprising that citizenship was 'felt more fully by men' and centred firmly around waged work and economic security.[140] This development gradually marginalized women from the most inclusive and generous forms of social policy: policies that linked full and inclusive benefits to the status of full-time worker and provider and placed women in the context of the 'ideal' postwar family of full-time provider and homemaker.

3 The Obligations of Family: Parents, Children's Labour, and Youth Culture

The Great Depression was characterized by tension and conflict over the economic and moral role of children within families, the relationship between children and parents, and between families and welfare officials. Captured partly by family court records, these conflicts emerged in the lived reality of the lives of working-class and unemployed families. As Neil Sutherland points out, working-class and most middle-class children in the Depression were still expected to contribute to the family economy by earning extra money or by helping with household labour. Even though the expectation of full-time schooling for young children had taken hold by the 1920s, most families found a variety of ways, through informal and formal labour, for their children to contribute to the family unit. The labour of children could prevent the family from falling into complete poverty.[1]

This chapter documents the myriad ways that children contributed, through various forms of labour, to the economic survival of their families. Participation of children in the family economy was not necessarily a smooth or conflict-free process. Conflict occasionally occurred between parents and truant officers, as parents attempted to negotiate with state authorities over their children's employment, or between parents and children, as family members argued over the apportioning of family resources. This chapter also explores the impact of high unemployment on the ability of the state to enforce children's obligations to parents and fathers' obligations to 'illegitimate' children in a period where expectations about children's independence, education, and responsibilities to the family unit were gradually changing. Finally, by examining Depression-era heterosexual youth culture, I will examine social concerns over declining marriage rates and the difficulties of enforcing support for children born to single mothers.

The role of children in the urban and rural family economy in the nineteenth century has been well documented.[2] The Great Depression marks a period of transition from the traditional, interdependent family economy, where working-class children were expected to leave school and work in order to contribute wages tó the family, to the 'modern' era of extended formal schooling for children and an economy structured around the male breadwinner wage. Expectations differed by ethnicity, region, and class, but until the end. of the Second World War, the majority of working-class and some rural families held that 'entrance' – the minimum educational requirement to attend high school – was the appropriate level of education for their children, and Nancy Christie argues that by the 1930s working-class women 'balked' at children having to work rather than attend school.[3] However, families' decisions about work and schooling were made in a period characterized by complex and competing ideologies. For example, the state encouraged children to contribute economically to the family economy by giving mothers' allowance benefits 'more readily' to mothers who encouraged children to work.[4] But, as Margaret Little points out, mothers' allowance was amended in 1934 to include women whose children were between the ages of sixteen and eighteen and still at school.[5] Ultimately, high unemployment, and an exceptionally high youth unemployment rate, made it increasingly difficult for children in the 1930s either to help support their families or to live independently.[6] Childhood and family history is not a simple story of the shift from a 'communal' or interdependent family and household structure to one based on increasing domesticity marked by extended periods of childhood dependency. Rather, assessing children's place in family life and in the paid labour force is best understood as a conflictual and uneven process between these patterns of development.[7] Despite the importance of youth within the family economy and social fears over promiscuity, lax morals, or criminal behaviour, very few programs or resources were directed towards alleviating the problem of youth unemployment. Youth might have been the target of concern or of fear, but as Cynthia Comacchio notes, they were never considered deserving of much more than 'supervision, containment, and regulation.'[8]

Stealing for Survival

Informal labour often came to the attention of the family court system when children were caught stealing food, money, wood, or coal to help meet their families' needs. A common children's chore in the nineteenth century was to take coal or wood from railway and factory yàrds because fuel was crucial for heating and cooking.[9] This was still a frequent activity in the interwar period. Family court records in Ottawa, for example, indicate that the police, the courts, and the railway companies struggled with the high incidence of coal theft in the 1930s. One young boy charged with theft told the court that he 'thought it was all right' because almost everyone he knew took the coal that spilled over from the chutes.[10] Companies into the early 1930s tolerated a certain level of coal theft by children, but as unemployment levels rose, they began to restrict the practice. In 1937, for example, Constable Martel told the family court judge that Mrs Martin, a mothers' allowance recipient on relief and head of a 'large family,' had 'in the past ... taken the coal herself and notified the company,' but had sent her son in December 1937 because she had been told by the company that 'they would not sanction her request, because if they did everybody would be asking.'[11]

Parents not only tolerated the theft of coal, they sent children out specifically to steal it. Both mothers and fathers justified this type of theft as one of the few ways that unemployed families could survive the winter months on meagre relief allowances. When Emile and Jean Cormier and Paul and Jean Martin were charged with stealing $5 worth of coal, they claimed that they were 'sent by their mothers.' When Mrs Martin was told by the family court judge that 'she should have gone to the proper authorities,' she replied, 'I was over at the relief office and they refused to give me coal ... [I] saw night coming and there was no coal or wood ... [I] sent the children to get some.' She, along with her sons, was given a suspended sentence, but the father of her sons' friends received less sympathy from the judge, who sentenced him to two days in jail because he was not on relief.[12] Parents condoned such theft as a necessary part of family survival. In 1938 several brothers were charged, along with three other boys, for stealing from the city wood yard. Their father, Antonio Probert, an unemployed labourer and father of five children, saw their actions as necessary and just, given their poverty. 'I have not much to say,' he told the judge in 1938, 'but necessity knows no law.' In a revealing exchange with the judge, Probert claimed that his priorities lay first with his family and that he had first tried to steal the wood himself, and he refused to accept the label of criminal for his actions.

JUDGE: Do you want to see your children brought up criminals?

PROBERT: I don't believe that is stealing. I enquired into it and this person told me that consciens would not be encouraged if I needed the wood. [sic]

JUDGE: I don't think you were thinking right when you did a thing like this?

PROBERT: It is not my thinking; it is my very highest authority.

JUDGE: The law says 'Thou shalt not steal'... I don't care who your authority is, God's commandments are still there.

Probert was given a suspended sentence and his sons were placed on probation, ensuring that social workers would monitor the proper moral development of the Probert children.[13]

Poor families did not see leftover coal as private property, and many families felt they had a right to use it in order to cook or stay warm. 'I thought it was all right,' remarked one father to a judge when his son stole two bags of coal. 'I don't think there was any harm.'[14] Court officials, when faced with the poverty of families, were ambivalent about applying severe criminal sanctions, usually treating this as a social problem by putting children on probation and giving a suspended sentence to those found guilty. The case of the Bird family illustrates this complex interplay between courts and families. In January 1938 Clifford and James Bird were charged with stealing three bags of coal valued at $1.50. The manager of the C.W. Bangs Company followed sleigh tracks to their house and reported the boys to the police. But when a female court official went in and confronted Mrs Bird, she admitted that 'she had sent two boys out for coal, and she started to cry. She said she had no fuel; she did not get her script. I did not know exactly how to act. I left her a scuttleful and took the rest back with me.' In court, Detective Gray, the investigating officer, confirmed her motivations: 'She said that was the reason ... they were so cold.' James Bird told the judge that the 'house was cold, and we had to get some coal ... we got it around the tracks. We got it under the platform, where the engines drop it off.' The boys were found guilty and placed on probation, while their mother was given a suspended sentence. Judge Balharrie lectured her: 'Your dire need at the present time isn't any excuse for your children being sent out to secure fuel.'[15] While judges in the family court system did not administer heavy penalties for these actions, neither did they condone the practice, upholding the legal distinction between private property and long-standing community practice. Such problems of 'crime' could then be used by the courts as a way to ensure ongoing regulation of potential 'problem' families through the court system. But it is still important to consider the myriad ways that families talked back to the courts: they refused to accept the label of criminal or deviant, they repeatedly denied the crime and created an alternate, community-driven definition of needs, and they stood up to questioning by family court judges.

Petty theft was also a common practice in the Great Depression, and a way for children or teenagers to add to the family income.[16] Many of the youth involved in petty crime were boys who were either too young to find paid work or who could not find temporary work in the depressed economy, yet still felt the pressure to help their families economically. Eric Best, age eleven, was caught stealing two tins of canned food in 1935. His family of four was on relief and lived in one room.[17] By the interwar years doctors, psychologists, social workers, and family court judges had developed theories of delinquency that, while not completely abandoning the idea of hereditary 'abnormality,' also sought explanations rooted in social and environmental factors. In particular, the negative influence of adolescent peer groups, especially those consisting of young, working-class boys, was believed to cause much of the 'age-based' delinquency.[18] Judges, police, and social workers in Ontario blamed 'gangs' and 'poor locale' for this problem, but it seems that economic desperation was one motivating factor for petty thefts.[19] Fifteen-year-old Alphonse Grandpré admitted to the arresting officer that he stole because his family of eight, on relief, needed money for food. Constable Soublière testified: 'The boy said they had nothing to eat at home, and he gave the $2.00 to his mother. The circumstances are very bad at home ... the mother said he had told her he had got work and he had got paid, he really did take the money home ... [t]here is not a thing in there, just a table, they are sleeping on the floor – the father left home six or seven years ago.' Judge McKinley recognized the boy's 'desire to help' his family and asked that the local Catholic church and the constable stay involved with his case and offer him 'encouragement.'[20]

For some children stealing was the easiest way to earn extra spending money or to find needed money for food or rent. The Lapointe family first came under the scrutiny of the Ottawa juvenile court in 1934, when Jacques was charged with breaking into the poorbox at the local Roman Catholic church while his father, a labourer with a family of five, was unemployed. His father testified: 'We try to do the best we can. I have five children ... I am not working at present.'[21] Parents, often the fathers of children caught stealing, seemed to tolerate theft as a sad necessity rather than a criminal offence. In May 1938 Sylvain Laporte of Eastview was given probation for receiving stolen goods. His father was an unemployed housepainter, and his brother was also unemployed and living at home. The twenty-two-year-old had attended the University of Ottawa for five months, but left because he needed to help support his family, who were on relief. His father explained that his son had stolen in order to obtain money and 'that he had been unable to provide the boy with spending money for some time.'[22] Both Lyle Birch and David Dinardi claimed they stole in order to get money to buy Christmas presents for their parents.[23] Of course, the defence of stealing money for Christmas presents may also have become a stock excuse for some children. In December 1936 Gerald Goldstein, who came from a Russian-Jewish family, was charged with two other boys with stealing a car battery; he claimed he stole it in order to get Christmas money for his mother.[24]

A well-understood and accepted black market in stolen goods, and a market for 'scrounged' objects such as junk metal and coal, existed in many communities.[25] When Raymond Laforte stole $34 worth of coke in February 1937, he intended to sell it to help his family. His father had deserted the family, his mother was on relief, and they were supplementing relief payments with his wages as a part-time pedlar.[26] Local adults from the neighbourhood, not just parents, approached children to steal and sell various goods, and it is apparent that children knew whom to approach in order to sell stolen goods. Walter Desjardins and Guy Chartrand were charged with stealing twenty-two potato bags from a market stand and selling them to two men for 20 cents per bag. Claimed one of the men: 'I am in the habit of buying from children on the market, empty bags, and baskets etc. I do that in the market regularly.'[27] Fourteen-year-old Muriel Dick was charged with two other girls in 1937 with stealing clothes and selling them to a local woman. Muriel told the court: 'She said if we got the things she liked she would pay us for it ... she was supposed to give me, for two dresses, twenty cents.'[28] In November 1930 Alain and Emile Charbonneau were charged along with two other boys with stealing coal from the CNR cars, which they sold to a local woman for 25 cents per bag. The judge was clearly frustrated with the level of theft and the involvement of adults and families, claiming: 'If these boys did not know that they could sell that coal they would never have stolen it ... I hope this [sentence] will be a warning to you and all the people in that district.'[29]

Children's Economic Contributions

Changes in patterns of youth employment and education were well under way by the Great Depression. By the 1920s most children were enrolled in school for a longer and more regular period of time than ever before. School enrollment even rose marginally in the Depression years, probably because of the high youth unemployment rates, and many parents were concerned with giving their children the opportunity to stay in school.[30] Some families struggled to keep their children in school despite a difficult financial situation. In Mount Elgin, William Prouse's farm was verging on bankruptcy in 1935 not only because of low crop prices, but also from the debts accumulated from educating his eight children. Only one child remained at home to work on the farm. In St Mary's, farmer Henry Gill went into debt to pay for his daughter's teacher training, while Mr V. Grant from East York wrote to Premier Henry for help finding a job in order to save his home from foreclosure and to keep his daughters in school.[31] Greater periods of education and training were important to both parents and children. In the Canadian Youth Commission survey of 1947, young adults expressed resentment over Depression-era financial hardships that had forced them to leave school earlier than planned so that they could help their parents. Families' and children's expectations were gradually changing in regard to work and education, as both parents and children desired a more extensive period of schooling and training.[32]

Yet most working-class families expected children to contribute to the family economy through either formal or informal labour, and most children fulfilled these expectations. Sociological surveys of the period overwhelmingly found that children were expected to take on some type of labour, though the extent and form of their economic contributions differed by ethnicity and class.[33] These expectations existed in rural areas, where, as Ruth Sandwell argues, the household remained 'a central locus of the economy,' but they persisted in urban families as well, where families needed children's wages to supplement the low incomes of male breadwinners.[34] Many children proudly took part in this type of familial labour. Basil Libby of South Porcupine delivered the *Toronto Star* for 20 cents a week at the age of fifteen and turned over the money to his mother. In 1938, while working at his first job in the local mines, he turned his pay cheque over to his mother, who gave him an allowance for clothes and gas. This tradition was followed until he turned twenty-one.[35] Charles Smith found a summer job on the CPR, moving and loading old railway ties outside of Chapleau in northern Ontario. Paid a dollar a day after the costs of room and board, he came home with $17 for his widowed mother and ten siblings. His eldest brother Harold had been pulled from school on his father's death in 1930 to become the main breadwinner, while his brothers Keith and Chester were, with the help of his father's union connections, able to get jobs on the CPR. When Keith died in 1937, his insurance was used to pay back taxes on the family home, which was about to be seized by the city of North Bay.[36] Martin Boudreau left school at sixteen to help support his parents and siblings, who were on relief. Over the course of ten months he shovelled snow for the city of Ottawa, worked for a week picking potatoes, and did occasional work for local farmers.[37] Family economic arrangements reflected a complex economy where children and parents held a variety of expectations. Children turned their wages over to their mothers until they were married, dropped out of school so that some siblings could continue their education, and moved away to find work and sent money home.

Younger boys and girls helped out by undertaking various types of informal and unpaid labour, such as picking berries or helping with domestic labour.[38] Gladys Clements and her two younger brothers in Elk Lake picked wild berries for their mother to preserve, and her brothers sold the surplus produce.[39] John Gore recalled that local children in Cobalt picked an abundance of wild blueberries to sell at the farmers' market every summer, claiming that this was 'how you put shoes on the children to go to school in the fall.'[40] Charles Smith was given a variety of household chores to help his mother: he was responsible for lighting the fire and providing breakfast to his younger siblings every morning, picking up four loaves of bread every day at the bakery, and shopping for inexpensive vegetables, soup bones, and meat every Saturday morning at the North Bay Farmers' Market.[41]

But this type of family strategy, while common, did not always run smoothly or easily. With the growth of mass culture and a greater variety of youth-oriented leisure activities such as dances and movies, conflicts arose between the expectations of parents and those of youth, who wanted to maintain a greater degree of independence and some control over their earnings. Occasionally, what was best for the 'collective well-being' of families did not match the desire for individualism or self-interest.[42] When the women's columnist for the *Farmer's Advocate* worried that too many young women were leaving rural life for the city, she suggested that young rural women should try to make extra money at home while still remaining on the family farm. In response, a young woman pointed out the repercussions: 'For goodness sake don't pile more work on our tired shoulders ... we girls must, partially at least, take the place of a hired man ... [b]ut, after working twelve or fifteen hours a day, helping to keep the home together and respectably kept, can we be asked to work another two or three hours in order to support ourselves?'[43]

Those children who did manage to find paid employment could get caught up in a power struggle over how much of their earnings to turn over to the family. These conflicts occurred while children were living at home, but could also extend to arguments over maintenance long after children had moved away or married. E. Wight Bakke's survey of unemployed families in Connecticut found that as parents increasingly relied on children's earnings in the face of male unemployment, the harder it became to discipline them.[44] Family court records partially capture some of these parent-child conflicts over distribution of income and resources. In September 1935 Maria Panayotou was charged with 'absenting herself from her home without cause.' Maria told the judge that the problems stemmed from conflict with her father over her wages. 'I have been working,' she claimed, 'but lately I have been laid off. This week I said I would get a swaggersuit, and my father claimed my pay, and said I would not get it. That is why I left and I did not do anything more.'[45] When Richard Ladouceur was charged with stealing a bike, a home visit from a probation officer revealed his resentment over the distribution of relief money in his family. He had a paper route and complained that his father spent the relief money and his earnings on the younger children, leaving him no money for his own use.[46] Yet, even with the struggle, tension, and conflict over changing roles and expectations, all family members took these economic obligations seriously. Parents expected children to participate, in some way, in the larger project of family and household survival.[47]

Conflicts with State Authorities

Expectations regarding children's labour could occasionally lead to conflict between parents and the state over the age at which children should be allowed to stay out of school and work at paid labour. While the state had generally won the battle over compulsory school enrollment by the 1920s, it was not until the 1960s that the 'deeply rooted' patterns of children's labour began to shift.[48] In the 1930s it was still quite common for children to leave school by the age of sixteen, or to attempt to leave even earlier, in order to find a job to help their family. For example, Chester Bain first came into contact with the family court system in January 1937, when he was absent from school. The judge helped him get a work permit because the family, with nine children, had been on relief since 1936. The family's total income consisted of Chester's odd jobs and $23.90 in relief every two weeks.[49] Even very informal labour could bring in much-needed cash. In Ottawa a young girl was discovered by a police officer in February 1938 selling paper butterflies to people on Bank Street. When Police Constable Glimmer took her home, he discovered that her mother, whose husband had deserted her and his four children, had sent out two of the children with a box of paper butterflies to sell on the street to supplement their relief.[50]

Children, mainly young boys, sought work in the 1930s and often came into conflict with school attendance officials and the family court system. In Montreal's Catholic schools, for example, truancy related to poverty and unemployment increased during the Great Depression, from approximately 9 per cent in 1920–21, to over 14 per cent in 1933–34.[51] Both children and their parents insisted on the need for their children to work, and in many cases, while state officials encouraged children to return to school, they were forced to acknowledge economic difficulties and issue special work permits for children between fourteen and sixteen years of age.[52] In some cases the children of deserted mothers were the only people bringing desperately needed money into the household economy. All members of the family, in these cases, were dependent on the labour of young children. In September 1936 Probation Officer Miss D. Cluff recommended that the family court give fifteen-year-old Lester Paulson a work permit. His parents were separated, and his mother supported the family through relief supplemented by keeping boarders. The court noted that Lester 'is the only one bringing in any money. He has a job as Messenger boy, and his salary is $3.00 per week. He is very poorly clad, and there is no money to buy books for him for High School, so that is would seem the best thing to give him a temporary permit while he has regular employment.'[53] In November 1938 Maurice Rivard was charged with truancy, but given a few weeks to find a job to help out his 'destitute' mother, who, after the desertion of her husband, was surviving on the wages of a son who sold newspapers.[54] Despite the economic necessity of children's paid labour, their work remained an issue of some concern to child welfare authorities. B.W. Heise, managing director of the Hamilton Children's Aid Society in 1933, and Mr F.C. Jackson, a social work student at the University of Toronto, developed a project that surveyed children working in the Hamilton 'street trades.' They found that most were young boys who made an average of $1.75 a week selling newspapers, often late at night. The main reason these children and their families gave for their work was parental unemployment.[55] Children did work late at night at various jobs, and often with their parents' permission. Thirteen-year-old Jack Collison was charged with truancy, for example, because he was too tired to attend school after helping his widowed mother sell newspapers late into the evening.[56] Margaret S. Pettigrew, chief attendance officer of the Toronto Board of Education, wrote to the Department of Labour, asking them to investigate a number of teenage boys who were working and attending school. She was concerned about complaints, for example, that Sunnyside Beach was employing schoolchildren during school hours and 'so late in the evenings that they cannot attend school the next morning.'[57] Despite these concerns, however, and a growing ideal of longer compulsory education, child welfare authorities had few options within a larger economic system where extreme poverty and unemployment meant that labour had to be given priority over school. Unemployment, poverty, and deprivation meant that children' economic contributions were ultimately more important to their families than their education. What family court records reveal is that officials, when investigating complaints of truancy, often issued work permits to children who were legally supposed to be in school until the age of sixteen or until fourteen with a special permit.

While boys and their parents came under scrutiny for work-related truancy, girls tended to come under the court's investigation for being kept home to help their mothers with housework and child care or to help look after parents who were ill.[58] If one or both parents had to enter a hospital or became ill, the families had little choice but to keep children home to manage the household. In February 1932 eight-year-old Ruth Epstein was charged with truancy. Her parents, both ill and on relief, had seven children including a newborn baby. Ruth was given permission to stay home and help her mother.[59] The case of the Lawson family illustrates the complex relationships of obligation and care in working-class and poor families. In 1934 the family of Darlene Lawson was investigated for truancy by a probation officer. Her father was an unemployed salesman, and her mother kept seven boarders; during a home visit, the mother admitted keeping her daughter home to help with the domestic labour. 'She claims that she took this large house to keep roomers and boarders, so that they would go off relief,' noted the probation officer, who felt that the 'girl is a clever child and should have the chance at school.' Her mother told the court that in addition to the work keeping boarders, 'it is the state of my health that is the matter. I cannot afford to go the hospital, and I kept her home to look after me. My husband is not working.' Darlene attempted to defend her mother and defend her contribution to the family: 'I would be willing to go to school but not when my mother is sick ... I stay at home myself when I see that my mother is sick.' Despite the court's insistence, Darlene and her mother continued to resist the court's order to send her back to school.[60] In 1936 the Kincaid family of Brockville came under scrutiny of the CAS and the family court for keeping their ten-year-old daughter at home to look after her three younger siblings while the mother was out at charwork. While the mother claimed her daughter did not have adequate clothes for school, the young girl said she had to look after the younger children. The mother promised the judge she would give up work so the children could go to school, though there was no indication of how the family would make up for the loss of income.[61] It seems that in many of these cases, parents promised the courts that children would return to school. In reality, however, children's labour was simply too valuable for parents to allow them to continue their education.

Though it was usually girls who worked at home, in some cases a combination of poverty, illness, and lack of clothing kept boys home to help their mothers. For boys, however, this was considered a temporary measure and not a central part of their domestic and gendered education.[62] Hugh Amherst and his wife had trouble keeping their ten-year-old son Morris in school and, in 1934, were charged with neglecting to send him to school: from September to March 1934 he was absent over fifty-two days. When Judge Balharrie asked Morris's father for an explanation, he replied, 'I leave home early in the morning to see if I can get work anywhere.' His wife was ill and sometimes kept their son at home to help her.[63] Howard MacMillan often stayed home from school to help his mother, a widow on relief who suffered from chronic bronchitis and intestinal disorders. Her doctor confirmed that because of her illnesses she required 'help at home for any heavy work.'[64]

Regardless of the possible intervention of state officials, the family economy remained dependent on the economic contribution of children well into the 1930s. These contributions could be a form of paid work, or they could take the form of informal or household labour. For many families in this period, but especially for families of the working class or those struggling with unemployment, the family retained a culture of 'support and obligation' between parents and children, both when children were young and after they had left the home.[65]

Adult Children, Parents, and Mutual Support

The obligations of children to help support their parents did not end in childhood: by law, adult children could be forced to make economic contributions to destitute parents. By the interwar years urbanization, industrialization, and increased geographic fragmentation of the family created a growing concern among social reformers that the elderly were becoming indigent and therefore at risk of becoming public charges.[66] In 1921 the United Farmers of Ontario government passed the Parents' Maintenance Act, which gave the elderly the right to charge their children for support payments of up to $20 a week. While most parents did not take their children to court, this law acted as a symbolic piece of legislation regarding familial duties and responsibilities and a 'useful club' for municipalities to force children to take on economic support for their parents.[67] Legislation like the Parents' Maintenance Act provided a basic framework for social welfare provision within an ideal version of family life as mutually cooperative and caring, where responsibility for the elderly lay first with family members and not with the state.[68] It also acted as a means-test for elderly relief applicants. Both aims of the Parents' Maintenance Act enforced a policy of limited state aid and attempted to keep support for individuals within the realm of the private family unit. Indeed, the Old Age Pension Act, which Ontario enacted in 1929, calculated children's earnings as part of applicants' incomes regardless of the actual amount received. Most local OAP boards in Ontario interpreted the legislation conservatively, making arbitrary deductions of $5 to $10 a month from the maximum. The state continued this policy of holding children economically responsible for the maintenance of elderly parents during the Great Depression, refusing to recognize the financial difficulties of unemployed families. By 1932 Welfare Minister George Martin announced that all children's income would be taken into consideration in an OAP application, regardless of whether or not they contributed to their parents' finances. In his 1942 review of Canadian social security policy, Leonard Marsh noted that the elderly often had trouble in qualifying for an old age pension because of the principle of interpreting eligibility through the terms of the Parents' Maintenance Act.[69]

Most local mothers' allowance boards acted in a similar way, calculating allowances based on the expected earnings of children.[70]

Surviving case files in family courts support the idea that parents used the Parents' Maintenance Act as a stick to force children who would not, or could not, financially support them. While some historians have suggested that the small number of existing case files means that prosecutions and convictions under the PMA were rare, it is clear that parents were aware of the power of the state to intercede in such situations and that judicial power could be used as a threat in order to force children to shoulder some form of economic support for their parents. Parents could, and did, approach the court system to investigate their children's financial situation and to negotiate for economic support on their behalf.

In the Great Depression, the principles underlying the Parents' Maintenance Act were encoded in relief applications. Like dependent wives, elderly parents were usually forced to lay a charge under the PMA or under non-support laws before authorities would grant them relief. Therefore, many charges under the Parents' Maintenance Act were never officially laid, but were used by judges, relief officials, and probation officers to means-test elderly relief applicants, keep relief costs down, and provide a stick for welfare officials to negotiate at least a minimal amount of support from adult children. Laying a charge could be the only option for elderly relief applicants and might not reflect a conflictual relationship among family members. Clearly, adult children in the 1930s were struggling to support themselves and their families and were unable to provide much extra to help support their parents. In 1936 Norman Mendelson asked the York family court to arrange for his son and daughter to contribute to his support, since relief would not be provided until they were interviewed. An investigation discovered that his children earned too little to increase their contribution towards his support. A caseworker from the family court arranged to go with the family to the welfare office to discuss their finances and arrange for relief.[71] Like the situation of women who had to submit to investigation or lay criminal charges of non-support to prove destitution and claim relief, elderly parents also had to convince the court of their utter poverty and the breakdown of the family system of economic support. Family courts did not accept the claims of the elderly without 'proper' investigation of family finances and relationships by those appointed as experts. Only when such experts, who were sanctioned by and imbued with the authority of the state, could interview, investigate, and determine the extent of dependency, would relief be granted.

When adult children were struggling financially, they resisted the attempts of both their parents and the state to force them to pay support. Sixty-year-old Daniel Peckham laid charges against four of his children in January 1938, and two of his children engaged in a protracted debate with the judge. His son-in-law refused to help, claiming that 'these people have had the meanness [sic] to go to you to try to force us to do something we have already tried to do to the best of our ability ... we will have nothing more to do with the matter.' He carefully laid out a series of financial problems in his own family. Similarly, Peckham's daughter wrote to Judge Balharrie, detailing her family's own untenable economic situation: 'The reason we are not doing anything to support him is because my husband has been out of work since last August and before that he was not even making a living by selling cars. Going farther into debt and not knowing where we were gong to get money to buy food and clothing for ourselves and two children, we decided to sell all our furniture, at a great loss and come to Toronto which we did.'[72]

In the case of the Gouin family in Toronto both the father, Gerard, and his son tried to force another sibling to help contribute to the father's income. The youngest son, Richard, defended himself by arguing that he only worked for $3.50 a week at Sears and could not afford more than a small contribution.[73] The state steadfastly continued the practice of assessing children's financial support even in the heart of the Depression, and even though these investigations quite often revealed the devastating impact of unemployment on several generations of families. In February 1939 Mrs Upshaw, a woman from Montreal, asked the York family court to get her two daughters, who lived in Toronto, to support her. Upon investigation, however, it was found that both daughters were married and had little income, and therefore could not be forced to support her.[74]

In some cases children openly resented their parents' claims for support, charging that they were 'lazy' or irresponsible with money. In June 1937 Harry Bartram, a fifty-two-year-old unemployed moulder, asked for maintenance from his three sons – a civil servant, a printer, and a pedlar – who were each ordered to pay $5 a week. One son, however, refused to pay and claimed that his father was lazy, spent money on alcohol, and used money from his sons to support his new wife and children. 'It is a strange disease that allows a man to work when the weather is fine,' he argued, 'but becomes so unbearable when winter sets in that he is unable to work. The above may appear to be sarcasm, but if you will take the trouble of referring to your correspondence files, you will discover that every year about this time a letter is sent.'[75]

The family courts offered elderly parents help in locating and negotiating with recalcitrant children, challenging notions of a golden age of extended family support. Clearly, some children actively resented the expectation of support held both by their parents and the state, and they refused to uphold the cultural norm of a mutual parent-child relationship.[76] In January 1937 Hector Lalonde asked that his son Laurent be charged under the Parents' Maintenance Act, as the son was single and employed, while his parents were on relief. In response, Laurent claimed that he had been laid off and was in rent arrears. His lawyer wrote to Judge McKinley claiming that the father 'is a comparatively young man of around 53 years of age and there is not evidence of disease or infirmity ... he makes no effort of any kind to secure employment, and is quite satisfied to sit by the stove in the home that he owns.'[77]

Most cases of parental support were settled fairly quickly after the courts intervened. Probation workers wrote up maintenance agreements or acted as mediators, or the elderly demonstrated to local relief boards they truly had no support and were therefore deserving of aid. After Mrs Myrtle Ball charged her four sons under the Parents' Maintenance Act in September 1933, they came to a mutual agreement: her son David offered not only to contribute $10 a month to her maintenance until his brothers found work, but also to take in one brother until he could find employment.[78] In 1936 seventy-eight-year-old Jack Thornton charged his three sons under the Parents' Maintenance Act. Though he received an old age pension of $20 a month, it was not enough to cover the cost of his home, which was $23 per month. After the intervention of the family court his two sons agreed to pay $2 a month each, while his other son refused, saying his obligations were too heavy at the moment.[79]

For many men, women, and children in the 1930s the institution of the family held possibilities for conflict, but it also embodied relationships of mutual economic support. These obligations were embedded within a culture of family support, where both young and adult children were expected to participate in the larger project of family survival. Support laws and welfare and relief policy drew on this culture, however, they did so not only to uphold the broader values of familial obligation, but also to ensure that the costs of family support remained, as much as possible, within the realm of the ideal, privatized family.

Yet the Great Depression also made evident that family support was not always enough to prevent poverty. By the end of the 1930s local, provincial, and federal authorities were increasingly aware of the failure of the capitalist labour market to adequately provide employment or redistribute income among families, children, or the elderly. The reality was that family members could not always provide the mutual economic assistance valourized in legislation such as the Parents' Maintenance Act or the means-tested benefit under the Old Age Pension Act, and despite child labour laws, youth had to find creative ways to contribute wages to the household. While postwar universal, non–means-tested welfare policies targeted at mothers, children, and the elderly certainly did not end poverty, these policies arose in part out of the economic hardships so clearly evident in the Great Depression.[80]

Youth and the Great Depression: Dating, Sex, and Economic Obligation

Popular concerns about the effect of high male unemployment on marriage rates and heterosexual relationships demonstrate how the depressed economy shaped fears and concerns about gender relationships in the 1930s. Unemployment did not just have an impact on finances, it also shaped the context in which men and women lived their private lives, their dating lives, and their sexual lives. High youth unemployment rates had a direct effect on marriage rates in the 1930s, as increasing numbers of young men and women delayed marriage because of unemployment. The marriage rate in Canada dropped from 7 per cent in 1930 to 6.4 per cent in 1931, reaching a low of 5.9 per cent in 1932. Between 1931 and 1934, the marriage rate reached a high of only 6.8 per cent, and it only dropped this low again in 1963, when it was 6.9 per cent.[81] In a cultural context of male breadwinner families, couples found it difficult to marry when male unemployment was so high that a man could not provide an income to support a wife and children. The Ontario Young Men's Christian Association (YMCA) was clearly concerned about this trend and in 1936 surveyed a group of unemployed unmarried men specifically on the question of marriage and its relationship to income. The vast majority of men (83 per cent) reported that they found it impossible to marry because of low wages and unemployment.[82] In an American sociological survey, young men and women of 'marriageable' age claimed to feel dissatisfaction and resentment over 'thwarted education and delayed marriages' brought about by the depressed economy.[83] Miss Elsie Markham of Birchcliffe was particularly incensed that her boyfriend, a bank clerk, could not make enough money to support a family. 'One must earn a certain salary before marrying and since the Depression this has been raised, so you see one isn't far ahead nor does the future seem very bright.'[84] Because of the expectation that a man should support his dependent wife and children, and because married women faced discrimination in the labour force, postponing marriage was the only available option for many. This postponement, however, led to delayed adulthood, since the status offered by marriage, for both men and women, signified maturity, responsibility, and an end to the dependency of childhood.

Delayed marriages were of some concern in the 1930s mainly because of the 'problem' of premarital sex and increasing rates of illegitimacy. Patterns of courtship had shifted in the twentieth century, from a more tightly controlled and community-regulated process to one of increasing freedom and access to privacy and youth-oriented public spaces. Consumerism both reflected and helped to create a heterosexual dating culture that celebrated women's sexuality in advertising for such products as deodorant, makeup, and fashion; while movies, automobiles, and dances were some of the many opportunities for youth to date in privacy or with other couples.[85] Domestic workers, who were not subject to parental supervision, made use of their freedom from family ties, using the homes of employers to have intercourse.[86] Social scientists blamed unemployment for a host of social and family problems and linked delayed marriages to premarital sex and illegitimate births, though it is difficult to know whether rates of premarital sex were actually increasing or whether public fears and concerns were rising. In Lothar Richler's collection of articles on unemployment, welfare, and public administration, for example, the loss of the 'right' to marriage and family was blamed for leading young men and women into a 'lowering of moral standards.'[87] In an Ontario YMCA survey, 68 per cent of single men believed that 'irregular' sex was increasing, and 52 per cent said it was linked to postponing marriage because of the Depression.[88]

Premarital sexual experimentation, such as 'petting,' was certainly not uncommon in the lives of young people in the 1930s. Comacchio argues that it was a 'usual' part of dating culture for working-class, immigrant, and rural couples, though it was done within the context of respectable or 'traditional' behaviour and expectations, which meant, particularly for women, a promise to marry. An illegitimate pregnancy could permanently rob a woman of her respectable status and condemn her and her child to poverty. However, it is difficult for historians to reconstruct the extent of premarital sex. Estimates from the nineteenth century suggest that anywhere from 8.3 to 20 per cent of women were pregnant upon marriage, a proportion suggesting that the extent of premarital sexual activity was much higher. Actual illegitimate births, however, comprised a much lower proportion: only about 2 to 4 per cent of all children were born outside of marriage in the nineteenth century. In the twentieth century official illegitimacy rates increased, and they continued to increase during the 1930s.[89] Social workers were worried about this, but they were unsure whether the cause was increased premarital sex or more accurate methods of birth registration.[90] Still, in Ontario, illegitimacy rates rose from 2.1 per cent in 1922 to 4.4 per cent in 1933, and they increased even more in Toronto, where they rose from 4 per cent in 1926 to 6.9 per cent in 1933.[91]

High unemployment for young men meant that marriage would likely be postponed even if an unplanned pregnancy occurred. When fifteen-year-old Melinda Bradford and her boyfriend Edward Carter discovered she was pregnant, they went to her family doctor and asked about an abortion. In court the doctor testified as to Carter's reluctance to marry: 'He didn't know how they could do that. He was more concerned about his education so he would have means of providing a livelihood.'[92] In 1938 Mark Raymond, a baker, was charged with seducing, under promise to marry, Bronwyn Wilson, a domestic worker. Her mother testified that he had proposed and set a wedding date, but he continually postponed it, saying 'he had some debts to clean up first.'[93] Raymond's lawyer J.D. McCallum interrogated her regarding her moral and economic expectations of marriage:

Q: What did you propose to live on – You knew how much Raymond was earning?
A: Yes.
Q: He told you he did not have any money?
A: Yes.
Q: He had no possible chance of getting married, did he tell you that?
A: He did not.[94]

Court records help to reveal the dating rituals and sexual negotiations of heterosexual relationships in the 1930s. The extent to which premarital sex took place has not been documented for the 1930s, and court records are limited in scope, only documenting relationships that ended up in court because of contested paternity and support payments. Yet court records do indicate that sex was a central element in heterosexual dating culture. The volume of records on illegitimate births and paternity suits suggests that unemployment only worsened the precarious financial situation of young, unmarried mothers.

The story of Joseph Bubka and Eva Crescenzi, a domestic worker from Hamilton, demonstrates the interplay between youth culture, social regulation, gendered obligations, and the impact of unemployment. In 1935 Bubka, a Hungarian-speaking basketmaker and taxi driver living in Grimsby, was charged with the seduction of Crescenzi. In court Eva testified that she met Joseph at a picnic in June 1934 in Hamilton, after which they began dating. She claimed that she had refused intercourse until he told her, 'I won't leave you. I would marry you at the end of the year anyways.' By June 1935 Crescenzi was 'in trouble,' and Bubka took her to the doctor to inquire into the possibility of an abortion. She ultimately refused to get a surgical abortion, though she did take some pills for 'delayed menstruation.' The doctor tried to persuade them to continue with the pregnancy, but Joseph refused, telling the doctor that he was working on a farm and could not support a child and a wife.[95]

Both young men and young women sought the services of abortion providers upon the discovery of an unwanted pregnancy, despite the danger and the illegality of abortion. While statistics are uncertain, given that abortions were rarely discovered unless they resulted in a severe illness or death, historians have estimated that anywhere from 10 to 15 per cent of all pregnancies in the first half of the twentieth century ended with an abortion. A 1935 survey by the Department of Maternal and Child Hygiene established that from one in five to one in seven pregnancies were aborted.[96] As McLaren notes, abortion had long been used as a method of birth control, often by married women, and was pursued mainly because of poverty or economic need. For unmarried women, especially, the economic consequences of having an illegitimate child were closely entwined with attempts to preserve sexual reputation and moral character.[97] With the high male unemployment rate, low-paying jobs for both men and women, and a drop in the marriage rate partly as a result of delayed marriages, women and men found that abortion was one way to deal with an unwanted pregnancy.

In many cases men were actively involved in helping women induce an abortion or in finding medical information. Indeed, police assumed men's involvement in the abortion, and they were often prosecuted, especially if the woman died.[98] When twenty-seven-year-old Mrs Fiona McGee of Sault Ste Marie pled guilty to the charge of attempting to procure a miscarriage, she told police that after her husband had deserted her and their five children she worked as a domestic for Mr Bartlett, where she became 'in the family way.' He ordered Blood's Iron Pills from Eaton's because, she claimed, 'I was told that would relieve my condition but it did not.' On their second attempt to end the pregnancy, they bought a catheter; Mrs McGee 'bled while using it,' called a doctor, and had a miscarriage on the way to the hospital. Though she admitted using the catheter to abort, there is no record of her sentence, and she remained free upon sentencing. Bartlett, a widower with two children, was convicted and sentenced to three months in jail. He testified that they had discussed her options together and that 'I thought I was doing everything for the best as Mrs McGee was afraid that her children would be taken from her if her condition was known.'[99] In January 1935 Bryan Morgan was found guilty of supplying Moira Smythe with 'noxious drugs, consisting of pills, capsules and bottles of medicine,' with intent to procure a miscarriage. Morgan testified that he 'knew a fellow who had got some girl into trouble and he had got some [medicine] at the same place ... to bring on a miscarriage.'[100] Surviving court records indicate the men, as well as women, asked friends for advice, asked doctors for help finding an abortion provider, or went to a drug store to buy medicine or equipment used to cause an abortion.

For many young unmarried men and women, supporting a child when one or both parents were unemployed was an onerous financial burden. When Edward Carter discovered that his girlfriend was pregnant, he consulted a doctor by himself and asked him for help obtaining an abortion, as he felt that without a job or education he could not undertake the financial obligation of a wife and child.[101] For Samuel Cliff and his girlfriend Hope Clark, a twenty-five-year-old clerk employed in a millinery store in London, an unexpected pregnancy led to an attempt to find an abortion provider. Cliff was found guilty of administering a drug to procure a miscarriage and jailed for one year after his girlfriend died from septicemia. An inquest revealed that after the drugs did not end her pregnancy, Clark borrowed $100 from a friend to go to Port Stanley for an abortion. The Crown's examination of Cliff questioned his sense of masculine duty and responsibility:

Q: Why did you not marry her?

A: I did not have a job.

Q: You did not mind sleeping with her and knocking her up. You are a fine fellow.[102]

While unemployment and low wages were not the only reasons that women and men attempted to seek out abortions, they clearly were important factors. Because of high youth and male unemployment rates, and the general trend towards delayed marriages in the 1930s, attempts to control sexuality and reproduction were necessary strategies for many young women.

If an unmarried woman became pregnant and private economic arrangements could not be made, the role of the state was twofold: first, determine paternity, and next, enforce the financial support of the woman and child by the father. In 1921 the Ontario government passed legislation regarding the legal status of illegitimate children. The Children of Unmarried Parents Act gave unwed mothers the right to ask the state to sue the putative father on their behalf. In her study of CUPA files from 1921 to 1969, Lori Chambers notes that a substantial minority of children (27 per cent) remained in the care of unwed mothers, who attempted to ensure support by launching a CUPA action.[103] This law was a complex blend of paternalistic and economic motivations. While partly based on concerns for the potential poverty of illegitimate children, legislators were more concerned with the regulation of female sexuality and male breadwinning duty. The Children of Unmarried Parents Act was also motivated by economic considerations that rested on privatizing child support so that women and children were less likely to become public charges. The state, in the form of welfare officials and family courts, was deeply concerned with the regulation of proper gender roles, sexual respectability, and individual economic responsibility. At a time when marriage itself seemed to be under threat, family court workers were deeply concerned with ensuring that traditional gender roles were bolstered and reinscribed through the court process.

Proof of paternity was a complex matter that rested on a court investigation of both women's and men's moral character. A woman's moral character was directly tied to her sexual character, which in turn was linked to values of female sexual modesty. Courts interpreted evidence of sexual assertiveness or more than one sexual partner as evidence of a lack of respectable moral character. In the courtroom women had to declare themselves chaste in order to 'prove' their respectability and to

claim the status of deserving mother. Women testified that they had
only ever had one sexual partner, for example, or that they had engaged
in sexual intercourse in return for a promise of marriage, or that their
partner had offered marriage upon discovering the pregnancy. Of
course, the physical reality of a pregnancy meant that it was impossible
for women to truly present themselves as morally pure. In courtroom
testimony, with defence lawyers challenging their morality, women
had to negotiate the hegemonic expectations of female chastity while
attempting to avoid the label of promiscuity. This was particularly difficult in a court system that, as Sangster has argued, saw only a fine line
between promiscuity and prostitution in women.[104]

Therefore, common defence strategies included insinuations that all
sexually active women were promiscuous and, therefore, prone to lie
about matters of sex.[105] Lawyers asked women about their sexual relationships with other men or asked if they had previously been pregnant
or 'caught.' When Ida Jeffries claimed she had intercourse with Don
Morgan in 1932, in the woods outside Trenton after going for a drive,
she was questioned by the defence about her sexual history:

Q: When did you first have connection with this young man?
A: The first time he came up to see me.
Q: Do you know Bob Phillips?
A: Yes.
Q: Did you spend a night at his cottage – right about this time?
A: No.

Ida's brother was also cross-examined about his sister's sexual relationships with men. 'I was trying to keep an eye on her,' he told the
court, 'but I couldn't say who she was with or anything like that.'
Similarly, the cross-examination of Lily Graham also focused on her
sexual history, with the defence asking about her sexual history with a
number of men and whether she had 'ever had a child' or been 'caught
this way before.'[106]

This type of interrogation could destroy both the claim of paternity
and the sexual reputation of young women. The sexual history of
fifteen-year-old Millie Pearson was the factor that decided against her
claim of paternity against Andrew Lord. Four of his friends testified in
court that they had participated in a sexual relationship with her, and
Lord claimed that she had been sexually assertive in their relationhip.
Perhaps even more damning to Pearson's case was the young woman's

admission of the frequency with which she met Lord for intercourse, claiming that it often took place while out car riding or in the wash-shed behind the service station where he worked on night duty. It continued until her mother took her to the doctor 'because there were rumours ... that I was in the family way,' though she denied having 'immoral sexual intercourse' with any other men. The judge found the testimony of her sexual activity compelling: 'I do not think the girl has much to her credit from her own standpoint ... in the face of that fact and the face of these boys' evidence, though it is denied by the girl, makes it sufficiently uncertain I could not find him the father of the child.'[107] As this case demonstrates, however, it is impossible to know the 'truth' behind these files. Women were compelled to claim as much sexual innocence as possible under the circumstances, knowing that to admit otherwise would result in a label of promiscuity and, ultimately, lack of economic support. Young men who claimed that their partners were sexually assertive or experienced, or who were able to find other men to testify to a woman's lack of sexual propriety, were likely to win their cases.

Intercourse under the promise to marry, or at least the promise to marry should a pregnancy occur, was one way that women could assert the public face of respectability despite a breach of premarital sexual morality. Ellen Parkins and Andrew Leggett, a truck driver from Belleville, had a son in August 1938. She testified that they 'went together' from July 1937 to March 1939 and that she agreed to intercourse with him when he 'said he would marry me if I got into trouble. He said it all along.' Both Perkins and her father claimed that Leggett had breached his promise of marriage. 'I told him I was going to have a baby and he said he would marry me and he kept it up until the middle of March ... and when I went to see him he said he would not marry me, he would go to jail first.'[108] Thus, delayed marriage, premarital sex, and single motherhood, according to court officials and social scientists, were connected in part to the problem of male unemployment. This understanding, however, coexisted with concern for the moral regulation of women's sexuality and maintenance of the heterosexual family structure.

While women bore ultimate responsibility for the long-term welfare of the child, and were questioned and judged most harshly by the courts, judges also questioned men's character and respectability when assessing paternity cases and support orders. Courts were concerned with men's sexual character and their commitment to the ideals of respectable marriage, and they sought to uphold the values of male duty and economic responsibility at a time when the link between masculinity and work was breaking down. In the Depression this proved particularly difficult, as young men were highly mobile in their search for work, and many found it impossible to pay support because they were unemployed. Orders under the Children of Unmarried Parents Act were difficult to enforce and rarely adequate; judges granted support payments based on the finances of the fathers and not the need of the woman or child. Furthermore, legitimate children and legal wives had first claim to a man's wage, and many fathers simply disappeared after receiving an ongoing support order. Enforcing the duties and obligations of men as breadwinners was an economic and moral imperative. The state blended a concern for maintaining male-headed families with the policy that women and illegitimate children should not be supported by public funds. While courts showed little concern for men's involvement in a child's upbringing, they did emphasize men's economic responsibility. The legislation enforced support payments but held no expectation of custody or access. Though this is not evidence that fathers lacked interest in their children's lives, it is clear that the state, and perhaps also men and women, defined the role of father as primarily an economic one. A father's duty to pay for child support was a central part of the meaning of respectable manhood and fatherhood.[109] Evaluation of proper manhood rested mainly on the degree to which men fulfilled their economic responsibilities, but also occasionally on their sexual conduct. In 1931, after Charles Wilbur, an unemployed labourer from Belleville, denied responsibility for the pregnancy of his girlfriend Emma Pettigrew, a domestic servant, he was cross-examined about the details of his sexual history and whether he had ever 'got any other girl pregnant.' The court then questioned him about the sexual content in a letter he had written to Pettigrew:

Q: 'I see by your letter you ain't so hot; it takes me to cool you down.' What do you mean by that?
A: That was only jokes.
Q: '... and I just wish I could see you in your night'?
A: Yes.
Q: '... it would be just too bad for you as you would sure take it off.'
A: It was only jokes.
Q: 'What with girls and other things I am all hot and if I got the chance to come up there you would not have to have your door

locked and your night because I sure get in an uproar living next to women.' Some more little jokes of yours?

A: Yes.

Q: To a girl with whom you had never been familiar.

A: Yes.

In this case, the judge found the evidence of a sexual relationship compelling and ordered a payment of $40 in expenses and $2 a week in child support.[110]

The sexual history of both parties and the history of the sexual relationship in question were tied to how the court understood and apportioned financial responsibility. In cases where the woman had clearly and willingly consented to a sexual relationship resulting in pregnancy, the court was more interested in 'dividing' blame than in assessing the adequate amount of provision for the child. Both William Holmes' and Maggie Clinton's morality and respectability were questioned by the court. Holmes, who was unemployed and married to another woman with whom he had a child, was questioned about his sexual morality, the number of times he had visited Maggie, and the number of times they had had intercourse. The judge in the case remarked: 'This could not have happened without her consent and she should not have consented to that sort of thing. She knows the chances she is taking as well as the boy and she should bear some responsibility as well as he. The question is how to divide it up.'[111] Similarly, the court attempted to find a way to lay sexual blame in the case of Irma Franklin and Victor Falls of Cookston. Claimed the judge: 'There is a responsibility on the girl as well as on the boy. She looks to be a normal girl; there was no rape, no force; by consent, she must share some the responsibility.'[112] A woman's consent to what was defined as immoral sexual behaviour meant, to the courts, that she should somehow 'pay' for her actions, and in most cases, this punishment took the form of small amounts of support. The Children of Unmarried Parents Act was never intended to alleviate children's or mothers' poverty, because the act was ultimately concerned with questions of blame, culpability, and punishment.[113]

Judges took seriously men's testimony about promises of marriage, using such promises as an indicator of men's moral character and as a means of reminding them of their duties and responsibilities as men. In the case of Clinton Harkness and twenty-year-old Ethel Simmons, for example, the judge encouraged male duty and responsibility by promoting marriage. Harkness told the court, 'I made up my mind I am not the guilty one; I did a few things I am sorry for now and I realize to try and prove myself not guilty would be useless.' Though Harkness was unsure about whether to marry, the Judge encouraged it: 'If you are fond enough of the girl and she will make a good wife and good home ... it will be for the child's sake, much better, and if you think you can be happy together the proper thing is marriage and I hope you will do it.'[114]

The court similarly encouraged Melvin Lewis to marry Laura Shipton, despite his reservations about her loyalty. Unemployment, a lack of money, and the necessity of being free to look for work also played a role in his reluctance to marry and support a child. 'I said, supposing I was working and asked you to marry me; she says, I would marry you ... if I married the young lady when I have doubts I was the father of the child it would not be right.' The court evidently thought his confusion was sincere, noting that he had 'some character' but advising him to 'accept her word' and settle the problem by marriage.[115]

While recognizing that Depression conditions made men's employment unstable and unpredictable, the courts criticized men's inability to find work and attempted to monitor their wages, savings, and job searches. Lloyd McCaffrey was lectured on his lack of moral integrity by the judge and the crown attorney after failing to make support payments between September 1934 and January 1935, by which point he owed close to $300. Though he made $15 a week as a telegrapher, he could not pay, he argued, because of living expenses, his need for new clothes and shoes, life insurance payments, and his desire to help support his parents. The court did not appreciate his financial priorities, as the following exchange between McCaffrey and the judge reveals:

Q: The difficulty is this man from his attitude does not appear to intend to pay anything and appears to have the idea he can get away with it.
A: I hardly think that is fair.
Q: It is fair. You have to pay and if you don't pay you go to jail.
A: I try to pay.
Q: You don't try to pay anything.
A: I need new clothes in the worst way.
Q: You cannot keep up life insurance and then your child you have to take care of it. You fellows run around and have a lot of fun and so goodbye [sic]. That cannot go. You have to take care of your child.

The judge reduced McCaffrey's support payments to $3 a week, but also threatened him with jail, admonishing him that his first economic responsibility was to his child. 'It is to your credit that you have some feeling for your father and mother ... [b]ut you are responsible for this child even more than you are responsible for your father and mother.'[116]

Because support payments were often extracted from men who had sporadic or no employment, family courts were in a position to supervise men, women, and children over an extended period of time. That the state was so deeply reluctant to consider state-subsidized care paid directly to unmarried mothers despite the expenses involved in tracking and monitoring young men over the course of years is testament to the overriding concern to keep support private and based on the values of individual responsibility and male breadwinner duty. To determine Melvin Lewis' support payments, Judge Deroche questioned him extensively on his work history, financial position, and employment prospects. He questioned his work ethic, why he had left a mining job in Kirkland Lake, and what he was currently doing to locate work. When Lewis did not pay any support or show up in court in December 1935, he was sentenced to ten days in jail. By January he had a job offer in northern Ontario, and the judge allowed him to go on the condition that he keep the court informed of his progress and that he return if he became unemployed.[117] Garrett Wilbur also had several chances to make support payments to Edna Stinson. In May 1931 Wilbur admitted owing $129 and not making any payments for three months. 'I have not been able to get a job,' he testified, 'since I lost my job down at the theatre. I tried all summer to get it. I was down at the Air Port trying to get a job.' He admitted marrying another woman shortly after 1931, but he was unable to support her either, and so they each went to live with their parents. 'If the man is telling the truth and has no work and no money I don't suppose we can make him pay,' decided the judge, putting off the case for seven months to give him a chance to find work. However, by June 1932 the court discovered that he had left for Florida and was $275.55 in arrears. Judge Deroche closely interrogated him on his lifestyle and on his and his parents' economic situation:

Q: What have you got to say?
A: I am not able to pay anything because I have not been able to get anything to do. I have been staying with my parents, I don't get any money, I just get my board. I have been trying to get something to do but have not had any luck.'

Q: What are your parents doing?
A: Nothing.
Q: Your father owns the Capitol theatre here and in Trenton?
A: Yes.
Q: You were in Florida.
A: Yes.
Q: You went by car?
A: Yes.
Q: And your expenses were paid down there?
A: Yes; I drove the car, he was not able to drive.
Q: You did nothing all winter but enjoy Florida sunshine, is that
   right? If a committal order was made they might find some way
   of making payments.[118]

The Children of Unmarried Parents Act did little to provide women
and their children with adequate resources and ultimately preserved
the inequities of female economic dependency. When women were not
regularly paid support, and most were not, they were locked in an un-
ending struggle to force the state to enforce private support. They had
few other options. Unmarried women with children were ineligible for
mothers' allowance. Jobs were scarce, and those that existed, mainly in
domestic service, were low paid and presented the additional problem
of securing costly child care. While men indeed would have had a
difficult time making support payments because of low wages or unemployment, and while judges were somewhat sympathetic to men's
economic constraints, women and children faced an even harsher economic reality. Unmarried women and their children had to rely on
charity or the support of family members for basic survival. Court records reveal that men were constantly in support arrears, and women
consistently asked the Children's Aid Society and the courts to trace
men's employment status and earnings. When Doris Secord gave birth
in 1938, she received no payments from the father and wrote to B.W.
Heise, director of the Ontario Children's Aid Society. 'Surely he is doing
some kind of odd jobs in that length of time. I've been informed that he
had signed up with some regiment of the army and I would like you to
investigate as I think I am entitled to some of the money. I am going to
be laid off work my self at Christmas time.' It was only during the war
that she finally received a dependents' allowance for her daughter.[119]
   Even if a man had agreed to provide support payments for an illegitimate child, a legal wife and child had first claim on the man's support,

because legal heterosexual marriage was sacrosanct in law and in social policy. When men were unemployed as well, the illegitimate child was even less likely to receive support. Jailing men in this situation would have been a financial disaster for two families, both of whom would be likely to end up on relief. In 1933 Elvin Sheppard of Trenton, a barber, was ordered to pay $ 2.50 per week in support to Maria Linquist, but a year later he had paid a total of only $10.50. CUPA investigator Captain Ruston testified that because he was married, unemployed, and his wife was pregnant, 'I did not feel we could press him very much for help.' When he appeared in court again in 1934 his defence lawyer claimed that the business was not prosperous and that his two children with his wife were suffering malnourishment because of his unemployment. Reluctantly, Ruston admitted that Sheppard's legal wife and children would suffer if he had to make support payments, since his family was only surviving on the occasional 10 cent hair cut he did in his home, plus medical, fuel, and food relief from the city. Ultimately, the court agreed that he had no way to support his firstborn, but illegitimate, child.[120] In such cases, women had few or no options for support.

Courts continually lowered payments in an attempt to force men to pay some degree of support for their illegitimate children. Barry Clark, a farmer from rural eastern Ontario, already had a wife and six children to support when he fathered a child born to his former housekeeper Olivia Mason. The court continually lowered his payments, but by September 1934 he had paid a total of only $5 and was hundreds of dollars in arrears. His farm was on the verge on bankruptcy, and he had had two more children with his wife. Threats of jail meant little, since this would have left his family on relief.[121] Similarly, the courts continually decreased the amount of support payments to get William Horton, an unemployed baker with a wife and another child, to pay Maggie Clinton of Deseronto. By March 1937 Horton had paid a total of only $9 in support and was in arrears of $224.05. He was also in debt for three months' rent, for coal supplies, and for his wife's doctor. 'Must the law take a man's life away?' Horton asked the judge. 'I work six and seven days a week and jobs are not easy to get … I don't know what I am going to do myself. If business does not pick up I will have to quit. I am getting behind every day.'[122]

Ultimately, the state did little more than attempt to encourage men to live up to their obligations as providers, especially if that duty could be fulfilled by making a one-time payment to the mother. 'Sometimes,' Judge Deroche told Edward Grimby, 'a fellow has some friends that can help him.' [123] The ultimate evidence of the state's concern for men's economic duty was the tendency to encourage men to make a lump sum maintenance payment in lieu of ongoing support. Judges encouraged this type of payment, which illustrates a fundamental difference in their view of male and female parenting. The active role of raising and nurturing a child belonged to the mother, while a lump sum payment gave a man the opportunity to 'start over' or 'wipe the slate clean.'[124] At the hearing of Jake Henderson and Maureen Fitzpatrick, on 27 May 1938, Judge Deroche encouraged Henderson to pay his debt of a $200 lump sum:

JUDGE: I am always advising these boys if their parents can help them
   to get it from your parents and pay it back to them.
HENDERSON: I cannot do that.
JUDGE: You will have to go on and pay and spend part of your life in
   jail ... if you can get off with $250 and pay them back, that is the
   way to do [sic]. The sooner you can get it fixed the sooner you can
   get out.
HENDERSON: All right.[125]

Judges usually advised men to get their fathers to pay the lump sum, or even to borrow it from their friends. Richard Stack was informed that his father should 'exert' himself to pay his son's debt of $265.38 or else find someone to 'put up the money and get rid of it.'[126] Lump sums were cheaper in the long run, the men were told, and also eliminated the potential of future jail sentences. Men's parental obligations were fundamentally economic, problems to be 'fixed' or be 'rid of' by the application of money.

While such payments may indeed have been helpful in covering women's medical debts and expenses, they rarely amounted to more than $300, hardly enough to maintain a woman and child for more than a short time, and certainly nowhere near a lifetime contribution towards raising a child. Men's fathering obligations were reduced to simple economic equations, and in these cases, a man's moral character was judged by his willingness to dispose of his economic obligations as quickly as possible. Women, of course, could not walk away from parenting duties quite so easily. Given that the fathers of men were asked to pay lump sums, and that fathers of young women often received the money for medical expenses, some of these payments look more like civil payment for property damages, rather than an attempt to regulate a paternal imperative among fathers of illegitimate children. Of course, given the difficulties women faced in collecting support payments, a payment of several hundred dollars was probably seen as a more secure alternative than years of waiting for support or constant appeals to the courts.

These case files illustrate the concern that unemployment might cause men to abandon their duties as breadwinners. Therefore, gender boundaries tightened around men's financial obligations to their dependents, even at a time when unemployment made it increasingly difficult for young men to make support payments. Yet, as the chapters on masculinity and employment indicate, men were connected to the home, family, and domestic life through their role as breadwinners. This understanding of men as loving fathers only held true in the context of legitimate marriage and a normative family structure.

Court records, newspapers, and records of social agencies illustrate the varied problems facing families in the Great Depression. These records document how economic crisis created tension between men and women, parents and children, and families and welfare officials. Less visible, of course, are the joyful times. While these records can, and do, capture moments of pride in making do or in feeding a family, less often do they capture moments of joy and fun. In the 1930s the growth and development of mass culture in its various forms coexisted with local or familial-based culture and leisure, and this was especially so at a time when money was tight. It is only after the Second World War that teenagers became 'cultural trendsetters' and that youth culture took on an enormous cultural and economic power.[127] So, for example, while movie attendance dramatically increased during 1930–34, and was obviously a popular pursuit for many, oral histories and memoirs reveal the creative ways in which children and youth found opportunities for pleasure and enjoyment in the midst of deprivation.[128] Dances, bonfires, church meetings, sports events, political meetings – these activities suggest that both grassroots and local culture, along with mass culture, played a role in shaping the lives of youth in this period.[129] Families in this period were also shaped by an ongoing tradition of respect for a mother's domestic work, by children's economic duties to parents, and by a belief in the reciprocal obligations between siblings, parents, and children. Sometimes these obligations and complicated relationships mediated conflict and tension, and sometimes they created them. It is perhaps the history of the 'good moments' that has yet to be written on children and the family in the Great Depression.

4 'A Family's Self-Respect and Morale': Negotiating Respectability and Conflict in Home and Family

All the bridges and viaducts the country is spending millions to build will not put the Government back when it needs it. It's the homes containing grateful citizens who will do that and what surer way to get it than by helping people to help themselves and keep their moral self-respect.[1]

'Home' was, and is, a physical space and material entity, and a symbolic shelter that was rooted in community and family relationships. In the Great Depression, home was also a physical shelter under attack, as rural and urban families struggled to make rent, mortgage, or property tax payments in order to prevent eviction and foreclosure. One's home was a physical emblem of respectability, a material structure that reflected one's status in the community. The home was a physical place where women worked, budgeted, and worried; where families fought and compromised; where husband and wives lived out duties, expectations, and obligations.

This chapter explores the material importance of the home as a physical space, as well as the kinds of conflicts that men and women negotiated in the household during years of high unemployment. Demands made by homeowners for protection from foreclosure in the 1930s reflect the association between homeownership, respectability, and rights of citizenship. Homeowners and renters alike were radicalized by the prospect of eviction, and many Ontario citizens lobbied the government for legislation protecting homeowners or resisted evictions through direct action. But the household was also a space where families negotiated strategies and conflicts for survival. Issues of concern and conflict involved decisions about budgeting, household management, or husbands who refused to look for work or register for relief. Families also faced difficult decisions regarding living arrangements such as doubling up with relatives or other families, splitting up, or placing children in institutional care. Finally, this chapter will examine the interplay between unemployment and domestic violence in the 1930s and the actions taken by the court system to regulate it.

This chapter draws on many examples from family and criminal court case files, which illustrate the complex interactions between men, women, children, and state authorities. Family courts had the power to intervene in personal lives: in cases of desertion, truancy, and juvenile crime in particular, courts acted in conjunction with social workers, the Children's Aid Society, doctors, psychologists, and others outside of the legal system to investigate, reform, and regulate family life.[2] Authorities could compel people to come in for marital advice or could show up unannounced at people's homes. Probation officers administered cases that never formally appeared before a judge. They gave marital advice, drafted behavioural agreements and pledges, and established financial arrangements.

Neither fully public nor fully private, families were built on unequal and complex relationships that could be both complementary and conflictual. Family members could mediate conflicts in a public way, engaging the intervention of court workers or relief officials. At times women and men deliberately asked the court system to intervene in family conflict, though they sought such intervention under conditions not of their own choosing. Women, for example, could approach social workers and probation officers to create a moral alliance against a husband who was spending money on alcohol or who refused to apply for relief. But women did not come to the family courts completely of their own accord, because the relief system was entwined with relief regulations stipulating that married female applicants for relief must first charge husbands with desertion or negligence. Similarly, relief was given to men in their position as household head, and in some situations, women had little control over how money was spent. Underlining the stories of negotiations between husbands, wives, relief authorities, and social workers in the 1930s are the twin themes of moral and economic regulation. The competing imperatives of social policy of this era were maintaining the gendered roles of male breadwinner and female dependent and restraining the costs of state-sponsored welfare.

Homes, Foreclosures, and Evictions

Closely linked with values of respectability and the demand for work was the pronouncement by many citizens that the sanctity of the home was under threat by high rates of unemployment. To both men and women, home ownership was a clear sign of moral worth within the community, giving both economic security and a sense of pride rooted in community respectability.[3] Homes were important not just because they were physical buildings or a place to live, but because they were powerful symbols of one's position in the social order. Homes were the most visible symbol of hard work and thrift – the moral qualities one needed to possess in order to be considered a good citizen.

While most homeowners were middle class, it was not rare for members of the working class to own their own home. For example, 44.4 per cent of working-class residents in Ontario owned their own homes in 1931, while 49 per cent of the middle class and 59.9 per cent of the self-employed were homeowners.[4] While most people on relief did not own property, Harry Cassidy's survey of relief recipients noted that in some areas of Ontario high numbers of relief recipients were homeowners: 22.2 per cent in East York, 20.3 per cent in St Catharines, and 18.3 per cent in Brantford.[5] The results of the National Employment Commission's survey of urban relief recipients also indicate that in some locations homeowners made up a substantial portion of those on relief: 33.4 per cent in Fort William and 16.2 per cent in Brantford.[6] People went to great lengths to purchase a home, often investing all of their savings, and as the Depression continued, they found themselves unable to pay mortgages and property taxes.[7]

Homeowners, particularly men, placed themselves within the circle of respectability by emphasizing such values as thrift and economic responsibility. Former Oshawa mayor John Stacey informed the city council that 90 per cent of people on relief were homeowners. This number was likely inflated for political purposes, given home ownership statistics elsewhere in the province, but it was an attempt to legitimize the demands of those on relief who considered themselves to be respectable citizens.[8] City councils and homeowners' associations worried that men were 'becoming ill in mind and body for want of their regular employment, and the happiness and peace of our home life is almost destroyed through the enforced idleness of the breadwinners.'[9] City councils and homeowners' associations continually asserted respectability, passed many resolutions that linked homeownership to pride and self-respect, and demanded that unemployed homeowners be given opportunities to pay tax arrears and mortgage payments through relief work. A home was where a family could 'live in a sanitary condition' and where a husband could fulfil the manly obligations to his family and 'bring my wife, and children up right.'[10] Women also found ways to appeal to the state as homeowners, since they were an essential part of the family economy, particularly when buying and maintaining a home. One woman told Premier Henry that she and her husband had 'built our place after working hours and holidays I worked like a man on our place to help my husband and saved every cent I could to help get along ... it is no fault of ours that we cannot meet our way.'[11] For married women the home was the centre of domestic production and of her responsibilities as a wife and mother. For many women staving off foreclosure was a crucial job in the Depression years, and women found a variety of ways to save, budget, and earn extra money to ensure the survival of the home.

Homeowners were praised for thriftiness and savings 'at a considerable sacrifice,' for paying taxes and taking 'a pride in the Municipality,' and for their 'praiseworthy efforts [at] maintaining themselves without recourse to relief.'[12] City councils and ratepayers' associations began a concerted campaign to force the government to change policy on mortgages and relief to offer homeowners the chance to stay in their homes. Solutions included allowing homeowners in tax arrears to work off their debts through relief work, thus placing them 'in the same position as a man who is on relief but who does not own his own home.'[13] The Fort William Public Welfare Board recommended changing the city rules, allowing the city to help homeowners on relief to pay their taxes after they were two rather than three years in arrears.[14]

In 1932, in response to the demands made by 'thrifty' and respectable homeowners, the Henry government passed the Mortgagers and Purchasers Relief Act to help prevent or delay foreclosures on mortgages taken out on houses, commercial buildings, or farms before 1932. Though limited in scope, applicants could be granted up to six months in interest and tax relief from a county judge. Foreclosure could only be undertaken on the permission of a judge, and magistrates were expected to help negotiate the concerns of both mortgagers and mortgagees.[15] In addition, one of the few federal initiatives to end unemployment and stimulate the economy was targeted at homeowners. The Home Improvement Plan, implemented in the late 1930s by the King government, was intended to convince 'responsible,' 'stable,' and respectable' working- and middle-class male homeowners to take out low-interest loans to renovate their homes and therefore stimulate the economy.[16]

While unemployment had the most severe impact on the unskilled, semi-skilled, and foreign-born members of the working class, members of the middle class, or those who had saved by investing in property, were not immune from its impact. To both middle-class and working-class citizens, a home was a marker of respectability. To members of the working class, especially, owning one's own home was public evidence of success and of adherence to values of hard work and independence.[17] It seemed blatantly unfair to many homeowners that in the Depression, when it was difficult or impossible to make mortgage or property tax payments, many municipalities classified them as ineligible for relief or public works programs. As John Stacey told Oshawa council, it was unfair to have to suffer utter destitution in order to be eligible for relief.[18]

Demands for aid by homeowners were also explicitly linked to the masculine status of men as breadwinners and taxpayers and as heads of the family. Men who had consistently fulfilled these gendered expectations of providing a home for their family suddenly found the very basis of their security and masculinity threatened. Men claimed they were 'hardworking labouring' men and long-time 'taxpayers.' They were providers, men who were 'bringing up families' or who had 'done our duties in every respect as citizens.'[19] As an Oshawa Daily Times editorial explained, the ineligibility of homeowners for relief 'seems like unfair discrimination against the men who, when times were good, was thrifty [sic] and endeavored to provide a home for his old age by investing his savings.'[20]

Veterans argued that they had made wartime sacrifices to protect their rights to private property and homeownership. Complained one veteran to Premier Henry, homeowning men had brought up families and paid taxes and should therefore receive 'our share in the relief works programmes,' especially those who 'have done our duties in every respect as Citizens, some seeing service in the War 1914–1918.'[21] As one man reminded Henry, 'we thought that when two of our boys went overseas, that they went to protect our home.'[22] The Ontario Provincial Command of the Canadian Legion determined, in 1934, that the ongoing evictions faced by veterans and their families were explicitly linked to sacrifices made in the First World War. Those in mortgage arrears, they argued, 'would be in a position to pay their taxes today had they not been loyal to their country's call.'[23]

As a result, relief regulations and legislation targeted at aiding homeowners enjoyed public support, as this type of relief or welfare was
aimed at the most respectable segment of the population. However, city
councils were not acting completely altruistically when they lobbied for
government money to be spent on mortgage and tax relief for property
owners. As increasing numbers of homeowners began to fall behind on
property taxes, municipal tax bases were depleted even further. Since
municipalities were partially responsible for relief, finding ways to help
people stay in their homes was one way of avoiding further expenses.
For example, the city council in Owen Sound decided to give relief
money to homeowners in the amount necessary to pay taxes, with
additional payments of $27 four times a year.[24]

Perhaps nothing linked those who faced unemployment together
more deeply than the fear of eviction or foreclosure. For while home
ownership was indeed the pinnacle of respectability, having a sense of
pride in one's home extended to tenants as well. Suzanne Morton argues
that workers in Halifax established respectability by establishing domestic privacy and by meeting common standards of good taste, reflected in
consumer purchases and the decoration of the home.[25] Both homeowners
and tenants took great pride in their possessions and the presentation of
their home. The possibility of foreclosure and eviction, and the reposses-
sion of furniture and belongings would, people claimed, destroy the
'family's self-respect and morale.'[26] The Peterborough *Evening Examiner*
bemoaned the loss of employment and the homes of 'regularly employed
factory workers,' whose 'thriftiness displayed in the buying of a bit of
new oilcloth for the door, a little sideboard, a settee and chair or two for
their front room, testify to the fine citizenship of such folks.'[27] Home, for
many, consisted of such material possessions as furniture, toys, and
carefully accumulated personal belongings, which were in danger of
being seized or thrown into the street upon foreclosure or eviction. As
Mrs Over of Port Stanley wrote to Premier Hepburn, 'our furniture has
no intrinsic value, the whole of it would hardly sell for enough to cover
this debt if put up for sale but it means home to us.'[28]

Material possessions and a comfortable home were physical symbols
of pride and respectability. 'Keeping face,' therefore, is a common theme
that appears in the memories of the Depression era. In Mary Quayle
Innis' *The Party*, Ethel, the female protagonist, determinedly throws an
elaborate and expensive party despite the threat of her husband's unemployment, simply to prove that 'Todd had his job the same as ever
and they could afford just as much as they ever had.'[29] One Toronto

resident remembered attending a large party in a private home, though the husband was unemployed and his children often had only tea and toast to eat, relying on the generosity of neighbours for meals. Though 'everybody knew,' the family had to 'put on a face.'[30] Similarly, a man who grew up in a middle-class section of Hamilton remembered his father talking about a neighbour who maintained their 'lovely home' by selling all their furniture piece by piece.[31] Still, this fate was better than that of Steve Metarski, who came to Canada from Eastern Europe and bought a house in Hamilton in the 1920s. By 1931 Metarski had lost his construction business, his house, and his furniture. He and his wife Sally moved into the basement and worked as domestic servants for the family that bought their house and lived upstairs.[32] Sociological studies found it was common for unemployed men and women to be constantly worried about the poor condition of their house and their furnishings. This was especially true for the unemployed middle class and for homeowners, who spent as much as possible on keeping up the appearance of the home in order to hide their deprivation.[33]

The fear of losing one's home was powerful, causing chronic worry, sleepless nights, and feelings of desperation. 'The thought that we might lose our Home if we do not soon make some payments ... this thought is with me day and night [and I] am unable to sleep thinking about it.'[34] Herman Emmons of Cataraqui wrote to Premier Henry: 'I am in great fear and anxiety of how I am going to get money to make my payment.'[35] Some families were evicted often and found themselves constantly moving, sometimes in the middle of winter.[36] Rules and regulations regarding eviction differed by community, but overall, little provision was made for those who were evicted in the early years of the Great Depression. Moreover, while some municipalities did eventually stipulate that evictions should be suspended in the winter or that alternative housing arrangements should be made with relief or welfare authorities, in reality, there were few options for affordable housing. Landlords could not be forced to accept relief recipients as tenants, and many property owners balked at renting homes at reduced rental rates. Families reported, and some bailiffs acknowledged, that alternative housing was often sub-standard, no better than 'rat holes,' with families offered houses filled with insects or with walls covered in newspaper.[37] Families awaited the arrival of sheriffs and bailiffs with trepidation, knowing that their belongings were often removed from their homes and left on the side of the street. In the cold months of February 1935 in northern Ontario, after owing $16 in rent, a family was forced from their home when the owner ordered all the windows and doors removed from the building.[38] In East York alone two to three hundred evictions were pending in the summer of 1936.[39] Eviction meant losing material possessions as well as shelter. One family in Timmins was left with only a table after bailiffs had seized their furniture.[40] Families lived from month to month in hopes of getting temporary work in order to put off another move. 'My wife, with her four-month-old baby, is still under the Doctor's care, and feels that she cannot, just now, face another eviction,' wrote Alfred Chaston, who convinced Premier Henry to find him temporary work on the parliament buildings so that he could buy himself one more month in his apartment.[41]

Eviction could not always be prevented, however, and its impact could be devastating. After her husband left Pierrette Gagnon and their two children to look for work, they were evicted, their furniture was seized, and they were left with no money for food.[42] In his memoir Lloyd Dennis remembers the material and psychological impact of his family's March 1934 eviction as 'an explosion, blowing away the family and its few possessions in every direction.' Eviction cut to the heart of the values cherished by so many working families. Eviction left the family dependent on friends and charity, destroyed the reputation of respectability, and disrupted community belonging. His mother, Dennis remembers, was like 'a whipped dog,' slinking 'up the road with her few belongings clinging to the back of an old truck' – a far cry from the woman who took pride in hosting Women's Institute meetings and quilting bees. His father was shamed that his neighbours would think 'that he was a negligent provider.' The eviction also split up their family, forcing his father and brother to seek road work on the Trans-Canada Highway, while he and his mother sold some of their belongings, gave away their animals, and went to live with friends.[43]

The disruption, anxiety, and anguish caused by eviction proceedings had an impact on all members of a family. Bailiffs moved the persons and belongings of small children, the ill, and the elderly, often leading to both physical and emotional distress. John McCabe of Toronto, who was charged with obstructing a sheriff's officer in 1936 during his tenth eviction, stated, 'It's too much ... nothing to look forward to, month after month. I want to live as I used to – to work and live peacefully.'[44] One of his children had died following a previous eviction. In another case, a grandmother became so upset during her extended family's eviction that she 'became hysterical and collapsed,' while a nine-year-old girl was so terrified when a bailiff entered her home that she temporarily ran away. The Toronto Board of Education was deeply concerned about the impact of continual evictions on school-aged children, reporting that children were 'demoralized' by the continual moving of houses and school districts.[45]

Eviction was not just an urban phenomenon. When farmers were faced with foreclosure, their families faced the potential loss of their home and also of their livelihood. While terrible farm conditions and foreclosures are usually associated with the drought-ridden prairies, farmers in Ontario also faced serious financial hardship in the 1930s. When crop prices were high in 1928 and 1929, many farmers became financially overextended through buying new land at high prices or investing in mechanization and electrification. In the Great Depression, falling prices and protective tariffs in American markets, combined with high taxes and mortgage payments, devastated many Ontario farmers. For example, the Smoot-Hawley tariff (1930) created a 50 per cent duty on cattle and 400 per cent duty on hogs. Prices were also low: beans that sold for $3.04 per bushel in 1929 sold for 48 cents per bushel in 1932.[46]

Letters to the premiers illustrate the fears of farmers and their sense of alienation and frustration. 'A few farmers passed out of this life with a rope around their neck last year in their barns,' wrote C.J. Blacknall to Premier Henry in 1933.[47] 'I do not think they [bank managers] should have the power when a man is doing all he can,' claimed P.D. McCabe to Henry.[48] Banks insisted that livestock be sold at low prices to make mortgage payments, and farmers were forced to sell not only stock, but also their furniture or even their woodpiles.[49] By the end of 1931 the Henry government announced a general policy of halting foreclosures on the approximately $35 million in farm mortgages held by the government. By fall 1932, which saw the lowest levels of farm income in the Depression, the Agricultural Development Board (established to give low-interest loans to farmers) could no longer make interest payments and had to borrow from the Treasury because so many farmers had defaulted on their loans.[50]

The Farmers' Credit Arrangement Act (1934), implemented by Prime Minister Bennett, provided a measure of credit relief to farmers in debt during the Depression by reducing interest and principal payments 'down to the productive level of the farm.'[51] The extant files document the devastating impact of lowered crop prices on farm families. Overwhelmingly, farmers reported that low prices of produce, high

George Henry (Ontario Premier, 1930–34). Ontario weathered the Great
Depression under two premiers: Conservative George Henry and Liberal
Mitchell Hepburn. When Henry became premier in December 1930,
succeeding former premier Howard Ferguson, Ontario families and
workers had already begun experiencing the impact of the depression.
In the 1934 election, Henry retained his seat but lost the election to
Hepburn. (Archives of Ontario, Acc.1750, S.321)

Mitchell Hepburn (Ontario Premier, 1934–42). Running a populist campaign, the Liberal party under 'Mitch' Hepburn defeated the Henry
Tories in the 1934 election with a resounding victory. Hepburn promised
prosperity, freedom of speech and assembly, progressive government
reforms, unemployment insurance, and economic assistance for farmers. (Archives of Ontario, Acc. 1750, S.323)

South Porcupine, Dome Mines, c.1931. Mines that remained open in Northern Ontario, such as this one near Timmins, held out the prospect of employment for men throughout Ontario. The phenomenon of transient male workers, however, deepened concerns of social disorder among residents, and also contributed to charges of non-support by women left without access to relief. (Archives of Ontario, RG 1/E.13, Book 1, 93)

Unemployment threatens the storks

'Unemployment Threatens the Storks,' by Ivan Glassco. As marriage and birth rates dropped throughout the depression, concerns grew over low rates of reproduction, the sexual values of youth, and the stability of the social order. Social scientists were worried, for example, that high unemployment and delayed marriages would result in increased premarital sex. (*Hamilton Spectator*, 7 October 1936)

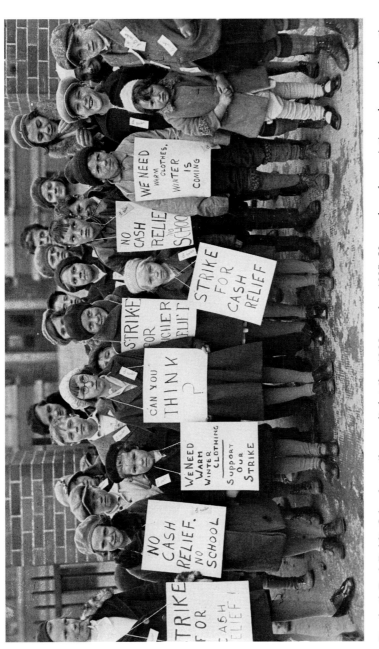

Danforth Park Public School, pupils on relief strike, 12 November 1935. Unemployed associations drew on the activism of women, men, and children. School strikes, involving the children of unemployed workers, drew publicity and framed demands in the language of familial duty, care, and responsibility. Children's signs emphasized the basic needs of unemployed families, such as adequate relief, cash, and warm clothing in winter. (City of Toronto Archives, Fonds 1266, Item 38454)

Local unemployed associations employed a variety of techniques to protest low relief rates. 'Possession' of a relief office or town hall, a kind of sit-in, drew publicity in local newspapers and offered a way to make their demands public. As the next two images show, such events were political and also deeply social, bringing together local families and community members. In the picture above, taken on 13 March 1935, the male and female members of the New Toronto Unemployed Association occupied the relief office, enjoying music, food, drinks, and cigarettes, while a photographer documented the protest. (City of Toronto Archives, Fonds 1266, Item 36139.)

Taken on 13 March 1935, at the same time as the previous photo-
graph, the New Toronto Unemployed Association clearly embraced
a role for children in activism. The presence of children in parades,
school strikes, picket lines, or the occupation of relief offices emphasized the interdependence of working families and that such
activism was undertaken in the name of family needs and concerns. (City of Toronto Archives, Fonds 1266, Item 36147.)

Taken on 15 March 1935, two days after the occupation of the relief office, the
New Toronto Unemployed Association used another popular protest tactic:
hanging the Minister of Public Welfare David Croll in effigy. Hanging well-
known political figures, relief officers, or town councilors in effigy was part of
a wider range of tactics, including picketing the homes of politicians or holding them 'hostage' until demands were met. Such activities were employed
to shame those public officials whom citizens held in contempt. (City of
Toronto Archives, Fonds 1266, Item 36144)

mortgage and interest rates, and low land values had resulted in near bankruptcy, forcing them to sell large amounts of livestock or to allow their buildings to fall into disrepair.[52] For Leo Reise of Saltfleet financial difficulties on his farm were exacerbated by winter unemployment, because for over seventeen years he had counted on casual paid labour to supplement his farm revenue.[53] Joseph Fair of Ancaster, for example, owed $3,500 on his mortgage and $1,465 in interest, $440 in back taxes, and more than $1,000 in other bank loans. In 1935 he made a profit of $385, out of which he paid taxes and interest, and also supported himself and three of his nine adult children.[54]

The case of the Simpson family of Cornwall serves to illustrate the depth of desperation felt by farming families. Calvin Simpson and his son Ron went to extreme measures to prevent eviction from their family farm. Both father and son, at one point or another, blamed each other or implicated themselves for setting a fire that destroyed the farm's barn. Court records reveal that in March 1939 Calvin was served with a notice of foreclosure on his farm. After trying and failing to borrow money from his sisters to pay for mortgage and machinery debts, the barn burned down. Inspector Desjardins of the Fire Marshall's Department testified in court that he overheard Calvin saying he would take the blame for setting the fire to protect his son. Ultimately, his son pled guilty to arson and was sentenced to two years less a day in the Ontario Reformatory. He stated that he committed arson because his father had no money to pay for the mortgage. 'I thought I was doing my father a favour,' he said. 'I thought there was a big insurance in it and he was going to get the money.'[55] The record remains unclear as to the 'real' story.

W.G. Nixon, the Liberal member of provincial parliament from Temiskaming, argued that farmers deserved some sympathy for their financial situation. 'I cannot see where any good purpose is to be served by putting a lot of fellows off their farms, and the Government taking over the property,' he told Premier Hepburn. He recommended a halt to all foreclosures, claiming that it made the government look bad because 'the sympathies of the rank and file are with the under dog.'[56] Nixon was particularly angered at the practice of foreclosing on farms in the winter months, noting that foreclosure often added to relief expenditures. In addition, he claimed: 'We must at the same time give particular thought to old pioneers who have, in many cases, made their farms out of bush lands and who, for this reason, find it very difficult to understand why the Government should not be willing to carry them further in order to give them another chance to redeem their homes.'[57] Hepburn's response did little to address Nixon's concerns. 'I am rather surprised at the contents of your letter,' he wrote to Nixon. 'You must realize it is a difficult job to liquidate some fifty Million [sic] Dollars of farm mortgages.'[58]

Often the only course of action for families facing eviction or foreclosure was to utilize the help of various political organizations, neighbours, and community members. The South York Liberal Young People's Association told Hepburn they were ready to defend an invalid mother with seven children from eviction due to tax arrears. 'If the worst come to the worst the members of our Association are prepared to picket the house and prevent the Bailiff from entering.'[59]

The devastation caused by evictions prompted many to inform politicians that losing homes, like losing jobs, was radicalizing the citizenry and turning people against the government. 'I cannot believe that either you or Mr Bennett know of the suffering and exploitation the unemployed are enduring at the hands of their more fortunate fellow citizens,' wrote a woman whose home had a second mortgage and was on the verge of being seized for tax arrears. 'Do you wonder in the face of suffering that people become radicals?'[60] Indeed, evictions did radicalize some communities, which, through local unemployed organizations, attempted to organize against and prevent evictions.

Eviction protests followed a variety of forms and encompassed a range of tactics. Mass meetings were called to develop practical plans to combat evictions and to lobby local politicians. Crowds of supporters and sympathizers, in some cases numbering up to four hundred people, gathered at or near the home of the person or family about to be evicted. During a York Township relief strike in 1936, for example, 150 people paraded to an eviction in progress, where they successfully blocked its completion.[61] Crowds and pickets prevented the authorities from entering; some crowds stayed the course of a day and an evening. Crowds 'protected' the home of the family of William Keefe, a retired veteran, for four weeks.[62] Once at the residence, supporters often occupied a house in advance of the bailiff's arrival, and through tactics of 'passive resistance,' such as sitting on the floor or on the furniture, they could delay the eviction proceedings.[63] Crowds also physically intervened in some eviction proceedings by grabbing furniture from the sheriff's hands and placing it back in the home.[64] The East York Workers' Association was well known for preventing and protesting evictions. At an August 1932 mass meeting, for example, member F.J. Lawton told the crowd that the EYWA would take matters into their own hands to prevent evictions: 'I wouldn't want to be a bailiff right now ... if he values his skin he wants to keep out of East York.'[65] Immediately on hearing that an eviction was taking place, an EYWA member with a truck was contacted, and members drove up and down the streets yelling 'Eviction!' Other members carried furniture back inside the home. A Hamilton unemployed organization also had a variety of methods for preventing evictions. Members physically threatened bailiffs, returned furniture in the back door as fast as it was carried out the front, and, remembers one activist, once drugged the coffee of a sheriff.[66]

In both Hamilton and East York the rights associated with 'Britishness' were used to protest evictions. At an eviction in 1932 in East York a group of two hundred veterans and their wives draped a Union Jack over the door and blocked it while the women sang the national anthem. In Hamilton, activist Peter Hunter remembered a popular tactic to protest an eviction. The family piled up their furniture and placed a copy of the popular poster of a British bulldog standing over a Union Jack on top. Below, a caption read: 'What We Have, We'll Hold.' The pile was 'guarded' by a group of unemployed First World War veterans.[67] And, like the relief protests and strikes considered in Chapter 5, symbolic actions evoking a 'charivari' were used to shame public officials and condemn unfair housing and relief policy. The Alderwood Workers' Association, for example, surrounded the home of Fred Braithwaite in Etobicoke, hanging the landlord and bailiff in effigy and placing a makeshift cardboard casket in front of the house containing a large doll – to symbolize death and starvation.[68]

In the face of large crowds, and active or passive resistance, sheriffs might temporarily give up, though they would usually return later with police assistance. Sometimes the presence of the police was enough to end a protest, but in other cases, physical assault and retaliation could occur. Men and women in crowds threw bricks or other objects at bailiffs, armed themselves with clubs, knives, or other weapons, and made verbal threats. The eviction of Mrs Janet Patterson, a widow with two sons living in East Toronto, exemplifies the anger and the resistance of the unemployed, as well as the uneven response of authorities. When Sheriff's Officer William Jeffreys arrived with several policemen to evict the family, they were greeted by a large crowd of protesters who attempted to prevent them from entering the home. Inspector Greenwood later testified that they used 'feet and fists and everything they could' to prevent the eviction; Jeffreys was eventually stabbed in

the leg and punched in the jaw. Twelve men, along with Mrs Patterson,
were charged with aggravated assault and obstructing a police officer,
though ultimately, eleven of the men were convicted only on the charge
of obstruction. The Pattersons were ultimately removed from their home,
placed in another home, and put on relief. While it was clear that some
court officials interpreted these protests as indicators of communist up-
rising or, as Assistant Crown Attorney W.O. Gibson claimed, a 'revolution,' a *Globe and Mail* editorial was slightly more circumspect, noting
that 'public opinion' was generally on the side of the 'unfortunate' and
that those on relief were usually not responsible for their situation and
should not be treated 'as members of the criminal class.'[69]

The *Toronto Star* interviewed several families in York Township who
were on the verge of eviction. Their stories illustrate how so many of
the unemployed were living on the edge of survival, skimping on food
and clothes so that they could pay the rent. The Gritsman family, with
three children, lived in a two-room house; unemployed for two years,
the husband, a truck driver, received a mere $5 a week in relief. George
McDowell, a machinist unemployed for two years, was eleven months
in rent arrears, received $4 a week in relief and milk tickets, and had
two sons under medical observation for malnutrition; their dinner the
previous night, he stated, had consisted of two strips of bacon, a piece
of bread, and a cup of tea. In the Knight household, a family of six received $3 a week in relief money; they split a loaf of bread for dinner.
Mrs Knight sewed baby clothes out of her husband's underwear. Albert
Crist, ineligible for relief because of the strict residency requirements,
averaged $4 a week doing odd jobs; Crist claimed his daughter was
suffering from malnutrition and that he had sold the family car, radio,
and living and dining room furniture to make ends meet, leaving only
a few chairs, a table, a bed, and a stove.[70]

Municipal authorities did attempt to find alternative housing for
those who were evicted, though shortages in affordable housing made
this difficult. Most protests did not permanently end an eviction pro-
ceeding. While sheriffs were instructed by Attorney General A. Roebuck
to show sympathy and 'humanity' by consulting relief authorities be-
forehand, he noted that creditors' claims could be 'dodged but not denied.'[71] Ultimately, the law put the rights of property owners and banks
before shelter for families. What protests did do was increase the visi-
bility of the suffering caused by evictions, create some public pressure
to ensure minimal housing and aid for those on relief, and win a temporary reprieve for those who were being evicted, so at least they did
not become permanently homeless.

The Household: Negotiation and Conflict

The location of one's home, and its physical condition, inspired pride and respectability while providing shelter and security. The home, idealized in prescriptive literature as the realm of the private female world and a safe haven for men from the harsh reality of the workplace, was actually, for most married men and women, a meeting place between male and female worlds. It was in the home that men and women came into conflict and attempted to negotiate appropriate gender roles, duties, and expectations. Here, men and women attempted to live out the expectations associated with what it meant to be a mother, father, husband, or wife. Yet neither men nor women were completely passive in the face of gendered expectations. Family court records and prosecution case files indicate that far from harmonious acceptance of such strongly ingrained stereotypes of the breadwinning father and domestic mother, men and women acted in conflict with these roles even as they ultimately accepted them as gender and familial ideals. Men and women often used the family court system, social workers, and judges to help mediate cases of conflict, and for women, especially, to help temper the power of individual men within families.

Budgeting and Managing

It was common practice in working-class families for men to turn over their wages to their wives for administration while keeping a small discretionary sum for themselves. Women were the family budgeters, and they were expected to act in the consumer interest of the family. Therefore, an honourable man trusted his wife to properly run the home while women depended on the male wage for the survival of the family.[72] In some cases this system worked smoothly. Many people remember handing their income as youths over to their mothers, who were understood to be the 'financial managers' of the home, and they also remembered their fathers doing the same. [73] Nancy Forestall's work on the mining community of Timmins shows that most men willingly turned over their wages to their wives, though at times, the women had to intercept them before they were spent elsewhere, namely, on alcohol.[74]

Conflict could erupt when one or both of the partners failed in fulfilling these gendered expectations. Women's ability to run a household was severely compromised by the Great Depression, and arguments over proper household budgeting were common. In response to women's complaints that they were not earning or turning over enough money to them, husbands criticized their wives' skills as homemakers or claimed that they spent money on frivolous items. Both men and women attacked each other's ability to fulfil the proper duties of home-maker or breadwinner, often blaming each other for their poor eco-nomic situation. This conflict is echoed in the work of E. Wright Bakke, whose survey of the psychological and sociological impact of un-employment on American families found that women tended to criti-cize men's inability to find work as laziness, while men 'retaliated' by condemning women's household management skills.[75] Men blamed their family's financial problems on their wives, whom they labelled as 'bad managers' or 'poor housekeepers' or 'extravagant spenders and poor shoppers.'[76] Such discourses of blame were apparent in the case of Lila and Sherman Voss. The Vosses came to the family court for advice on a separation agreement because of ongoing conflict involving his unemployment and her household management. She complained that she was forced to work to support the family, while he accused her 'of trying to live far beyond her means and of trying to keep up financially with a sister of hers who is comfortably off.' Mrs Voss denied this, claiming 'she had to work to keep the home or they would starve.' Voss told the probation officer that he had suffered a great deal of unemploy-ment in the past year and that he was a good husband because he did not drink or smoke, and he turned over his money to his wife when he could.[77] Similarly, Bonny Steinberg claimed that her husband Martin, a salesman, had stopped supporting her and their child since their separation a year earlier. Mr Steinberg blamed their separation on his wife's elaborate material expectations. He told the probation officer that his 'wife wanted two rooms furnished elaborate,' yet he was 'only employed temporary at Brown Bread.' Mrs Steinberg was unhappy with the quality of relief goods her husband had arranged for her and, noted the probation officer, 'refused bread and milk tickets.' The proba-tion officer advised the husband to arrange for further relief, convinced Mrs Steinberg to accept it, and encouraged Mr Steinberg to keep trying to find a job.[78] 'She spends too much money' or her 'spending extrava-gances' were common male complaints in response to women's frustra-tions at lack of income, employment, and relief.[79]

Conflicts erupted over how to spend limited wages or relief money and over who was allowed to make financial decisions. The wife of Isaac Bitmann clearly placed the health of her child and herself before her husband. When he complained that his wife quarrelled with him and would not give him food, she claimed that they only received

enough from the relief department to feed herself and her child.[80] The
solutions of family court officials varied, but they generally had faith
that adherence to traditional gender roles would reduce or eliminate
conflict within families. To them, the roots of conflict were ultimately
interpersonal, not economic. In the fall of 1938 Claire McNamara reported to Probation Officer John Young that her husband Michael, an
electric appliance and junk salesman, refused to support the family
properly by not giving her enough money to run the home. Young visited the home and recommended the couple not discuss money matters, that Mr McNamara give his wife a monthly allowance and leave
the household management to her and that the wife not 'criticize any of
her husband's business deals.' When Mr McNamara found a permanent job in Toronto the family moved there to be with him.[81]

Surveys of youth in the post–Second World War era suggest that children were shaped by ongoing marital conflict over money. Youth interviewed by the Canadian Youth Commission, for example, remembered
'anxiety' and 'friction' in their families and 'squabbles which were mostly
over money matters.' Fully 25 per cent said they had suffered the effects
of limited finances, particularly overcrowding, poor housing, and having to leave school earlier than they had wished.[82] Recommendations by
the CYC for greater government intervention in the economy and public
ownership of some industries reflected this concern over the impact of
unemployment on family life. This generation of young adults solidly
supported the idea of government-created full employment and the
establishment of living wages and social insurance on 'a basis of right
rather than of charity.'[83] These views were clearly shaped not just by the
the Second World War, but by watching parents, family members, and
friends struggle with unemployment in the Depression years.

The Effects of Alcohol

In many cases, marital conflicts ensued when couples argued over
issues of alcohol consumption. Temperance campaigns and social reformers often used drinking as a 'code word' for domestic violence and
a way to indirectly critique male power and women's economic dependence within marriage. In the nineteenth century drinking was
labelled a particularly male vice.[84] But, as both Linda Gordon and Ellen
Ross have pointed out, alcohol consumption had real material consequences for women and families. Budgets that were already strained
were made tighter by men's expenditures on alcohol. Drinking used up

money that could have gone for food or rent, or it could exacerbate problems of domestic violence, increase poverty, and lead to neglect of families.[85] Late-nineteenth-century budget studies have shown that some working-class men spent enough money per week on alcohol to feed a family of five for two to three days.[86] Denyse Baillargeon found that in Depression-era Montreal 20 per cent of wives felt their family had been affected by their husband's drinking. Whether women and children were forced to receive charity, or whether the money spent on alcohol could have been spent on food or rent, alcohol consumption often had a negative impact on a family's standard of living.[87]

Women attempted to force their husbands to meet the obligations expected of a provider, such as turning over wages promptly and responsibly. Yet, because women had little or no formal economic power, turning to the family court was the only way for some women to force unwilling men to turn over their wages or relief payments. Judges and probation officers met with couples, attempted to negotiate the boundaries of proper behaviour, and if all else failed, could charge a man with failure to adequately provide for his family. For many families in the 1930s approaching the courts was a necessity, because careless spending of money on alcohol kept them in financial distress. Court records reveal that women could not stretch budgets to pay rent or buy food and clothing when wages or relief payments were used to buy liquor. In November 1934, for example, Mrs McCallum reported to Judge Balharrie that her husband earned $18 a week in a drug store but they were in debt because he drank, leaving them on the verge of eviction.[88] The money spent by Luc Brasseur on alcohol placed his family in rent arrears, while Bertha Eves contacted the family court because her husband, an unemployed salesman, was drinking so much that she and her two children were forced onto relief.[89] When men collected relief money in cash, the money could end up being spent completely on alcohol.[90]

Drinking was particularly dangerous to family survival, especially that of women and children, if it led to the loss of employment. In such cases wives and children often had to find paid labour, though Annette Charbonne's work as a private music teacher – like the underpaid work of most women – could not make up for the income her husband lost when he was fired from his job for drinking.[91] In 1935 Jemima Cowan complained that her husband, a First World War veteran who ran an ice cream and candy store, spent his money on alcohol, leaving her to fear that he would lose his business. She asked the court to convince him to abstain, give his business to her, or sell it, and split the profit in half.[92] Mrs Agatha Garrisi complained that her unemployed husband Steve drank and abused her. The situation had deteriorated to the point where the children had to support the household. It was Mrs Garrisi's twenty-two-year-old daughter Grace who reported to the caseworker that her mother spent most of her time in bed, forcing Grace and her brother to earn the family's income and leaving her younger sisters to do most of the housework. Their father drank constantly and only rarely worked.[93]

Court records do not always reveal the many reasons why men drank or did not turn relief money or wages over to their wives. For some the problem may well have been alcoholism. For others a 'rough' working-class culture, exacerbated by poverty, may have contributed to the problem.[94] For many men, however, the high rates of unemployment, the shame of being unable to provide, or the humiliation of their wives' wages were identified as problems by caseworkers, by women, and by men themselves. The Depression shattered many men's ability to provide, and for some, alcohol was a way to cope and reduce the stress of unemployment. Men often explained their drinking in reference to tension caused by unemployment, and court officials and doctors also understood excessive drinking in these terms.

When Effie and Stuart MacPherson came in to see Probation Officer Miss MacDonald together at the York family court, he claimed that his wife '[drove] him to drink' by nagging him about his unemployment. He told the probation officer that 'since he has been unemployed his wife has been working and he says that ever since she started to work he had not "heard the end of it" and as soon as she gets home from work there is trouble.' The arguments over his drinking and her earnings – she took in laundry for $1.25 a day – continued until a separation was agreed upon.[95] In March 1934 Chantal Lafleur reported to Probation Officer Alexander Renton that her husband drank, was unemployed, and was not properly supporting her and her two children. Dr Gundry from the Brockville Mental Hospital wrote to Judge McKinley that Lafleur was an unemployed baker, who 'complains that he had had a great deal of hard luck and has got very discouraged. During periods of discouragement he says that he drinks to forget his troubles. He is apparently an individual whose personality is so unstable that he is unable to stand up against the troubles of life without recourse to liquor.'[96]

In November 1936 Ellen MacIntyre approached the family court office to complain that her husband John, a salesman, lost his job in October and had been drinking heavily in response. The next month

Mrs MacIntyre wrote to Judge McKinley, asking him to give some advice to her husband, whom she claimed was a good father and man when sober. She asked about how to get him a job at the Public Works Department, as they were in rent arrears and on the verge of eviction. 'But if something does not turn up in the line of work for him I don't know just what will happen,' she wrote. 'He is very anxious to secure work and his nerves are bad, as he is discouraged and getting very restless not having work to do ... John would not like me writing and explaining all details, as he keeps all this to himself.'[97]

Court officials and others were often sympathetic when men's drinking was linked to unemployment. Drinking was understood as a social problem connected with environmental factors rather than simply a moral failure. In October 1931 Laura Garrow complained for the second time since 1929 that her husband was failing to provide because of his drinking. A letter of November 1931 to Judge McKinley from their minister, Reverend Williams of the United Church, sympathized with their financial problems: 'I can well imagine that a long period with employment bringing in a minimum of money, and being less than his ability to accomplish, plus a physical condition, having to do with digestive matters, might well bring about a state of apparent chronic irritation ... drives him out to seek his false comfort in Hull.' In April 1932 the Garrows found a job looking after apartments for a wage plus free rent, but a year later the apartments were sold, and they had to move and go on relief. By May 1933 Mr Garrow was drinking again, but once he began work in October he stopped.[98]

Work-related stress and alcohol were also hurting the marriage of Wilma and Roger Howse, who ran a restaurant in Ottawa. She called the police in June 1938 because he was drinking, shouting, swearing, and breaking furniture in the home. During a home investigation, the family court worker discovered severe financial problems and linked these to Mr Howse's drinking. Their coffeeshop business had a large overhead of eight employees and $100 in rent per month, they both worked long hours, and, according to the probation officer, 'this had undermined their health. Both are a bundle of nerves.'[99]

The courts had a number of methods for dealing with alcohol-related conflicts. Upon a report from the Relief Board or a family member, the family court initiated a home visit or asked the couple to attend a meeting at the family court office. The husband was then asked to promise to abstain from alcohol or to sign a temperance pledge. If the drinking continued, courts could fine or put a man in jail, either for causing a public disturbance or for failing to support his family properly or to look for work. Relief cheques could also be administered through the court instead of being given directly to men, thus guaranteeing that women would have access to relief money before it was spent on alcohol. While there are many records of relief funds being administered by third parties, there are none where the relief cheque was given directly to the wife. Even in cases where a husband would not or could not work, his wife was considered a dependent. By the 1930s the court system had assumed the previously informal role played by women themselves in controlling male drinking. Where women once confronted men in bars or chided them in public, women were now turning to courts to ask judges and probation officers to intervene and regulate men's behaviour. Though not always successful, such options gave women a degree of control over their husband's economic power, though only by accepting the ongoing surveillance of the courts.[100]

Separations, Relief, and Refusing to Look for Work

Most families depended on the wages of a male breadwinner for survival. Without a male wage, women found it extremely difficult to make do, even with their own paid work or informal waged labour. As a result, when men withheld wages, refused to look for employment, or refused to work for relief, they could be charged with neglect under legislation designed to enforce men's duties as breadwinners. Under provincial legislation such as the Deserted Wives' and Children's Maintenance Act or Criminal Code legislation on non-support women found some tools to enforce male support. By asking the courts to intervene when men refused to look for work or to get relief, women forced the courts to take seriously the economic impact of dependence on the male breadwinner on themselves, their children, and the survival of the household. The courts and the relief system were not separate entities, but worked in tandem to regulate gender and familial obligations as well as access to economic resources.

Relief policies were built on assumptions of male breadwinning and female dependence, and obligations predicated on gender, age, and marital status were encoded into its terms of provision. These varied sets of obligations created categories of 'dependents' and 'providers,' where relief was distributed on the basis of the heteronormative family ideal. The assumptions of specific familial duties reveal the complexities of family life, as well as the contradictions within a relief system that was intended to regulate access to economic support while also upholding a 'proper' family life. Husbands were generally expected to perform some kind of labour in return for relief, and when a couple was separated, or a man had previously deserted, women found themselves relegated to the role of dependent through their status as legally married wives. Viola Mulroney, for example, was forced to prosecute her husband for non-support after six years of separation when she was laid off from her work as a government charwoman.[101]

Many local relief boards insisted that a husband work for his wife's relief even if they were no longer living together. If necessary, she was expected to charge him with non-support on the basis of her status as a married woman. For women, charges of desertion acted as a means test, proof they had done everything possible to keep economic support within the confines of the private family. Resistance from the husband, who no longer saw himself as the family breadwinner, or difficulties in tracing him, could then lead to a delay in relief provisions for women and their children. Antonia Hanik of Toronto faced serious problems getting relief after she separated from her husband, from whom she received no support. The House of Industry refused to give her supplies unless he went to get them or unless the family court office wrote them a statement saying they were officially separated. After a meeting with the probation officer, Mr Hanik agreed to work at the House of Industry so his children could get some relief supplies.[102]

If women refused to agree to these rules, they were often denied relief. Patricia McMurtry, a domestic servant separated from her abusive husband, was informed by the Relief Office in Toronto that she could not get relief until she tried to force her husband to support her. Since she refused to reconcile with him or even meet with him, she was denied relief.[103] Relief boards only accepted the word of family court officials that women were separated or unable to force their husbands to support them, rather than the claims of the women themselves. Expert testimony was thus rendered a necessity in order to qualify as deserving of aid. In July 1937 Karen Jarenchuk, a mother of three, faced intransigent relief authorities in Toronto, who insisted that her husband Paul had not truly deserted her, but was secretly earning money and sending it to her. Only after a probation officer tracked down the husband, and found that he was not making enough to support his family and pay his own room and board did Mrs Jarenchuk get access to relief.[104] Clearly, responsibility for a woman's support lay first with the husband. As Judge Balharrie told Gaston Letourneau, the state was no

longer responsible for his wife once he had a job. Despite their separation, 'your wife has been taken off relief, and the responsibility for her
maintenance is yours.'[105] The state's main concerns were economic efficiency in order to privatize the costs of family support and maintaining female dependence on the breadwinner rather than the state.

Another conflict in marriages arose when husbands refused to look
for work or to work for their relief according to municipal regulations
and rules. In cases such as these the courts intervened to hold men to
their family obligations. Men were placed by the state and the court
system in a double bind. Humiliation and shame were intentionally
built into the relief system to act as a disincentive, but the courts forced
reluctant men to apply for relief, claiming it was their duty as a husband and father to do so. Husbands and wives argued over whether or
not to apply for relief; in October 1931 Michael Legrand argued with his
wife over the necessity of applying for relief, and left the home, forcing
her to approach the family court for help in locating him.[106] It was in
cases like this that family courts could intervene to add external pressure to the men. When Nina Rosario complained to the court that her
husband, an unemployed labourer, refused to apply for relief, the probation officer made Mr Rosario promise to apply immediately, telling
his wife that if he did not, she was to inform the court right away.[107] In
March 1936 Michael Plouffe refused to go to the Relief Office in Westboro
to get his relief for his wife Lila, though he went the following week. In
October 1937 the probation officer wrote Plouffe a letter, stating: 'I had
a phone call from your wife today, and she told me that you had refused to appear before the Council to make application for relief. If you
will come into my office, before Thursday, I would like to discuss this
matter with you.'[108] Wrote one woman to the Ottawa family court in
frustration: 'At present the children and myself are on relief and he's
not on but I have to keep him on what little I get, and he got his rent
voucher around the tenth and he hasn't went out to work it yet, and I
don't suppose he will …I would really like to know if you could have a
talk to him and see what's to him and see what's to be done as there is
no future as far as I can see, and we haven't even got enough off [sic]
anything to keep going much longer.'[109]

Women clearly grew frustrated with unemployed husbands, but ex-
pressions of this frustration or attempts to force men to find work could
often lead to male violence. Mrs Hood had her husband charged with
wife assault, in March 1934, after he beat her when she tried to wake
him up in the morning. 'I have a terrible time to get him up but he does

not try to get work.[110] When men were unemployed, even the most supportive of wives eventually questioned their husbands' desire to find work or their honesty in being unable to find employment.[111] Gilbert Lapointe's wife claimed that her son 'had no suitable clothing for school,' and, wrote the probation officer, 'bitterly denounces the father for the condition of extreme poverty in the home.' [112]

Historians can interpret this refusal to work in multiple ways. First, such actions can be understood as a form of domestic violence, a way for men to maintain a degree of power and control over economically dependent women within a patriarchal family structure.[113] There are numerous examples of men using relief funds without consulting their wives, to disastrous effect. Conflicts also erupted over how to spend limited wages or relief money and over who was allowed to make financial decisions. In August 1938 Ingrid Kassel complained that her husband had been unemployed for several years, leaving them on relief. Yet he had recently purchased a truck without her knowledge, prompting the relief department to cut off their aid. They separated, and the office gave Mrs Kassel a letter to help her get relief from the welfare department. Four months later, his second-hand clothing store and truck were both seized by bailiffs.[114]

In many cases, non-support reflected the shame and humiliation that some men felt when they failed to live up to dominant norms of masculinity. This is not surprising, since humiliation was intentionally built into relief regulations, and since those on relief were often publicly humiliated. The shame felt by unemployed and poor men, or by men asked to apply for relief, was intimately connected to humiliation and the loss of pride. As Elspeth Probyn argues, shame is linked to 'interest,' or in other words, the desire for recognition and acceptance from one's peers and the larger community.[115] For some women doing the physical and emotional labour necessary to protect their husband's sense of pride for as long as possible was just another duty as wife and mother. Lloyd Dennis recalled his unemployed father telling the town clerk, 'I don't need any bloody hand-outs from the government. I want work, not charity.' It was his mother who eventually convinced him that he would have to change his mind. Several months later, his father had to 'swallow his pride' and wait outside while his wife shopped with food vouchers in the local store.[116] For Birdie White the winter of 1933–34 in rural Ontario brought the family close to applying for relief. Her memories of her parents discussing the necessity of relief are muffled, anxious, and painful. 'And always,' she writes in her memoirs, 'the conversation would come round to that dreaded word, "Relief," and Dad's voice would be raised in a defiant No!' Her father, ashamed even that his mother received an old age pension, refused to accept relief even though his wife argued that they needed food rations for the family. To him, it was a 'disgrace' and not to be openly discussed.[117] These examples indicate that for many men acceptance of relief was a public admittance and public exposure of failure: failure to live up to the role of breadwinner, failure to live up to the expectations of manhood, and the failure of economic dependency. This shame was felt so deeply by men because the sense of exposure engendered by relief reflected a fear of being 'found out' as a failure by others. In addition, when such shame was connected not to a specific action of wrongdoing but to a failure to measure up to deeply held ideals and expectations, and when it was connected to material deprivation, it was not only intimate others who witnessed failure. Rather, failure was reflected back in ongoing ways through the judgmental eyes of relief inspectors, welfare officials, or family court judges. Such a terrible exposure provoked, in many, a desire for hiding or cover, and that might include a rejection of the breadwinner role, a role that Benson argues men in the 1930s were 'blocked from fulfilling.'[118] Walter Shipman, for example, insisted that he was not refusing to support his wife and family, but that the Depression had left his job situation hopeless: 'I haven't had very much heart at all to make a living but I have done all I can.'[119] Regardless of the reason for men's failure to provide, however, women were left to find ways to make up for the lack of money, either by insisting on a visit to the Relief Office, finding employment, or as a last resort, approaching the family courts for help. Inevitably, it was women who bore the most drastic material consequences of such actions.

Family Survival Strategies: Doubling Up, Splitting Up, and Placing Children in Care

One strategy used by working-class families when the economy worsened was to double up households, create intergenerational households, or live with relatives, which allowed families to save money or to stay together. This was generally a temporary measure rather than the creation of a long-lasting household structure and was done in response to economic crisis.[120] The extended family was both a source of conflict and of mutual support. At times, such strategies seemed to work well, allowing single mothers, for example, to draw on the free labour of older relatives while they worked to supplement mothers' allowance or relief. Irma Ambrosino, who worked as a hosiery mender in Ingersoll and received mothers' allowance, lived with her mother, her two children, and two boarders after her husband deserted her. Her mother looked after her children, while she paid for her board.[121] Similarly, Glenda Burton lived with her three sons and her mother in downtown Toronto. She worked as a domestic at the University Club, while her mother did the cooking and housework for the household.[122] Beth Adams, a widow, had sold her farm to her eldest son in 1929, but due to low crop prices he was only able to pay her $20. She moved in with her son and daughter-in-law in town, while her son on the farm supplied them with fuel and potatoes. The mothers' allowance investigator noted that the families 'appear to get along nicely together.'[123]

Overcrowded households could, however, create or exacerbate conflicts between family members. For some couples, domestic conflicts arose from the interference of in-laws who voiced opinions regarding the unemployment of their son-in-law or their daughter-in-law's budgeting skills. Edwin Maroney had been arrested twice previously for drunkenness when his mother complained that, in December 1934, he was drinking and staying out late. He lost his job as a government stenographer in 1931 and moved, with his wife, to live with his parents. This, Judge McKinley stated, 'had caused trouble as his Mother and wife do not get along.'[124] For Ella Morton, a twenty-five-year-old woman from York County, trouble in her marriage to David, a truck driver, began when they and their two children moved in with her in-laws in 1934. She felt that they would get along 'much better' if he would provide her with their own home. In a meeting with Probation Officer Miss Mayhew, David admitted his wife's insistence on a home of their own was 'reasonable.' He promised to find them a house within the next three months, but noted that he could not get one immediately because of his low wages and his need to help his unemployed brother.[125] In May 1934 Ada Maliszewski approached the court to complain that living with her mother-in-law was making her life 'unpleasant,' because her husband collected relief and gave it to his mother to manage rather than to her. The probation officer noted she had no 'cause for complaint,' since he was unemployed and could not afford to provide her with their own home, and that she 'won't listen to reason.' After she charged her husband with assault in December 1934, they separated, and she refused to reconcile until he provided their own home.[126]

Another strategy that some families used to save money was to separate temporarily. This type of separation could involve informally placing children with relatives while one or both parents worked. Alternatively, a couple might decide to split up and return to live, either by themselves or with their children, in the home of their parents. This strategy often allowed men to leave their families while they travelled to look for work. Flora Ballard lived with her husband in Toronto until he was laid off, after which she moved with their two children to live with her mother; the wife of Victor Maclean lived with her mother while he worked as a farm labourer and at odd jobs.[127] The Allen family of Fort William provides a good example of the complex ways that families negotiated living apart. In 1933 the parents moved outside the city to live on a land settlement farm, taking the younger children with them, while the older children (usually six at any one time) stayed in the city to work and to finish high school. Hilda Allen (O'Brien), one of the older sisters who remained in the city, remembered the financial difficulties precipitating the separation as difficult on her parents, especially her father. 'Dad was a proud, stubborn Scotchman who was used to doing well and then suddenly there wasn't anything to do well with ... one neighbour described my Dad as a very disappointed man.'[128] Her younger sister Ruth Allen (Aho) was only six when the family moved to the farm. She remembered 'times being tough' and her older siblings, who stayed in the city, generously helping to support the entire family.[129] The combination of siblings earning wages in the city while finishing their education, and parents in the country providing food, allowed the family to creatively negotiate the Depression economy.

In some cases, however, these kinds of family arrangements could result in social welfare investigations and accusations of neglect. In Ottawa James McDonald was charged by the Children's Aid Society with neglecting and abandoning his three children. After his wife's death in 1930, his sister and his eldest daughter helped to keep house and look after the two younger children, but in 1933, and again in 1936, they were removed from his care against his wishes. A.G. Monroe of the CAS told the judge that 'Mr M. thinks we are trying to steal his children, so I went to get some further facts.' In the courtroom, several of his landladies reported that the children were dirty and loud, that they had no shoes for school, and that they often ran out of food. One sympathetic landlady testified that he was 'doing his best,' that he had no furniture, and they all took turns sleeping on a stretcher. When the judge discovered that the eldest daughter was not home helping, the judge called her to the stand to ask why. Sixteen-year-old Marge replied: 'I was discouraged at seeing the messy house all the time ... I am willing to stay if there was some furniture ... I am willing to do anything.' In return for her presence in the home, the judge promised to try to get the family some furniture.[130]

In some cases, children were placed in institutional care. Child protection agencies, both Children's Aid Societies and private agencies, reported increases in the number of children who were under supervision or had been removed from homes in the 1930s. Both Cassidy's survey on unemployment in Ontario, and *Child and Family Welfare*, the organ of the Canadian Council on Child and Family Welfare, noted that children were increasingly being placed in institutional care, and they blamed this increase on unemployment and financial stress.[131] For example, in 1931 the Toronto Children's Aid Society reported an 84 per cent increase in the number of children placed in institutional care over the years 1928–31.[132]

While in some cases child protection agencies would have acted against the wishes of the parents in removing children from their homes, men and women sometimes requested that the family courts arrange to temporarily remove their children, as a strategy to cope financially. Clara Conklin, in a letter to Judge Balharrie, complained of her husband who drank, assaulted her, and refused to work for relief rent. 'I've lived this life for five years in the hope he might turn out to be a man ... would the children be better off out for adoption where they can at least get the needs in life or place them in a home or institution and try and make a home for children and self and leave him out ... perhaps you can help us.'[133] Georgette Ruskin asked Probation Officer Deborah Cluff to help her place her baby in a boardinghouse while she found a domestic service job. Though her husband was abusive, drank, and refused to find employment, Cluff advised the woman to give her husband a second chance.[134] In 1940 Jean Savard was charged by the Children's Aid Society with failure to provide for his five children, whom he had placed in an orphanage in 1937 while his wife was ill in the Brockville Mental Hospital. He paid little money for their upkeep, since his only income was a monthly $14 pension from United States Army, though he often sent clothing.[135]

Occasionally, the family courts did facilitate the placing of children in institutional care on behalf of parents who could not afford to raise them, indicating that this was sometimes accepted by the courts as a suitable strategy. Wilma and Victor Clark, for example, lost their furniture because of rent arrears, and they were unable to get relief in Ottawa because they were from Hull. The court planned to return them to Hull, get them help from a priest, and place some of the younger children in an institution.[136] Glenda Burton, a mothers' allowance recipient, was deserted by her husband and supported herself and her three children on the allowance and occasional work as a domestic servant. When she became ill in 1931, however, she temporarily placed her seven-year-old son in the Essex County Shelter.[137]

Separating, placing children in institutional care or to live with relatives, or doubling up households or extended families were all temporary ways to manage poverty or unemployment. These strategies are difficult to document, given that many were done on a fluid or informal basis and would not have been captured by census takers, family courts, or social welfare agencies. It was the situations that precipitated some form of family conflict or charge of neglect, not those that ran relatively smoothly, that brought the attention of the court system.

Domestic Violence

Conflicts over money, budgeting, and alcohol, combined with the stresses of living in poverty, the disruption of unemployment, and the humiliation of being on relief, sometimes escalated from verbal conflict to physical violence. Historians of domestic violence have pointed out that violence occurred within the context of a set of understandings about gender roles. In particular, Nancy Tomes has argued that men and women both recognized the 'prerogatives' of male breadwinner status and that violence occurred when women were perceived to have failed to uphold their wifely duties. Similarly, arguments over money, budgeting, and alcohol also played a role in men's explanations for violence.[138] Family court records confirm that during the interwar era, domestic violence was treated as a social problem rather than a crime and that courts were focused on the regulation of male breadwinner families through ongoing counselling and probation. Court officials performed a regulatory function, attempting to end or control violence by convincing men to control their behaviour or to act as responsible providers. Men were commonly asked to promise, for example, to keep their 'hands off' their wives, while in the case of Garth Douglas, the court and his wife Myrna agreed to drop assault charges if Mr Douglas promised to not do it again and if he went north to find work.[139]

In many cases of domestic violence that appeared before the family court, unemployment was understood to be a key factor in abuse.[140] Judges, doctors, and court workers, along with women and men, linked the stress of high unemployment and its impact on masculinity and male authority to the persistence of violent male behaviour. By the 1930s unemployment had become an explanatory element with which courts adjudicated incidents of violence. In some cases, as well, a threat of criminal charges was used by wives and by the courts as a way to force men to look for work or to work for relief. In the case of Harold and Elsie Sparrow, Mrs Sparrow testified that her husband punched her, beat her with a shoe, and a few days later, kicked her onto the verandah and locked her out. She claimed that this had occurred 'quite a few times,' saying, 'You cant say anything to him, you cant get him out of bed in the morning, he was bad enough when he was working, now he is out of work he is ten times worse ... I never know when the man will strike me [sic].'[141] In February 1939 Marie Corrin claimed that her husband Norman stayed in bed 'and will not go and look for work,' which led to an argument and to him slapping her face.[142]

Probation officers, judges, and court officials linked unemployment to male violence. Victoria Ficco told the family court that her husband Henry had spent all the relief money on alcohol, causing a quarrel and then an assault. Probation Officer Miss Macdonald noted: 'Man says that he has not had steady work for sometime [sic]. He says that he worked for the Massey Harris Co. for 18 years but now he cannot get work and he gets discouraged and when his wife does not cooperate he gets into a temper and admits that he is sometimes unreasonable.'[143] Dr Cleland of the Brockville Mental Hospital blamed psychological problems resulting from unemployment for the domestic violence of Randolph Holmes, an unemployed welder who in the spring of 1932 had been charged with assault, negligence to provide, and drunkenness. While he was unemployed, his wife Darla supported the family of six by taking in laundry, which was supplemented by relief. After an examination, Dr Cleland wrote that Holmes was 'introversive, tending to daydream, and, at present, is worrying much about being out of work. This feeling of inadequacy leads him, at times, to take temporary refuge in alcohol, and when in this state he is evidently not accountable for his actions ... we believe that he will probably get along fairly well as soon as he gets work.'[144]

Feminists have long debated the impact of poverty on the existence of violence against women. While a radical feminist analysis locates the explanation for violence in male power and privilege, both anti-racist and socialist feminists have argued for a more complex analysis of the relationship among power, gender, violence, class, and race. In particular, socialist feminists have argued that while domestic violence is clearly enacted in a culture that privileges masculine power and control, for poor, unemployed and working-class men, violence may be 'the only form of power they can assert over others.'[145] Given the paucity of statistics, the burying of domestic violence cases in a variety of court proceedings, underreporting, and overrepresentation of the poor in family court files, it is impossible to know the extent of domestic violence in the interwar era, let alone how it might have been related to male unemployment. Historical studies, however, indicate that domestic violence is closely connected to the stress and frustrations engendered by poverty and unemployment. As Linda Gordon has argued, violence was not rooted solely in male power, but in familial conflicts and 'power struggles in which individuals are contesting real resources and benefits.' The impact of unemployment on a masculine identity rooted in power over women and children, and independence and self-sufficiency, was a contributing factor to family tensions in general and violence in particular.[146]

Related familial conflicts revolved around the gendered roles that men and women expected each other to play. Unwomanly actions, such as spending too much time with a male boarder or going out to work, could also be used by men as an explanation for violence; such actions display the fear evoked by women asserting even small degrees of economic or sexual independence.[147] In January 1930, for example, Mrs Sanders reported that her husband Gerald had assaulted her that morning because she wanted 'to go to work ... and [he] did not want her to go.'[148] The type of work that married women did in the home – such as keeping boarders – could also lead to anger and jealously. In the case of Mr and Mrs Malkie arguments and jealousy over her means of keeping the family afloat during her husband's unemployment led to wife assault. Jenna Malkie complained that her husband beat her after she had gone to the room of a male boarder; her husband demanded the man leave the home, leaving them without any income. In December 1937 their eleven-year-old daughter Irena wrote a letter to Miss Mayhew claiming that her mother could not find a job and that her father was working and spending his money on Polish newspapers when they needed clothes and schoolbooks. 'I am writing this because my mother can't write or talk very good English.'[149]

Joanna Noakowski consistently asked the York family court to discipline her husband for violence, who was charged and jailed for ten days for assaulting her in 1935. She and her interpreter, a neighbour, returned several times to complain of further abuse. Despite the warnings from the relief officials and the family court, Mrs Noakowski moved her three children into a home with another man. When called into the office, according to the probation officer, she 'defied me at every turn. Said she would live where she liked and with whom she liked ... [s]he wept and stormed and said that she would leave the children here for us to look after.'[150] Clearly, lack of facility in English and poor economic circumstances did not make Mrs Noakowski a passive victim in her dealings with the courts.

In some cases, though rare, violence turned into murder. In Dresden, in 1937, William Tubman was charged with beating to death his wife Eve. They had one eight-year-old son as well as a boarder living with them. The Crown's address to the jury explained the murder by stating that their marriage had been in trouble as a result of unemployment, financial difficulties, and Mr Tubman's jealousy over a male boarder. The crime was committed, the attorney intimated, because the deceased was covered by a $720 insurance clause.[151] In Owen Sound twenty-three-year-old Melville Wilkie admitted to killing his wife Gertrude and their six-month-old daughter Norma in a house fire that he set while they slept. 'His sole reason for setting the death-dealing blaze,' reported the Daily Times on his court-room statement, 'was to obtain $1,100 insurance that he hoped would put his business in a stronger position and stave off threatening creditors.'[152]

Though the extent of domestic violence is difficult to ascertain, court records indicate that it was a serious problem in the 1930s. While male violence was condemned by the courts, and men were occasionally fined or sent to jail for short periods, the permanency of the marriage bond was emphasized, and judges encouraged couples to stay together even in the case of repeated abuse. Women had few options within the context of this family model. Annalee Golz has found that the majority of men convicted of wife assault up until the 1920s were given a suspended sentence and a pledge to keep the peace.[153] In court records of the 1930s this trend is also clear. In family court records most cases of domestic violence were addressed or discovered in the context of other family concerns, such as relief problems or alcohol, so incidents of violence were often addressed in an unofficial and non-criminal way. In their response, courts maintained some continuity with the nineteenth century, when the legal system attempted to keep couples together by forcing men to pledge to 'keep the peace.' This response fits with the overall aim of the courts and the relief system in this era to treat violence, desertion, and non-support with social rather than criminal sanctions. This trend was solidified in the 1930s, as unemployment and its effects on masculinity were increasingly understood to be contributing factors in family conflict and men's violence.

These tales support the work of historians who have recognized that women were not simply passive, defeated victims in the face of male violence. When they had the opportunity to do so, women sought court-related interventions to end abuse. Though it is difficult to assess whether women's main motivation in seeking intervention was rooted in a belief in their right not to be beaten, it is clear that women attempted to find ways to end violence in the home while ensuring that they and their children would be adequately supported.[154] The ways that violence, poverty, and women's legislated economic dependency were deeply intertwined with the courts and the relief system is compellingly illustrated in the case of an unnamed woman from northern Ontario who, the local newspaper reported, faced a 'perplexing' problem. She was separated from an abusive husband who was willing to take her back, and as a result, she was ineligible for relief. The men on the town council were divided on the issue. Mayor J.P. Bartleman reflected the prevailing view that men were responsible for supporting women, and women were responsible for staying married, even to abusive men. He remarked: 'There are lots of women who won't live with their husbands. Are we going to keep all of them?' Ultimately, the relief system was not structured to deal with problems such as family violence, which was seen as a problem in the way of efficient administration of male unemployment. By defining male patterns of employment and unemployment as the norm at the centre of relief, structural gender inequalities remained outside the concern of relief provision.[155]

Understanding the role of family relationships and the family economy in the 1930s is encapsulated by understanding the multiple meanings of the word *home*. Home could symbolize security, respectability, and cooperation – or conflict, violence, and poverty. Men and women fought, in a variety of ways, to keep houses they owned or prevent eviction from those they rented. Foreclosures affected working-class, middle-class, and rural families and farmers; evictions touched the lives of many more. In a time when a home was symbolic of respectability, its loss not only created numerous material problems and instability, but also signified a decline of status.

A respectable home was much more than a physical structure. Gendered duties and responsibilities, which made up the elements of family survival, were negotiated between husbands and wives within domestic space. Many families were able to negotiate budgeting, wages, and relief money, and handle the stress of unemployment with some success, and their stories did not appear in court records or rarely in the records of social welfare agencies. However, even in memoirs and in sociological studies of the period, quarrels, frustration, anger, and worry appear as common elements of family life during the Great Depression.[156] For conflicts involving abuse, alcohol, or non-support, many cases ended up in the court system, and women played an important role in seeking the intervention of state authorities. The results of such intervention were not always beneficial. Courts and relief systems understood financial obligations as resting solely on the male breadwinner, and for this model of family life to work, families were expected to stay together – even in abusive circumstances. Both relief and court authorities upheld the ideal, male-headed family, one centred on a private familial network of economic obligations. The ideal, respectable family that underpinned the ideology of relief provision was one where its members lived together, did not argue, supported each other without question, and functioned within a series of well-understood and accepted obligations. But this idealized family form ignored the complex reality of familial conflict and ultimately provided an opportunity for a casework approach to family problems within the relief system. The state's desire to maintain efficiency and lower the costs of relief administration could converge, but also conflict, with its desire to maintain and support a model family norm. The concern for preserving model family units and for controlling costs of public relief shaped the various conflicts in Ontario's families, as well as the kind of help that both men and women could expect to receive.

5 Militant Mothers and Loving Fathers: Gender, Family, and Ethnicity in Protest

On 9 October 1933 Mr Thomas Frith of Pembroke, Ontario, wrote his fourth of six letters to Ontario Premier George Henry. Unemployed and supporting a family, he unsuccessfully petitioned Henry for a job:'I am getting fed up with everything. It looks strange to me that men that never did anything for the government can be holding down permanent jobs and the likes of me face poverty ... I would just like too [sic] know how you would like it yourself if you fought 3½ years for your government ... do you think you would be getting a fair deal if they didn't give you a little work to keep your wife and family?'[1] Thomas Frith was only one of thousands of unemployed Ontario citizens who wrote to the premiers of Ontario in the years of the Great Depression. For many this was the only way they actively criticized or protested against high unemployment and government policy. Union organizing was difficult in times of unemployment and labour surplus, and the Depression had a disastrous effect on the power of unions to organize on behalf of workers.[2] However, focusing solely on the history of industrial strikes is to miss the complexity of political action that emerged in the Depression years. This chapter looks at how protest took a variety of forms, ranging from collective political action to individual letters of complaint to politicians. These forms of protest were, in turn, shaped by gender, class, and ethnicity. Critiques of unemployment policy and demands for jobs, a living wage, unemployment insurance, and dignified treatment of the unemployed dominated the Communist Party, the Workers' Unity League, local unemployed organizations, and the Co-operative Commonwealth Federation. In addition to the socialist critique of unemployment and capitalism, veterans' groups or individuals writing to newspapers and to politicians criticized federal and provincial initiatives on employment and relief policy. Suggestions ranged from reforming the capitalist economy through state-sponsored social welfare to proposals for a radical restructuring of the social and political order.[3] The gendered politics of breadwinner ideology and domesticity framed the rhetoric and action of unemployed organizations and relief worker unions, veterans' organizations, and individual citizens during the Depression years.

The collective action initiated by unemployed organizations in the 1930s was a dynamic form of political activism rooted in communities across the province. Through the Workers' Unity League and the National Unemployed Workers Association, the Communist Party had some success in organizing workers in previously unorganized industries, relief camps, and among the unemployed.[4] A number of associations in Ontario municipalities became known as radical and effective protestors; unemployed groups protested relief cuts, demanded adequate and nutritious relief food, and compensation for gasoline, water, and hydro bills. Activists in these groups, as historian John Manley notes, encouraged the unemployed to view the concessions that they won as 'rights.' Though the movement depended for its survival on the participation of the foreign-born, it was 'fluid,' representing a variety of ethnic groups and political ideologies.[5] The political responses of those experiencing unemployment cannot easily be divided into dichotomous categories of radical or conservative. For example, local unemployed associations combined members of the CP, CCF, Liberal, and Conservative parties, as well as those with no formal political affiliation.[6] The makeup of individual associations differed by region, and it is not always possible to discern the political ideologies of the organization or trace the ideological position of the rank-and-file members. Such groups were not strictly regulated, and they incorporated a variety of ideological responses to meet immediate local needs and demands.[7] Though dismissed by one prominent historian as unions 'comprised of members who want to get out,' as Bryan Palmer has pointed out, they attempted to maintain the dignity of their members in the midst of unemployment and uncertainty.[8] An analysis of the tactics of local and collective action illustrates the engagement of the unemployed with the development of state welfare policy and provincial and federal politics.

Similarly, the Legion's work on behalf of veterans, while sometimes narrow in scope, voiced concerns over social welfare and, in the early 1930s, explicitly joined the interests of unemployed veterans with those of workers and the unemployed in general. Concerned with inadequate pension and disability payments in the 1920s, a powerful ex-servicemen's lobby developed with the growth of the Royal Canadian Legion. Through its national and provincial organizations, the Dominion and Ontario Command, the Legion criticized unemployment policy and argued that employment was a fundamental entitlement that veterans had earned through patriotic loyalty to the state. Both unemployed unions and veterans' organizations demonstrate that Ontario citizens drew on methods, rhetoric, and action from across the political spectrum to demand action on welfare and economic reform.

Most people, however, did not belong to a relief workers' union, a veterans' group, or even a political party. For this reason the thousands of letters written by ordinary Ontario citizens, who were trying to cope with inadequate relief, unemployment, or low wages, to the Depression-era premiers of Ontario, George Henry (1930–34) and Mitchell Hepburn (1934–45), are a valuable source of information on the struggles faced by Ontario families, as well as the way in which men and women made claims on the state.[9] These letters contain criticisms of government policy, complaints against those on relief, solutions to the economic crisis, or requests from unemployed, working-class men and women, usually of British background, for jobs or financial aid. The only Canadian study looking at similar sources is *The Wretched of Canada*, a collection of letters written to Prime Minister R.B. Bennett. The editors, Michael Bliss and L.M. Grayson, argue in their introduction that such letters were written by the poorest of the population, people whose lives were 'a single-minded struggle for survival' and who had 'too much individualism … too little political sophistication to fight back in a radical protest against a whole economic and social system.'[10] While some letters to politicians were indeed desperate pleas for help, many were clearly articulated demands for economic justice based on notions of entitlement. Letters written by breadwinners, wives and mothers, veterans, and Anglo-Canadians used the idea of a reciprocal relationship between citizen and state, and the language of respectability, service, and duty, to claim entitlement to jobs and financial aid.

Relationships of gender, class, and ethnicity shaped local, collective, and individual protest. Men and women argued for economic security and protection of home and family through state-sponsored support of the breadwinner role and a family wage, while wives and mothers argued that unemployment and inadequate relief compromised their job to raise and protect a family. Thus, class-based concerns for economic survival were entwined with ideology surrounding the gendered roles of breadwinner, wife, or mother. Furthermore, for families of Anglo-Celtic descent, which comprised the vast majority of Ontario residents in the 1930s, *Britishness* became a signifier of respectable citizenship and therefore a powerful basis from which to claim the right to employment.[11] The language of rights and entitlement, while more inclusive than that of charity, was most strongly associated with the notion of contractual reciprocity. Though this helped to expand social welfare provision and government responsibility, it did not ultimately challenge the contract-based ideology of citizenship that based the reward of social provision on individual service and duty to the state.[12] Moreover, in a society where full participation in state and society was predicated on employment and the value of economic independence, the highest form of citizenship was gendered masculine, since entitlement to jobs was firmly entrenched as a masculine right.

Fighting Unemployment: Fathers and Breadwinners

The tension between the themes of charity and entitlement was central to the actions and rhetoric of men's protest, and it shaped men's concerns as fathers, breadwinners, and husbands. Unemployed men were expected to fight against unemployment and to protest the conditions of relief. Though dependency was associated with shame, this was tempered by a sense of entitlement to economic and family security. Many men made forceful claims on the state in a manner that traditional notions of the shame-filled and quiescent 'reliefee' simply cannot explain. Emotions such as shame or humiliation can work in diverse ways. While the shame associated with dependence and feminization could lead to desertion of families or rejection of the breadwinner role, this emotion could also be turned towards protest and complaint. Deborah Gould argues that such emotions can lead to 'quiescence' in the face of injustice and domination, or they can 'animate political activism.'[13] Shame was a powerful motivator for social change when it was experienced by a collective group of unemployed men who felt the injustice of unemployment and who saw work as an entitlement.[14]

Material concerns over wages, working hours, and working conditions were central to male protest, but men also were concerned with such 'domestic' issues as adequate and nutritious food and proper clothing for their children. The masculine role of breadwinner and the consequent right to a living wage conferred respectable status on men and their families. The ideology of the family wage was rooted in working-class men's desire to retain dominance in the family and the job market, but it was also a rational decision by working families to improve standards of living within the home and to regulate labour.[15] The family wage ideal encompassed demands for economic security, adequate wages, and a dignified standard of living. Men's primary identities as workers and providers were destabilized by the economic crisis, and Depression-era protests attempted to reinforce the association between masculinity and work. Thus, men's most vocal and powerful demands involved agitation for increased government intervention in the economy. This demand for work rather than charity was not simply an economic argument, however, because men's demands were still rooted in the rhetoric of fatherhood and family duty.[16]

Men were workers, but they took pride in their role as good husbands and loving fathers, and their sense of family respectability played an integral part in the language of their protests and demands.[17] Breadwinning status, the family wage, masculine identity, respectability, and pride framed demands for employment and underlined demands for dignified and adequate relief provision as part of the rights of citizenship.[18] To be a man was to have the right to demand good wages and a secure job that would lend dignity to family life.

Unemployment robbed men of their ability to provide for their family and made it difficult for wives to manage a household. As a result both men and women protested the disintegration of breadwinning status. The 'private' sphere of the family and the 'public' sphere of paid employment were not oppositional categories.[19] The role of provider and wage earner existed in conjunction with the domestic setting of the home, and the categories of breadwinning and domesticity were both central to the meaning of fatherhood.[20] For working-class men, however, this concern for family life did not revolve around seeking 'expert' advice on companionate marriage and child psychology. Rather, unemployed men upheld the importance of the family wage and of women's maternal roles to the survival of the family unit. In turn, these domestic concerns could motivate collective protest against local relief authorities.[21]

The method and quality of relief distribution was a prime target of local protest. Though the federal government funded 'emergency' relief, each municipality was responsible for administering its own policy. By 1932 large public works projects were replaced by direct relief, and most Ontario cities expected men to submit to work tests in return for relief vouchers, goods, or cash. Because these tests were designed to 'prove their genuine willingness to labour' – and were not a form of public works – men were not remunerated at standard wage rates.[22] In addition, while Ontario set uniform maximum food allowances and relief rates in 1932, municipal variations still existed because local governments had no obligation to provide a minimum standard of aid. Municipalities dispensed relief in kind, cash, or vouchers, and some local governments told recipients that relief was a loan that had to be repaid.[23] When relief vouchers had to be redeemed at specific stores, housewives had limited consumer choice and budget control. Most recipients therefore wanted relief in cash, paid directly to the unemployed. Problems arose when municipal governments forced men to work for relief and refused to pay for their labour at the same rate as workers not on relief.

As labour records on municipal relief worker protests indicate, relief workers were moved to protests, petitions, and strikes not just by poor working conditions and inadequate relief, but also by anger over such 'domestic' concerns as food, clothing, bedding, nutrition, and health. Of some seventy-seven relief strikes and protests recorded in the Department of Labour Strikes and Lockouts files, for example, almost half (49 per cent) involved issues of adequate food, clothing, or housing, alongside disputes over wages and methods of relief distribution.[24] Of these, fourteen strikes were motivated *primarily* by domestic concerns. That so many relief strikes and protests involved concerns related to the domestic sphere underlines the close association between the home and work in the rhetoric and actions of the unemployed.

Concern over the adequacy and quantity of food was a crucial area of concern for unemployed men. When relief was distributed in vouchers or in kind, unemployed men questioned the difficulty their wives faced shopping, budgeting, and cooking with limited food supplies or poor quality goods. Eight strikes revolved solely around the cost, quality, and choice of food. In Kitchener, for example, a relief strike erupted over bread tickets when one hundred men in the local Unemployed Workers Association protested against the city's policy of making bread tickets redeemable only at specific stores. The men returned to work once the relief board guaranteed they could redeem their tickets 'wherever they chose.'[25] A staple of working-class and poor families, bread was again at the centre of a strike in Oshawa in 1933, after the city council attempted to give Dominion grocery stores, rather than a variety of local bakeries, sole responsibility for supplying relief bread. The general quality and quantity of relief food was central to many other strikes, as were the 'exorbitant' prices commanded by stores accepting relief vouchers. In Toronto 250 men protested against the new civic relief store at city hall, demanding it provide more nutritious food. Their wives, they claimed, found the food to be of poor quality and taste[26]

Men motivated to protest by lack of food for their families could be a threat to the social order, but they could also elicit a degree of sympathy from the mainstream press. In York Township several hundred men gathered in front of council chambers, claiming that 'unless food was provided, there would be nothing left but to loot grocery stores.' With some sympathy, though couched in patronizing terms, the *Globe and Mail* noted that 'the spectacle of hundreds of men asking only for food for themselves and their weak dependents when their last dollar of savings has been spent is one that a civilized community cannot witness unmoved.'[27] Struggles over cooking and budgeting were made public problems through protests, strikes, and parades. That food played such a central role in unemployed protest is not surprising. Food was not important simply for its fundamental nutritional value, but because the quality and quantity of food signified health and status. Its purchase and preparation tied the domestic labour of women to the waged work of men, and low-quality relief provisions were a visible and painful reminder of inadequacy.[28]

While food was of immediate concern to poor families, inadequate relief compromised family survival in other ways. Relief authorities did not budget for such 'extras' as adequate clothing, shoes, mattresses, cooking utensils, or children's schoolbooks. Luxuries not covered by direct relief in Ontario ranged from animal feed, tobacco, wallpaper, and curtains to toothpaste, shaving cream, razors, and ammunition.[29] Fifty Mimico relief workers struck for stoves, bedding, kitchen utensils, and free schoolbooks for their children, while inadequate clothing allowances for families led to strikes in Port Arthur and in Sturgeon Falls.[30] In Kitchener striking relief workers had the support of the local fire chief when they protested the situation of Paul Ferret. Denied a cooking stove by the relief board, Ferret had been badly burned while attempting to cook in his furnace.[31] Relief workers in Longbranch went on strike three separate times in 1934 when the council refused to turn on the water for families who could not pay water bills and when at least six families on relief were discovered sleeping on the floor without mattresses or blankets.[32] Again and again those on relief attempted to expand the definition of what was a necessity and what was a luxury. Items defined as luxuries by city or town councils were often outright necessities (ammunition in northern or rural areas, for example), while others were needed for maintaining a small measure of personal dignity.

The rights and responsibilities attached to breadwinner status and fatherhood were made explicit in the Fathers' Association, which, along with the Mothers' Association, seems to have been organized in Toronto in the early 1930s and was politically active in the city of Oshawa. The local press gave these organizations a fair degree of coverage in 1932, especially when Fathers' Association leader F.W. Watkinson was condemned as 'preaching a lot of red stuff.'[33] The organization itself was divided ideologically, which became clear when a public debate developed between Watkinson and members of the association, who insisted they were not communist and believed in revolution only through 'constitutional means.' Precipitating the debate was a speaker from Toronto who, the local paper reported, 'advocated action ... by methods akin to those adopted in revolutions of past history.'[34] What makes the Fathers' Association so interesting was that it was politicized about family as well as class issues. It publicly criticized the impact of poor relief standards on the family and the lack of control that housewives had over food because of relief store restrictions. The group was based, noted the local paper, 'on the ideas of protection of the family in times of economic stress.'[35]

Relief workers' actions challenged the popular stereotype of the shame-filled and humiliated man emasculated by unemployment. Unemployed unions developed a wide range of provocative tactics and forms of direct action such as sit-ins at public buildings or 'collective violence' such as holding mayors, councillors, and relief officials 'hostage' until municipal officials met certain demands.[36] In most cases crowds of men participated in this collective violence, though it was not uncommon for women to be involved as well. In Cooksville, in June 1933, over one hundred striking relief workers protested in front of municipal hall while a delegation met inside with the council. When the reeve addressed the crowd and announced that council would not agree to their demands, the crowd responded with calls of 'Tar and feather him!' and 'We'll steal before we starve!' The crowd then rushed and struck the reeve, ripped out fence rails, 'pounded at windows' of the town hall, and let air out of a councillor's car tires. Members of the strike executive, Albert Crooks and Fred Bailey, tried to control and disperse the crowd before stepping in to protect the reeve.[37]

Occasionally, spontaneous protest erupted when even the most humiliating provisions of relief were restricted or denied. In Tillbury the town council decided to cut relief vouchers to men and their dependents until more funding was received from the provincial government. When at least thirty men showed up to receive their cheques, and relief chairman Clark Foster failed to appear, an 'impromptu mass meeting' was staged in the town hall and a councillor was 'verbally attacked.'[38] Similarly, in Pembroke in March 1936 the mayor and town council members were held in the town hall for several hours by twenty-five unemployed men until relief cuts were restored, and a week later, windows in municipal offices were smashed in a protest.[39]

Protests involving physical violence were organized in reaction to both domestic and wage-related concerns such as cuts in food and clothing allowances. These ranged from staging sit-ins in town halls to holding relief officers and local politicians hostage in municipal offices until certain demands were met.[40] The 'violence' of these actions was largely symbolic and evocative of charivari tactics, suggesting that the underlying motivation was an attempt to publicly shame or humiliate public officials.[41] Protesters picketed the homes and public offices of aldermen, city councillors, and relief officials, and public figures were mocked or burned in effigy. In 1936 in Guelph, when Mayor Mahoney refused to reconsider cuts in relief allowances, approximately six hundred relief workers occupied city hall and threatened to keep council members in chambers all night, though they ultimately left when ordered to do so. Afterwards, approximately a hundred workers paraded to the store owned by Alderman Frank, 'where they sang several songs,' charivari style, to publicly shame him.[42] This tactic succeeded, winning the protesters a reversal in the city's reductions. A wave of relief strikes swept the Toronto area in July 1936, with strikes and protests occurring in York, North York, Etobicoke, Mimico, Long Branch, and Lakeview.[43] Lakeview strikers held relief administrator R.S. Moore and four of his staff prisoner in the relief office, where they also hung Public Welfare Minister David Croll in effigy.[44] In Etobicoke seventeen men were charged with seizure, confinement, and unlawful assembly when they held the reeve and two relief administrators hostage in a local school's boiler room, where they dangled a rope in front of them, then threatened to tar and feather them.[45] And in 1934 six members of the Longbranch Workers' Association imprisoned relief officer J.S. Tiffin in his office in a move to protest the lack of mattresses, bedding, and stoves in the homes of many families on relief.[46] The Canadian Labour Defense

League defended those relief workers who were criminally charged, outlining the impact of unemployment policy on their families: 'Relief schedules allow nothing for mattresses or stoves, yet these very necessary things wear out ... children are forced to sleep on old mattresses placed on boxes, old coats are used for bed-clothes; many sleep right on the floor. Many homes are using stoves that leak, creating the danger of suffocation from escaping gas.'[47] These collective protests were rational, in that the participants had a fairly well-articulated set of specific and general demands. But they were also shot through with powerful emotions rooted in a rejection of shame and the forging of collective anger centred on a conception of justice and fairness.[48]

Local protests and relief worker strikes never won major concessions for unemployed families. Because relief administration was local, cash-strapped municipalities did not have adequate resources to deal with the magnitude of unemployment. Local authorities could not meet major political demands, for example, for non-contributory unemployment insurance. But some strikes were successful and resulted in concessions that improved the lives of the unemployed on relief. For example, in 18 per cent of all strikes, full or partial demands were met.[49] Action by local authorities regarding the provision of food or social services could quickly end a strike. For example, a relief strike in St Catharines over the 'inadequate, inferior' food supply distributed by a combination of vouchers and goods resulted in a greater variety and increase in food rations and a guarantee that light, water, and medical services would be supplied by the township.[50] In Longbranch in 1934 strikers forced municipalities to turn water back on, while in North Bay in 1935 they won emergency orders for bread and the right to choose where to redeem relief script.[51] In Espanola in 1936 strikers forced the town to abandon cuts in relief, maintain clothing vouchers, guarantee the provision of electricity, and promise to investigate conditions of slum housing.[52] The politically active East York Workers' Association managed to increase municipal relief rates to 14 per cent over the provincial maximum.[53] As these examples show, unemployed organizations were often successful in forcing municipal authorities to maintain or expand material aid, though they ultimately tried to link these local protests to larger political issues involving federal unemployment policy and occasionally a critique of the capitalist economy.

Broader demands by relief worker unions centred on preserving the democratic right to protest without penalty, non-contributory un-employment insurance, and the demand for a voice in welfare policy.

One frequent request was for a meeting of workers' representatives with the premier or minister of public welfare, another was for investigations of poor housing or relief administration. In 11 per cent of all strike cases workers accepted a meeting with public officials and returned to work. The consistent demands made by the unemployed to present their concerns before politicians indicate that they saw themselves as full and responsible citizens, with a right to a voice in government policy. The post–Second World War state axiom of never again returning to economic depression was partially based on the depth of unrest and anger in families and local communities during the Great Depression.

Citizen Soldiers and Manly Veterans

Men who held the status of First World War veteran were able to make even more powerful claims of entitlement to jobs and adequate relief. Veterans' calls for economic justice were deeply entwined with gendered notions of entitlement, citizenship, and patriotic duty.[54] With front-line action – the highest form of war service – reserved for men, along with an entrenched sense of masculine entitlement to employment, ex-servicemen clothed calls for adequate aid with patriotic loyalty and breadwinning status. Veterans' criticisms of the government were rooted in post–First World War mobilization against poor retraining programs and inadequate disability pensions.[55] Veterans argued that they had sacrificed in the name of Canada and the British Empire and had acted with courage, honour, and duty. In return, they believed they deserved adequate recognition and compensation by the state, in the form of preferential access to employment and adequate financial support when out of work. Veterans were central participants in the dynamic public debate over the extent of the government's responsibility for the support of its citizens, even as their arguments for entitlement excluded many.[56] To simply dismiss veterans as conservative is to overlook their complex relationship with the state, and to miss the rich variety of their demands for government aid. In letters written by veterans directly to Ontario politicians, and in the records of veterans' organizations, it is possible to see how these men influenced government policy through protest, organization, and resistance. Were veterans' claims and demands for welfare exclusionary in nature, or were they rooted in broader ideals of entitlement? Ultimately, veterans' claims for social welfare were ambiguous, for veterans and their organizations drew on both discourses, sometimes simultaneously. Veterans argued for policies such as universal health care or unemployment insurance, but they also couched many of their demands in a discourse of loyalty to and sacrifice for the British Empire. Claims for welfare were therefore in constant engagement with contemporary economic conditions, as well as political debates about social welfare in general.[57]

Veterans were insistent that their wartime sacrifices, including the years of lost wages during active service and separations from their families, had never been properly rewarded. Complained Thomas Frith, 'the Government as no [sic] more use for me now they have got the best out of me I was one of the first too go [sic] when the country was in trouble now we are left with nothing only the relief we get.'[58] The unfulfilled promises made by the Canadian state to ex-servicemen were powerful symbols in Mary Reynolds' protest play of 1936, *And the Answer Is...*' Set against the backdrop of 'A War Memorial,' the 'Man in the Cap,' a poor unemployed veteran, bitterly bemoans the horrors of war and its aftermath: 'An' I'm one of the lucky ones. Wasn't killed in the war – wasn't even hit – a grateful country don't need to pay me no pension. Discharged fit ta go back ta m'job, and since me discharge I've spent most a me time lookin fer me job. Nearly twenty years hard scratchin'/ Some luck, I betcha [sic].'[59] In Frank Love's play *Looking Forward* a character named Betty condemns the war, its connection to capitalism, and its devastating effect on her father and other veterans:

MOTHER: If them rich people hadn't been willing to lend their money
   we couldn't have won the war, then where would we have been?
BETTY: We'd be on relief the same as we are now. The only difference
   would be that a different set of bloodsuckers would be collecting
   the interest, that's all. What did father get for the best four years
   of his life, a belly full of gas and a bag full of cheap groceries every
   week ... [t]he men who did the fighting have to go down to the
   Pogey House where they are treated like a lot of criminals.[60]

As with many criticisms of the unemployment crisis, veterans called for government intervention in the economy and the creation of full employment 'at a living rate of wage.'[61] Veterans in particular argued for their right to employment, claiming that war service gave them added entitlement to employment.[62] As Dominion Legion president L.R. LaFlèche claimed in 1930, 'No enfranchized [sic] loyal British subject and Canadian citizen has a greater right if as great to influence the prospect of this nation's future [sic].'[63]

By the early 1930s the Legion made unemployment the focus of its concern. The Ontario Provincial Command decried the problem of veterans' unemployment, calling for increased taxation of the wealthy and preferential hiring for veterans in government and industry, employment at fair wages, and generous social insurance covering unemployment, old age, and illness. At the 1934 Dominion Convention the unemployment committee condemned the material and psychological effect of unemployment on families, especially the 'branding of those compelled to accept relief as a class apart and outcast, and the perpetuation of conditions likely to create a permanent and dependent pauper class deprived of moral economic privileges and rights.'[64] Meetings of the Ontario Provincial Command in the early part of the Depression linked the economic problems of ex-servicemen with the concerns of the unemployed and the working class in general. For example, a unanimous resolution at the 1933 annual convention announced that the 'Legion supports any movement which has for its goal the social and economic welfare of the producing classes as opposed to the accumulation of wealth by exploitation both of Natural and Human resources.' [65]

Legion leaders and members reflected the deeply entrenched cultural tension between charity and entitlement, as they argued for generous pension rights, enforcement of preferential hiring in the civil service and in public works, and access to adequate relief.[66] 'I don't want charity I want a position,' wrote J.W. Alfred Rowe of Windsor to Premier Henry. 'I feel with all my services to the Empire that I am deserving.'[67] The Legion leadership, however, was reluctant to support a 'war bonus,' monetary compensation given to all veterans for wartime service. In November 1933 Sir Arthur Currie, the first Canadian-born commander of the Canadian Corps, claimed that 'the great mass of returned men in Canada never had the thought that because they fought for their country they were entitled to preferred treatment by their county, in comparison with other citizens.'[68] Yet a bonus for war service was popular among rank-and-file veterans.[69] Even though Legion leaders publicly condemned a bonus policy, they continually expanded the definition of entitlement as the Great Depression continued, by arguing for special rights in the newly created categories of 'pre-aged' and 'burnt-out' veterans.[70] While insisting that veterans were not asking for special entitlements, these categories were so expansive that leaders came close to arguing for compensation for war service. Even Currie believed that 'every man who experienced the hardships of war is paying some penalty.'[71] It was not far from his statement to the position of the Ottawa Legion president who claimed that the government should grant all unemployed ex-servicemen a well-paid pension, even if 'in the majority of cases this would be a life pension.'[72]

Veterans linked their status as soldiers to the respectability associated with manly breadwinning and family duty. The demand for jobs wove together veterans' arguments of sacrifice with the deeply entrenched masculine entitlement to paid labour. 'I myself am a returned man with four years of service for my country,' argued William Kinsman. 'It certainly does not make me feel very nice to think I helped to defend a country that will not help me in times when I and my family need it badly.'[73] F.J. Shaw demanded a job, arguing to Premier Henry that it was 'unjust and unfair that I should have to appeal to charity organizations to procure the bare necessities of life for my wife and children.'[74] When wartime sacrifice was combined with the manly duties of supporting a family, the claim to a rightful job could create a powerful sense of entitlement among veterans.

For veterans there was a close relationship between the prosperity and stability of the home and the security of the state. Osborne Dempster, an unemployed mason whose family was on relief in Toronto, had to sell his furniture to pay rent arrears and avoid eviction. 'It will be a strong man patriotically who this winter will drown out the cries of his children for bread with the strains of the "Maple Leaf Forever,"' he told Premier Henry. 'My children are receiving less nourishment than I received while in a Soviet prison in Moscow.'[75] In 1934 the Dominion unemployment committee criticized the 'decreasing relief benefits with increasing living costs resulting in more general malnutrition and ill-health in the home of the unemployed' and the 'insecurity of tenure of homes.' The committee also pointed out 'the increasing determination of the unemployed to defend their homes by any available means against the social injustice of enforcing degrading and perilous poverty upon them.'[76] Unemployed veterans continually linked the economic security of their family and home to wartime service. Their role in the Great War was a central part of the organic relationship between citizen and state and not separate in time and space from the current economic difficulties. Re-establishment and integration into civilian life, as Morton and Wright point out, was seen by veterans as an ongoing government responsibility.[77]

To privilege work and economic independence premised on bread-winning and family provision was the most powerful demand that veterans could make. Yet, even as relief was characterized as a 'degrading' form of 'pauperism,' veterans increasingly portrayed it as a 'right' they had earned through war service.[78] Many veterans with small disability pensions were ineligible for municipal relief, which the Legion deemed 'pathetic.'[79] The Legion therefore argued for more generous relief top-ups to veterans, and by 1933, 14,368 veterans were in receipt of extra 'departmental relief' given by the federal Department of Pensions and National Health.[80] After listening to delegations of ex-servicemen's representatives, the Hyndman Report, initiated late in the Bennett government's term to address veteran unemployment, claimed that the term 'relief' should be changed to that of 'unemployment assistance.' It also recommended that veterans receive cash relief, in an amount equal to or higher than that given to relief recipients in the 'civilian population.'[81]

The intersection of masculine entitlement to employment with that of service and duty to the state was a powerful argument for jobs and recognition. The idealized soldier had fulfilled his duty to protect his nation, home, and family by going to war. This vision of the ideal soldier was visible in war propaganda that downplayed the atrocities of the war and celebrated male adventure, the 'saintliness ... of sacrifice,' and the power and success of 'Johnny Canuck's' incredible feats of valour, strength and stoicism.[82] In wartime rhetoric the masculine image of the boyish and youthful soldier coexisted with the soldier as an icon of hardiness, mythic courage, and heroism, all of which were linked to the imaginary Nordic strength of the Canadian nation. 'Men from the mountain the rock and the river / Men from the forest the lake and the plain / Strike for our flag and defend it forever,' declared one wartime jingle.[83] Canadians and soldiers were 'a hardy race of men ... a race that is stalwart brave and free.'[84]

On return from war, however, this iconic masculinity was threatened by the reality of disability and unemployment. In the 1930s the ideal of manhood epitomized by the youthful soldiers had been neutered by their age, disability, psychological stress, and unemployment. As the Depression progressed, veterans' organizations increasingly portrayed ex-servicemen as 'burnt-out' and unable to compete with younger, healthier men because of their age and disability. By 1930 the Legion had successfully convinced the government to implement the War Veterans' Allowance Act, which recognized that men who served overseas and who suffered no obvious disability on demobilization had still experienced 'premature aging' or 'physical and mental deterioration.'[85] General Alex Ross claimed that veterans were unable to compete with 'vigorous youth' in the labour market and that 'a man who served overseas, even though unscathed, suffered a marked depreciation in physical energy.'[86] The images of lost youth, boyishness, and innocence, displayed alongside images of men who had fulfilled the expectations of citizenship and obeyed the call to service, created a compelling picture of wounded ex-servicemen in crisis. However, these contradictory images of wounded and heroic masculinity were not easily reconciled. Re-establishment propaganda proclaimed that 'once a soldier always a man,' yet pre-aged, wounded or disabled veterans were the very antithesis of the strong, healthy, and masculine 'boys' who initially went off to war.[87] Legion leaders emphasized a fractured manhood while simultaneously celebrating the manliness and courage of former soldiers. 'When *men* were needed to save our nation,' wrote the Legion's unemployment committee to Premier Hepburn in 1934, 'the boys responded to the call unselfishly, upholding the best traditions of our Empire … Promises of Freedom and Security have been broken or Forgotten.'[88] There is evidence that veterans themselves resisted fully embracing a discourse that emphasized their weakness, finding such characterizations of their position humiliating and frustrating. In response to a political speech by a Legion leader that all veterans had been psychologically damaged by war, an anonymous soldier took offence, claiming that such assertions were distorted and that he was a 'Front Line Survivor – and still *normal*!!'[89] Similarly, an anonymous columnist in the *Legionary* challenged perceptions that he was not 'normal,' arguing that war service created men of great 'character,' 'courage,' virility,' and 'self-confidence' and that if veterans were unable to readapt to civilian life it was 'by reason of the failure of many "subnormal" citizens to fulfill war promises.' He included a poem he had written: '*Normal* men, proud and strong / Rallied to the flag; marched along / Weak and old men forced to stay / With other men* of softer clay. (*Eligibles).'[90]

The discourse of wounded manhood was unstable, since the very reasons advanced for aid undermined the ideal of a strong, healthy, and independent masculinity. Veterans saw themselves as deserving citizens who were too proud to accept charity, while at the same time arguing that it was not shameful to demand government aid after serving in war. Perhaps this is why their calls for aid were so strongly clothed in the discourses of contract and entitlement, which were associated with independent manhood and which helped to maintain images of masculine strength despite the untenable economic position of many veterans.[91] Their fulfilment of the masculine call to sacrifice deserved special recognition, veterans believed, particularly when high unemployment made it increasingly difficult to support their families. As one unemployed veteran with an ill wife and four children told Premier Henry, 'Give some of the rest of us who have wallowed in the mud of Flanders a chance to make a few dollars and keep the Respectability of ourselves and our families.'[92]

Veterans lobbied for and won a number of concessions from the national government. Though the response was piecemeal and uneven, Ottawa slowly began to acknowledge that support for veteran re-establishment was an ongoing federal responsibility. The Depression years saw a gradual loosening of eligibility requirements surrounding pensions and the establishment of and continual amendments to war veterans' allowances. Persistent criticisms of inadequate relief and high unemployment won 'unemployment assistance' for veterans, cash-based payments intended to make up the difference between municipal relief rates and pensions. Preference in public works and the civil service and expanded job training were other examples of government responses to veteran unemployment problems.[93] But veterans, like the unemployed in general in the 1930s, did not win a cohesive plan to fight unemployment, let alone expansive social insurance. The long and often tedious process of political negotiation between veterans, their leaders, and the state illustrates the extent to which veterans were treated by the government as political participants and not entirely as supplicants. However, the more radical of veterans' demands for social welfare programs for all unemployed men and families emerged mainly from provincial and local branches in the early part of the 1930s. As the Great Depression progressed veterans' organizations focused on the formal lobbying process in Ottawa, and they increasingly agitated on the basis of veterans' specific needs. Still, their demands, along with other types of protests in the 1930s, helped to create a public consensus around state-sponsored welfare and therefore played an important role in the shaping the postwar war welfare state.

Protesting Unemployment: Wives and Militant Mothers

When Mrs Georgina Ketcherson led a delegation of one hundred 'indigent mothers' to confront Windsor city council over the lack of suitable children's clothing and the poverty of their families, she was participating in a larger politics of widespread maternal activism.[94] Unemployed men, as relief recipients, transients, or veterans, were clearly visible in unemployed protest. But women also participated in relief politics as mothers upholding the necessity of men's employment and the family wage, as auxiliaries in relief worker unions, and as vital participants in protests, demonstrations, and rallies. Women's concerns over unemployment were also visible in the thousands of letters of anger, protest, and complaint they wrote to premiers Henry and Hepburn. Their letters articulated the concept of a reciprocal relationship between citizen and state and demanded that the government take on the moral responsibility to nurture and protect its citizens. While men referred to their status as rightful workers and breadwinners, married women made claims on the state rooted in their position as wife, mother, and dependent. Married women in particular were labelled in public discourse as economic dependents of men, while their domestic reproduction and caregiving work was connected to the unpaid sphere of home and family.[95]

Women in 1930s Canada drew on a historical precedent of female militancy, ranging from protests in the tradition of the 'moral economy' to street-level protests in radical immigrant or socialist communities. In most cases motherhood was a motivator and justification of political action for women across boundaries of geography, class, ethnicity, and time.[96] This does not mean that all women enacted politicized motherhood in the same way: the nature and extent of women's demands were shaped by expectations of how the state might respond and by constraints of class, region, or race. Demands made by peasant women in eighteenth-century bread riots in Europe, maternal feminists in the nineteenth and twentieth centuries, and communist housewives all clearly differed, both in the nature of the demand and in the way that demand was expressed. Yet the figure of the politicized mother shares some commonalities: the primary connection between women and children, the validation of motherhood and domestic labour as central to the survival of the family unit, and the belief that the role of motherhood justified political action. Women's demands on the state came from two main positions in the 1930s: those located on the class and ethnic margins of Anglo-Celtic Ontario and those located on the margins of class but in the ethnic centre. In both cases women were able to draw on powerful notions of motherhood, but those who made claims to social and economic rights based on British identity drew political strength from myths of nation-building, history, and citizenship.

Women clearly upheld the association between masculinity and work, arguing that their husbands needed employment to fulfil their obligations as husbands and fathers. When Mrs Alice Boulton wrote to Premier Henry for the second time to criticize government unemployment policy, she asked for 'work to keep us human'; by this, she meant a job for her husband, so that he could adequately support her and their ten dependent children.[97] Women asked for jobs for husbands and aid for children to maintain the pride, dignity, and security of the family. 'My husband feels terrible he loves his family, is willing to work hard,' wrote a mother of seven whose university-educated husband lost his job as a salesman. Her husband, and many other men, she claimed, were 'people who have always paid their way ... people unaccustomed to hardship [and] are losing everything they ever worked for through no fault of theirs.'[98] Though the claims that women made for their families' right to economic security were less direct than those made by men, their requests for help were not forms of begging or charity. Male breadwinners claimed entitlement predicated on a broad public consensus around their right to paid employment. But women still argued for economic security, even within a position of subordination and the framework of a familial status that defined them primarily as dependents. Women's maternalist arguments do not mean that women were not workers, but the male breadwinner ideal remained dominant within public discourse.[99] Men were most masculine when they were employed. 'It is awful,' noted Mrs A. McKenna, 'when a man is willing to work and can't get work at anything.'[100] Unlike men's employment, which was understood as central to their gender identity, women's work in the labour force was often attacked, sometimes tolerated as an economic necessity, but not understood to be deeply connected to their status or identity as women, mothers, and wives.[101]

Even though the rhetoric of the family wage excluded women from the public sphere, women drew on the rights associated with it to criticize government unemployment and relief policy and to argue for their families' right to economic security. One woman wrote: 'It is almost winter and our men have had no work for ages and we have no winter clothes and no prospects of any my own children have no clothes ... [i]ts work we want not relief. We don't our living [sic] for nothing we want work and lots of it.'[102] Women repeatedly insisted on their children's need for adequate food and clothing, as well as schoolbooks and medicine, reminding the premiers that their husbands required jobs to meet these necessities and demanding that the state provide work.

Mrs Wallace Gow of Sturgeon Falls wrote to Premier Henry, demanding work for her husband and sons. 'The situation we mothers are up against,' she wrote, was kitchens with 'barren cupboards' and men with empty 'lunch pales [sic].'[103] Protesting on behalf of husbands and children by using this rhetoric of 'militant mothering' was one way that women could subvert assumptions of female domesticity to make claims on the state.[104] The arguments made by women on behalf of their families may not have challenged traditional gender roles, but their letters voiced political resistance to unemployment policy. They demanded political accountability, and they threatened to withhold their vote in the next election. As one woman admonished Henry, after writing him three times in vain to request a farm loan and schoolbooks for her daughter, there was 'one vote here the last time and will be three this time if i get no help i give none [sic].'[105]

'Militant mothering' was not only present in the way that individual women made demands on the state, but also in organized protests in the Depression years. Women expected their husbands to protest against inadequate wage and relief rates, framing these actions within the proper duties and responsibilities of manhood. After the arrest of Stratford relief strikers in 1936 one of the several wives who wrote to Premier Hepburn in protest asked, 'Surely it is no crime to ask for more food that our children may not suffer from malnutrition?'[106] Another wife from Stratford, in a series of letters to the judge, the attorney general, and the premier, asked, 'Why should our children and I be denied having a good husband and father in our home just because he protested against the low standard of relief?'[107] Even Attorney-General Gordon Conant, in a memo to Premier Hepburn regarding the unsuccessful prosecution of relief protestors in 1938, wondered 'whether we should ... abandon this appeal. It may look a little vindictive to take these people to the Supreme Court of Canada.'[108] As women exhorted men to fulfil their manly obligations to support them and their families, they employed images of the male breadwinner and provider. The Longbranch Workers' Association led relief workers on a strike in protest against low food, fuel, and clothing allowances and to request 'useful' municipal works and cash wages of 50 cents an hour. Fifteen women and approximately a hundred men picketed relief projects and quickly surrounded the men still working, adopting the tactic of shaming individual men and questioning their masculinity. 'The women noisily exhorted the strikers to "be men" and "stand by their families," while the men at a distance, alternately jeered and cheered.'[109]

'Militant mothering' was also evident in the collective action of women themselves. Both the Communist Party and the CCF organized women around housewife and consumer concerns, but the radicaliza- tion of domestic duties was not intended to 'emancipate' women from hierarchical gender roles.[110] Women often acted within auxiliary roles while still participating in much of the direct political action. Even in protest literature protest itself was often gendered male. In Frank Love's play *Looking Forward* Betty, the young radical, portrays men as the true leaders of resistance to relief cuts: 'Charity, *charity*. The dividends of the working class. I wish I was a man.' Yet she still upholds the centrality of women to radical struggle:

> And if my man goes to jail because he stands up for his rights I'll be proud of him. And will I sit home and cry? I will not. I'll take his place in the streets and carry on the struggle.
> This is not a time for the women to be sitting at home moping. Their place is in the streets with their men fighting shoulder to shoulder. If my man goes to jail I'll see that there are ten more to take his place.[111]

Women's protest in the 1930s embraced traditional 'female' concerns, such as rising food prices, children's welfare, and household budget- ing. However, women also spoke to crowds and at meetings, with pre- miers and politicians, and even participated in collective violence, demonstrating the intimate link between the home and the economy. In the historical tradition of 'furious mothers and housewives,' women's actions were based on a belief in their 'right' to feed their families.[112] Women's protests were therefore more than a reaction to immediate material needs. While rooted in pressing material concerns, women also vocalized a powerful belief in their right to claim an affordable standard of living, economic security, and adequate food, clothing, and shelter for their families.

The gendered nature of protest and the evocation of militant moth- ering by women activists and the media is illustrated in the *Toronto Star's* story of Mrs William Wilkinson from North York, the only woman delegate at the Workers' Economic Conference held in Ottawa in August 1932 by the National Council of Unemployed Committees.[113] The *Star* portrayed the protestors at the conference as vaguely intimidating, re- porting on their 'violently worded' resolutions, 'fiery speeches,' and the singing of 'the Red Flag.' Mrs Wilkinson gained some notoriety during the delegation's meeting with Prime Minister Bennett, where she reportedly pounded on his desk and argued with him over his government's inaction regarding unemployment. 'Mr Bennett,' she reportedly said, 'we women of Canada are not going to let our children starve for you or any other government in Canada.' In response to Bennett's attempts to console her, she proclaimed, 'I'm not here speaking for myself … but for other women all over Canada. This can't go on … [i]f we are bitter, it is you have made us bitter. We women can't go on bringing kids in this world just for them to starve.'[114] Mrs Wilkinson's militancy was portrayed as an extension of her maternal role, as a proud and strong woman fighting for her husband and her family. 'It's a far cry from a little home in North York to the chambers of the highest executive in the land,' claimed the newspaper. 'But foremost in her mind and back of that was the thought of her family of five and of her anxious husband in their little home.' Her family, reported the paper, was proud of her, and though they once had had a 'comfortable' home, they were struggling to feed, clothe, and maintain the family on inadequate relief.[115]

The full extent of women's involvement in relief politics in the Great Depression is not well documented, though women supported relief camp strikes, and participated in the consumer activism of housewives in groups organized by socialist organizations. In the spring of 1935, for example, CCF and Communist Party women, along with members of the Women's Christian Temperance Union, worked as a joint Mothers' Council in Vancouver, leading fifteen hundred strikers with baby carriages to Stanley Park, where they formed a giant heart to support 'our boys.'[116] In the mid-1930s communist groups successfully organized housewives into neighbourhood groups and associations across the country, which lobbied for better relief and protested against rising food costs, especially milk and meat; and the Jewish Communist movement led a kosher meat boycott in Toronto in 1933, which initially involved seven hundred Jewish women who organized protests, rallies, mass meetings, and pickets.[117] Such forms of housewife activism were also common in the United States. In 1935 meat boycotts erupted in Chicago, New York, and Detroit, where women's groups, often led by communist leaders, picketed stockyards and butchers, assaulted strike breakers, kerosened meat, and lobbied municipal and federal governments.[118]

Women actively participated in relief protests and strikes, formed mothers' committees, and organized around domestic interests and consumer issues. In Oshawa the Mothers' Association protested relief conditions, the relief store, and inadequate relief food. Newly elected president Mrs T. Gardner criticized the relief officers and the mayor for 'telling me what to feed my family and preparing my budget … [w]e can go and ask for what we want nicely first, but if we don't get what we want then we can try something else.' At the inaugural meeting Mrs C. Smoker, a nurse, proclaimed that rickets and tuberculosis were jeopardizing the health of unemployed families. She also listed the degrading features of relief, including low-quality provisions, prying interviews, insults by the relief officer Miss Farncomb, and having to line up in public to receive rations. For their efforts, the local paper warned its readers that these families were turning to 'communistic views' and should be carefully watched.[119]

Women supported their striking husbands in a variety of visible ways. They voted on strike actions, attended demonstrations, mass meetings and parades, picketed relief works, and lobbied all levels of government. When relief workers in St Catharines demanded a voucher system rather than relief in kind, 'girls led a parade' of about 125 men through the streets.[120] The Etobicoke Workers' Association held a three hundred–person parade in October 1933, where men, women, and children marched and carried banners protesting inadequate relief conditions.[121] Women were therefore a physical and vocal presence in local protest, both to their husbands and to strike organizers, who took their concerns seriously, and to government officials and local authorities who often received them in deputations. In York Township the second relief strike of the summer began in July 1932, sparked by the problems women had cooking and preparing nutritious meals on the relief vouchers. Women picketed a number of relief projects, urging all the men to quit work in solidarity with the strikers. When, as the *Toronto Star* reported, a woman called one of the workers 'yellow,' he retorted, 'Go home and wash your dishes.' 'We haven't any dishes to wash,' she snapped. 'We never eat.'[122]

Women assumed a leadership role in local protest that was rarely found in traditional political parties. The York Township strike executive, for example, consisted of five men and two women.[123] During a one-day strike by men in Oshawa over inadequate relief store food, the strikers were addressed by Mrs Lillian Williams and Mrs A. Vipond, whose speeches centred on the poor quality of food given to families on relief.[124] During the July 1932 York Township relief strike, at a meeting of twelve hundred people one woman announced that she took exception to Premier Henry's statement that 'no one would starve,' declaring, 'I have four children … and not one of them has gained a pound since Christmas.'[125] Women also addressed women's concerns separately. York Township's United Women's Association held mass meetings for and by women during the June 1936 relief strike. Mrs McGregor told the crowd, 'If we stick together we will be able to do things for this strike that even men can't do.'[126] York Township discussed sending more than a thousand wives of relief workers to Ottawa to meet Liberal members of Parliament and demand a better standard of living for their families.[127] Women played an important role in negotiations between strikers and state representatives. An agreement between Minister Croll and three female members of Toronto Township's General Workers' Union, for example, ended a relief strike in 1936, when the government promised to investigate relief grievances and to immediately renew relief vouchers.[128] Women provided traditional auxiliary support to unemployed associations, much as they did for unions and political parties. When fourteen strikers were arrested in 1936 for forcibly confining the reeve and relief administrator in Etobicoke, relief workers planned a one-hour work stoppage during which women throughout the Toronto suburbs held teas and draws to raise money for their defence.[129]

While women acted as auxiliaries in organizations and in protests, they also took a prominent role in direct action. Groups of women participated in protests that verged on violence, willingly placing their bodies between strikers and the police or physically attacking relief officials and municipal politicians. In Blind River, in 1936, fifty-three women 'mobbed' the office of Relief Officer K. Hanger after a 10 per cent reduction in relief, while in the same year in Lakeview forty women 'besieged Relief Officer R.S. Moore in his own office, demanding food vouchers for themselves and their children.'[130] Women were also involved in direct street action. In May 1933 women and children were part of a crowd that 'stormed' the Hamilton unemployed hostel to demand payment of 48 cents an hour for their two days of work a week and for reinstatement of single men to the relief rolls.[131] In a London, Ontario, relief strike in the spring of 1935 'mothers and wives' of relief strikers were prevented by police from breaking down the door to the township offices. In response a large group of women in a crowd of about twelve hundred people again tried to force the police barricade. In the resulting fracas, 'Mrs Cleverly was struck on the face by Police Constable Snell. Mrs Patterson's foot was badly jammed in the door by police,' and Councillor Hardue 'was set upon by a striker's wife and forced to flee for shelter.'[132] During an Oshawa relief strike in March 1936 ten to twelve female members of the unemployed association tried to get city salvage workers to quit in sympathy by resorting 'to physical force to remove the men from their jobs.'[133]

Women and children were used as a physical presence in picket lines to create a degree of protection for male protestors in the belief that the police were less likely to physically harm a woman. This tactic was used in labour strikes as well as relief strikes, and it could generate some protection from the violence of local police.[134] In Fort William and Port Arthur local authorities faced protests by men and women against shipping relief workers to the relief camp at Lac Seul to work for 20 cents a day. A report at an executive meeting of the Ukranian Farm Labour Temple Association noted that 'in order to prevent police from beating up our men, women and children must be put out in front on station platform.'[135] At the 1934 Gogama relief strike, near Sudbury, strikers barricaded the highway and placed wives and children between male strikers and the police. The police refused to attack them, and the *Sudbury Star* reported that five officers had been taunted and had their 'hats knocked off by the women.' The Sault Ste Marie *Star* reported that relief strikers placed barriers across the highway, with twenty-five women and children in front, acting as a further barrier between strikers and the police. When police attempted to push through the blockade, a woman fell across a fence and the police quickly retreated.[136]

Children, home, and family were central symbols in strikes and protests, connecting women and children to union tactics and political action. Women often kept children home from school in support of a strike or protest or took children to picket at relief offices and municipal offices.[137] Parents brought their children to participate in an all-night sit-in at the New Toronto Relief Office in 1935, for example, unafraid to involve entire families in community politics.[138] The presence of children asserted the importance of the working-class family unit and the connection between the economy and the family. Children's presence in sit-ins and strikes reminded state authorities that unemployment and relief policies affected the lives of children and families, and they also served to remind policy makers that men were fathers and husbands as much as workers. For example, when the Etobicoke Workers' Association called a relief strike in October 1933, demanding a 50 per cent increase in relief, cash payments, and the creation of public works, over five hundred children were kept home from school. Women and children played a central role in the 1935 East York strike, when a thousand relief workers struck over relief cuts in food allowances and inadequate money for medical treatment. Young children picketed at the Danforth Park School, wearing sandwich boards with such slogans as 'No cash relief no school' and 'We need warm winter clothing / Support our strike.' Mothers kept over a thousand pupils home in East York for a week in support of the strike.[139] The language of protest drew on images of suffering families and children in crisis. The Lakeview Workers' Association incorporated images of innocent children and family duty when they protested against relief cuts by picketing at the side of the highway wearing sandwich boards with such captions as 'We protest the Liberal government starving our children on relief' and 'Liberal government called Henry government baby starvers – then gave us a cut in relief.'[140] During the Etobicoke relief workers strike in the fall of 1933 women and children were visible in the parade of three hundred people, carrying banners that read 'Give us this day our daily bread.'[141] Similar symbols were popular with the East York Workers' Association, which supported school strikes, and children picketing with sandwich boards imploring Toronto citizens: 'Can you think?'[142]

Women, and to a lesser extent children, were therefore connected to the public activism of unemployed men. The rhetoric and action of unemployed protest was structured around the preservation of women's maternal duties and men's breadwinner status. In unemployed protest women's participation in strike action and crowd violence demonstrates the important connection of women's domestic role to the survival of the working-class family and to 'class struggle' itself.[143] It is crucial to understand this type of female protest as a kind of political resistance. The arguments made by women on behalf of their families did not challenge traditional gender roles, but their actions demonstrate that they did not see themselves as passive victims.[144] Married women were not accorded the same level of respect and status as men, but their demands for respectability and security should be recognized as a crucial factor in transforming state obligations for social welfare. Though women were largely absent from higher-paying administrative positions or policy making in welfare programs, and they were labelled dependents in social welfare provision, they were nevertheless central in 'shaping the broad outlines of the welfare state.'[145] The rights of mothers and wives were central to the actions and rhetoric of relief politics and protest in the 1930s.

'British Justice': Citizenship, Ethnicity, and Rights

Strikes and rallies led by unemployed and relief worker unions, the lobbying of veterans' groups for state support of ex-servicemen, and

individuals writing letters to politicians criticizing government unemployment policy were all forms of protest undertaken by unemployed men and women in Ontario during the Great Depression.
Political action took many ideological forms, and protests were a messy
mix of radical and conservative ideology, often criticizing the inequalities of capitalist production by adopting the language of British rights
or male privilege.

Relief worker and unemployed unions, for example, while usually
organized by the communist-led Workers' Unity League, were actually an uneasy balance of political, ethnic, and ideological alliances.
Veterans' groups, women's organizations, members of the Co-operative
Commonwealth Federation and the Communist Party, church groups,
city councillors, and members of the provincial or the federal parliament all participated in local demonstrations. The ideology of particular groups was also shaped by regional patterns of immigration and
ethnicity. In some areas protests were clearly cross-ethnic, with participants from a variety of more recent immigrant and Anglo-Celtic groups.
The Crowland relief strike of 1935, for example, involved workers from
various European backgrounds, including Polish, Ukranian, Hungarian,
and Italian, and it was supported by the Communist Party, the CCF,
and Polish groups that had ties to the Roman Catholic Church.[146] The
East York Workers' Association, known for its radicalism, was homo-
geneous, with its members either British immigrants or Canadians of
British background. Windsor's local unemployed council drew its early
membership from Ukrainian, Hungarian, and Croatian immigrant
workers, but it had grown popular with 'Anglo-Saxon' workers by
1931.[147] Beamsville Reeve Alex Grott claimed that most men participating in the relief strikes during the summer of 1935 were married
Canadian workers with children.[148] Moreover, in many areas the activism of First World War veterans led to a vocal presence dominated
by those who claimed strong loyalties and ties to Great Britain. The
Workers' Ex-Servicemen's League was affiliated with the Communist
Party, and it also used the rhetoric and symbolism of patriotic Britishness
to protest unemployment. One favourite phrase for protest banners
read 'Heroes in 1914 are called bums in 1934.'[149] It may be that the unemployed associations not officially affiliated with the National Council
of Unemployed Committees and the Communist Party, though they
used increasingly 'militant' and class-conscious language and tactics,
were more attractive to Anglo-Celtic workers.[150] For public authorities
and state officials concerns around radical challenges to the capitalist

economic system were intimately connected with anti-immigrant rhetoric and anti-communism; many times, these were conflated.

A great deal of tension existed in the language and forms of local, community, and individual protest. While many individuals insisted that they were not 'reds,' communist organizations were quite successful in organizing the unemployed, and the appearance of radical demands in unemployed organizations worried some state officials and political pundits. Newspapers, politicians, and some members of the population reacted fearfully to communist-led protest, particularly when participants were labelled as the immigrant 'other.' Newspapers were quick to point out when agitators were not of British descent. 'The foreign element has been more obtrusive,' wrote the North Bay Nugget on the eve of an unemployed demonstration.[151] A demonstration in Timmins, in April 1931, broke up soon after communist demonstrators were 'confronted with an unsympathetic gathering of citizens.'[152] In Kirkland Lake, in October 1932, a parade held by four hundred unemployed men and 'mostly composed of the foreign-born section of the populace' was charged by police, and at their behest the 'English-speaking citizens' helped 'disperse' the crowd.[153] In communities where tension already existed between Anglo-Celtic and 'foreign citizens,' emotions, racism, and anti-communist rhetoric ran high. In a relief strike in Sudbury, in May 1933, for example, communist and anti-communist factions of the unemployed clashed at a meeting and demonstration in a public park. Tensions were also exacerbated by the high level of involvement of Finnish workers in local politics, leading to anti-immigrant rhetoric.[154] Even Peter Hunter, in his memoir describing his work as an unemployed organizer for the Communist Party in Ontario, identified 'foreigners' as workers of Eastern European and not British birth. He recalls that he escaped without harm from a protest in Hamilton because police policy was to arrest known reds and 'foreign-born' workers. Hunter, however, was born in Scotland, and arrived in Canada at the age of ten.[155]

Yet in other circumstances radical and conservative language coexisted. Many people participated in various forms of radical protest, often in communist-led unions or unemployed organizations, but did not join the Communist Party. Nevertheless, they used a radical discourse that expressed the depth of their frustration and anger at government intransigence, the exploitation by employers, and the inequalities of capitalism. The Globe and Mail reported during a relief strike in 1932 that a woman addressed a rally of over two thousand people and 'decried the alleged indifference in administrative circles which termed "red" those who struck out for their rights. "If fighting for enough to eat is being a Red or Communist, alright they can call me what they like ... if the governments continued their present form of indifference they would be forced to use force," she said.'[156] Both David Roediger and John Manley point out that a militant language of class struggle and critique of capitalism 'gained acceptance' among the unemployed during the Great Depression. Communist Party organizing helped shape the language and forms of protest among the unemployed and within unemployed organizations, even among those who never identified as Marxist.[157]

Nevertheless, ethnicity shaped organizations and protest in ways other than identifying communists as foreigners or 'others.' Concepts of Britishness framed demands for rights and critiques of state policy. Veterans believed, for example, that their role in sacrificing for the British Empire and the Canadian state gave them a greater claim than others to state aid in times of economic distress. For unemployed Anglo-Celtic men and women, claims to British identity and history were a powerful way to set apart the demands of 'true' citizens of Canada from those less entitled to make claims on the state. It is not surprising that in a time of social and economic upheaval an affirmation of Canadian national identity appeared in popular discourse. Though historians have discussed the growth of Canadian cultural and political nationalism beginning in the 1920s, few have looked at how national identity was articulated and experienced outside of the intellectual elite. If a nation is an 'imagined community,' then it is crucial to understand how nationality was shaped and understood at the popular level.[158] In the letters written to Ontario premiers, as well as in the rhetoric and symbolism of some unemployed and veterans' organizations, citizens used the discourse of Britishness and nationalism to place themselves – along with the politicians they were addressing – within a collective, though narrowly defined, Canadian identity.

Anyone who was white and of British heritage was considered to be a true Canadian and therefore worthy of financial aid and economic justice. In the case of the East York Workers' Association, the British ancestry of local workers was linked to a 'strong sense that this was *their* country and that they had the right to the necessities of life.'[159] Those who were 'Canadian by birth,' which generally meant those of British heritage, were understood as the most deserving citizens of Canada.[160] For many, true Canadian identity was established through

generations of established Anglo-Celtic ancestry. In letters to the pre-
miers, for example, the United Empire Loyalists and the early pioneers
symbolized the belief in an organic community where generations of
Canadians were linked together in the creation of the Canadian nation.
An unemployed man on the verge of foreclosure wrote to Premier
Henry to ask for help in saving his family's home, saying, 'My wife is a
Canadian of three generations back and myself I am forty-five years in
Canada a British subject at that.'[161] United Empire Loyalist 'stock' was a
vital signifier of status to both men and women; Loyalists represented
the imperial tie between Canada and Great Britain, and the early pioneers symbolized British sacrifice, courage, and industry.[162] In this idealized version of Canadian history, intellectual and amateur historians
claimed that Loyalists and pioneers had 'tamed' the Canadian land by
conquering French-Canadian and Aboriginal peoples and that they had
brought progress, liberty, civilization, and Anglo superiority to the new
nation. But while these debates and the mythmaking occurred at both
elite and middle-class levels of culture, many of these ideals were also
reflected in popular thought. One woman, in her appeal to Premier
Hepburn for aid, explicitly linked both herself and the government to
'pioneer British stock' from 'the Stirring days of Alexander McKenzie.'[163]

By drawing on the constructed identity of Britishness women could
be true Canadians on an equal basis with men, argue for greater recognition and entitlement, and claim a crucial place for themselves within the
national narrative.[164] The native-born, according to female letter writers,
played a crucial role in building the nation and should therefore receive
recognition from the state. Genealogy became a calling card and signifier of special status. 'I am no foreigner,' wrote a widow who was facing
foreclosure. 'I was born in Ontario from parents that [were] also born in
Ontario. My grandfather was a U.E.L. my grandparents on my mothers
side were Irish. My husband was also a good Canadian born in Canada
from English blood.[165] Another woman wrote, 'Are we not true, loyal
Canadians from the same descent as your wife Mrs Henry. Her ancestry
Laura Secord [sic] was mine also as well as Sir Allen McNab and the
other faithful early settlers.'[166] Single mothers could call on Canadian
nationality to argue their respectable status more forcefully. A woman
turned down for mothers' allowance wrote, 'We are respectable citizens
of Canada and have been for generations back. I am bringing up my
family deasent and respectable [sic] and educating them the best I can ...
I feel I have been dealt out of my rights by some-one who thinks it there
[sic] duty to save government money.'[167] At the popular level in the 1930s

Britishness, loyalty, sacrifice, and duty were crucial signifiers of national belonging and markers of full citizenship. This definition of citizenship based on a shared British background was particularly appealing to women in this period. The liberal construction of citizenship, with its emphasis on the political and economic independence of the male worker-citizen, was essentially masculine in nature. A definition of citizenship linking Anglo-Celtic background with the experience of motherhood enhanced women's citizenship status and created an effective tool of protest.[168]

This use of Britishness as a claim to entitlement was one way for the poor and the unemployed to claim respectability and to make demands for economic and political justice. The narrow definition of who constituted a true Canadian excluded the non-Canadian-born and those 'foreigners' who were not of British background. Those who were excluded from claiming Canadian identity were therefore unable to demand these rights with the same degree of power, as they were not considered full members and citizens of the Canadian state.[169] 'Is there a chance,' asked one unemployed man, 'for a good honest Canadian Citizen to make an honest living for himself and Family?' The government, he complained, allowed 'our own Canadians to be shut out and all classes of foreigners placed in their positions.'[170] Writers complained with bitterness and hostility that 'foreigners' were taking away Canadians' rightful place in the labour force, making them scapegoats for unemployment and poverty. One unemployed woman stated, 'It is impossible for a single man, during the last five years, to have any hope of marriage...[i]t is the foreigner and the Jew who are taking our trades and work from us, who can afford to marry and start a home.'[171]

The narrow category of Canadianness was also reflected in public policy that played on anti-immigrant and racist rhetoric to deal with the unemployment crisis. Deporting or threatening to deport noncitizens who were dependent on public relief was one way that governments attempted to control 'foreign' radicalism and to limit relief expenditures. It was Department of Immigration policy under both Bennett and King to deport immigrants on relief, aided by the municipalities, which were expected to report them and request deportation.[172] In the two-year period from March 1931 to March 1933 there were 14,154 deportations, while there were fewer than 25,000 in the three decades spanning the years 1900–30.[173] Deportations reached a high point in 1932, when 7,647 people were deported, 5,217 for being public charges.[174] Municipalities generally upheld a policy of excluding immigrants from relief. In Sarnia, for example, central European immigrants were denied relief and fired from local public works projects.[175] In 1932 Oshawa declared that un-naturalized aliens in the country for less than five years who were on relief would be deported. Only two aldermen voted against that resolution, though it was protested by Ukranian residents, some local ministers, lawyers, and politicians, and the local Orthodox churches.[176] It was primarily the Communist Party and the CCF that protested deportations of unemployed or radical immigrants, but they were also joined by a number of mainstream churches, judges, lawyers, unions, university professors, and journalists. However, in the early years of the Great Depression, this concern over civil liberties was tempered by popular opinion that blamed immigrants for stealing jobs from Canadians.[177]

Ethnicity, Britishness, and sacrifice combined to give the protests and demands of First World War veterans even greater political currency. Veterans used the rhetoric of duty to the Canadian nation and the British Empire to frame their political demands. One of the enduring myths of the Great War is that of the birth of the independent Canadian nation in the victories of the battlefield.[178] Veterans' rhetoric rested on these myths of Canadian heroism after the war. 'The freedom of the nation rests upon sacrifice,' claimed the Canadian Legion. Soldiers wrote 'Canada's name high on the world's roll of honour' and won Canada 'international prestige.'[179] Soldiers had served the Empire and helped to create a new nation, and they saw themselves as the embodiment of true Britishness, Canadian loyalty, and civic patriotism. Earlier war propaganda had explicitly linked Britishness to Canadian soldiers and emphasized the common interests of the Empire and Canada. 'So if you are white / You will join the fight / And rally round the/ (Come and enlist boys) guns.' Canadian soldiers were 'British boys,' upholding 'old Britain's pledge' and 'the Empire's honor true.'[180] Veterans' special link to the Canadian nation bolstered their arguments for preferential treatment, marked them as 'rightfully deserving,' and stood them in contrast to 'foreigners' stealing jobs and the dangers of communism. Veterans, among other Canadians, blamed immigrants and aliens for stealing jobs during the Depression. Wrote an unemployed veteran and Legion member from Fort Frances, 'I have often wondered whether it might not be quite appropriate to emblazon a few foreign ensigns on the fly of the Union Jack, for it seems to me a foreigner has more privileges and is thought more of in our workshops than true British subjects who have fought for our good old flag.'[181]

Anti-alien sentiment ran high among Legion leaders and members, a tradition that extended back to the early years of the veterans' movement.[182] The 1931 report of the Ontario unemployment committee resolved that all un-naturalized aliens or all those naturalized after July 1931 be fired from government jobs and replaced by veterans.[183] In 1932 the Dominion Command protested the potential layoffs of nearly six hundred veterans by the CNR in Winnipeg and in other locations across Canada. The Legion demanded that all un-naturalized persons be fired and argued that union seniority should be determined by the date of naturalization. Dominion Legion chairman A.E. Moore claimed that the foreign-born had 'stolen' seniority from veterans by securing jobs during the war years, thereby establishing seniority that 'rightfully belonged to men on active service.'[184]

Connected closely with anti-immigrant sentiment and emphasis on British loyalty was a dedicated anti-communism within the ranks and leadership of the Legion. The *Legionary* proudly reported the work of local members in helping police 'maintain law and order when threatened by subversive elements' and in upholding 'British law and British institutions.' Branch members from all over the province were sworn in as special constables to help the police suppress riots and 'inflammatory demonstrations.'[185] In Sudbury in response to fear that 'Reds' were trying to incite the population, especially the 'alien-born,' police swore in forty Legion members as a temporary police squad. By June 1932 the police had called this unit in more than six times, and they engaged twice in 'active combat ... ending in the complete rout of the demonstrations.'[186] In Windsor the local Legion branch unanimously endorsed a resolution supporting city council's decision to ban all 'Red parades' or assemblies, claiming that such groups, 'particularly if influenced by foreign quarters,' were 'contemptible' and a threat to 'human freedom.'[187] The Port Arthur branch, 'determined to oust the Red menace from their locality,' sent a sixty-man delegation to city council with a proposal to end all 'sinister Red activities.' The delegation convinced the council to implement a by-law restraining all parades and demonstrations and to outlaw the distribution of 'communistic literature.'[188]

Within such conservative, anti-immigrant, and anti-communist rhetoric, however, some veterans suggested alternative ways to alleviate the economic crisis. To most veterans, like to other Canadian citizens, patriotism and loyalty were not blindly upheld without the expectation of state compensation, and they could be used to make powerful claims of entitlement to economic security. As Lieutenant W.J. Osborne Dempster pointed out in a letter to Premier Henry in October 1931, 'I am no extremist or radical but conditions as they exist in Toronto today are very similar to those that existed in Petrograd in October 1917 making the bolshevik revolution possible ... starvation breeds revolution ... [w]ould you Mr Premier in the case of an emergency which may come expect us, who bore the brunt in 1914 to 1918 and are now paying two fold for our loyalty today, to again man the breach?.'[189]

Patriotism, loyalty, and Britishness could therefore be a way, though a narrow and limited one, to claim respectability and full citizenship – and to demand changes in the social and economic structure. Veterans' link to the Canadian nation, rooted in the traditions of the Empire, was not simply a conservative means of preserving the status quo. Mixed with anti-immigrant sentiments were demands for improving the economic conditions of loyal Canadian citizens, particularly the patriotic citizen-soldiers who had fought for their country and the Empire. Veterans were quick to denounce 'Bolshevism,' but they also condemned government inaction on unemployment, supported unemployment insurance, and fought for subsidized health care. Veterans embraced 'British justice' and life under the 'old old flag – the Union Jack,' but this Britishness was tied to the right to economic and social security.[190]

Popular protest during the Great Depression was rich, visual, and varied. Unemployed unions led relief strikes, parades, and rallies, and unemployed men and women demanded government action to create jobs, increase relief, and develop government-sponsored social welfare. Framing these was the discourse of rights, entitlement, and citizenship. The relationship between citizen and state was understood as one of mutual obligation; in return for fulfilling the duties of citizenship, citizens argued that the state owed its citizens more than paltry, humiliating, and intrusive relief. Rather, it owed its citizens the opportunity to find employment, and when unemployment was 'no fault of their own,' adequate social welfare. In effect, the state's obligation was to nurture and protect its citizens when they could no longer do so themselves.

These demands were shaped by the language of gender, class, and ethnicity. The values of duty, obligation, and citizenship were understood and enacted through the identities of husbands and fathers, wives and mothers, workers, and citizens. Unemployed men and women were both concerned about the ability of men to support a family, and they made demands for government intervention revolving around the right of men to a living wage. These demands were also expressed in terms of women's rights and obligations to properly manage family and household. The demands of both organized groups and individuals revolved around the ideology of breadwinning and domesticity.

Ethnicity shaped relief protest in the 1930s. For many Ontario citizens, Anglo-Celtic heritage became a marker of entitlement to state support and to the rights of citizenship. For veterans, in particular, Britishness and loyalty to Empire and nation became a powerful claim for state aid. Conversely, anti-immigrant discourse blamed 'foreigners' for stealing jobs, and this discourse was reflected in popular rhetoric as well as in government policy of deportations and exclusionary relief policies. Thus, anti-immigrant rhetoric and anti-communism were often conflated: Britishness was a way to not only mark oneself as a 'true' Canadian citizen, but also to set oneself apart from, yet simultaneously draw on, radical communist-organized protest that was associated with 'reds' and 'foreigners.'

Entitlement to employment or social welfare was not understood by most Ontario citizens as a universal human right, but as part of a reciprocal relationship between the citizen and the state. Those that properly fulfilled the duties of citizenship and were clothed in the rhetoric of dutiful husbands, wives, and Anglo-Celtic ethnicity could ultimately make the most powerful claims on the state.

Conclusion: Survival, Citizenship and State

Despite the revival of popular and academic literature on the Great Depression that began in the 1970s, historical study of this era has remained fragmented and incomplete. The period from 1929 to 1939, though historically connected to post–First World War political developments such as wartime government and bureaucratic state expansion, and to post–Second World War welfare state development, still remains in the consciousness of its survivors as an era of its own, an era marked by deprivation, uncertainty, and struggle. By drawing together a number of fields, including the history of social welfare policy, women's history, and labour history, *Respectable Citizens* explores the ways in which families in Ontario negotiated the material impact of unemployment, the meaning of citizenship, and the emerging welfare state.

The everyday lives of men, women, and children in Ontario during the 1930s often looked rather bleak, as they faced high unemployment, inadequate relief, and provincial and federal governments that insisted that the Great Depression was only a temporary economic slow-down. But families developed imaginative, creative, and complex survival strategies, many of which remain historically visible. Men, women, and children all found numerous ways to contribute to family survival, though their interests were not always complementary, and expectations of duty, care, and obligation could often lead to conflict. At the centre of the functioning of the home lay the domestic labour of women. Yet the history of women's labour in the Great Depression has often been subsumed behind the iconic image of the unemployed man attempting to find work at all costs. The daily and often backbreaking labour of women in the domestic economy, downplayed in the phrase 'making do,' was in fact central to the functioning of the family unit. In the daily activities of shopping, cooking, budgeting, providing emotional support to unemployed husbands and children, and undertaking formal or informal waged labour, women's work remained a crucial part of family survival in the Depression period. It propped up and supplemented low male wages, inadequate relief, and poorly funded welfare policies such as mothers' allowance.

While the experiences of men have never been invisible in the historical imagination of the 1930s, the specific impact of unemployment and relief on masculine identity and on men's position as fathers and husbands has not been studied to any great extent. The relief system, woefully underfunded and unable to respond to the magnitude of unemployment, was designed to uphold the values of independence and male breadwinning and to ensure that the federal government would not undertake responsibility for unemployment. While some men certainly experienced shame, despair, and frustration, others responded with anger and passion. The gendered rhetoric of the 'right' to male breadwinning was central to agitation for government job creation and social welfare policy and, as such, became a fundamental part of post–Second World War welfare state policy.

Though historians have discussed unemployment in terms of policy development, there remains much to be said on the impact of joblessness on masculinity, family structure, and marital relationships.[1] A social history of unemployment draws not solely on policy, but on historical work on family conflicts over alcohol or domestic violence in other periods, particularly the nineteenth century. Clearly, there is some continuity in the family economy, traditions of children's labour, conflicts surrounding alcohol, and violence and desertion from the nineteenth to the twentieth centuries. Yet massive unemployment, particularly for men and for youth, and a chaotic and humiliating relief system that was accompanied by a court system concerned with regulating family life, created particular problems and challenges in these years, which helped to reimagine the nature of the relationship between citizen and state. Surviving court records, while mired in the language of relief policy and government legislation – and reflecting the views of poor and working-class family life by middle-class experts – do provide an opportunity to understand the ways that women, men, and children negotiated poverty and state intervention. A kind of what Joan Sangster calls 'cheap justice' for the poor, such courts offered clients, generally women, at least an opportunity to argue for financial support, to mediate conflict, or to end violence in the home.[2] Even if resistance to poverty and state power was often not expressed in terms that modern observers might consider progressive, the consistent talking back to those in power, and the repeated requests and demands for various kinds of aid, indicate that Ontario's poor and unemployed were not simply passive observers or victims of economic decline.

Yet the history of the Depression era is not just a social history of domestic labour, masculinity, or even employment: this era is shaped by the gradual development of the welfare state and popular conceptions of citizenship and national identity. Deeply felt values of bread-winning, maternalism, and state obligation helped to shape the degree and nature of government intervention and state-sponsored welfare. The Great Depression was a crucial period in the expansion of the scope of federal responsibility for social welfare and unemployment. Canadian historians have focused on this transition from the perspective of intel-lectual or political history, looking at the role of the churches, women's and reform groups, or the state itself in creating welfare policy. Yet this transformation also emerged from citizens' demands for a living wage, work for men as breadwinners, economic security for women and chil-dren, and the rights of Canadians of 'British' descent and First World War veterans.

The transition to greater government involvement was connected to ideas about citizenship and nation, ideas that were at least partly rooted in popular conceptions of a contractual or reciprocal relationship be-tween citizen and state. As a result, postwar welfare policy had am-biguous and limited results and, as historians have shown, remained tied to hierarchies of gender, class, and race. The idea of 'contract' or reciprocity was framed by narrow understandings of service and duty. Calls for wider state responsibility for welfare and employment were rarely universal, though they did challenge narrower notions of state responsibility. Liberal understandings of citizenship and male economic independence framed many of the popular concepts of welfare state formation. Canadian historians have convincingly argued that broader social welfare reform was born in the 'cradle' of the veterans' demands after the First World War.[3] Yet veterans' claims on the state were, to a certain extent, set apart from those of 'civilians' and based on an entitle-ment rooted in loyalty to Empire, nation, and gendered duties of cour-age and duty. 'Britishness,' though a vague and fluid concept, was used by veterans and Anglo-Celtic citizens to demand greater rights to eco-nomic security. This does not mean that those not of British descent were passive in the Depression years. Their voices in court records, for example, reveal an active and dynamic engagement with the state. Yet those who had the strongest claims to citizenship and to a place in the social fabric of the nation were those who could claim some kind of connection, no matter how tenuous, to a British background.

Similarly, hierarchical gender roles based on the roles of male bread-winner and female homemaker were rarely challenged in popular dis-course, state policy, or in radical left politics. Maternalist duties and the breadwinner ethos were celebrated and upheld throughout the Great Depression, and women working in the paid labour force were criti-cized at best and fired and attacked at worst. These ideals were encoded in welfare state policy and helped to ensure that the most generous postwar welfare benefits, such as unemployment insurance, were struc-tured around the patterns of male employment.

Such considerations of the limitation of the welfare state must not downplay the extent of this state transformation in the postwar years or the agency of unemployed workers, especially since the poor, the un-employed, and the disenfranchised played crucial roles in that trans-formation. Expanding welfare policies, though limited, did indeed lead to the possibility of claiming greater rights to entitlement rather than acquiescence to charity.[4] The ability to make these claims emerged from the activism of men and women in the Great Depression, as they en-gaged in an explicitly political process in a deliberate attempt to im-prove their material welfare.

Historians must be careful not to overstate the claim that women were made 'invisible' by the emerging welfare state and its emphasis on the male breadwinner role. Certainly, the increased emphasis on the formal, paid labour of men in welfare policy was an important trend that does partly answer the question of why gender relationships were not made more egalitarian by the economic crisis and why the postwar era saw such a concerted revival of domesticity. Women were indeed marginalized, but not completely so. Domestic concerns, as evidenced by men's connection to their roles as fathers and husbands, and their understanding of the importance of domestic labour to relief politics and family survival, were embedded in demands for greater social and economic entitlement. While the male breadwinner role did survive the Great Depression and was bolstered in the postwar economy, women were not made completely invisible for a number of reasons.

First, despite a moral panic that married women working would cause social and gender disorder, women continued to enter the labour force in ever-increasing numbers in the postwar period.[5] Second, family

allowance legislation offered a degree of recognition for women's traditional maternal and domestic work. Though not overly generous, the
allowance was a universal program and not needs-based, targeted at
and paid to mothers, and for some families, it provided a degree of
economic flexibility.[6] Finally, the very existence of the demand for full
employment and expanded welfare only achieved such political popularity because it was predicated on the necessity of men's breadwinning status. Thus, while masculinity itself was threatened by high
unemployment, it was men's status as actual or potential breadwinners, and their position as husbands and fathers, that caused concern
over the erosion of social and gender norms, and ultimately, of social
disorder. Demands based on the need to adequately support a family
were central to unemployed men's and women's criticism and activism
in the Great Depression, and these demands won some sympathy, and
occasionally, as the actions of unemployed unions demonstrated, some
basic concessions. Without the entwined nature of maternalism and
fatherly domesticity, the demands for government intervention in economic and social welfare would neither have been so powerful nor
so popular.

Notes

Introduction

1 Hazel Jameson, *$10 And A Dream* (Winlaw, BC: Polestar, 1988), 158; interview, Mary Cleeson (note: name has been changed on request).

2 Glen H. Elder Jr, *Children of the Great Depression: Social Change in Life Experience* (Chicago: University of Chicago Press, 1974), 4. Elder notes that memory is like an 'anaesthetic' that tends to downplay the hard times. On this theme of the 'value' of Depression hardship, see Michiel Horn, 'The Great Depression: Past and Present,' in Michiel Horn, ed., *The Depression in Canada: Responses to Economic Crisis* (Toronto: Copp Clark Pitman, 1988): 274–89; various reminiscences in Michiel Horn, ed., *The Dirty Thirties: Canadians in the Great Depression* (Toronto: Copp Clark, 1972): 696–7; Robert Collins, *You Had to Be There: An Intimate Portrait of the Generation that Survived the Depression, Won the War, and Re-Invented Canada* (Toronto: McClelland and Stewart, 1997).

3 See Bryan Palmer, *Working-Class Experience: Rethinking the History of Canadian Labour, 1800–1991* (Toronto: McClelland and Stewart, 1992) for a history of depressions and recessions in the economy.

4 James Struthers, *No Fault of Their Own: Unemployment and the Canadian Welfare State, 1914–1941* (Toronto: University of Toronto Press), 83; Michiel Horn, *The Great Depression of the 1930s in Canada* (Ottawa: Canadian Historical Association Booklet no. 39, 1984), 10.

5 Horn, *'Great Depression,* 4–9.

6 Don Spanner, '"The Straight Furrow": The Life of George S. Henry, Ontario's Unknown Premier' (Doctoral dissertation, University of Western Ontario, 1994), 239.

7 James Struthers, *The Limits of Affluence: Welfare in Ontario, 1920–1970* (Toronto: University of Toronto Press, 1994), 3.

8 Communities such as Sault Ste Marie and Sudbury, e.g., had high unemployment rates, as did Windsor, Fort William, Port Arthur, Oshawa, and East York. Spanner, 'Straight Furrow,' 177–95; Harry Cassidy, *Unemployment and Relief in Ontario, 1929–1932* (Toronto: Dent, 1932), 34. In 1938, 12.5% of the population in East York was on direct relief, compared with 1.3% in Teck Township (Kirkland Lake) and 1.1% in Timmins. Archives of Ontario (AO), RG 29–135, Ontario Department of Public Welfare (DPW), General Welfare Assistance Branch Statistics, 1931–62, Box 2, file 9.

9 Struthers, *No Fault of Their Own*.

10 *Less eligibility* refers to the policy of keeping relief rates lower than the wages of the lowest paid labourers in order to preserve the work ethic. This policy was central to the British Poor Law and to Canadian unemployment policy. See, e.g., Struthers, ibid., 6–7.

11 John Taylor, 'Relief from Relief,' in Horn, *Great Depression*, 251; Struthers, *No Fault of Their Own*, 153–5. See also Mary Mackinnon, 'Relief Not Insurance: Canadian Unemployment Relief in the 1930s,' *Explorations in Economic History* 27/1 (1990): 46–83. Mackinnon argues that in London labourers formerly employed in the building trades were overrepresented on relief rolls. Cassidy's survey documents that unskilled and semi-skilled workers dominated the relief rolls, forming 75.9% of the numbers on relief in East York and 83.9% in St Catharines. Cassidy, *Unemployment and Relief*, 49–50. Trade unions reported that unemployment in the construction industry rose from 2.9% in 1928 to 65.8% in 1933. National Employment Commission, *Final Report* (1938), 32.

12 Cassidy, *Unemployment and Relief*, 41, 48.

13 Struthers, *No Fault of Their Own*, 74.

14 Horn, 'Great Depression,' 275–83, 273.

15 Cassidy, *Unemployment and Relief*, 83–5.

16 Struthers, *No Fault*, 68–9; Margaret Hobbs, 'Gendering Work and Welfare: Women's Relationship to Wage-Work and Social Policy in Canada during the Great Depression' (Doctoral dissertation, University of Toronto, 1994), 92; Lorne Brown, *When Freedom Was Lost: The Unemployed, the Agitator and the State* (Montreal and Buffalo: Black Rose, 1987).

17 H. Blair Neatby argues that the Great Depression also led to a crisis of faith in traditional political and economic institutions. See his *The Politics of Chaos: Canada in the Thirties* (Toronto: Gage, 1972).

18 See Hobbs, 'Gendering Work and Welfare,' 4. Hobbs discusses the image
of the 'Martyr mother.' See also Lois Rita Helmbold, 'Beyond the Family
Economy: Black and White Working-Class Women during the Great
Depression,' *Feminist Studies* 13/3 (1987), 629–48.

19 This study has incorporated several different types of Ontario court records
(RG 22), which are held at the Archives of Ontario. The court records used
were all covered, with the exception of the Farmers' Creditors Arrangement
Act Files, by the terms of the Freeedom of Information Act. This includes
Family Welfare Court records from the domestic relations courts, case files
under the Children of Unmarried Parents Act (CUPA), and prosecution
case files and records of indictments. In accordance with the legal terms of
the FOI Act, I have agreed to remove all personal characteristics that could
identify the individuals in question. I have also agreed to remove all
original file numbers from the case files. I have changed the names, but
have substituted names that reflect the ethnic heritage of the people in the
files. I have also retained the names of public officials that appear in the
records. Surviving case files from the 1930s in the domestic relations courts
exist for York County (Toronto) and Carleton County (Ottawa). The York
County records are substantive (fifty-eight boxes) and have no file index
for names, type of case, or date. I sampled two boxes per year for the years
1929–1939 for a total of sixty-eight boxes; in each box, I examined every
tenth file. I also kept note of the case files that involved all non–Anglo-Celtic
names in order to keep track of the documentation of ethnic diversity in
these sources. The collection of records from Carleton County are arranged
alphabetically for the years 1922–63; I examined all sixty-three boxes and
pulled every file from the 1930s.

   Prosecution case files from the 1930s have survived from the following
Ontario counties: Leeds and Grenville, Wentworth, Wellington, Prescott
and Russell, Essex, Middlesex, Simcoe, Algoma, Kent, and Ontario. These
contain files pertaining to all criminal matters, ranging from relief fraud
to rape, and in areas without specialized domestic relations courts, they
contain records of family welfare cases such as non-support and desertion.
I looked at all files from the 1930s in each of the above-mentioned counties.

   CUPA case files are archived separately. Examples of these cases have
survived in Hastings County (Belleville) and York County; all files from
the 1930s were examined. Finally, a small selection of Mothers' Allowance
case files (RG 29-35) are preserved in the Ontario Archives. Like court
records, these files are also restricted under FOI terms, and all names and
original file numbers have been changed.

20 Interviews were done, in 1997, with the following people: Ruth Aho, Borden Blood, Gladys Clements, Mary Cleeson (pseudonym), Earl Craig, Basil Libby, Myrtle McGeragle, Hilda O'Brien, Dorothy Osmars; and in 2001 with Agnes Campbell.

21 Veronica Strong-Boag, *A New Day Recalled: Lives of Girls and Women in English Canada, 1919–1939* (Toronto: Penguin, 1988); Nancy Christie and Michael Gauvreau, *A Full-Orbed Christianity: The Protestant Churches and Social Welfare in Canada, 1900–1940* (Montreal and Kingston: McGill-Queen's University Press, 1996); Nancy Christie, *Engendering the Welfare State: Family, Work and Welfare in Canada* (Toronto: University of Toronto Press, 2000); Cynthia R. Comacchio, *Nations Are Built of Babies: Saving Ontario's Mothers and Children, 1900–1940* (Montreal and Kingston: McGill-Queen's University Press, 1992); Katherine Arnup, 'Educating Mothers: Government Advice for Women in the Inter-War Years,' in Katherine Arnup, Andree Levesque, and Ruth Roach Pierson, eds., *Delivering Motherhood: Maternal Ideologies and Practices in the Nineteenth and Twentieth Centuries* (London and New York: Routledge, 1990), 190–210; Palmer, *Working-Class Experience*; Desmond Morton, *Working People: An Illustrated History of the Canadian Labour Movement* (Toronto: Summerhill, 1990); Joan Sangster, *Dreams of Equality: Women on the Canadian Left, 1920–1950* (Toronto: McClelland and Stewart, 1989); Joan Sangster, *Earning Respect: The Lives of Working Women in Small-Town Ontario, 1920–1960* (Toronto: University of Toronto Press, 1995); Joy Parr, *The Gender of Breadwinners: Women, Men, and Change in Two Industrial Towns, 1880–1950* (Toronto: University of Toronto Press, 1990); Donald Avery, *'Dangerous Foreigners': European Immigrant Workers and Labour Radicalism in Canada, 1896–1932* (Toronto: McClelland and Stewart, 1979); Ruth Frager, *Sweatshop Strife: Class, Ethnicity, and Gender in the Jewish Labour Movement of Toronto, 1900–1939* (Toronto: University of Toronto Press, 1992).

22 Hobbs, 'Gendering Work and Welfare,' 1. See, e.g., Barry Broadfoot, *Ten Lost Years, 1929–1939: Memories of Canadians Who Survived the Depression* (Toronto: Doubleday, 1973); James Gray, *The Winter Years: The Depression on the Prairies* (Toronto: Macmillan, 1966); Ronald Liversedge, *Recollection of the On-to-Ottawa Trek* (Toronto: McClelland and Stewart, 1973); Michael Bliss and L.M. Grayson, eds., *The Wretched of Canada: Letters to R.B. Bennett, 1930–35* (Toronto: University of Toronto Press, 1971); Victor Hoar, ed., *The Great Depression: Essays and Memoirs from Canada and the United States* (Toronto: Copp Clark, 1969). One popular account that appeared much later is Pierre Berton, *The Great Depression, 1929–1939* (Toronto: Penguin, 1990).

23 For monographs or articles specifically on the Great Depression, see Horn, *Dirty Thirties* and *Depression in Canada*; A.E. Safarian, *The Canadian Economy in the Great Depression* (Toronto: University of Toronto Press, 1959); Neatby, *Politics of Chaos*; J.R.H. Wilbur, *The Bennett New Deal: Fraud or Portent?* (Toronto: Copp Clark, 1968); J.R.H. Wilbur, *H.H. Stevens* (Toronto: University of Toronto Press, 1977); Donald Forster and Colin Read, 'The Politics of Opportunism: The New Deal Broadcasts,' *Canadian Historical Review* (hereafter *CHR*) 60/3 (1979): 324–49; Neil McGenty, 'Mitchell F. Hepburn and the Ontario Election of 1934,' *CHR* 45/4 (1964): 293–313. For work with substantial sections on the Depression, see Robert M. Campbell, *Grand Illusions: The Politics of the Keynesian Experience in Canada, 1945–75* (Peterborough: Broadview, 1987); Alvin Finkel, *The Social Credit Phenomenon in Alberta* (Toronto: University of Toronto Press, 1989); John Herd Thompson and Allen Seager, *Canada, 1922–1939: Decades of Discord* (Toronto: McClelland and Stewart, 1985); Martin Robin, *Shades of Right: Nativist and Fascist Politics in Canada, 1920–1940* (Toronto: University of Toronto Press, 1991); Larry Glassford, *Reaction and Reform: The Politics of the Conservative Party under R.B. Bennett, 1927–38* (Toronto: University of Toronto Press, 1992), Kenneth McNaught, *A Prophet in Politics* (Toronto: University of Toronto Press, 1959); Allen Mills, *Fool for Christ: The Political Thought of J.S. Woodsworth* (Toronto: University of Toronto Press, 1991); H. Blair Neatby, *William Lyon Mackenzie King*, vols.1 and 2 (Toronto: University of Toronto Press, 1959); John Saywell, *'Just Call Me Mitch': The Life of Mitchell F. Hepburn* (Toronto: University of Toronto Press, 1991); Spanner, 'Straight Furrow'; William Beeching and Phylis Clarke, *Yours in the Struggle: Reminiscences of Tim Buck* (Toronto: NC Press, 1977); Terry Crowley, *Agnes MacPhail and the Politics of Equality* (Toronto: Lorimer, 1990); Lita-Rose Betcherman, *The Little Band: The Clashes between the Communists and the Political and Legal Establishment in Canada, 1928–32* (Ottawa: Deneau, 1980); Michiel Horn, *The League for Social Reconstruction: Intellectual Origins of the Democratic Left in Canada, 1930–1942* (Toronto: University of Toronto Press, 1980).

24 Brown, *When Freedom Was Lost*; Liversedge, *Recollections of the On-to-Ottawa Trek*; Patricia Schulz, *The East York Workers' Association: A Response to the Great Depression* (Toronto: New Hogtown Press, 1975); John Manley, '"Starve, Be Damned!" Communists and Canada's Urban Unemployed, 1929–1939,' *CHR* 79/3 (1998): 466–91; John Manley, 'Communism and the Canadian Working Class during the Great Depression: The Workers' Unity League, 1930–36' (Doctoral dissertation, Dalhousie University, 1984); Taylor, 'Relief from Relief'; Irene Howard, 'The Mothers' Council of

Vancouver: Holding the Fort for the Unemployed, 1935–38,' *BC Studies* nos. 69–70 (1988): 249–87; Peter Archibald, 'Distress, Dissent and Aliena-tion: Hamilton Workers in the Great Depression,' *Urban History Review* 21/1 (1992): 2–32; Marcus Klee, 'Between the Scylla and Charybdis of Anarchy and Despotism: The State, Capital and Working Class in the Great Depression, Toronto, 1929–40' (Doctoral dissertation, Queen's University, 1998). Outside of Ontario, see the variety of articles on the labour situation and unionization, such as Allen Seager, 'Class, Ethnicity and Politics in the Alberta Coalfields, 1905–1945,' in *'Struggle a Hard Battle': Essays on Working-Class Immigrants* (DeKalb: Northern Illinois University Press, 1986), 304–24; J.H. Thompson and Allen Seager, 'Work-ers, Growers and Monopolists: The Labour Problem in the Alberta Beet Sugar Industry during the 1930s,' in Horn, *Depression*, 30–50; Evelyn Dumas, *The Bitter Thirties in Quebec* (Montreal: Black Rose, 1975). Sections of Frager's *Sweatshop Strife* and Sangster's *Dreams of Equality* are con-cerned with labour organization and gender in the Great Depression.

25 Denyse Baillargeon, *Making Do: Women, Family and Home in Montreal during the Great Depression*, trans. by Yvonne Klein (Waterloo: Wilfrid Laurier University Press, 1999). There are several important articles and a doctoral dissertation by Margaret Hobbs on campaigns against working women, as well as scattered work on the domestic economy and the household. See Hobbs: 'Gendering Work and Welfare'; 'Equality and Difference: Feminism and the Defence of Women Workers During the Great Depression,' *Labour / Le Travail* (hereafter *L/LT*) no. 32 (1993): 201–23; 'Rethinking Antifeminism in the 1930s: Gender Crisis or Workplace Justice? A Response to Alice Kessler-Harris,' *Gender and History* 5/1 (1993): 4–15; see also Margaret Hobbs and Ruth Roach Pierson, '"A Kitchen That Wastes No Steps": Gender, Class and the Home Improvement Plan, 1936–40,' *Histoire Sociale / Social History* (hereafter *HS/SH*) 21/41 (1988): 9–37; Laura Hollingsworth and Vappu Tyyska, 'The Hidden Producers: Women's Household Production during the Great Depression,' *Critical Sociology* 15/3 (1988): 3–27; sections of Sangster's *Earning Respect*; Mary Patricia Powell, 'A Response to the Depression: The Local Council of Women of Vancouver,' in Horn, *Depression in Canada*, 12–29. On masculin-ity, see Mark Rosenfeld, '"It Was a Hard Life": Class and Gender in the Work and Family Rhythms of a Railway Town,' in Bettina Bradbury, ed., *Canadian Family History: Selected Readings* (Toronto: Copp Clark Pitman, 1992), 241–80; sections of Parr, *Gender of Breadwinners*; sections of Cynthia Commachio, 'A Postscript for Father: Defining a New Fatherhood in Interwar Canada,' *CHR* 78/3 (1997): 305–408.

26 Alvin Finkel's *Business and Social Reform in the Thirties* (Toronto: Lorimer, 1979) is one of the few books to focus solely on the Great Depression in Canada, though James Struthers' work on unemployment policy is largely concerned with this period. His *No Fault of Their Own*, which argues that the principle of less eligibility was written into unemployment insurance, is a seminal work on unemployment and the development of relief policy. Works on social welfare policy that have sections on the Depression include: Dorothy Chunn, *From Punishment to Doing Good: Family Courts and Socialized Justice in Ontario, 1880–1940* (Toronto: University of Toronto Press, 1992); Margaret Little, *'No Car, No Radio, No Liquor Permit': The Moral Regulation of Single Mothers in Ontario* (Toronto: Oxford University Press, 1998); Christie, *Engendering the State*; Mackinnon, 'Relief not Insurance.' On social work, see James Struthers, '"Lord Give Us Men": Women and Social Work in English Canada, 1918–1953,' in Allen Moscovitch and J. Albert, eds., *The Benevolent State: The Growth of Welfare in Canada* (Toronto: Garamond, 1987), 126–43; James Struthers, 'A Profession in Crisis: Charlotte Whitton and Canadian Social Work in the 1930s,' in Horn, *Depression in Canada*, 229–44.
27 Bliss and Grayson, *Wretched of Canada*; Collins, *You Had to Be There*. See also reminiscences in Michiel Horn and Barry Broadfoot, *Ten Lost Years*. Horn writes, 'If, as we are often told, Canadians tend to be cautious, with a low appetite for risk taking and a high propensity to save, many explanations no doubt exist. Among them, however, the memory the Depression surely occupies a place.' Horn, *Great Depression of the 1930s*, 20.
28 Finkel, *Business and Social Reform*; Allan Moscovitch and Glenn Drover, 'Social Expenditures and the Welfare State: The Canadian Experience in Historical Perspective,' in Moscovitch and Albert, *Benevolent State*, 13–43.
29 On the 'progressive' welfare state, see Dennis Guest, *The Emergence of Social Security in Canada* (Vancouver: University of British Columbia Press, 1985). On the fluidity of public and private involvement in social welfare, see Mariana Valverde, 'The Mixed Social Economy as a Canadian Tradition,' *Studies in Political Economy* 47 (1995): 33–60; Jane Lewis, 'Gender, the Family and Women's Agency in the Building of "Welfare States": The British Case,' *Social History* 19/1 (1994): 37–55.
30 Historians have discussed the influence of government, business, and party politics; the role of intellectuals, religion, and the social sciences; and the desire of the state to preserve the capitalist economic order and avoid social disorder. See Christie and Gauvreau, *A Full-Orbed Christianity*; Doug Owram, *The Government Generation: Canadian Intellectuals and the State* (Toronto: University of Toronto Press, 1986); Struthers, *No Fault of Their*

Own; Finkel, *Business*; Kenneth McNaught, *A Prophet in Politics* (London: Oxford University Press, 1959), Walter Young, *Anatomy of a Party: The National CCF, 1932–6* (Toronto: University of Toronto Press, 1969); Horn, *League for Social Reconstruction*; Leslie Pal, *State, Class and Bureaucracy: Canadian Unemployment Insurance and Public Policy* (Montreal and Kingston: McGill-Queen's University Press, 1988); Rodney Haddow, *Poverty Reform in Canada, 1958–78* (Montreal and Kingston: McGill-Queen's University Press, 1993); Ann Shola Orloff, *The Politics of Pensions: A Comparative Analysis of Britain, Canada and the United States, 1880–1940* (Madison: University of Wisconsin Press, 1993).

31 Jane Ursel, *Private Lives, Public Policy: 100 Years of State Intervention in the Family* (Toronto: Women's Press, 1992). In the American context, see Mimi Abramovitz, *Regulating the Lives of Women: Social Welfare Policy from Colonial Times to the Present* (Boston: South End, 1988).

32 Ruth Roach Pierson, 'Gender and the Unemployment Insurance Debates in Canada,' *L/LT* no. 25 (1990), 95–7. See Barbara Nelson, 'Origins of the Two-Channel Welfare State: Workmen's Compensation and Mothers' Aid,' in Linda Gordon, ed., *Women, the State, and Welfare* (Madison: University of Wisconsin Press, 1990); Margaret Little, *'No Car, No Radio'*; Margaret Little, 'Claiming a Unique Place: The introduction of Mothers' Pensions in British Columbia,' in Veronica Strong-Boag and Anita Clair Fellman, eds., *Rethinking Canada: The Promise of Women's History* (Don Mills: Oxford University Press, 1993), 285–303; James Struthers, '"In the Interests of the Children": Mothers' Allowances and the Origins of Income Security in Ontario, 1917–30,' in *Limits of Affluence*, 19–49. For a Canadian overview, see Patricia Evans, '"Divided Citizenship"? Gender, Income Security and the Welfare State,' in Patricia Evans and Gerda R. Wekerle, eds., *Women and the Canadian Welfare State* (Toronto: University of Toronto Press, 1997), 91–116.

33 Frances Fox Piven, 'Ideology and the State: Women, Power and the Welfare State,' in Gordon, *Women, the State, and Welfare*, 250–64; Evans, 'Divided Citizenship?' 95; Linda Gordon, 'What Does Welfare Regulate?' *Social Research* 55/4 (1988): 609–30; Ann Shola Orloff, 'Gender and the Rights of Social Citizenship: The Comparative Analysis of Gender Relations and Welfare States,' *American Sociological Review* 58 (1993): 305.

34 See Michael Willrich, 'Home Slackers: Men, the State, and Welfare in Modern America,' *Journal of American History* 87/4 (2000): 460–89; Anna R. Igra, 'Likely to Become a Public Charge: Deserted Women and the Family Law of the Poor in New York City, 1910–36,' *Journal of Women's History* (hereafter *JWH*) 11/4 (2000): 59–81; Christie, *Engendering the State*, 107–11, 128–9, 243–44.

35 See Gordon, 'Family Violence, Feminism, and Social Control,' 178–98, and
    Virginia Sapiro, 'The Gender Basis of American Social Policy,' in Gordon,
    Women, the State, and Welfare, 36–54.
36 James Struthers, 'How Much Is Enough?' in *Limits of Affluence*, 77–116;
    Little, *'No Car, No Radio'*; Lynn Taylor, 'Food Riots Revisited,' *Journal of
    Social History* (hereafter *JSH*) 30/2 (1996): 483–96; Howard, 'Mothers'
    Council of Vancouver'; Frager, *Sweatshop Strife*; Sangster, *Dreams of
    Equality*; Dominique Marshall, 'The Language of Children's Rights, the
    Formation of the Welfare State, and the Democratic Experience of Poor
    Families in Quebec, 1940–1955' *CHR* 78/3 (1997): 409–39; Dominique
    Marshall, *The Social Origins of the Welfare State: Quebec Families, Compul-
    sory Education, and Family Allowances, 1940–1955* trans. by Nicola Doone
    Danby (Waterloo: Wilfrid Laurier University Press, 2006); Shirley
    Tillotson, 'Citizen Participation in the Welfare State: An Experiment,
    1945–57,' *CHR* 75/4 (1994): 241–51; Magda Fahrni, *Household Politics:
    Montreal Families and Postwar Reconstruction* (Toronto: University of
    Toronto Press, 2005).
37 Linda Gordon, *Pitied But Not Entitled: Single Mothers and the History of
    Welfare, 1890–1935* (Cambridge: Harvard University Press, 1994), 241–51.
38 Cynthia Comacchio, 'Another Brick in the Wall: Toward a History of the
    Welfare State in Canada,' *left history* 1/1 (1993): 108.
39 Historically, citizenship was conceived of as necessary to being fully
    human. The ancient conception of the *polis* was a public arena, separate
    from women, slaves, and foreigners, and a place where some men could
    engage as social, political, and moral beings. J.G.A. Pocock, 'The Ideal of
    Citizenship since Classical Times,' *Queen's Quarterly* 99/1 (1992): 36–8.
    Note that in the period covered by this book, Canadians were British
    subjects, though many used the language of Canadian citizenship. For a
    detailed examination of the historical concept of citizenship in Canada, see
    Janine Brodie, 'Three Stages of Canadian Citizenship,' and Veronica
    Strong-Boag, '"The Citizenship Debates": The 1885 Franchise Act,' in
    Robert Adamoski et al., eds., *Contesting Canadian Citizenship: Historical
    Readings* (Peterborough: Broadview, 2002): 43–68 and 69–94.
40 T.H. Marshall, *Citizenship and Social Class* (London: Pluto Press, 1992), 8.
41 Nancy Fraser and Linda Gordon, 'Contract versus Charity: Why Is There
    No Social Citizenship in the United States?' *Socialist Review* 22/3 (1992):
    52–6, 58.
42 David Roediger, *The Wages of Whiteness: The Making of the American
    Working Class* (London: Verso, 1991); Adamoski et al., *Contesting Canadian
    Citizenship*.

43 Pocock, 'Ideal of Citizenship,' 36; Fraser and Gordon, 'Contract vs Charity,' 64. For a critique of rights discourse, see Frances Olsen, 'Statutory Rape: A Feminist Critique of Rights Analysis,' *Texas Law Review* 63 (1984); Catharine MacKinnon, 'Feminism, Marxism, Method and the State: Toward Feminist Jurisprudence,' *Signs* 8 (1983): 635–58.

44 Elizabeth Schneider, 'The Dialectic of Rights and Politics: Perspectives from the Women's Movement,' in Gordon, *Women, the State, and Welfare*, 226–49; Gordon, *Pitied But Not Entitled*.

45 Marhsall, *Citizenship and Social Class*, 8.

46 Linda Gordon, *Heroes of Their Own Lives: The Politics and History of Family Violence, 1880–1960* (New York: Penguin, 1988); Gordon, *Pitied But Not Entitled*.

47 Some historians have argued that maternalism as a concept should be reserved for those middle-class women who politicized the role of government to carve out a space for themselves in the public sphere, a role that was based in part on regulating the lives of marginalized women. For this approach, see Sonya Michel, 'Introduction,' *Social Politics* 7/1 (2000): 1; Seth Koven and Sonya Michel, *Mothers of a New World: Maternalist Politics and the Origins of the Welfare State* (New York: 1993), 6.

48 Sangster, *Dreams of Equality*; Howard, 'Holding the Fort'; Annelise Orleck, 'We Are that Militant Thing Called the Public'; Frager, *Sweatshop Strife*; Gillian Creese, 'The Politics of Dependence: Women, Work and Unemployment in the Vancouver Labour Movement before World War II,' *Canadian Journal of Sociology* 12/1–2 (1988): 121–4; Elizabeth Faue, *Community of Suffering and Struggle: Women, Men and the Labor Movement in Minneapolis, 1915–45* (Chapel Hill: University of North Carolina Press, 1991).

49 See Avery, *Dangerous Foreigners*; Beeching and Clark, *Yours in the Struggle*; Gregory S. Kealey and Reg Whitaker, eds., *R.C.M.P. Security Bulletins: The Depression Years* (St John's: Canadian Committee on Labour History, 1997); Dumas, *Bitter Thirties in Quebec*.

50 See Pauline Greenhill, *Ethnicity in the Mainstream: Three Studies of English Canadian Culture in Ontario* (Montreal, Kingston, and London: McGill-Queen's University Press, 1993); Howard Palmer, 'Reluctant Hosts: Anglo-Canadian Views of Multiculturalism in the Twentieth-Century,' in R. Douglas Francis and Donald B. Smith, eds., *Readings in Canadian History: Post-Confederation*, 2nd ed. (Toronto: Holt, 1986), 185–201; Katie Pickles, *Female Imperialism and National Identity: Imperial Order Daughters of the Empire* (Manchester and New York: Manchester University Press, 2002).

51 Numerous historians have looked at the interplay between elite culture, national identity, and broadcasting policy, both in the interwar years and

in the postwar era. See Carl Berger, *The Writing of Canadian History: Aspects of English Canadian Historical Writing since 1900* (Toronto: University of Toronto Press, 1986); Neatby, *Politics of Chaos*, 17–19. Mary Vipond explores this theme in the English-Canadian intellectual elite. See her 'Nationalism and Nativism: The Native Sons of Canada in the 1930s,' *Canadian Review of Studies in Nationalism* 9/1 (1982): 81–95, and 'The Nationalist Network: English Canada's Intellectuals and Artists in the 1920s,' ibid., 7/1 (1980): 32–52. See also Marc Raboy, *Missed Opportunities: The Story of Canada's Broadcasting Policy* (Montreal and Kingston: McGill-Queen's University Press, 1990); Mary Vipond, *Listening In: The First Decade of Canadian Broadcasting* (Montreal: McGill-Queen's University Press, 1992); Richard Collins, *Culture, Communication and National Identity: The Case of Canadian Television* (Toronto: University of Toronto Press, 1990).

52 Special issue, *Gender and History* 5/2 (1993); Cecilia Morgan, 'History, Nation and Empire: Gender and Southern Ontario Historical Societies, 1890–1920s,' *CHR* 82/3 (2001): 491–528.

53 Benedict Anderson, *Imagined Communities: Reflections on the Origins and Spread of Nationalism* (London: Verso, 1983); Carl Berger, *The Sense of Power: Studies in the Ideas of Canadian Imperialism* (Toronto: University of Toronto Press, 1970).

54 In 1931 Ontario's population numbered 3,431,683. Of these, 74% were of British background (English, Irish, Scottish, other), and 25% were of European background. In the European category, 36% were of French background. *Conspectus of the Province of Ontario* (Toronto: King's Printer, 1947), 210, Table 9.

55 Barbara Roberts, *Whence They Came: Deportation from Canada, 1900–35* (Ottawa: University of Ottawa Press, 1988).

56 Catherine Hall has pointed out that in English history Britishness signalled order and civilization in the conflict between missionaries and blacks; for missionary women, the work was based on bringing whiteness, and therefore 'order, civilizations and Christianity' to the colonies, and it was a newly developed sphere for women, though one based on restricted, middle-class conceptions of both race and gender. Hall, *White, Male and Middle-Class: Explorations in Feminism and History* (New York: Routledge, 1992). Antoinette Burton has also shown how English feminists used the discourses of imperialism to claim 'political citizenship,' in *Burdens of History: British Feminists, Indian Women, and Imperial Culture, 1865–1915* (Chapel Hill: University of North Carolina Press, 1994).

57 This discussion has been enriched by work within whiteness studies. See, e.g., Noel Ignatiev and John Garvey, *Race Traitor* (New York: Routledge, 1996); Richard Dyer, *White* (London: Routledge, 1997); George Lipsitz, *The Possessive Investment in Whiteness: How White People Profit from Identity Politics* (Philadelphia: Temple University Press, 2006); David Roediger, *Towards the Abolition of Whiteness: Essays on Race, Politics and Working-Class History* (London: Verso, 1994); David Roediger, *Colored White: Transcending the Racial Past* (Berkeley: University of California Press, 2002).

58 Franca Iacovetta and Wendy Mitchinson, eds., *On the Case: Explorations in Social History* (Toronto: University of Toronto Press, 1998); CHR Forum, '"On the Case: Explorations in Social History": A Roundtable Discussion,' *CHR* 81/2 (2000): 266–92.

59 Chunn; *From Punishment to Doing Good*; Mariana Valverde, *The Age of Light, Soap and Water: Moral Reform in English Canada, 1885–1925* (Toronto: McClelland and Stewart, 1991); Wendy Mitchinson, 'The Women's Christian Temperance Union: "For God, Home and Native Land" – A Study in Nineteenth-Century Feminism,' in Linda Kealey, ed., *A Not Unreasonable Claim: Women and Reform in Canada, 1880s–1920s* (Toronto: Women's Press, 1979): 151–67.

60 Chunn, *From Punishment*, 49.

61 Ibid., Appendix C, 200-1. The relevant parts of the Criminal Code were sections 238 and 242; ibid., 52, 55. In 1910, e.g., Toronto and Ottawa developed separate juvenile courts that were staffed by volunteers and members from the CAS.

62 Chunn, *From Punishment*, 62–3.

63 Ibid., 20-1.

64 On oral history and memory, see Alessandro Portelli, *The Battle of Valle Guila: Oral History and the Art of Dialogue* (Madison: University of Wisconsin Press, 1997); Michael Fritsch, *A Shared Authority: Essays on the Craft and Meaning of Oral and Public History* (Albany: State University of New York Press, 1990); Selma Leyedesorff et al., eds. *Gender and Memory* (Toronto: Oxford University Press, 1996).

65 See Anthony Platt, *Child-Saver: The Invention of Delinquency* (Chicago: University of Chicago Press, 1969). For an analysis that views such welfare legislation as direct patriarchal repression, see Ursel, *Private Lives, Public Policy*.

66 Sangster, *Regulating Girls and Women*, 8. See Michel Foucault, 'Truth and Power,' reprinted in *The Chomsky-Foucault Debate on Human Nature* (New York and London: New Press, 2006): 140–71.

67 See Chunn, *From Punishment*; Jaques Donzelot, *The Policing of Families* (New York: Pantheon, 1979).

68 Klee, 'Between the Scylla and Charybdis,' 80. Klee notes that in the family court case files for Toronto there was a 'slightly disproportionate' number of non-Canadian-born people in the files, mainly those born in Great Britain or other European nations. In Carleton County the 1931 census indicates that 64% of the population was of British background, while 28% was of French heritage. Dominion Bureau of Statistics, *Census of Canada, 1931*, vol. 7, *Population by Areas*, 309, Table 6. After sampling files from nine boxes in this record group, the numbers indicated that French-Canadian families were overrepresented by 11.2% in family court case files. On the demography of urban francophones in the Ottawa area, see Fernand Ouellet, 'L'évolution de la présence francophone en Ontario: une perspective économique et sociale,' in Cornelius J. Jaenen, ed., *Les Franco-Ontariens* (Ottawa: Les Presses de l'Université d'Ottawa, 1933), 162–5. In the case of the Female Refuges Act in Ontario, most young women were of Anglo-Celtic background. Sangster, *Regulating Girls*, 123.

69 See Mariana Valverde, 'On the Case: A Roundtable Discussion,' *CHR* 81 (2000): 267.

70 Sangster, *Regulating Girls*, 10.

71 Jane Humphries, 'The Working Class Family, Women's Liberation, and Class Struggle: The Case of Nineteenth-Century British History,' *Review of Radical Political Economics* 9/3 (1997): 25–40; Steven Penfold, '"Have You No Manhood in You?" Gender and Class in the Cape Breton Coal Towns, 1920–26,' in Marc Rosenfeld and Joy Parr, *Gender and History in Canada*, 270–94. For the ways in which women made domestic concerns central to protest, see Temma Kaplan, *Crazy for Democracy: Women in Grassroots Movements* (New York and London: Routledge, 1997); Elizabeth Janeway, *Powers of the Weak* (New York: Knopf, 1980).

72 Marshall, *Social Origins of the Welfare State*; Michel Foucault, 'Omnes et Singulatim: Toward a Critique of Political Reason,' in *Chomsky-Foucault Debate*, 172–213. For an early interpretation of women's power from the ground up, see Janeway, *Powers of the Weak*.

73 Orloff, *Politics of Pensions*, 10–11; Michael Gardiner, *Critiques of Everyday Life* (New York: Routledge, 2000), 2–20.

74 Anna Davin, 'Imperialism and Motherhood,' *History Workshop* no. 5 (1978): 9–66; Koven and Michel, 'Introduction,' *Mothers of a New World*, 2, and chapters in that book, particularly Marilyn Lake, 'A Revolution in the Family: The Challenge and Contradictions of Maternal Citizenship in Australia,' 378–95. Comacchio, *Nations Are Built of Babies*; Arnup,

'Educating Mothers'; Valverde, *Age of Light, Soap and Water*. There is a
sizeable literature on colonialism and intimacy. For just a few examples,
see Jean Barman, 'Taming Aboriginal Sexuality: Gender, Power, and Race in
British Columbia, 1850–1900,' *BC Studies* nos. 115–16 (1997): 237-66; Anne
McClintock et al., eds., *Dangerous Liaisons: Gender, Nation and Postcolonial
Perspectives* (Minneapolis: University of Minnesota Press, 1997).

75   Comacchio, 'Another Brick in the Wall,' 105.
76   See Gerald Markowitz and David Roediger, eds., *'Slaves of the Depression':
Workers' Letters about Life on the Job* (Ithaca and London: Cornell University
Press, 1987); E.P. Thompson, 'The Crime of Anonymity,' in Douglas Hay,
ed., *Albion's Fatal Tree: Crime and Society in Eighteenth-Century England*
(London: Lane, 1975).

1 'Giving All the Good in Me to Save My Children'

1   Laurel Cornell, 'Where Can Family Strategies Exist?' *Historical Methods*
20/3 (1987): 120.
2   Louise Tilly, 'Beyond Family Strategies, What?' ibid., 118.
3   Ibid., 118, 124.
4   See Bettina Bradbury, 'Gender at Work at Home: Family Decisions, the
Labour Market, and Girls' Contributions to the Family Economy,' in
Readings in Canadian History, 187–206; Nancy Christie, 'By Necessity or by
Right: The Language and Experience of Gender at Work,' *L/LT* no. 50
(2002): 117–48.
5   For a classic outline of the concept of separate spheres, see Nancy Cott,
The Bonds of Womanhood: 'Woman's Sphere' in New England, 1780–1835 (New
Haven: Yale University Press, 1997); Barbara Welter, 'The Cult of True
Womanhood,' *American Quarterly* 18 (1966): 151–74.
6   Sangster, *Earning Respect*, 127. Sangster argues that women's domestic
labour greatly increased in the Depression.
7   Strong-Boag, *New Day Recalled*, 125; Sybille Meyer, 'The Tiresome Work of
Conspicuous Leisure: On the Domestic Duties of the Wives of Civil
Servants in the German Empire,' in Marilyn Boxer and Jean Quataert, eds.,
Connecting Spheres: Women in the Western World, 1500 to the Present (New
York: Oxford University Press, 1987), 156–65.
8   Hollingsworth and Tyyska, 'Hidden Producers,' 6. The authors argue that
25% of Canadian households as late as 1971 could not support a family on
male wages alone.
9   Baillargeon, *Making Do*, 8.

10 Ellen Ross argues that in turn-of-the-century London, mothers' work was not just central to female identity but to the mother-child relationship. Children 'owed' their mothers both money and respect for the labour they did on their behalf. See Ellen Ross, *Love and Toil: Motherhood in Outcast London, 1870–1918* (New York: Oxford University Press, 1993), 8. See also Cynthia Comacchio, *The Dominion of Youth: Adolescence and the Making of Modern Canada, 1920–1950* (Waterloo: Wilfrid Laurier University Press, 2006).

11 Interview, Mary Cleeson.

12 Magne Stortroen, *An Immigrant's Journal* (Cobalt: Highway Bookshop, 1982), 61, 78.

13 Charlie Angus and Brit Griffin, *'We Lived a Life and Then Some': The Life, Death, and Life of a Mining Town* (Toronto: Between the Lines, 1996), 64. See also Lloyd Dennis, *Marching Orders: A Memoir, Growing Up in Rural Ontario during the Depression* (Toronto: Umbrella Press, 1997), 114.

14 Interviews: Dorothy Osmars, Borden Blood.

15 Neil Sutherland, *Growing Up: Childhood in English Canada from the Great War to the Age of Television* (Toronto: University of Toronto Press, 1997), 51–2. See also Ross, *Love and Toil*, for a similar theme in memoirs of children born in nineteenth-century London.

16 Susan Porter Benson, 'Living on the Margin: Working-Class Marriages and Family Survival Strategies in the United States, 1919–1941,' in Victoria de Grazia and Ellen Furlough, eds., *The Sex of Things: Gender and Consumption in Historical Perspective* (Berkeley: University of California Press, 1996), 212–43; See also Goodwin et al., *Passionate Politics*, 14; Baillargeon, *Making Do*, 9; Ross, *Love and Toil*, 6–9.

17 *Farmer's Advocate*, 28 Jan. 1937.

18 *Northern News*, 19 May 1932. See also *Chatelaine* for numerous articles in this vein.

19 Luxton, *More Than a Labour of Love*, 46. For a similar perspective on farm women in Saskatchewan in the Depression, see Cristina G. Bye, '"I Would Like to Hoe My Own Row": A Saskatchewan Farm Women's Notion about Work and Womanhood during the Great Depression,' *Frontiers* 26/3 (2005): 135–6.

20 Baillargeon, *Making Do*, 108–9.

21 Barbara R. Brooks, 'Using Left-Overs in Effective Fashion,' *Porcupine Advance*, 11 Aug. 1932.

22 *Evening Examiner*, 20 Nov. 1930.

23 AO, RG 22-1333, Carleton County Juvenile and Family court, Adult Case Files (hereafter CC FamCt), Box 7, 1937.

24 Ibid., Box 60, 1938.

25 Ibid., Box 63, 1933.

26 Archives of Ontario (AO), RG 3-9, Mitchell F. Hepburn, Public General Correspondence (hereafter Hepburn Papers), Box 180, File: Unemployment Relief, no. 2, Mrs Pat O'Ray to Hepburn, Sept. 1934, Mrs Arthur Oddy to Hepburn, 21 Aug. 1934.

27 AO, RG 3-8, George S. Henry, General Correspondence (hereafter Henry Papers), MS 1747, File: Unemployment Relief, no. 3, Mrs Wallace Gow, on behalf of the mothers of Sturgeon Falls, to Henry, 29 Sept. 1931.

28 See Ross, *Love and Toil*, 32–3, on the importance of meat.

29 *North Bay Nugget*, 26 April 1933; *Three Meals A Day: Suggestions for Good Food at Low Cost* (Ottawa: Metropolitan Life Insurance Co., 1930); *Porcupine Advance*, 26 Oct. 1933.

30 *North Bay Nugget*, 24 Jan. 1931.

31 Ibid., 3 Jan. 1931.

32 Berton, *Great Depression*, 217; Ross, *Love and Toil*, 40.

33 She usually bought inexpensive brisket to make soup, which, though labour intensive, saved money. She washed and cut the meat, boiled it until soft, grated in onions, carrots, and celery, and saved the broth for further use. Chicken dumplings were made in a saucepan of boiling water, flour, baking powder, raisins, suet, and sugar; a ball of dough was placed into a cotton cloth, dropped into water for two and a half hours, then sliced and fried for leftovers. Interview, Mary Cleeson.

34 *North Bay Nugget*, 20 Jan. 1933.

35 *Oshawa Daily Times*, 25 Aug. 1932.

36 *North Bay Nugget*, 17 May, 20 Jan. 1933.

37 Ibid., 11 Oct. 1933.

38 Hollingsworth and Tyyska, 'Hidden Producers,' 15. The authors note that in 1930 the value of canned goods produced was $55 million, but by 1932 it had dropped to $33 million. Quoted from the *Labour Gazette*, Nov. 1934, 15. A similar trend occurred in the United States.

39 Interview, Earl Craig; Sangster, *Earning Respect*, 127.

40 Interview, Anges Campbell. For women with large families, preserving fruits and vegetables was a labour-intensive chore. See also Catherine Gidney, 'The Dredger's Daughter: Courtship and Marriage in the Baptist Community of Welland, Ontario, 1933–1944,' *L/LT* no. 54 (2004): 144.

41 Kathy McClelland-Wierzbicki, *The Great Depression in Northern Ontario, 1929–1934* (Sudbury: Laurentian University, 1981), 9.

42 City of Thunder Bay Archives (hereafter TBA), 4101, Series 76, Fort
    William Council and Committee Minutes (hereafter FWMin), Report of
    License and Relief Committee, 5 June 1932; ibid., 6 June, 1933.

43 *North Bay Nugget*, 11 June 1932.

44 See, e.g., Suzanne Morton, *Ideal Surroundings: Domestic Life in a Working-
    Class Suburb in the 1920s* (Toronto: University of Toronto Press, 1995),
    128–9; Parr, *Gender of Breadwinners*, 190–2.

45 Eric Muncaster, 'Community Gardening,' *Child and Family Welfare* 10/1
    (1934): 45–9.

46 Interviews: Basil Libby, Mary Cleeson. Even Tory Premier George Henry,
    after losing the election in 1934, reportedly told his daughter, 'I'll be able
    to help you in the garden now.' To this she responded, 'I've been looking
    for a good man.' Cited in Spanner, 'Straight Furrow,' 365, from the *Mail
    and Empire*, 20 June 1934.

47 Angus and Griffin, *We Lived a Life and Then Some*, 65.

48 Parr, *Gender of Breadwinners*, 191; Morton, *Ideal Surroundings*, 29; Robert
    Colley Angell, *The Family Encounters the Depression* (Gloucester: Peter
    Smith, 1965), 115. Angell notes that one of the men in his survey of
    Michigan families had a successful garden that allowed him to 'swell'
    with 'pride.'

49 Joan Sangster, 'Making a Fur Coat: Women, the Labouring Body, and
    Working-Class History,' *International Review of Social History* 52/2 (2007):
    241–70.

50 Struthers, *No Fault of Their Own*, 72; AO, RG 29-74, DPW, J.S. Band Files,
    Box 9, Relief Memoranda, File 66, 1933, memo, 31 Dec. 1932.

51 *Porcupine Advance*, 26 Oct. 1933.

52 Cassidy, *Unemployment and Relief*, 186.

53 Struthers, *Limits of Affluence*, 102.

54 *Oshawa Daily Times*, 16 Nov. 1932; *Evening Examiner*, 20 Nov. 1930; *North
    Bay Nugget*, 28 March and 3 Jan. 1931. For most women, buying fresh food
    in bulk would have been impossible. While 90% of urban households in
    Ontario in 1935 had electricity, only 12.6% of these had fridges, while only
    27.3% had electric stoves. Hobbs and Roach Pierson, 'Kitchen that Wastes
    No Steps,' 30.

55 *Porcupine Advance*, 26 Oct. 1933.

56 Ibid., 15 Dec. 1932.

57 Comacchio, *Nations Are Built of Babies*, 218–24; Charles Webster, 'Health,
    Welfare and Unemployment during the Depression,' *Past and Present*
    no. 109 (1985): 204–30; Lewis, *Women in England*, 28–9.

58 Comacchio, *Nations*, 224.

59 Hepburn Papers, Box 180, 1 Ambrose Hearn to Hepburn, 3 Sept. 1934.
60 Cassidy, *Unemployment and Relief*, 183.
61 Ibid., 190–2.
62 Struthers, *Limits of Affluence*, 184–5. Advisory Committee on Direct Relief
    to the Provincial Government of Ontario, *Report on Provincial Policy on
    Administrative Methods in the Matter of Direct Relief in Ontario* (Toronto:
    Herbert H. Ball, King's Printer, 1932). This report is commonly known as
    the 'Campbell Report,' after its chairman, Wallace R. Campbell. It is held
    at the Archives of Ontario, RG 29-74, DPW, J.S. Band Files, Box 1, File no. 3,
    Chronological Corresondence.
63 Dorothy King, 'Unemployment Aid and Direct Relief,' in Lothar Richtar,
    ed., *Canada's Unemployment Problem* (Toronto: Macmillan, 1939), 99.
64 Baillargeon, *Making Do*, 7.
65 Advisory Committee, *Report on Provincial Policy*, 17. See also Struthers,
    Limits of Affluence, 88.
66 Cassidy, *Unemployment and Relief*, 185.
67 TBA, FWMin, Licence and Relief Committee, 26 Sept. 1933; McClelland-
    Wierzbicki, *Great Depression*, 9; Dennis, *Marching Orders*, 124.
68 *North Bay Nugget*, 17 Jan. 1931.
69 Stafford, *Always and After*, 125–6.
70 Baillargeon, *Making Do*, 133.
71 Thunder Bay Historical Museum Society, Oral History Project, 1977
    (hereafter TBHMS), Interview, 17 March 1977, with Mrs Edith Grace
    Taylor (born 1891). There is no reference as to whether she lived in Fort
    William or Port Arthur. Hollingsworth and Tyyska, 'Hidden Producers,'
    14.
72 *North Bay Nugget*, 28 Feb. 1931. See also Katrina Srigley, 'Clothing Stories:
    Consumption, Identity and Desire in Depression-Era Toronto,' *JWH* 19/1
    (2007): 82–104.
73 Baillargeon, *Making Do*, 133.
74 Berton, *Great Depression*, 217.
75 McClelland-Wierzbicki, *Great Depression*, 5, quoting Mary Warmington.
76 Baillargeon, *Making Do*, 95; Elizabeth A. Roberts, 'Women's Strategies,
    1890–1940,' in Jane Lewis, ed., *Labour and Love: Women's Experiences of
    Home and Family, 1850–1940* (Oxford: Basil Blackwell, 1986), 223–47;
    Martha May, 'The "Good Managers": Married Working-Class Women and
    Family Budget Studies, 1895–1915,' *Labor History* 25/3 (1984): 351–72.
77 Sangster, *Earning Respect*, 128.
78 *North Bay Nugget*, 15 Nov. 1933.
79 Mrs Rose Jessop, TBHMS, interview, 1977.

80 Most women workers were concentrated in the field of domestic service, which encompassed one-fifth of all female workers; this field was the only women's profession that increased during the Great Depression. See Leonard Marsh, *Canadians In and Out of Work* (Toronto: Oxford University Press, 1940); Alison Prentice et al., eds., *Canadian Women: A History* (Toronto: Harcourt, Brace and Jovanovich), 235.

81 Henry Papers, MS 1759, Mrs Anne McCormack to Henry, 26 Oct. 1933; Mrs Christien Thatcher, TBHMS interview, 1977.

82 AO, RG 22-3390, Middlesex County Prosecution Case Files (hereafter Middlesex Case Files), Box 23-28, 1938. No outcome was noted in this case.

83 Ibid., Box 12, 1935–6.

84 AO, RG 3-10, Hepburn Papers, Box 225, File: M. F. Hepburn, personal, no. 2, Mrs George W. Amos to Hepburn, n.d. July 1934.

85 AO, RG 22-5836, York County Juvenile and Family Court, Occurrence Files (hereafter YC FamCt), Box 194.

86 Hollingsworth and Tyyska, 'Hidden Producers,' 12–13.

87 Bruce County Museum and Archives, Bruce County Historical Society, Oral Histories of Bruce County; Mrs Jane Mill, TBHMS interview, 8 March 1977.

88 Richard Harris, 'The End Justified the Means: Boarding and Rooming in a City of Homes, 1890–1957,' *JSH* 26/2 (1992): 332; Baillargeon, *Making Do*, 97.

89 Hollingsworth and Tyyska, 'Hidden Producers,' 19.

90 Baillargeon, *Making Do*, 97.

91 Harris, 'Boarding and Rooming,' 350; Peter Baskerville, 'Familiar Strangers: Urban Families with Boarders, Canada, 1901,' *Social Science History* 25/3 (2001): 321–46.

92 Baskerville, 'Familiar Strangers,' 329.

93 AO, F1405, Series 61-001, MU 9959, Multicultural History Society of Ontario Papers, Delhi Tobacco Belt Project.

94 Hepburn Papers, Box 180, File: Unemployment Relief, no. 2, Mrs M. Cook to Hepburn, 23 June 1934.

95 AO, RG 22-5790, Wentworth County Prosecution Case Files (hereafter Wentworth Case Files), Box 10, 1931.

96 See also Myers, *Caught*, 190–1.

97 Wentworth County Case Files, Box 12, 1932.

98 YC FamCt, Box 184, 1934.

99 Ibid., Box 186.

100 Women's domestic and informal labour was done inside the home and therefore not counted by census takers. These women were classified as

homemakers, not 'gainfully occupied' workers. Hobbs, 'Gendering Work and Welfare,' 332–3. See also Luxton, *More Than a Labour of Love*, 173–4.

101 Cassidy, *Unemployment and Relief*, 186; E. Wight Bakke, *The Unemployed Worker: A Study of the Task of Making a Living without a Job* (New Haven: Yale University Press, 1940), 118.

102 *Farmer's Advocate*, 26 March 1931.

103 *Northern News*, 19 May 1932.

104 *North Bay Nugget*, 19 March and 16 Dec. 1932.

105 See Fahrni, *Household Politics*; de Grazia and Furlough, *Sex of Things*. A mass culture of consumption was increasingly linked with both class identity and status after the 1920s. See Palmer, *Working Class Experience*, 229–36; Morton, *Ideal Surroundings*, 44–50. For the variety of ways that couples engaged in leisure and consumption as a form of recreation, see Gidney, 'Dredger's Daughter'; Donica Belisle, 'Toward a Canadian Consumer History,' *L/LT* no. 52 (2003): 181–206.

106 *North Bay Nugget*, 1 April 1931.

107 Henry Papers, MS 1736, File: Advertising 1930. American historian Alan Brinkley argues that over the course of the Depression, New Deal reformers moved from an emphasis on government regulation of the economy to a focus on consumption 'as a route to economic growth.' The economic crisis was understood as a problem of underconsumption rather than of overproduction. Brinkley, *The End of Reform: New Deal Liberalism in Recession and War* (New York: Vintage, 1995): 69–71.

108 Hobbs and Roach Pierson, 'Kitchen That Wastes No Steps,' 24–32.

109 *Chatelaine*, Oct. 1933, 13.

110 Bliss and Grayson, *Wretched of Canada*, 145.

111 *Farmer's Advocate*, 30 Aug. 1934.

112 Henry Papers, MS 1747, File: Unemployment Relief, no. 3, Mrs Wallace Gow to Henry, 29 Sept. 1931; Hepburn Papers, Box 180, Mrs W. King to Hepburn, 16 Sept. 1934; Henry Papers, MS 1759, File: Department of Public Welfare, Mrs Charles Townsend to Henry, 30 Aug. 1933; Hepburn Papers, Box 180, Mrs W.H. Mitchell to Hepburn, 2 Oct. 1934.

113 Henry Papers, MS 1761, File: Unemployment Relief, no. 1, Juliet Framer to Henry, 28 March 1933.

114 CC FamCt, Box 16, 1938.

115 Ibid., Box 20, 1934.

116 Bliss and Grayson, *Wretched of Canada*, 118.

117 Baillargeon, *Making Do*, 99.

118 See Hobbs: 'Gendering Work and Welfare,' 60; 'Equality and Difference,' 201–23; 'Rethinking Antifeminism,' 4. And see Katrina Srigley, 'The

Enduring Family: Employed women, Unemployed Men, and Memories of the Great Depression,' Paper presented to the Canadian Historical Association, Quebec City, May 2001.

119 Beth Light and Ruth Roach Pierson, *No Easy Road: Women in Canada, 1920s to 1960s* (Toronto: New Hogtown Press), 252. The proportion of the married female workforce increased from 7.18% in 1921 to 10.03% in 1931. Hobbs, 'Gendering Work and Welfare,' 41.

120 *Census of Canada, 1931*, vol. 1, *Summary*, 203.

121 *Evening Examiner*, 11 Oct. 1930. For an interesting look at the politics of woman blaming, see also Todd McCallum, 'Vancouver through the Eyes of a Hobo: Experience, Identity, and Value in the Writing of Canada's Depression-Era Tramps,' *L/LT* no. 59 (2007): 29–30.

122 Alice Kessler-Harris, 'Gender Ideology in Historical Reconstruction: A Case Study from the 1930s,' *Gender and History* 1/1 (1989): 31–49.

123 Hobbs, 'Rethinking Antifeminism' and 'Equality and Difference.' For an argument that race is as central to understanding work as is gender, see Katrina Srigley, 'In Case You Hadn't Noticed!: Race, Ethnicity, and Women's Wage-Earning in a Depression-Era City,' *L/LT* no. 55 (2005): 69–105.

124 AO, RG 7-1, Department of Labour, Minister–Correspondence (hereafter DOL Min), Box 6, File no. 240, Anonymous Correspondence, 1939, anonymous to N.O. Hipel, Minister of Labour, 13 July 1939.

125 Ibid., File no. 205, 'M,' General Correspondence, 1939, clipping from *Globe and Mail*, 16 June 1939, anonymous.

126 Ibid., Box 5, File no. 216, 'R,' General Correspondence, 1937–38, Miss Vera Rogers to Hepburn, 22 March 1938; ibid., Box 4, File no. 148, Anonymous Correspondence, 1937–38, 'An Employee' to Hepburn and MacBride, 28 Feb. 1938.

127 See Hobbs, 'Gendering Work and Welfare,' 42–3.

128 DOL Min, Box 7, File no. 320, 'S,' General Correspondence, 1939,N.O. Hipel to Mr V. Salomaa, Deputy Clerk of Timmins, 1939.

129 Henry Papers, MS 1738, memo, 18 June 1931, File: Civil Service Positions, J. McCutcheon, Civil Service Commissioner to Henry. See also Bird, 'Hamilton Working Women,' 129, for other women who used this strategy to find or keep jobs after marriage.

130 McCutcheon, File: Civil Service Positions, memo, 18 June 1931.

131 Henry Papers, MS 1745, File: Reports, Married Women in the Service, 1931.

132 DOL Min, Box 6, File no. 228, Welfare and Municipal Affairs, 1937–38, Christina Bunnett to Dr Faulkner, DPW, 4 Jan. 1938; Hutcheon, Secretary for MacBride, to Faulkner, 12 Jan. 1938.

133   Ruth Milkman, 'Women's Work and Economic Crisis: Some Lessons of the Great Depression,' *Review of Radical Economics* 8/1 (1976): 73–97; Sangster, *Earning Respect*, 119–22.

134   *Census, 1931*, vol. 13, *Monograph on Unemployment*, 235.

135   Leonard Marsh, *Employment Research* (Oxford: Oxford University Press, 1935), 240–4.

136   *Census, 1931*, vol. 13, 237; Hobbs, 'Gendering Work and Welfare,' 233–5.

137   Dionne Brand, '"We Weren't Allowed to Go into Factory Work until Hitler Started the War": The 1920s to the 1940s,' in Peggy Bristow et al., eds., *'We're Rooted Here and They Can't Pull Us Up': Essays in African Canadian Women's History* (Toronto: University of Toronto Press, 1994): 175–7. See also Srigley, 'The Enduring Family'; Brenda Clegg, *Black Female Domestics during the Depression in New York City, 1930–1940* (New York and London: Garland, 1995).

138   Canada, *Report of the Royal Commission on Price Spreads* (Ottawa: J.O. Patenaude, 1937), 130. At two men's clothing factories in Sainte-Thérèse, Quebec, e.g., 100% of female workers were classified as inexperienced, despite the legal maximum of 50%. Canada, *Price Spreads*, 129.

139   Canada, *Royal Commission on the Textile Industry* (Ottawa: J.O. Patenaude, 1938), 148–9. Female employees at a Vallyfield, Quebec, textile mill even drew up a petition asking the provincial government to spare their jobs by asking the company to disregard the minimum wage. Alison Prentice et al., *Canadian Women*, 234–5.

140   In 1934 Section 11(6) of the Minimum Wage Act was implemented, prohibiting employers from firing women and hiring men at lower wages.

141   DOL Min, Box 4, memo, 25 Feb. 1937, File no. 128, A.W. Crawford, Chairman of Minimum Wage Board to R. Irwin, Secretary to David Croll; ibid., memo, 14 March 1936, Crawford to Irwin.

142   Srigley, 'Enduring Family.' Srigley's interviews with married women in Toronto suggest that women of a variety of ethnic backgrounds upheld the ideal male breadwinner family, despite their participation in the paid labour force.

143   *Census, 1931*, vol. 13, 17.

144   Hollingsworth and Tyyska, 'Hidden Producers,' 21. Broadfoot, *Ten Lost Years*, 195, 277–8, 279–80, 282; Stansell, *City of Women*, 172–92; Lori Rotenberg, 'The Wayward Worker': Toronto's Prostitute at the Turn of the Century,' in Janice Acton et al., eds., *Women at Work: Ontario 1850-1930* (Toronto: Canadian Women's Educational Press, 1974), 42; Sangster, *Regulating Girls and Women*, 3, 33, 85–129; Strange, *Toronto's Girl Problem*.

145 Stansell, *City of Women*, 179–83; Cindy Patton, 'Outlaw Territory: Criminality, Neighborhoods and the Edward Savtiz Case,' *Sexuality Research and Social Policy: Journal of the NSRC* 2/2 (2005), 63–75.

146 CC FamCt, Box 70, 1938.

147 Myers, *Caught*; Dubinsky, *Improper Advances*; Stansell, *City of Women*.

148 AO, RG 22-1090, Algoma District Prosecution Case Files (hereafter Algoma Case Files), Box 11, 1930.

149 AO, RG 4-32, Ministry of the Attorney General (hereafer MAG), Criminal and Civil Case Files, 1938.

150 Wentworth Case Files, Box 9, 1930.

151 Middlesex Case Files, Box 17-30, 1931. There is no record of how long the husband and wife were incarcerated, though the two women arrested along with her were given a sentence of four months in the Mercer Reformatory.

152 Strange, *Toronto's Girl Problem*, 93–4; Rotenberg, 'Wayward Worker,' 46–8.

153 YC FamCt, Box 200, 1936.

154 Sangster, *Regulating Girls and Women*, 89.

155 Angus McLaren and Arlene Tiger McLaren, *The Bedroom and the State: The Changing Practices and Politics of Contraception and Abortion in Canada* (Toronto: McClelland and Stewart, 1986), 76; Sangster, *Regulating Girls*, 102; Janice Newton, 'From Wage Slave to White Slave,' in Linda Kealey and Joan Sangster, eds., *Beyond the Vote: Canadian Women and Politics*, (Toronto: University of Toronto Press, 1989), 217–39.

156 Lara Campbell, 'The Strong Ones Were Women,' unpublished M.A. paper, University of Toronto, 1993, 19; *Canadian Forum* 16 (1937): 5.

157 In the 1931 Census, 285,541 Canadian households (13%) were listed as female headed, including widows, single mothers, and deserted or separated women. This number did not capture single mothers living at home with birth families, families who doubled up, or even temporary desertions or separations, depending on the questions asked by the census taker. It is also important to note that most female heads had children or other dependents to support. A total of 195,457 children and other dependents were officially supported solely by women in 1931. *Census, 1931*, vol. 12, *The Canadian Family*, 100.

158 Henry Papers, MS 1760, File: Relief Asked For, letter, n.d. Feb. 1933.

159 AO, RG 29-35, DPW, Mothers' Allowance Case Files (hereafter Mothers' Allowance Files), Box 1, 1935–38.

160 Little, *'No Car, No Radio, No Liquor Permit,'* 71, 66.

161 DPW, Mothers' Allowance Files, Box 1, 1930–39.

162 Ibid., Box 3, 1936.

163 Ibid., Box 3, 1929–37.

164 Henry Papers, MS 1757, File: Mothers' Allowance Commission, Mrs Ethel Burley of Bowmanville to Henry, 1 May 1933.

165 In 1935 the waiting period was reduced from five years to three. In 1946 it was reduced to one year, and in the 1950s to six months. Little, 'No Car, No Radio,' 85, 122.

166 Henry Papers, MS 1745, File: Relief Asked For, Mrs Clarence Green to Henry, 9 June 1931.

167 CC FamCt, Box 9, 1930-32.

168 Little notes that lobbyists and recipients in British Columbia saw Mothers' Pensions as a payment for service rendered. 'Claiming a Unique Place: The Introduction of Mothers' Pensions in British Columbia,' in Strong-Boag and Felman, *Rethinking Canada*, 285–303.

169 Quoted in Little, 'No Car, No Radio,' 81.

170 Hepburn Papers, Box 190, File: Public Works Department, Mothers' Allowances, Mrs R.H. to Hepburn, 21 Feb. 1935. Quoted in Struthers, *Limits of Affluence*, 99.

171 Some literature argues that the welfare state can provide a potential escape from individual dependence on men by providing a direct relationship to the state. Carol Pateman, *The Disorder of Women: Democracy, Feminism and Political Theory* (Stanford: Stanford University Press, 1989), 196; Evans, 'Divided Citizenship?' 95; Gordon, 'What Does Welfare Regulate?'; Orloff, 'Gender and the Social Rights of Social Citizenship,' 305.

172 Hepburn Papers, Box 180, File: Unemployment Relief, no. 2, Mrs J.W. to Hepburn, 6 Sept. 1934.

173 DPW, Mothers' Allowance Files, Box 2, 1923–39; ibid., Box 3, 1933–38.

174 Henry Papers, MS 1745, File: Relief Asked For, Mrs Clarence Green to Henry, 9 June 1931. See also Mothers' Allowance Files in MS 1742 (1931) and MS 1757 (1933).

175 CC FamtCt, Box 7, 1934.

176 DPW, Mothers' Allowances Files, Box 2, 1931–37.

177 Ibid., Box 1, 1936–39.

178 Little, 'Blurring of Boundaries' and 'Manhunts and Bingo Blabs: The Moral Regulation of Ontario Single Mothers,' *Canadian Journal of Sociology* 19/2 (1994): 233–47; Struthers, *Limits of Affluence*, 43.

179 Struthers, *Limits of Affluence*, 48.

180 Henry Papers, MS 1742, File: Mothers' Allowances Commission, Mrs Caroline Callahan to Henry, 30 Oct. 1931.

181 Ibid., MS 1757, File: Mothers' Allowances Commission, Mrs Ruth Coulter to Henry, 5 March 1933.

182 CC FamtCt, Box 13, 1937–38.

183 Ibid., Box 16, 1937.

184 Ibid., Box 22, 1936.

185 MAG, Criminal and Civil Case Files, 1933, I.A. Humphries, Department of the Attorney General, to W.G. Martin, Minister of Public Welfare, 13 Sept. 1933.

2 'If He Is a Man He Becomes Desperate'

1 Michael Kimmel, *Manhood in America: A Cultural History* (New York: Free Press, 1996): 2–6.

2 Steven Maynard, 'Queer Musings on Masculinity and History,' *L/LT* no. 42 (1998): 185.

3 Gail Bederman, *Manliness and Civilization: A Cultural History of Gender and Race in the United States, 1880–1917* (Chicago and London: University of Chicago Press, 1995), 11.

4 Thank you to Shirley Tillotson, Dalhousie University, for encouraging me to develop this idea.

5 Bederman, *Manliness and Civilization*, 5.

6 Joy Parr notes that for men the 'simultaneity of these ways of being was inescapable.' *Gender of Breadwinners*, 245.

7 R.W. Connell, 'The Big Picture: Masculinities in Recent World History,' *History and Theory* 22/5 (1993): 611; Jeanne Boydston, *Home and Work: Housework, Wages and the Ideology of Labor in the Early Republic* (New York: Oxford University Press, 1990): 142–63.

8 See Paul Willis, 'Shop Floor Culture, Masculinity and the Wage Form,' in J. Clarke et al., eds., *Working Class Culture: Studies in History and Theory* (New York: St Martins's Press, 1979), 185–98; Kimmel, *Manhood in America*.

9 Hobbs, 'Rethinking Antifeminism,' 4. Numerous historians have documented this tightening of gender definitions. Marc Rosenfeld, e.g., notes that during the Depression in the railway town of Barrie definitions of masculinity emphasized 'hard work and endurance.' Similarly, Jonathan Katz, George Chauncey, and Lillian Faderman have all argued that economic crisis created a greater emphasis on heterosexual norms. Rosenfeld, 'It Was a Hard Life,' 265; Jonathan Ned Katz, *The Invention of Heterosexuality* (New York: Penguin, 1995); Lillian Faderman, *Odd Girls and Twilight Lovers: A History of Lesbian Life in Twentieth-Century America* (New York: Penguin, 1991), 93–4; George Chauncey, *Gay New York: Gender, Urban Culture, and the Making of the Gay Male World, 1890–1940* (New York: Basic Books, 1994) 331–54.

10 *Northern News*, 11 Jan. 1934.

11 Hobbs, 'Rethinking Antifeminism,' 7.

12 Gordon and Fraser, 'Contract vs Charity,' 55; Pateman, *Disorder of Women*, 185.

13 Anna Clark, 'The New Poor Law and the Breadwinner Wage: Contrasting Assumptions,' *JSH* 34/2 (2000): 261–81; Martha May, 'Bread before Roses: American Workingmen, Labor Unions, and the Family Wage,' in Ruth Milkman, ed., *Women, Work and Protest: A Century of U.S. Women's Labor History* (Boston: Routledge and Kegan Paul, 1985), 1–21; Sally Alexander, 'Men's Fears and Women's Work: Responses to Unemployment in London between the Wars,' *Gender and History* 12/2 (2000): 401–24.

14 *Evening Examiner*, 18 Nov. 1930.

15 *Porcupine Advance*, 11 Aug., 17 Nov., 24 Aug. 1932; *North Bay Nugget*, 2 Jan. 1932, quoted in Struthers, *No Fault of Their Own*, 75.

16 Collins, *You Had to Be There*, 27–9.

17 Ibid., 22.

18 Broadfoot, *Ten Lost Years*, 70, also quoted in Struthers, *No Fault of Their Own*, 71; Hobbs, 'Gendering Work and Welfare,' 60; Christie, *Engendering the State*, 212.

19 Henry Papers, MS 1759, File: Department of Public Works, East Block, Russel Morris to Henry, 24 June 1933.

20 Hepburn Papers, Box 225, File: Hepburn, personal, no. 6, Mr. Herbert T. [sic] to Hepburn, 14 Aug. 1934.

21 Henry Papers, MS 1760, File: Relief Asked For, Harold Foate to Henry, 18 Jan. 1933.

22 *Porcupine Advance*, 12 Jan. 1932.

23 The town of Gravenhurst placed a public notice in the local newspaper, outlining a number of rules for relief recipients: they were not allowed to own a liquor permit or a car licence, and they were required to plant their land with vegetables in order to qualify for aid. Henry Papers, MS 1761, File: Unemployment Relief, no. 1, newspaper clipping from 1933. In Fort William relief officer F. Blain was instructed by city council to tell relief applicants that their telephone would be discontinued upon application for relief. TBA, 4095-72, Licences, Police, Relief and Welfare Committee Minutes, 5 Feb. 1932. In Timmins, when one man approached the council for wood, the relief officer claimed that 'the man could supply his own wood if he would only show a little energy.' *Porcupine Advance*, 12 Jan. 1932.

24 Hepburn papers, Box 190, File: Public Welfare Department, general, no. 2, Frank Hitchings, Clover Leaf Grocery to Hepburn, 15 Aug. 1935.

25 *Porcupine Advance*, 11 Aug. 1932.

26 Ibid., 31 March, 1932. North Bay debated forcing the unemployed to both register and make a declaration of unemployment under oath, presumably to weed out potential defrauders, and in August 1930 all the unemployed in Fort William were required to formally register at the police court building. *North Bay Nugget*, 13 Jan. 1932; TBA, Series 4, 124, Box 209, File: Labor Situation, 1929–30.

27 Don McLeod, TBHMS, interview, March 1977.

28 *Child and Family Welfare* 1/2 (1934): 50.

29 *Porcupine Advance*, 15 June 1933.

30 Bakke, *Citizens without Work*, 212. In their sociological survey of Chicago families, Cavan and Ranck found that one widely disliked feature of the relief system was the 'young inexperienced' case workers who, many men and women felt, had no experience in raising families. Ruth Shonle Cavan and Katherine Howland Ranck, *The Family and the Depression: A Study of One Hundred Chicago Families* (Freeport: Books for Libraries Press, 1969), 159.

31 Unemployed men ran the food depots of Toronto's Department of Public Welfare (DPW). Struthers, *Limits of Affluence*, 89. In Northern Alberta, relief was administered by the RCMP, while in East Windsor, it was administered by managers from the Ford Motor Company. Struthers, *No Fault of Their Own*, 49, and *Limits of Affluence*, 83–9.

32 Henry Papers, MS 1759, File: Public Works, J. Frise to Henry, 12 Dec. 1933.

33 AO, RG 21, MS 671, Box 3, Oshawa City Council Minutes, 18 Nov. 1929.

34 F.A. Matatall and Hector Menard, *Report on the Cost of Relief and Its Administration in the City of Ottawa*, 16 July 1934. Held in RG 29-74, DPW, J.S. Band Files, File: 74-1-58, Reports and Surveys, Box 7.

35 Struthers, *No Fault of Their Own*, 149.

36 Christie, *Engendering the State*, 200–1. See also Hobbs, 'Gendering Work and Welfare,' 226–40, for an analysis of the gendered nature of statistics on unemployment.

37 Struthers, *Limits of Affluence*, 319n45, 91. At this school men received lectures on 'sociological subjects' and took courses in accounting. DPW, J.S. Band Files, Box 6, File: D.A. Croll, newspaper clipping from the *Globe and Mail*, 3 Nov. 1934.

38 *Porcupine Advance*, 17 Nov. and 15 Dec. 1938.

39 See Palmer, *Working-Class Experience*; Morton, *Working People*; Peter Baskerville and Eric Sager, *Unwilling Idlers: The Urban Unemployed and Their Families in Late Victorian Canada* (Toronto: University of Toronto Press, 1988).

40 Alexander, 'Men's Fears,' 404; Cynthia R. Comacchio, *The Infinite Bonds of Family: Domesticity in Canada, 1850–1940* (Toronto: University of Toronto Press, 1999): 117.

41 Cassidy, *Unemployment and Relief*, 41, 48.

42 Kimmel, *Manhood in America*, 192.

43 Alexander, 'Men's Fears,' 411–12; Hobbs, 'Rethinking Antifeminsim,' 6, 8.

44 *North Bay Nugget*, 27 Feb. 1932; Hepburn Papers, Box 190, File: Public Welfare Department, general, no. 2, Mrs R.H. Wilson to Hepburn, 14 Jan. 1935.

45 Hepburn Papers, Box 228, File: Liquor Control Board, re: positions, Henri Saint-Jacques to Hepburn, 27 July 1934.

46 Ibid., Box 247, File: Public Works Department, George Wilson to Hepburn, n.d., 1935.

47 Collins, *You Had to Be There*, 23. Collins notes that in the early 1930s, 1% of all deaths in Canada were caused by suicide, a rate not reached again until the 1960s. In Ontario suicides increased in number from 207 in 1928 to 327 in 1931. M.C. Urquhart, *Historical Statistics* (Cambridge: Cambridge University Press1965), 658, Series Y178-201.

48 Louis I. Dublin, *Suicide: A Sociological and Statistical Study* (New York: Ronald Press, 1963), 65. See also Louis I. Dublin and Bessie Bunzel, *To Be or Not to Be* (New York: Harrison Smith and Robert Haas, 1933).

49 Dublin, *Suicide*, 66. The Lynds' sociological study of American life in the Depression also speculates, though with very small numbers, that a jump in suicide rates in 1930 and 1931 was connected to economic conditions. Robert S. Lynd and Helen Merrell Lynd, *Middletown in Transition* (New York: Harcourt, Brace, 1937): 137-8, 543, Table II.

50 *Porcupine Advance*, 31 Jan. 1932.

51 H.L. Beales and R.S. Lambert, *Memoirs of the Unemployed* (East Ardsley: E.P Publishing, 1973), 174.

52 *Porcupine Advance*, 19 March 1931. The front page of the Peterborough *Evening Examiner* (22 Oct. 1930) reported that J. Victor Stanly, a fifty-year-old branch manager for the Bank of Toronto, shot himself in response to the news of heavy stock losses, leaving behind a note that stated 'he could not stand life any longer.' See also *North Bay Nugget*, 22 April 1931; *Northern News*, 20 Sept. 1934; *Porcupine Advance*, 4 Aug. 1932. In Stirling, Ontario, travelling salesman Pat Hayerty ingested five grams of strychnine and almost died. He was 'apparently despondent over the few sales that he had been making and claimed that that was the reason for his rash act.' *North Hastings Review*, 12 Nov. 1930. The *Evening Examiner* (24 Sept. and 13 Nov. 1930) also reported on two murder-suicides that occurred in

the United States that were connected to men's unemployment and inability to support a family.

53 CC FamCt, Box 69, 1936.

54 Baillargeon, *Making Do*, 126; Bakke, *Citizens without Work*, 184; Parr, *Gender of Breadwinners*, 90–2; Sangster, *Earning Respect*, 127. In the British survey, *Memoirs of the Unemployed*, by Beales and Lambert, e.g., only one man admitted to taking responsibility for household labour and child care while his wife worked.

55 George Prevost and his twelve-year-old son paddled a homemade log raft eight miles across Lake Nippissing to get food for their family. *Northern News*, 22 June 1933.

56 *Porcupine Advance*, 15 Oct. 1931.

57 Hepburn Papers, Box 190, File: Public Welfare Department, general, no. 2, Cecil Tensely to Hepburn, 16 Feb. 1935.

58 *Oshawa Daily Times*, 19 Oct. 1932.

59 *Porcupine Advance*, 23 Dec. 1935.

60 There was no reference to exactly how these men accomplished this kind of theft.

61 AO, RG 22-2990, Leeds and Grenville Counties Prosecution Case Files (hereafter Leeds/Grenville Case Files), Box 4, 1934–45; ibid., 1936.

62 Middlesex Case Files, Box 24-39, 1939.

63 Eva Garcia, '"Taking Care of One's Own": Gender, Unemployment Relief, and the London Welfare Board, 1930–40,' Master's thesis, University of Guelph, 1997, 50, 76. However, note that even a temporary suspension of relief would have been disastrous for families who had no other source of income.

64 Middlesex Case Files, Box 50-37, 1937.

65 Ibid., Box 20-34, 1935.

66 Lillian Petroff, *Sojourners and Settlers: The Macedonian Community in Toronto to 1940* (Toronto: Multicultural History Society of Ontario, 1995), 89.

67 Middlesex Case Files, Box 50-37, 1937.

68 Algoma Case Files, Box 12, 1935.

69 'Dear Comrade Lousia,' wrote the young woman, 'I think I could manage about five of the Revolutionary Youth Papers ... Dad was arrested the other day ... [h]e asked her for a fuel order and she refused. He locked the door and demanded the order.' Middlesex Case Files, Box 21-35, 1937.

70 MAG, Criminal and Civil Case Files, 1938.

71 Robin Jarvis Brownlie: *A Fatherly Eye: Indian Agents, Government Power and Aboriginal Resistance in Ontario, 1918–1939* (Don Mills: Oxford University Press, 2003) and '"A Better Citizen than lots of White Men":

First Nations Enfranchisement – An Ontario Case Study, 1918–46,' *CHR* 87/1 (2006): 29–52.

72 Brownlie, *Fatherly Eye*, 110.

73 Middlesex Case Files, Box 21-35, 1936, M.F. Vickers to Mayer Lerner, 3 Feb. 1936, stating that McMahon had served in the First World War, 54th Battalion, and was a man of 'fine character' and 'exceptional bravery.'

74 MAG, Criminal and Civil Case Files, 1938.

75 Henry Papers, MS 1752, File: Department of Public Welfare, Samuel Johnston to Henry, 11 May 1932.

76. Ibid., MS 1759, File: Department of Public Welfare, George Davenport to Henry, 20 July, 1933.

77 Bertram Brookner, 'Mrs Hungerford's Milk,' in Donna Phillips, ed., *Voices of Discord: Canadian Short Stories from the 1930s* (Toronto: New Hogtown Press, 1979), 95, 99–100, 109–10.

78 Frank Love, 'Looking Forward,'in Richard Wright and Robin Endres, eds., *'Eight Men Speak: A Political Play in Six Acts' and Other Plays from the Canadian Workers' Theatre* (Toronto: New Hogtown Press, 1976), 17.

79 Mary Quayle Innis, 'Staver,' in Phillips, *Voices of Discord*, 173–81.

80 Faue, *Community of Suffering and Struggle*.

81 Oscar Ryan, 'Unity,' in *Eight Men Speak*, 103. On Section 98 of the Criminal Code, see Roberts, *Whence They Came*, 22, 125–8.

82 Henry Papers, MS 1759, File: Department of Public Works, George Davenport to Henry, 20 July, 1933.

83 Parr, *Gender of Breadwinners*, 200–1. Elaine Tyler May claims that high male unemployment and shared breadwinning roles could have led to more egalitarian gender relationships in the postwar period, but that domesticity was too highly prized for that to happen. But the value of domesticity was only part of the story: the connection of masculinity to both work and to family helped the breadwinner role survive the Depression era. Elaine Tyler May, *Homeward Bound: American Families in the Cold War Era* (New York: Basic Books, 1988), 37–57. For a Canadian perspective, see Robert Rutherdale, who argues that 'masculine domesticity' in the postwar era was linked to higher wages, higher employment rates, and the consumer economy, all of which were signifiers of abundance and material success in the post-depression era. Robert Rutherdale, 'Fatherhood, Masculinity, and the Good Life during Canada's Baby Boom, 1945–65,' *Journal of Family History* (hereafter *JFH*) 24/3 (1999): 351–73.

84 Eric Strikwerda, '"Married Men, Should, I Feel, Be Treated Differently": Work, Relief and Unemployed Men on the Urban Canadian Prairie, 1929–32,' *left history* 12/1 (2007): 30–51.

85 Henry Papers, MS 1759, File: Department of Public Works, James Young to Henry, 27 Dec. 1933.

86 *North Bay Nugget,* 20 May 1931; TBA, Series 4, City Clerk's Files, Box 209, 1929–30, 'Labour Situation,' Unemployment Committee, 29 Nov. 1929. As early as December 1930, Port Arthur city council passed a resolution banning all single men, except those who were the sole support of their families, from working on city relief projects. TBA, Series 17, Port Arthur City Council Minutes, 8 Dec. 1930.

87 *Evening Examiner,* 25 Nov. 1939. See also Strikwerda, 'Married Men,' 37.

88 Note the concern in the *Canadian Congress Journal,* e.g., over how unemployment could harm female morality by leading to prostitution or by hurting women's health, and therefore the health of future generations of children. *Canadian Congress Journal* 9/11 (1930): 27; ibid., 10/12 (1931): 38. See also letters of concern regarding prostitution in Bliss and Grayson, *Wretched of Canada,* 92–3, 83–4.

89 *North Bay Nugget,* 14 Jan. 1931.

90 Henry Papers, MS 1759, File: Department of Public Works, F.W. Gibbard to Henry, 15 and 30 April, 30 May, n.d. Sept. 1933.

91 Ibid., MS 1761, File: Uemployment Relief, no. 1, Edward Lymen to Henry, 14 Jan. 1933.

92 Ibid., MS 1759, File: Department of Public Works, T.H. Gray to Henry, 3 Oct. 1933.

93 Griswold, *Fatherhood in America,* 1993; Comacchio, 'Postscript for Father,' 305–408. This chronological understanding of fatherhood should be qualified by noting that, even in the Victorian era, men were deeply concerned about the security and comfort of their children and family, and historians have begun to challenge the stereotype of the universal and disinterested father. John Tosh, 'Domesticity and Manliness in the Victorian Middle Class: Edward White Benson,' in Michael Roper and John Tosh, eds., *Manful Assertions: Masculinities in Britain since 1880* (London and New York: Routledge, 1991), 44–73; Laura McCall, '"Not So Wild a Dream": The Domestic Fantasies of Literary Men and Women, 1820–60,' in Laura McCall and Donald Yacovone, eds., *A Shared Experience: Men, Women and the History of Gender* (New York: New York University Press, 1998): 176–89.

94 Comacchio, 'Postscript,' 395.

95 Henry Papers, MS 1745, File: Relief Asked For, Mr A.E. Owen to Henry, 6 June 1931.

96 Ibid., MS 1744, File: Positions, General, June 1931 to Jan. 1932, D.G. Firth to Henry, 16 and 17 Sept. 1931; ibid., MS 1761, File: Soldier's Aid Commission, Grant MacMillan to Henry, 30 June 1933.

97 CC FamtCt, Box 62, 1936.

98 Oscar Ryan, E. Cecil-Smith, Frank Love, and Mildred Goldberg, 'Eight Men Speak: A Political Play in Six Acts,' in *Eight Men Speak*, 21–89.

99 DOL Min, Box 1, File no. 70, Miscellaneous, 1934–35, Albert Sawdon to David Croll, Minister of Public Welfare, 14 Nov. 1934.

100 Ibid., Box 4, File no. 146, General Correspondence, 1937–38, A.E. Allen to M.M. MacBride, Minister of Labour, 7 Jan. 1938.

101 Klee, 'Between the Scylla and Charybdis of Anarchy and Despotism,' 238.

102 Ibid., 194–9.

103 DOL Min, Box 4, File no. 131, 1935–37, George Gilpin, c/o Commercial Travellers Association, Toronto to David Croll, 14 Nov. 1936.

104 Ibid., Box 6, File no 222, 'T,' General Correspondence, 1937–38, Bert Tipping to MacBride, 26 Jan. 1938.

105 Wentworth Case Files, 1931; see also ibid., Box 17, 1939, and Box 15, 1936.

106 Henry Papers, MS 1760, File: Resolutions, Miscellaneous, City of London, 7 Sept. 1933.

107 AO, RG 7-4, DOL, Disputes and Strikes 1937–38 (hereafter DOL Dis&S), Container 1, File: Dispute, Holand Coal Company, Holland to Hepburn, 30 Nov. 1937.

108 Brown, *When Freedom Was Lost*; Strikwerda, 'Married Men,' 38–9; McCallum, 'Vancouver through the Eyes of a Hobo,' 30.

109 Alexander, 'Men's Fears,' 410.

110 *Evening Examiner*, 22 Sept. 1930.

111 Henry Papers, MS 1757, File: Navy League, Sam Harris, President, Navy League of Canada to Henry, 27 March, 1933.

112 'The Psychology of the Unemployed from the Medical Point of View,' in Beales and Lambert, *Memoirs of the Unemployed*, 275.

113 DOL Min, Box 1, File no. 18, Unemployment Relief, clipping from *MacLean's*, 'A Remedy for Wage Fund,' 15 Aug. 1930.

114 Hepburn Papers, Box 250, File: Comments on Relief, Mrs Charles Lickman to Hepburn, 29 July, 1935.

115 Penfold, 'Have You No Manhood in You?' 273; Parr, *Gender of Breadwinners*. See also Chapter 5 of this book, which argues that almost half of Ontario's relief strikes involved 'domestic' concerns.

116 Henry Papers, MS 1747, File: Unemployment Relief, no. 3, Lt. W.J. Osborne Dempster to Henry, 8 Oct. 1931.

117 Hepburn Papers, Box 180, File: Unemployment Relief, no. 2, L. Walton to Hepburn, 24 June 1934.

118 Hugh Garner, 'On the Road in the Thirties', in M. Horn, ed., *The Dirty Thirties: Canadians in the Great Depression.* (Toronto: Copp Clark, 1972), 711.

119 Liversedge, *Recollections of the On-to-Ottawa Trek*, viii–ix.

120 Berton, *Great Depression*, 164.

121 Broadfoot, *Ten Lost Years*, 134–5, 139; Liversedge, *Recollections*, 91.

122 Ellen Stafford, *Always and After: A Memoir* (Toronto: Penguin, 1999), 173–4.

123 Betcherman, *Little Band*, 107–8.

124 CC FamtCt, Box 2, 1931.

125 Ibid., Box 26, 1938.

126 Igra, 'Likely to Become a Public Charge'; Willrich, 'Home Slackers; Chunn, *From Punishment to Doing Good*.

127 Chunn, *From Punishment*, 153.

128 By the year 1935–36, there were 10,000 beneficiaries of Mothers' Allowance in Ontario, and 7.3% of these were deserted women. Little, 'No Car, No Radio, No Liquor Permit,' 101, 97, Table 4.4.

129 There were 9,140 transients in Kirkland Lake in 1931. Michael Barnes, *Kirkland Lake: On the Mile of Gold* (Kirkland Lake: Economic Development and Tourism Department, 1994), 89. Gold prices increased in the early to mid-1930s: in Teck Township, e.g., which included Kirkland Lake, gold mine production increased from $17 million in 1930 to $34 million in 1934. Ibid., 93.

130 Ibid., 102.

131 *Porcupine Advance*, 5 May and 19 Jan. 1932.

132 MAG, Criminal and Civil Case Files, 1938.

133 CC FamCt, Box 18, 1930.

134 Chunn, *From Punishment*, 169.

135 Christie, *Engendering the State*, 109. For a later twentieth-century take on the fear of men abandoning their breadwinner roles, see Susan Faludi, *Backlash: The Undeclared War against American Women* (New York: Crown, 1991); Barbara Ehrenreich, *The Hearts of Men: American Dreams and the Flight from Commitment* (Garden City: Anchor Press, 1983).

136 AO, RG 22-3833, Ontario County Juvenile and Family Court, Domestic Case Files (hereafter OC Case Files), Box 7, 1939.

137 YC FamCt, Box 222, 1939.

138 Annalee Golz, 'Family Matters: The Canadian Family and the State in Postwar Canada,' *left history* 1/2 (1993): 9–50.

139 Christie, *Engendering the State*; Jennifer A. Stephen, *Pick One Intelligent Girl: Employability, Domesticity, and the Gendering of Canada's Welfare State* (Toronto: University of Toronto Press, 2007); Ann Porter, *Gendered States: Women, Unemployment Insurance, and the Political Economy of the Welfare State in Canada, 1945–1997* (Toronto: University of Toronto Press, 2003);

Roach Pierson, 'Gender and the Unemployment Insurance Debates.' Much has been written on this issue in an international context. For just a few examples, see Laura Levine Frader, *Breadwinners and Citizens: Gender in the Making of the French Social Model* (Durham and London: Duke University Press, 2008); Kristin Stromberg Childers, 'Paternity and the Politics of Citizenship in Interwar France,' *JFH* 26/1 (2001): 90–111.

140 Alexander, 'Men's Fears,' 419; Christie, *Engendering the State*, 13. Gillian Creese, 'The Politics of Dependence: Women, Work and Unemployment in the Vancouver Labour Movement before World War II,' *Canadian Journal of Sociology* 13/1–2 (1988): 136–40. Creese sees the Great Depression as a 'contradictory legacy.' Increased working-class female militancy led to increased involvement for women in community politics, but demands for a living wage and employment did not challenge the division of labour. For a discussion of the way in which the postwar welfare state addressed the role of motherhood in social policy, see Dominique Jean, 'Family Allowances and Family Autonomy: Quebec Families Encounter the Welfare State, 1945–1955,' in Bradbury, *Canadian Family History*, 401–37; Marshall 'Language of Children's Rights'; sections of Little, *'No Car, No Radio, No Liquor Permit.'*

3 The Obligations of Family

1 Sutherland, *Growing Up*, 114.
2 John Bullen, 'Hidden Workers: Child Labour and the Family Economy in Late Nineteenth-Century Urban Ontario,' in Bradbury, *Canadian Family History*, 199–219; Ross, *Love and Toil*; Bettina Bradbury, *Working Families: Age, Gender and Daily Survival in Industrializing Montreal* (Toronto: McClelland and Stewart, 1993).
3 Christie, *Engendering the State*, 7. By 1918 middle-class families tended to expect their children to complete high school. Sutherland, *Growing Up*, 74–7.
4 Christie, *Engendering the State*, 152.
5 Little, *'No Car, No Radio, No Liquor Permit,'* 85.
6 Ibid., 95; Comacchio, *Dominion of Youth*, 9, 36. Comacchio notes that unemployed youth made up approximately 1/5 of the unemployed workforce in the Depression.
7 Bruce Bellingham, 'The History of Childhood since the Invention of Childhood: Some Issues in the Eighties,' *JFH* 13/2 (1988): 347–58.
8 Comacchio, *Dominion of Youth*, 37–9, 152.
9 Bullen, 'Hidden Workers,' 201; Sutherland, *Growing Up*, 119–20.

10 CC FamCt, Box 11, 1940.

11 Ibid., Box 48, 1937.

12 Ibid., Box 16, 1937.

13 Ibid., Box 2, 1938.

14 Ibid., Box 14, 1940.

15 Ibid., Box 9, 1938.

16 Ellen Ross points out that in late nineteenth- and early twentieth-century London, older children, especially boys around the age of thirteen, were often caught stealing. Ross, *Love and Toil*, 151.

17 CC FamCt, Box 2, 1935.

18 Comacchio, *Dominion of Youth*, 35; Myers, *Caught*, 78–80.

19 Klee, 'Between the Scylla and Charybdis,' 133–72.

20 CC FamCt, Box 16, 1939.

21 Ibid., Box 2, 1934.

22 Ibid., Box 40, 1938.

23 Ibid., Box 20, 1935, and Box 2, 1938.

24 Ibid., Box 28, 1936.

25 Sutherland, *Growing Up*, 124. See also R.E. Pahl, *Divisions of Labour* (Oxford: Basil Blackwell, 1984), 91–2.

26 CC FamCt, Box 40, 1937.

27 Ibid., Box 13, 1936.

28 Ibid., Box 20, 1937.

29 Ibid., Box 14, 1930.

30 Sutherland, *Growing Up*, 114; Patrick J. Harrigan, 'The Schooling of Boys and Girls in Canada,' *JSH* 23/4 (1990): 805; Christie, *Engendering the State*, 8; Comacchio, *Dominion of Youth*, 51. The Canadian Youth Commission reported that between 1911 and 1941, the average number of years spent in school increased from 7.96 to 10. Average time spent in school was longest in British Columbia (10.73 years) and Ontario (10.55 years). CYC, *Youth, Marriage and the Family* (Toronto: Ryerson Press, 1947), 22.

31 Henry Papers, MS 1759, V. Grant to Henry, 19 Sept. 1933.

32 CYC, *Youth, Marriage and the Family*, 84.

33 Glen H. Elder Jr, *Children of the Great Depression: Social Change in Life Experience* (Chicago: University of Chicago Press, 1974); Bakke, *Unemployed Worker*, 116–17.. Cavan and Ranck, *Family and the Depression*, 92.

34 R.W. Sandwell, 'The Limits of Liberalism: The Liberal Reconnaissance and the History of the Family in Canada,' *CHR* 84/3 (2003): 423–50; Comacchio, *Dominion of Youth*, 144–5.

35 Interview, Basil Libby.

36   Charles Smith, *I Remember, I Remember: An Autobiography* (North Bay: Charles Smith, 1989), 58–60, 53–4. This self-published memoir is held at the North Bay Public Library.
37   CC FamCt, Box 2, 1937.
38   Sutherland, *Growing Up*, 122.
39   Interview, Gladys Clements.
40   Angus and Griffin, *We Lived a Life and Then Some*, 65.
41   Smith, *I Remember*, 55–7.
42   Sandwell, 'Limits of Liberalism,' 437.
43   *Farmer's Advocate*, 9 and 23 Sept. 1937.
44   Bakke, *Citizens without Work*, 206; Myers, *Caught*, 136, 153.
45   CC FamCt, Box 61, 1935. A swaggersuit refers to a style of coat that became popular in the Great Depression. It was basically a loose jacket with a full back and a stand-up collar, along with a diamond-shaped gusset placed under the arm. See Jean L. Cooper, 'Assignment: Study Garment-Swagger Coat-4/29/01,' available at http://www.staff.lib.virginia.edu/~jlc/Assign9.htm.
46   CC FamCt, Box 46, 1936.
47   See Elder, *Children of the Great Depression*, for a detailed discussion, based on psychological and sociological data, on the expectations placed on children in 1930s Oakland, California.
48   Sutherland, *Growing Up*, 114.
49   CC FamCt, Box 9, 1937.
50   Ibid., Box 54, 1938.
51   Wendy Johnston, 'Keeping Children in School: The Response of the Montreal Catholic School Commission to the Depression of the 1930s,' in Horn, *Great Depression in Canada*, 162–87. These numbers include those children kept home because of lack of food and clothing.
52   School attendance regulations mandated that children be in school up to the age of sixteen years, though they could be issued a special work permit between the ages of fourteen and sixteen. See also Comacchio, *Dominion of Youth*, 130, 135.
53   CC FamCt, Box 63, 1936.
54   Ibid., Box 66, 1938.
55   *Child and Family Welfare* 8/5 (1933).
56   CC FamCt, Box 16, 1935.
57   DOL, RG 7-1, Box 5, File no. 209, 'P,' General Correspondence, Pettigrew to MacBride, 5 May 1938.
58   Ross, *Love and Toil*, 152–4; Sutherland, *Growing Up*, 115–18.
59   CC FamCt, Box 65, 1932.

60 Ibid., Box 44, 1934.
61 Ibid., Box 16, 1936.
62 Sutherland, *Growing Up*, 117.
63 CC FamCt, Box 2, 1934.
64 Ibid., Box 47, 1939.
65 James Snell, 'The Family and the Working-Class Elderly in the First Half of the Twentieth Century,' in Lori Chambers and Edgar-Andre Montigny, eds., *Family Matters: Papers in Post-Confederation Canadian Family History* (Toronto: Canadian Scholars' Press, 1998), 50; Bakke, *Unemployed Worker*, 115–18.
66 Struthers, *Limits of Affluence*, 61.
67 Ibid.; James Snell, 'Maintenance Agreements for the Elderly: Canada, 1900–51,' *Journal of the Canadian Historical Association* 3 (1992), 197–216.
68 James G. Snell, *The Citizen's Wage: The State and the Elderly in Canada, 1900–1951* (Toronto: University of Toronto Press, 1996), 8.
69 Guest, *Emergence of Social Security*, 77.
70 Struthers, *Limits of Affluence*, 68, 71, 44–5.
71 YC FamCt, Box 203, 1936.
72 CC FamCt, Box 60, 1938.
73 YC FamCt, Box 210, 1937.
74 Ibid., Box 222, 1939.
75 CC FamCt, Box 2, 1936.
76 See also Snell, *Citizen's Wage*, 75–8.
77 CC FamCt, Box 44, 1937.
78 Ibid., Box 67, 1938.
79 YC FamCt, Box 200, 1936.
80 See Snell, *Citizen's Wage*; Jean, 'Family Allowances and Family Autonomy'; Marshall, 'Language of Children's Rights'; Golz, 'Family Matters.'
81 F.H Leacy, *Historical Statistics of Canada* (Ottawa: Statistics Canada, 1983), Series B75–81.
82 This survey is discussed in H.A. Weir, 'Unemployed Youth,' in Lothar Richter, ed., *Canada's Unemployment Problem* (Toronto: Macmillan, 1939), 142–5.
83 Cavan and Ranck, *Family and the Depression*, 178.
84 Hepburn Papers, Box 176, Miss Elsie Markham to Hepburn, 8 Oct. 1934.
85 Strong-Boag, *New Day Recalled*, 85–6; Comacchio, *Dominion of Youth*, 71; Steven Seidman, *Romantic Longing: Love in America, 1830–1980* (New York: Routledge, 1991); Comacchio, *Infinite Bonds of Family*, 74–5.
86 See, e.g., the records in AO, RG 22-2335, Hastings County Juvenile and Family Court (hereafter HC FamCt), Children of Unmarried Parents Act

(CUPA) Files, Box 5, 1934 and 1932; Magda Fahrni, 'Ruffled Mistresses and Discontented Maids: Respectability and the Case of Domestic Service, 1880–1914,' *L/LT* no. 39 (1997): 69–97.

87 Weir, 'Unemployed Youth,' 141.

88 Ibid., 144.

89 Little notes that in the interwar years, illegitimacy increased from 4.2% of births in 1936 to 5.2% in 1945. *'No Car, No Radio, No Liquor Permit,'* 121. See also Peter Ward, *Courtship, Love and Marriage,* on illegitimacy in nineteenth-century English Canada, 33.

90 *Child and Family Welfare* 10/5 (1935): 16.

91 Ibid.

92 AO, RG 22-4890, Simcoe County Prosecution Case Files (hereafter Simcoe Case Files), Box 17, 1935.

93 Middlesex Case Files, Box 23-38, 1938.

94 Ibid.

95 Wentworth Case Files, Box 14, 1935.

96 Mitchinson, *Nature of Their Bodies,* 144; McLaren and McLaren, *Bedroom and the State,* 51; Comacchio, *Nations Are Built of Babies,* 71–2.

97 Angus McLaren, 'Illegal Operations: Women, Doctors, and Abortion, 1886–1939,' *JSH* 26/4 (1993): 799.

98 Ibid., 803–5.

99 Algoma Case Files, Box 12, 1930–31.

100 Ibid., Box 12, 1935.

101 Simcoe Case Files, Box 17, 1935.

102 Middlesex Case Files, Box 24-29, 1938.

103 Lori Chambers, 'Illegitimate Children and the Children of Unmarried Parents Act,' Lori Chambers and Edgar-Andre Montigny, eds., *Ontario since Confederation: A Reader* (Toronto: University of Toronto Press, 2000), 235–59.

104 Sangster, *Regulating Girls,* 114–24.

105 See Lori Chambers, *Misconceptions: Unmarried Motherhood and the Ontario Children of Unmarried Parents Act, 1921–1969* (Toronto: Osgood Society for Canadian Legal History, 2007), 10, 31.

106 HC FamCt, CUPA Files, Box 5, 1932.

107 Ibid., 1934.

108 Ibid., 1939.

109 Chambers, 'You Have No Rights,' 121. Chambers argues that access increased the likelihood of men paying support, but it is still important to remember that only 16% of men in the years of her study, 1921–69, made full payments. (Of these, 67% had access to their children). Almost 50% of the men disappeared without paying.

110 HC FamCt, CUPA Files, Box 5, 1932.

111 Ibid., 1935.

112 Ibid., 1935.

113 See Chambers, *Misconceptions*, 3.

114 HC FamCt, CUPA Files, Box 5, 1929.

115 Ibid., 1934.

116 Ibid., 1934.

117 Ibid., 1934.

118 Ibid., 1931.

119 York County, Metropolitan Toronto Juvenile and Family Court (hereafter YC FamCt, CUPA Files, Box 107, 1938.

120 HC FamCt, CUPA Files, Box 5, 1933–34.

121 Ibid., 1931.

122 Ibid., 1935.

123 Ibid., 1937.

124 Ibid., 1932.

125 Ibid., 1937.

126 Ibid., 1936.

127 Cynthia Comacchio, 'Dancing to Perdition: Adolescence and Leisure in Interwar English Canada,' *Journal of Canadian Studies* 32/3 (1997): 26.

128 Ibid., 31n37. Comacchio shows that movie receipts went from an already unprecedented $38,479,500 in Canada in 1930 to $107,718,000 in 1934 and that Ontario counted for almost half of them. Bryan Palmer notes that the trend towards mass culture slowed briefly before the onslaught of the postwar consumer era. Palmer, *Working-Class Experience*, 232. For more on recreation in the interwar years, see 'At Play: Fads, Fashions, and Fun,' in Comacchio, *Dominion of Youth*, 162–88.

129 Interviews: Gladys Clements, Mary Cleeson. Florence Jackson, *North Wind Blowing Backwards* (Cobalt: Highway Bookshop, 1977), 4–6; Hartley Trussler, *Hartley Trussler's The Best of North Bay*, ed. By Michael Barnos (North Bay: North Bay and District Chamber of Commerce, 1992), 141.

4 'A Family's Self-Respect and Morale'

1 Henry Papers, MS 1744, Mrs Alice Boulton to Henry, 27 June 1931.

2 Chunn, *From Punishment to Doing Good*, 20; Sangster, *Regulating Girls and Women*.

3 Parr, *Gender of Breadwinners*.

4 Richard Harris, 'Home Ownership and Class in Modern Canada,' *International Journal of Urban and Regional Research* 10/1 (1986): 79. Harris

notes that 61.4% of Ontario residents owned their own homes in 1931. In Canada in 1931, 45.6% of urban households, 85.1% of farm households, and 78.8% of rural households owned their own homes.

5 Cassidy, *Unemployment and Relief*, 50.

6 National Employment Commission, *Final Report* (Jan. 1938), 70, Table E-XIV-Housing. In some areas of the country, numbers were even higher, such as in Burnaby, B.C., where 46.5% of those on relief were homeowners.

7 Homeownership declined in the Depression: 61.4% of Ontario residents owned their homes in 1931, while only 56.5% were homeowners in 1934. Harris, 'Home Ownership and Class,' 73.

8 *Oshawa Daily Times*, 7 Sept. 1932.

9 Henry Papers, MS 1760, File: Resolutions, the Toronto Ward Two Property Owners Joint Executive to Henry, 24 April 1933.

10 Hepburn Papers, Box 225, File: M.F.Hepburn, private, no. 3, Mrs George Amos to Hepburn, July 1934; Henry Papers, MS 1759, File: Department of Public Works, V. Grant to Hepburn, 19 Sept. 1933.

11 Henry Papers, MS 1760, File: Relief Asked For, Mrs Thomas Pearl to Henry, 18 March 1933.

12 Ibid.: File: Resolutions, Peterborough City Council to Henry, 7 Feb. 1933; Kitchener City Council to Henry, 14 June 1933; Hamilton City Council to Henry, 13 June 1933. On how taxation, charitable giving, and notions of citizenship were connected in the developing welfare state, see Shirley Tillotson, 'A New Taxpayer for a New State: Charitable Fundraising and the Origins of the Welfare State,' in Raymond Blake, Penny E. Bryden, and J. Franks Strain, eds., *The Welfare State in Canada: Past, Present and Future* (Concord: Irwin, 1997), 138–55.

13 Henry Papers, MS 1760, File: Resolutions, Miscellaneous, 15 June 1933, Resolution passed by Town of Sandwich, East Windsor.

14 TBA, Series 73, 4097, Fort William Public Welfare Board Minutes, June 1936.

15 AO, RG 49-63, Press Clipping Service, Legislative Assembly, MS 755, Reel 42, no. 3365, *Mail and Empire*, 19 April 1933; Spanner, 'Straight Furrow,' 285–90.

16 Hobbs and Roach Pierson, 'Kitchen That Wastes No Steps,' 14. The plan was only affordable for those who earned at least $1,200 per year, not the majority of the working class.

17 Sangster, *Earning Respect*, 113.

18 *Oshawa Daily Times*, 7 Sept. 1932. As of 1 August 1933 the Ontario government decided homeowners owing one year in taxes could get relief under the heading of shelter. AO, RG 29-74, DPW, J.S. Band Files, Box 9, Relief Memoranda, File no. 66, memo, n.d. Aug. 1933.

19 Henry Papers, MS 1762, File: Unemployment Relief, Homeowners, Herman Emmons to Henry, 4 Sept. 1933; ibid., MS 1747, C. Peterson to Henry, 15 Sept. 1931.

20 *Oshawa Daily Times*, 28 Sept. 1932, 4. See also *Globe and Mail*, 24 Oct. 1932, 2.

21 Henry Papers, MS 1747, File: Unemployment Relief, no. 3, C. Peterson to Henry, 15 Sept. 1931.

22 Ibid., MS 1762, File: Unemployment Relief, Homeowners, Henry Van Wurden to Henry, 8 Sept. 1933.

23 *Report of the Ontario Provincial Command, Annual Convention* (hereafter *ROPC AC*), 1934.

24 *Globe and Mail*, 8 May 1933, 3.

25 Morton, *Ideal Surroundings*, 32–8.

26 Henry Papers, MS 1755, File: Legislation, Mortgage, W.H. Prentice to Henry, 18 March 1933.

27 *Evening Examiner*, 23 Dec. 1930.

28 Hepburn Papers, Box 225, File: Personal, no. 1, Mrs Over to Hepburn, 2 Sept. 1934.

29 Mary Quayle Innis, 'The Party,' in *Voices of Discord*, 151.

30 Broadfoot, *Ten Lost Years*, 146.

31 Ibid., 153.

32 Ibid., 8–9.

33 Elder, *Children*, 53; Bakke, *Citizens without Work*, 10–13.

34 Henry Papers, MS 1760, File: Relief Asked For, Ervin Smale to Henry, 1 May 1933.

35 Ibid., MS 1762, File: Unemployment Relief, Homeowners, Herman Emmons to Henry, 4 Sept. 1933.

36 C. Gunning, *North Bay: The Lean Years, 1929–1939: A Decade of Adversity* (North Bay: Bond Printing, 1996): 151.

37 *Globe and Mail*, 2 May 1933, 31; 1 May 1933, 8; 10 May 1937, 2. For more on the tensions between property owners, municipals councils, and relief authorities, see *Globe and Mail*, 10 May 1937, 2; 10 April 1933, 3; 19 April 1933, 3; 17 April 1934, 5; 23 April 1934, 6.

38 Gunning, *North Bay*, 178–9.

39 Schulz, *East York Workers' Association*, 34.

40 *Porcupine Advance*, 29 Nov. 1934.

41 Henry Papers, MS 1759, File: Department of Public Works, Alfred Chaston to Henry, 8 May 1933.

42 CC FamCt, Box 29, 1939.

43 Dennis, *Marching Orders*, 126–9.

44 *Globe and Mail*, 1 Aug. 1936, 10; 6 Jan. 1937, 4; 22 Aug. 1935, 2; 18 Sept. 1933, 9.

45 Ibid., 1 Sept. 1937, 4; 21 Sept. 1934, 4; 14 Sept. 1938, 4.

46 Saywell, *'Just Call Me Mitch,'* 86, 34, 86.

47 Henry Papers, MS 1755, File: Legislation, Mortgages, C.J. Blacknall to Henry, 20 March 1933.

48 Ibid., MS 1760, File: General Correspondence, P.D. McCabe to Henry, 13 Jan. 1933.

49 Ibid., MS 1755, File: Legislation, Mortgages, anonymous to Henry, n.d. June 1933.

50 Saywell, *'Just Call Me Mitch,'* 86, 334; Spanner, 'Straight Furrow,' 206–7.

51 Berton, *Great Depression*, 415; Wilbur, *Bennett New Deal*, 45–6; Horn, *Great Depression*, 19.

52 AO, RG 22-5751, Wentworth County, Official Receiver's Farmers' Creditors Arrangement Files, Box 1, no. 136, 1936.

53 Ibid., Box 1, no. 112, 1936.

54 Ibid., Box 1, no. 92, 1936.

55 AO, RG 22-4490, Prescott and Russell Counties Prosecution Case Files (hereafter Prescott/Russell Case Files), Crown Attorney, Box 6, 1939. Unfortunately, there was in fact no insurance policy on the barn.

56 Hepburn Papers, Box 293, File: W.G. Nixon, MLA, Temiskaming, to Hepburn, 29 Aug. and 13 Oct. 1938.

57 Ibid., Nixon to Hepburn, 2 Feb. 1938.

58 Ibid., Hepburn to Nixon, 22 Sept. 1938.

59 Ibid., Box 247, File: Public Welfare Department, 30 Jan. 1935.

60 Henry Papers, MS 1762, File: Unemployment Relief, Homeowners, Mrs Knut Hansen to Henry, 21 July 1933.

61 National Archives of Canada (NAC), RG 27, DOL, Strikes and Lockout Files, vol.380, no. 25, 1936.

62 *Globe and Mail*, 15 July 1933, 11; 24 April 1936, 2; 9 June 1936, 9; 1 March 1933, 9; 10 April 1933, 9.

63 Ibid., 19 April 1933, 3; 17 April 1933, 3.

64 Ibid., 7 Oct. 1933, 2; 5 July 1933, 2.

65 *Toronto Daily Star*, 3 Aug. 1932.

66 Hunter, *Which Side Are You On?*

67 Schulz, *EYWA*, 34; Hunter, *Which Side*, 21.

68 *Globe and Mail*, 15 July 1933, 11.

69 Ibid., 1936: 8 July, 9; 9 July, 4; 17 July, 2; 21 July, 2; 28 July, 10; 29 July, 4.

70 AO, RG 49-63, Press Clippings Service, Legislative Assembly, MS 755, Reel 592, *Toronto Star*, 10 May 1932.

71 *Globe and Mail*, 30 Nov. 1935, 4 and 11.
72 As Neil Sutherland shows, the practice of women being the household financial managers did not fade until after the Second World War. *Growing Up*, 132. In the postwar Canadian Youth Commission survey it is interesting to note how quickly this shift in thinking occurred. The survey reported that youth aged between fifteen and twenty-four, regardless of ethnic or religious affiliation (French, English, Protestant, Catholic, and Jewish youth were surveyed), overwhelmingly felt that the father should 'manage' the family income, though women and children should be 'consulted.' CYC, *Youth Marriage and the Family*, 92.
73 Interviews: Dorothy Osmars, Basil Libby, Earl Craig, Mary Cleeson.
74 Nancy Forestall, 'The Miner's Wife: Working-Class Femininity in a Masculine Context, 1920–50,' in Kathryn McPherson and Cecilia Morgan, eds., *Gendered Pasts: Historical Essays in Femininity and Masculinity in Canada* (Toronto: Oxford University Press, 1999), 148–9.
75 Bakke, *Citizens without Work*, 210, 114. Bakke's study of families in New Haven was one of a number of surveys done in the 1930s by social scientists in order to develop an understanding of the impact of unemployment on the family, and to develop a cohesive social science of human relationships and the economy. Thus, families tended to be categorized by their degree of cohesion or 'disorganization' and assessed on the basis of how they 'properly' or 'improperly' adjusted to the reality of unemployment. See also Angel, *Family Encounters the Great Depression*, 90; Lewis, *Women in England*, 27. Lewis shows that husbands often had 'harsh words' for the budgeting skills of wives, though in cases where they themselves had to manage household budgets, they did so quite poorly.
76 YC FamCt, Box 191, 1935, Box 218, 1938.
77 Ibid., Box 179, 1931.
78 YC FamCt, Box 179, 1933.
79 AO, RG 22-1090, Algoma District Prosecution Case Files, Box 13, 1939; CC FamCt, Box 65, 1938.
80 YC FamCt, Box 188, 1934.
81 CC FamCt, Box 54, 1938.
82 CYC, *Marriage and the Family*, 84–5.
83 CYC, *Youth and Jobs*, 15, 26.
84 Gordon, *Heroes of Their Own Lives*; Kathryn Harvey, 'Amazons and Victims: Resisting Wife Abuse in Working-Class Montreal, 1869–79,' *Journal of the Canadian Historical Association* 2 (1991): 133–4; Valverde, *Age of Light, Soap and Water*, 59–60; Mitchinson, 'Women's Christian Temperance Union.'

85 Gordon, *Heroes*, 144–5; Ross, *Love and Toil*, 42–3.
86 Ross, *Love and Toil*, 43.
87 Baillargeon, *Making Do*, 104.
88 CC FamCt, Box 53, 1931.
89 Ibid., Box 7, 1936-7; YC FamCt, Box 173, 1931.
90 CC FamtCt, Box 42, 1936.
91 Ibid., Box 13, 1939.
92 YC FamCt, Box 188, 1935.
93 Ibid., Box 170, 1932.
94 See Ross, *Love and Toil*, 49; Elaine Frantz Parsons, 'Risky Business: The Uncertain Boundaries of Manhood in the Midwestern Saloon,' *JSH* 34/2 (2000): 283–307.
95 YC FamCt, Box 170, 1930.
96 CC FamtCt, Box 46, 1934.
97 Ibid., Box 57, 1936.
98 Ibid., Box 29, 1929.
99 Ibid., Box 31, 1938.
100 Parsons, 'Risky Business,' 293–94; Ross, *Love and Toil*, 44.
101 CC FamCt, Box 49, 1937.
102 YC FamCt, Box 179, 1932.
103 Ibid., Box 222, 1939.
104 Ibid., Box 210, 1937.
105 CC FamCt, Box 41, 1934.
106 Ibid., Box 45, 1934.
107 YC FamCt, Box 210, 1937.
108 CC FamCt, Box 64, 1936.
109 Ibid., Box 15, 1938.
110 YC FamCt, Box 181, 1934.
111 Beverly Stadum, *Poor Women and Their Families: Hardworking Charity Cases, 1900–30* (New York: State University of New York Press, 1992), 98; Benson, 'Living on the Margin,' 223.
112 CC FamCt, Box 61, 1939.
113 Annalee Golz, 'Uncovering and Reconstructing Family Violence: Ontario Criminal Case Files,' in Iacovetta and Mitchinson, *On the Case*, 297.
114 YC FamCt, Box 218, 1938.
115 Elspeth Probyn, *blush* (Minneapolis: University of Minnesota Press, 2005); Silvan Tomkins, 'Shame-Humiliation and Contempt-Disgust,' in Eve Kosofsky Sedgwick and Adam Frank, eds., *Shame and Its Sisters: A Silvan Tomkins Reader* (Durham: Duke University Press, 1995).
116 Dennis, *Marching Orders*, 114–15, 124–5.

117 Muriel E. Newton White, *The Sunset and the Morning* (Cobalt: Highway Bookshop), 14, 105.

118 Sara Ahmed, *The Cultural Politics of Emotion* (New York: Routledge, 2004); Probyn, *blush*; Benson, 'Living on the Margin,' 219–20.

119 Wentworth Case Files, Box 13, 1932.

120 Cassidy, *Unemployment and Relief*, 244. Cassidy notes that social service agencies observed many families moving in together when the Great Depression hit. In her study of Hanover, Ontario, Parr notes that Knechtal employees responded in a similar fashion. In 1926, 96% lived in single-family homes, but by 1938, one-third shared their dwelling with another family to save money. Parr, *Gender of Breadwinners*. Baillargeon claims that in Montreal this strategy was a blend of economics and pre-industrial cultural tradition, though even in her sample, the maximum time a couple lived with parents or in-laws was two years. Baillargeon, *Making Do*, 159, 163. See also Snell, 'Family and the Working Class Elderly,' 500; Susan McDaniel and Robert Lewis, 'Did They or Didn't They? Inter-generational Supports in Families Past: A Case Study of Brighs, Nfld., 1920–45,' in Chambers and Montigny, *Family Matters*, 492; Chad M. Gaffield, 'Canadian Families in Cultural Context: Hypotheses from the Mid-Nineteenth Century,' in *Canadian Family History*, 139; Mary S. Hartman, *The Household and the Making of History: A Subversive View of the Western Past* (Cambridge: Cambridge University Press, 2005).

121 DPW, Mothers' Allowance Case Files, Box 1, 1930–39.

122 Ibid., Box 1, 1935.

123 Ibid., Box 1, 1935–37.

124 CC FamCt, Box 50, 1934.

125 YC FamCt, Box 170, 1936.

126 Ibid., Box 182, 1934.

127 Ibid., Box 200, 1936; Henry Papers, MS 1760, Victor Maclean to Henry, 20 Feb. 1933.

128 Interview, Hilda Mae (Allen) O'Brien.

129 Interview, Ruth (Allen) Aho.

130 CC FamCt, Box 54, 1936.

131 Cassidy, *Unemployment and Relief*, 255.

132 *Child and Family Welfare* 8/1 (1932): 22. See also, ibid., 8/5 (1933): 16–19.

133 CC FamCt, Box 15, 1938.

134 Ibid., Box 64, 1936.

135 Ibid., Box 69, 1937–40. The CAS had paid $15 a month for the children, and the town of Eastview had paid a total of $1,660.80.

136 Ibid., Box 17, 1938.

137 DPW, Mothers' Allowance Files, Box 2, 1935. See also Sangster, *Earning Respect*, 129.

138 Golz, 'Uncovering and Reconstructing Family Violence'; Nancy Tomes, 'A Torrent of Abuse: Crimes of Violence between Working-Class Men and Women in London, 1840–75,' *JSH* 11/3 (1978): 329–45.

139 CC FamCt, Box 45, 1938; YC FamCt, Box 215, 1938.

140 As Gordon notes in *Heroes of Their own Lives*, in the Depression era in the United States, unemployment was of central concern to the courts.

141 Wentworth County Case Files, Box 12, 1933.

142 YC FamCt, Box 222, 1939.

143 Ibid., Box 170, 1931.

144 CC FamCt, Box 33, 1932.

145 Lynne Segal, *Slow Motion: Changing Masculinities, Changing Men* (New Jersey: Rutgers University Press, 1990): 256. See also Janet Mosher, 'Caught in Tangled Webs of Care: Women Abused in Intimate Relationships,' in Carol T. Baines et al., *Women's Caring: Feminist Perspectives on Social Welfare* (Toronto: Oxford University Press, 1998), 139–59; D. Levinson, *Family Violence in Cross-Cultural Perspective* (Newbury Park: Sage, 1989); K. Yllo and M. Bograd, eds., *Feminist Perspectives on Wife Abuse* (London: Sage, 1988).

146 Gordon, *Heroes*, 3; Segal, *Slow Motion*, 256; Sangster, *Regulating Girls*, 65.

147 Sangster, *Regulating Girls*, 70.

148 CC FamCt, Box 69, 1930.

149 YC FamCt, Box 186, 1932.

150 Ibid., Box 191, 1935.

151 AO, RG 22-2690, Kent County, Ontario Crown Attorney, Prosecution Case Files, 1937.

152 *Evening Examiner*, 13 Nov. 1930.

153 Golz, 'Uncovering and Reconstructing,' 293.

154 For the various ways that women fought back against male violence, see Anna Clark, *Women's Silence, Men's Violence: Sexual Assault in England, 1770–1845* (London: Pandora, 1987); Gordon, *Heroes*; Tomes, 'Torrent of Abuse'; Kathryn Harvey, 'Amazons and Victims.'

155 *Porcupine Advance*, 1937.

156 See Cavan and Ranck, *Family and the Depression*, 57.

5 Militant Mothers and Loving Fathers

1 Henry Papers, MS 1759, File: Department of Public Works, Thomas Frith to Henry, 9 Oct. 1933.

2 Desmond Morton, *Working People: An Illustrated History of the Canadian Labour Movement* (Toronto: Summerhill, 1990), 142. In 1930 there were just sixty-seven strikes in Canada, and twenty ended in favour of employers. Stuart Jamieson, *Times of Trouble: Labour Unrest and Industrial Conflict in Canada, 1900–66* (Ottawa: Minister of Supply and Services, 1976), 214. Despite a series of strike waves in 1934 and 1937, historians have characterized these as 'desperation strikes' to prevent wage rollbacks or to maintain or demand union recognition. Jamieson identifies a strike revival between 1935 and 1940, peaking in 1937, due partly to the American Wagner Act and the development of the CIO. See also Brown, *When Freedom Was Lost*, 31; Gregory Kealey and Douglas Cruikshank, 'Strikes in Canada, 1891–1950,' in Gregory Kealey, ed., *Workers and Canadian History* (Montreal and Kingston: McGill-Queen's University Press, 1995), 375. The authors note that fifteen of nineteen strikes were in Ontario in 1934, mainly in Toronto, and were on the basis of union recognition.

3 See, e.g., Struthers, *No Fault of Their Own*; Horn, *League for Social Reconstruction*; Sangster, *Dreams of Equality*; Carmela Patrias, 'Relief Strike: Immigrant Workers and the Great Depression in Crowland, Ontario, 1930–1935,' in Franca Iacovetta and Robert Ventresca, eds., *A Nation of Immigrants: Women, Workers and Communities in Canadian History, 1840s–1960s* (Toronto: University of Toronto Press, 1998), 322–58; Lorne Brown, 'Unemployed Struggles in Saskatchewan and Canada, 1930–1935,' *Prairie Forum* 31/2 (2006): 193–216.

4 See Brown, *When Freedom Was Lost*, 25; Manley, 'Starve, Be Damned!' 471–3. The first unemployed workers' union was founded in September 1929 in Vancouver, and by fall 1931 there were six in Saskatoon alone. NUWA was launched in 1930, initially targeting transient male workers in Vancouver; it was attached to the WUL in 1931, but renamed the National Council of Unemployed Committees in 1932, when it removed itself from the WUL to attract workers who did not identify as Marxist.

5 Manley, 'Starve, Be Damned!' 473. Associations in the Toronto suburbs of North York, Etobicoke, Mimico, and Longbranch were particularly active.

6 Palmer, *Working-Class Experience*, 245; Schulz, *EYWA*. Premier Hepburn, the Liberal cabinet, and the police were convinced that unemployed activism was cunningly organized by communist agitators. This assumption rested on the belief that the unemployed were easily manipulated rather than actively seeking ways to negotiate relief. See Saywell, *'They Call Me Mitch,'* 265–7.

7 Relief strikes were documented by the federal Department of Labour, which kept a record of relief strikes, industrial strikes, and hunger

marches in Canada. These records document seventy-seven relief strikes in Ontario, including seventy-three strikes, three strike threats, and one case of direct action against relief officials outside of a strike. Note, however, that this database did not include every incident of protest across the country. NAC, RG 27, DOL, Strikes and Lockout Files.

8 Morton, *Working People*, 150; Palmer, *Working-Class Experience*, 246.

9 These letters are housed at the Archives of Ontario in the collection of the Premiers' Papers, and include letters to members of Parliament, municipal politicians, and directly to the various ministers of public welfare and of labour. Henry Papers, Correspondence; Hepburn Papers, Public Correspondence; Hepburn Papers, Private Correspondence.

10 Bliss and Grayson, *Wretched of Canada*, xxv.

11 For demographics on the Ontario population, see Ontario Bureau of Statistics, *A Conspectus of the Province of Ontario* (Toronto: King's Printer, 1947), 210, Table 9. Also, it is important to note that 96% of the population were British subjects, as opposed to 'aliens.' Ibid., 212, Table 12.

12 See Fraser and Gordon, 'Contract vs Charity'; Roach Pierson, 'Gender and the Unemployment Insurance Debates in Canada.'

13 Deborah Gould, 'Rock the Boat, Don't Rock the Boat, Baby: Ambivalence and the Emergence of Militant AIDS Activism,' in Jeff Goodwin et al., eds., *Passionate Politics: Emotions and Social Movements* (Chicago: University of Chicago, 2001), 135–55.

14 Jeff Goodwin, 'Introduction: Why Emotions Matter,' *Passionate Politics*, 7–28; Peter N. Stearns and Jan Lewis, eds., *An Emotional History of the United States* (New York: New York University Press, 1998), 1–2, on how emotions can 'create history.'

15 See Humphries, 'Working Class Family'; May 'Bread before Roses; Ron Rothbart, '"Homes Are What Any Strike Is About": Immigrant Labor and the Family Wage,' *JSH* 23/2 (1989): 267–84. May argues that the family wage was initially rooted in improving family living standards, but as the ideology became accepted by cross-class reformers, including representatives from both state and labour, it was increasingly about enforcing male dominance in the home and the labour force.

16 See Joan Sangster's description of the Peterborough Unemployed Workers' Unity League, organized in 1933. Sangster, *Earning Respect*, 126.

17 Rothbart, 'Homes,' 278. Even with the advent of mechanization and mass production, values of dignity and worth in labour proved to be remarkably elastic concepts used by workers and the unemployed. See Ava Baron, 'On Looking at Men: Masculinity and the Making of a Gendered Working-Class History,' in Ann-Louise Shapiro, ed., *Feminists' Revision*

History, 158; Palmer, *Working-Class Experience*, 57–9, 155–63; Ava Baron, 'An "Other" Side of Gender Antagonism at Work: Men, Boys, and the Remasculization of Printers' Work, 1830–1920,' in A. Baron, ed., *Work Engendered: Toward a New History of American Labor* (Ithaca: Cornell University, 1991), 47–69; Bryan Palmer, *A Culture in Conflict: Skilled Workers and Industrial Capitalism in Hamilton, Ontario, 1860–1914* (Montreal: McGill-Queen's University Press, 1979); Gregory Kealey, *Toronto Workers Respond to Industrial Capitalism, 1867–1892* (Toronto: University of Toronto Press, 1980).

18 For the nineteenth century, see articles in Baron, *Work Engendered*. In particular, see Mary Blewett, 'Manhood and the Market: The Politics of Gender and Class among the Textile Workers of Fall River, Massachusetts, 1870–1880,' 92–113; Eileen Boris, '"A Man's Dwelling House Is His Castle": Tenement House Cigarmaking and the Judicial Imperative,' 114–41; and Ileen De Vault, '"Give the Boys a Trade": Gender and Job Choice in the 1890s,' 191–215.

19 Robert Rutherdale argues that fathers have historically been 'more than income earners' in their families. Rutherdale, 'Fatherhood and Masculine Domesticity during the Baby Boom: Consumption and Leisure in Advertising and Life Stories,' in Chambers and Montigny, *Family Matters*, 310.

20 Robert R. Griswold, *Fatherhood in America: A History* (New York: Basic Books, 1993); Rutherdale, 'Fatherhood and Masculine Domesticity,' 309.

21 Humphries, 'Working Class Family,' 38.

22 Struthers, *No Fault of Their Own*, 74. The Ontario government required that all those receiving direct relief do some work 'equivalent to the amount of relief given' in return. RG 29-74, DPW, J.S. Band Files, Box 9, Relief Memoranda, File: Offical Memoranda, 'Memorandum as to Direct Relief,' n.d. Dec. 1933.

23 Struthers, *Limits of Affluence*, 87; Clifford J. Williams, *Decades of Service: A History of the Ontario Ministry of Community and Social Services, 1930–80* (Ontario: Ministry of Community and Social Services, 1984),:18.

24 NAC, RG 27, DOL, Strikes and Lockout Files. Of the thirty-seven cases focused on work and wages, however, nine (24%) utilized the rhetoric or symbolism of gender, home, and family, such as women leading parades or using women and children as barricades, or male relief workers demanding a family wage.

25 Ibid., vol. 358A, Box 54, 1933.

26 Ibid., vol. 351, Box 66, 1932. *Globe and Mail*, 11 May 1938, 4.

27 AO, RG 49-63, Press Clippings, Legislative Assembly, MS 755, Box 592, from Toronto *Globe*, 'Relief Troubles Acute,' 16 May 1932.

28 See Ross, *Love and Toil*, 32–3, 45.

29 AO, RG 29-74, DPW, J.S. Band Files, Box 6, Relief Memoranda, File no. 66, Memo, 31 Dec. 1932.

30 NAC, RG 27, vol. 366, Box 65, 1934; vol. 381, 'Strikes, Jan.–Oct.,' 1936.

31 Ibid., vol. 394, Box 21, 1937.

32 Ibid., vol. 366, Box 27, 1934.

33 *Oshawa Daily Times*, 17 Nov. 1932.

34 Ibid., 2 Dec. 1932.

35 Ibid., 21 Oct. 1932.

36 Cruikshank and Kealey, 'Strikes in Canada,' 358–9. See also Liversedge, *Recollections of the On-to-Ottawa Trek*, 73–82, on the occupation of the Vancouver Hudson's Bay store and museum.

37 NAC, RG 27, vol. 359, Box 30, 1933.

38 *Windsor Daily Star*, 21 April 1938.

39 NAC, RG 27, vol. 380, Box 12, 1936.

40 Ibid., vol. 372, Box 15, 1935.

41 On the role of the charivari, see Bryan Palmer, 'Discordant Music: Charivaris and Whitecapping in Nineteenth-Century North America,' *L/LT* no. 3 (1978): 5–62; E.P. Thompson, '"Rough Music" or English Charivari,' *Annales* 27 (1972): 285–312; Loretta T. Johnson, 'Chivaree/Shivaree: A European Folk Ritual on the American Plains,' *Journal of Interdisciplinary History* 20/3 (1990): 371–87.

42 NAC, RG 27, , vol. 380, Box 26, 1936. See also *Globe and Mail*, 27 April 1939, 28, where men in Scorborough Township denounced the local reeve and councillor and picketed the reeve's home with signs protesting the reeve's 'five cent meals.'

43 A wave of relief strikes also occurred in summer 1935 in response to the increased provincial supervision of municipalities where relief rates had increased over the maximum ceilings. The strikes in 1936 were likely the last attempt to push the municipalities and the province to increase or maintain adequate relief rates, but as James Struthers notes, there was little they could do because David Croll, in April 1936, imposed special property taxes to punish municipalities that offered relief above the maximum amount. Struthers, *Limits of Affluence*, 93–6.

44 NAC, RG 27, vol. 380, Box 28, 1936.

45 Ibid., vol. 380, Box 28, 1936.

46 Ibid., vol. 366, Box 60, 1934.

47 AO, RG 4-32, Attorney General Case Files, 1934.

48 See Charles Tilly, *From Mobilization to Revolution* (Reading: Addison-Wesley, 1978), and George Rudé, *The Crowd in History: A Study of Popular*

Disturbances in France and England, 1730–1848 (New York: Wiley, 1964), on the rationality of crowds; Stearns and Lewis, *Emotional History of the United States*, 1–14 and Goodwin, 'Introduction: Why Emotions Matter,' 1–24, for a good overview of how scholars have understood rationality and emotion in collective protest.

49 In eleven cases, strikers won nothing at all, and in eight cases, strike actions and protests resulted in police charges, imprisonment, or families being cut from relief. In 36% of cases, no outcome at all was noted. Nothing was won in 14% of all cases, or 22% of all cases where the outcomes were noted; strikers were worse off in 10% of all cases after strike action, or 16% of cases where the outcome was noted. Full or partial demands were met in 18% of cases, or 27% of cases with known outcomes.

50 NAC, RG 27, vol. 353, Box 151, 1932.

51 See ibid., vol. 366, Box 6, 1934, and vol. 375, Box 54, 1935.

52 Ibid., vol. 380, Box 30, 1936.

53 Struthers, *Limits of Affluence*, 92. The provincial maximum in 1934 was set at the standard of the 1932 Campbell Report plus 25%. The Ontario government arrived at this formulation in 1934 after assessing rising food costs. Municipalities could raise the amount of relief to a maximum of 25% over the original rates set out in the Campbell Report. See Dorothy King, 'Unemployment Aid and Direct Relief,' in Richtar, *Canada's Employment Problem*, 100.

54 See Roach Pierson, 'Gender and the Unemployment Insurance Debates'; Jonathan Vance, *Death So Noble: Memory, Meaning and the First World War* (Vancouver: University of British Columbia Press, 1997).

55 Desmond Morton, 'The Canadian Veterans' Heritage from the Great War,' in Peter Neary and J.L Granatstein, eds., *The Veterans Charter and Post-World War II Canada* (Montreal: McGill-Queens' University Press, 1998), 23. By 1919 the Great War Veterans Association advocated such welfare state polices as public housing, minimum wage, nationalization of primary resources, profit controls, and age, sickness, and unemployment insurance. Jeffrey A. Keshen, *Propaganda and Censorship during Canada's Great War* (Edmonton: University of Alberta Press, 1996), 204.

56 As Desmond Morton points out, while veterans' groups were often on the 'the political right,' they also maintained an 'egalitarian, radical edge.' Morton, 'Canadian Veterans' Heritage,' 22.

57 In *Protecting Soldiers and Mother: The Political Origins of Social Policy in the United States* (Cambridge: Belknap Press of Harvard University Press, 1992), Theda Skocpol argues that while American Civil War pensions approached de facto old age and disability pensions, these benefits

were ultimately linked to war service and not to broader support of the male breadwinner role.

58 Henry Papers, MS 1759, File: Department of Public Works, East Block, T. Frith to Henry, 31 Aug. 1933.

59 Mary Reynolds, 'And the Answer Is ...' in Wright and Edres, *Eight Men Speak*, 143.

60 Love, 'Looking Forward,' in *Eight Men Speak*, 16. F.W. Watt argues that protest literature in the 1930s moved Canadian fiction away from a literary 'culture of nation-building' to one of realism. F.W. Watt, 'Literature of Protest,' in Carl F. Klink et al., eds., *Literary History of Canada: Canadian Literature in English*, vol. 6 (Toronto: University of Toronto Press, 1965), 473–89.

61 *ROPC AC*, 1934.

62 *Legionary* 10/3 (1935): 4; 10/6 (1935): 8.

63 Ibid., 5/2 (1930): 1.

64 *ROPC AC*, 1931 and1933; *Legionary* 9/4 (1934): 7.

65 *ROPC AC*, 1933.

66 Legion submissions also influenced the recommendations of the Hyndman Report, initiated in the waning days of R.B. Bennett's power. Partially adopted by the King government in 1936, the report reserved jobs issuing door-to-door radio licences for unemployed veterans and gave wage subsidies for veterans' job training.

67 Henry Papers, MS 1744, File: Positions, General, June 1931 to Jan. 1933, J.W. Alfred Rowe to Henry, 9 Aug. 1931.

68 *Legionary* 8/12 (1933): 7–8.

69 In Jan. 1919, when the Great War Veterans' Associationcalled for a $2,000 war bonus despite opposition from the leaders, its membership increased from 20,000 to 200,000. Morton, 'Canadian Veterans' Heritage,' 24. On the popularity of bonuses and the relationship between American veterans and protest, see Stephen R. Ortiz, 'Rethinking the Bonus March: Federal Bonus Policy, the Veterans of Foreign Wars, and the Origins of a Protest Movement,' *Journal of Policy History* 18/3 (2006): 275–303; Jennifer D. Keene, *Doughboys, the Great War and the Remaking of America* (Baltimore: Johns Hopkins University Press, 2001); Paul Dickson and Thomas B. Allen, *The Bonus Army: An American Epic* (New York: Walker, 2004).

70 Morton and Wright, *Winning the Second Battle*, 214.

71 *Legionary* 4/7 (1929): 5.

72 Ibid., 12/4 (1936): 30.

73 Hepburn Papers, Box 180, File: Unemployment Relief, William Kinsman to Henry, 17 Dec. 1934.

74 Henry Papers, MS 1745, File: Returned Men, F.J. Shaw to Henry, Aug. 1931.
75 Ibid., MS 1747, File: Unemployment Relief, no. 3, Lt W.J. Osborne Dempster to Henry, 8 Oct. 1931.
76 *Legionary* 9/4 (1934): 7.
77 Morton and Wright, *Winning the Second Battle*, 141.
78 *Legionary* 10/6 (1935): 8; 10/3 (1935): 1.
79 Ibid., 10/4 (1935): 9.
80 Morton and Wright, *Winning*, 218, 214.
81 NAC, RG 27, DOL, Deputy Minister's Office, vol. 187, File: 614.06:6, Unemployment of Ex-Servicemen, 1935–42, 'Response of the Canadian Legion to the Hyndman Committee Report,' 8 June 1935.
82 Keshen, *Propaganda and Censorship*, 17.
83 *Canadians Never Budge, 1918*, in Jean-Michel Viger, ed., 'Songs of the Canadian Soldier: The Great War, 1914–1918,' unpublished manuscript, held at the Dominion Command Library, Ottawa.
84 Ibid., *Canadian Battle Song, 1918*. On ideas about Canada and the 'Nordic races,' see Marilyn Barber, 'Introduction,' in J.S. Woodsworth, *Strangers at Our Gates*, 2nd ed. (Toronto: University of Toronto Press, 1972 [1909]).
85 *Legionary* 4/10 (1930): 5. Under Prime Minister Mackenzie King, the War Veterans Allowance Act extended old age pensions to those soldiers who had been judged 'broken down or burned out,' usually at age sixty-five, five years earlier than the OAP. However, the WVA Act was administered as an allowance, not a pension. It was discretionary, means-tested, and allowed a maximum of $40 per month for married men. Dennis Guest, *The Emergence of Social Security in Canada* (Vancouver: University of British Columbia Press, 1985), 95.
86 *Legionary* 9/6 (1934): 4.
87 Morton and Wright, *Winning*, Military Hospitals Commission, poster reproduction.
88 Hepburn Papers, Box 180, File: Unemployment Relief, Canadian Legion Unemployment Committee to Hepburn, Dec. 1934.
89 *Legionary* 6/11 (1932): 7.
90 Ibid.
91 Fraser and Gordon, 'Contract vs Charity,' 54–6.
92 Henry Papers, MS 1759, File: Department of Public Works, East Block, F. Kelly, 24 May 1933.
93 Morton and Wright, *Winning*, 209–20.
94 RG 49-63, Press Clipping Service, Legislative Assembly, MS 755, Box 6336, *Globe*, 27 Oct. 1933.

95 Evans, 'Divided Citizenship?' 91, 95; Roach Pierson, 'Gender and the Unemployment Insurance Debates'; Pateman, *Disorder of Women*, 182–5, 192–5.

96 Frager, *Sweatshop Strife*; Sangster, *Dreams of Equality*; E.P. Thompson, 'The Moral Economy of the English Crowd in the Eighteenth Century,' *Past and Present* no.50 (1971): 76–136; Rusty Bitterman, 'Women and the Escheat Movement: The Politics of Everyday Life on Prince Edward Island,' in Strong-Boag and Fellman, *Rethinking Canada*, 47–58; Dana Frank, 'Housewives, Socialists, and the Politics of Food: The 1917 New York Cost-of-Living Protests,' in K. Sklar and T. Dublin, eds., *Women and Power in American History*, vol 2 (Englewood Cliffs, NJ: Prentice-Hall, 1991), 101–13; Carolyn Strange, 'Mothers on the March: Maternalism in Women's Protest for Peace in North America and Western Europe, 1900–85,' in Guida West and Rhoda Lois Blumberg, eds., *Women and Social Protest* (New York: Oxford University Press, 1990), 209–24; Alexis Jetter et al., eds., *The Politics of Motherhood: Activist Voices from Left to Right* (Hanover: University Press of New England, 1997).

97 Henry Papers, MS 1744, File, Positions, General, June 1931 to Jan. 1932, Mrs Alice Boulton to Henry, 27 June 1931.

98 Ibid., MS 1745, File: Relief Asked For, , Mrs W.A. Rowland to Henry, 1 Oct. 1931.

99 See Gordon, *Heroes of Their Own Lives*; Bird, 'Hamilton Working Women'; Hobbs, 'Equality and Difference,' 201–3; Kessler-Harris, 'Gender Ideology in Historical Reconstruction'; Klee, 'Between the Scylla and Charybdis'; Hobbs, 'Rethinking Antifeminism,' 4–15. In certain industries such as restaurant service, Klee has shown that married women had a strong identity as family providers.

100 Hepburn Papers, Box 180, File: Unemployment Relief, no. 1, Mrs A. McKenna to Hepburn, 16 July 1934.

101 Hobbs, 'Rethinking Antifeminism'; Christie, *Engendering the State*, 209–15.

102 Hepburn Papers, Box 180, File: Unemployment Relief, no. 1, Mrs W.H. Mitchell to Hepburn, 2 Oct. 1934.

103 Henry Papers, MS 1747, Mrs Wallace Gow to Henry, File: Unemployment Relief, no. 3, 9 Sept. 1931.

104 See Sangster, *Dreams of Equality*; Howard, 'Holding the Fort for the Unemployed'; Annelise Orleck, '"We Are That Mythical Thing Called the Public": Militant Housewives during the Great Depression,' *Feminist Studies* 1 (1993): 147–72.

105 Henry Papers, MS 1736, File: Agricultural Development Board, Mrs Agnes Sullivan to Henry, 26 Aug. 1931.

106 Hepburn Papers, Box 203, File: Provincial Secretary's Department, Mrs J. Jones to Hepburn, 14 May 1936.
107 Ibid., Mrs Lionel Moulton to Hepburn, 10 May 1936.
108 MAG, Criminal and Civil Case Files, Box 11, 1938.
109 NAC, RG 27, vol. 375, Box 57, 1935.
110 Sangster, *Dreams of Equality*, 91–164.
111 Love, 'Looking Forward,' 17.
112 Taylor, 'Food Riots Revisited,' 492.
113 The Workers' Economic Conference was one of a number of conferences held for local unemployed organizations across the country by the NCUC. It was held at the same time as the Bennett government hosted the Imperial Economic Conference. Bennett tried to prevent delegates from arriving by having the RCMP stop and search trains, and he met with conference delegates surrounded by RCMP bodyguards. The rally, where city police led a charge against protestors, had been banned. Manley, 'Communism and the Canadian Working Class,' 564–7.
114 *Toronto Daily Star*, 2 and 3 Aug. 1932.
115 Ibid., 3 Aug. 1932.
116 Sangster, *Dreams of Equality*; Howard, 'Holding the Fort.'
117 Frager, *Sweatshop Strife*, 163.
118 Orleck, 'We Are that Mythical Thing.'
119 *Oshawa Daily Times*, 29 Oct. 1932.
120 NAC, RG 27, vol. 359, Box 29, 1933.
121 Ibid., vol. 358, Box 64, 1933.
122 Ibid., vol. 380, Box 86, 1932.
123 Ibid., vol. 380, Box 25, 1936.
124 Ibid., vol. 351, Box 66, 1932.
125 Ibid., vol. 351, Box 86, 1932.
126 Ibid., vol. 380, Box 25, 1936.
127 Ibid., vol. 380, Box 28, 1936.
128 Ibid., vol. 380 Box 40, 1936.
129 Ibid., vol. 380, Box 28, 1936.
130 Ibid., vol. 380, Box 17, 1936.
131 Ibid., vol. 359, Box 27, 1933.
132 Ibid., vol. 374, Box 30, 1935.
133 Ibid., vol. 380, Box 11, 1936.
134 Klee, 'Between the Scylla and Charybdis,' 301. See also Bitterman, 'Women and the Escheat Movement.'
135 MAG, Criminal and Civil Case Files, 1935.
136 NAC, RG 27, vol. 366, Box 53, 1934.

137 Patricia Schulz argues that the EYWA found the school strike to be an effective form of protest because it affected provincial education grants, which were based on daily attendance figures. Schulz, *EYWA*, 28.
138 *Globe and Mail*, 16 March 1935, 13.
139 NAC, RG 27, vol. 375, Box 56, 1935; *Globe and Mail*, 13 Nov. 1935, 11.
140 NAC, RG 27, vol. 374, Box 14, 1935.
141 Ibid., vol. 358A, Box 64, 1933.
142 Ibid., vol. 375 Box 56, 1935.
143 Penfold, 'Have You No Manhood in You?' 277–88.
144 As Linda Gordon points out, when women made demands for relief, they rejected charity, 'invent[ed] rights,' and claimed the status of rightful citizens. Gordon, *Pitied But Not Entitled*, 627.
145 Frances Fox Piven and Richard A. Cloward, 'Welfare Doesn't Shore Up Traditional Family Roles: A Reply to Linda Gordon,' *Social Research* 55/4 (1988): 633.
146 Patrias, 'Relief Strike,' in Iacovetta, *Women, Workers and Communities*, 323, 327.
147 Schulz, *EYWA*, 4, 18. Schulz shows that by the 1920s, East York was a predominantly Anglo-Saxon area, characterized by working-class families and homeownership. Most members of the organizations were of Anglo background. See also Manley, 'Communism,' 545–6.
148 NAC, RG 27, vol. 374, Box 36, 1935.
149 Ibid., vol. 366, Box 65, 1934. See also Manley, 'Communism,' 574.
150 Manley, 'Communism,' 539–40. A detailed historical analysis of the ethnic membership and political ideologies of the leaders and members of unemployed organizations must be undertaken to fully document community protest in the 1930s.
151 *North Bay Nugget*, 22 April 1931.
152 Ibid., 22 April 1931.
153 *Oshawa Daily Times*, 20 Oct. 1932.
154 NAC, RG 27, vol. 359, Box 23, 1933.
155 Hunter, *Which Side Are You On Boys?* 14–15.
156 NAC, RG 27, vol. 351, Box 86, 1932.
157 Manley, 'Starve, Be Damned!' 418, 540n11; Manley, 'Communism,' 476, 538n12. Manley notes that most of the 'tens of thousands' that participated in unemployed organizations in Canada in the 1930s were not Communist Party members. See also this same theme in letters written to President Roosevelt, in Markowitz and Roediger, 'Slaves of the Depression,' 15.
158 See Berger, *Writing of Canadian History*; Vipond, 'Nationalism and Nativism' and 'The Nationalist Network'; Raboy, *Missed Opportunities*;

Collins, *Culture, Communication and National Identity*. But see Cecilia
Morgan, 'History, Nation and Empire.' Morgan uses middle-class
Anglo-Celtic historical societies to explore how middle-class Canadians,
particularly those from Southern Ontario, developed ideas of nation and
empire. See also Anderson, *Imagined Communities*.

159 Schulz, *EYWA*, 56.
160 Henry Papers, MS 1761, File: Unemployment Relief, no. 1, Edward
Lymen to Henry, 14 Jan. 1933.
161 Ibid., MS 1762, File: Unemployment Relief, no. 1, Thomas Holliday to
Henry, 7 Aug. 1933.
162 Morgan, 'History, Nation and Empire,' 500–17; Berger, *Sense of Power*,
99–101. See also Angela Wollacott, *To Try Her Fortune in London: Australian
Women, Colonialism, and Modernity* (New York: Oxford University Press,
2001), for a look at the 'interchangeability' of Australian, English, and
British identity, 142–3.
163 Hepburn Papers, Box 225, File: M.F. Hepburn, private, no. 3, Miss Matilda
E. Milland to Hepburn, 3 July 1934.
164 Antoinette Burton, *Burdens of History: British Feminists, Indian Women, and
Imperial Culture, 1865-1915* (Chapel Hill: University of North Carolina
Press, 1994); Ann Curthoys, 'Identity Crisis: Colonialism, Nation and
Gender in Australian History,' *Gender and History* 5/2 (1993): 65–76.
165 Henry Papers, MS 1750, File: Mothers' Allowances Commission,
Mrs Susan B. Silver to Henry, 24 Feb. 1932.
166 Ibid., MS 1760, File: Relief Asked For, Mrs C.R. Cline to Henry, 2 Aug. 1933.
167 Ibid., MS 1745, File: Relief Asked For, Mrs A.H. MacKenzie to Henry,
29 Dec. 1931.
168 To see a similar argument in the context of imperial politics, see Davin,
'Imperialism and Motherhood,' 9–66.
169 Though it is difficult to assess the exact ethnic background of letter
writers, a careful study of the letters reveals very few non–Anglo-Celtic
names. It is important to note, however, that some names might have
been Anglicized upon immigration and also that some letter writers
could have been of African-Canadian or aboriginal background. See also
David Roediger, *The Wages of Whiteness: Race and the Making of the
American Working Class* (London: Verso, 1991). See Laura Tabili, *We Ask for
British Justice: Workers and Racial Difference in Late Imperial Britain* (Ithaca:
Cornell University Press, 1994), 4–15 for a look at how British tropes of
fair play could be used by subordinated groups to claim equality.
170 Henry Papers, MS 1744, File: Positions, General, June 1931 to Jan. 1932,
Bill Coleman to Henry, 19 Nov. 1931.

171 Ibid., MS 1750, File: Mothers' Allowances Commission, Miss Annie Meighan to Henry, 26 Aug. 1932.

172 Roberts, *Whence They Came*, 160–9.

173 Brown, *When Freedom Was Lost*, 37.

174 Urquhart, *Historical Statistics of Canada*, 29, Series A 342–7.

175 Donald Avery,'*Dangerous Foreigners': European Radical Workers and Labour Radicalism in Canada, 1896-1932* (Toronto: McClelland and Stewart, 1979), 111.

176 *Oshawa Daily Times*, 19 Aug. 1932. This affected twenty to twenty-five families, or approximately fifty people including dependents. See also ibid., 20 and 25 Aug. 1932.

177 Roberts, *Whence They Came*, 146–7, 164.

178 See John Swettenham, *Canada and the First World War* (Toronto: Ryerson Press, 1969); Desmond Morton, *When Your Number's Up: The Canadian Soldier in the First World War* (Toronto: Random House, 1993), 169; Desmond Morton and Jack Granatstein, *Marching to Armageddon: Canadians and the Great War, 1914–19* (Toronto: Lester and Orpen Dennys, 1989). See also the criticism by Vance, *Death So Noble*, 10–11.

179 *Legionary* 4/8 (1930): 6; 4/7 (1929): 13.

180 *The Call (n.d.); British Boys (1916)*, in Viger, 'Songs of the Canadian Soldier,' 107, 49.

181 *Legionary* 13/6 (1938): 12.

182 In 1918, e.g., after several days of 'anti-alien rhetoric' at a GWVA convention in Toronto, veterans led a series of attacks against the city's Greek restaurants. Morton and Wright, *Winning the Second Battle*, 82.

183 *ROPC AC*, 1931. In 1930 the Fort William branch of the Legion recommended that all non-naturalized people who had participated in the local May Day Parade be deported. *Legion* (Jan. 1986): 17.

184 *Legionary* 6/12 (1932): 7.

185 Ibid., 11/1 (1935): 20; *Globe and Mail*, 2 May 1932, reported on special constables in the cities of Oshawa and St Catharines.

186 Ibid., 7/1 (1932): 26.

187 Ibid., 4/11 (1930): 26.

188 Ibid., 5/2 (1930): 29.

189 Henry Papers, MS 1747, File: Unemployment Relief, no. 3, Lt Dempster to Henry, 8 Oct. 1931.

190 *ROPC AC*, 1934. In 1934, e.g., the OPC went on record as 'being favourable to the principle of state medicine,' and in 1938, the Dominion Command pressed the federal government for legislation for low-rent housing. See *ROPC AC*, 1934; *Legionary* 9/4 (1934).

Conclusion

1 Margaret Hobbs' work, while mainly concerned with the role of women in the labour force, does frame the Great Depression in the context of a gender crisis. Hobbs, 'Gendering Work and Welfare.' Denyse Baillargeon also addresses the impact of unemployment on masculine identity and marital relationships. Baillargeon, *Making Do.*
2 Sangster, *Regulating Girls*, 13.
3 Morton, 'Canadian Veterans' Heritage,' 15–31.
4 Struthers, *Limits of Affluence*, 4.
5 E.g., women made up 17% of the labour force in 1931 and 27.3% by 1961. See Prentice et al., *Women in Canada*, 474. Calculated from Statistics Canada, Labour Force Annual Average, 1993. Table 1, A16–A17.
6 Jean, 'Family Allowances and Family Autonomy,' 430.

References

Archival Collections

Archives of Ontario

F 819, Ontario Association of Children's Aid Societies Papers
F 837, Ontario Welfare Council Papers
RG 3 Office of the Premier
 RG 3-8, George S. Henry, General Correspondence
 RG 3-9, Mitchell F. Hepburn, Public General Correspondence
 RG 3-10, M.F. Hepburn, Private General Correspondence
RG 4 Ministry of the Attorney General
 RG 4-2, Correspondence Files
 RG 4-32, Criminal and Civil Case Files
RG 7 Department of Labour
 RG 7-1, Department of Labour, Minister–correspondence
 RG 7-4, Department of Labour, Disputes and Strikes
 RG 7-12, Ontario Ministry of Labour, Deputy Minister of Labour, Correspondence
RG 8-5, Provincial Secretary's Correspondence
RG 18 Records of Royal Commissions of the Province of Ontario
 RG 18-97, Inquiry into the Handling of Unemployment and Direct Relief at Sturgeon Falls (1933)
 RG 18-100, Commission to Inquire into the Handling of the Unemployment Relief Fund in the Township of York (1931)
 RG 18-109, Committee of Inquiry into Dismissal of Ex-Servicemen from the Public Service of the Province of Ontario (1935)

RG 21, Municipal Records, MS 671 Box 3, City of Oshawa Municipal Records, Council Minutes

RG 22 Court Records

RG 22-1090, Algoma District Prosecution Case Files

RG 22-1333, Carleton County Juvenile and Family Court, Adult Case Files

RG 22-1890, Essex County, Prosecution Case Files

RG 22-2335, Hastings County Juvenile and Family Court, Children of Unmarried Parents Act Case Files

RG 22-2490, Huron County, Ontario Crown Attorney, Prosecution Case Files

RG 22-2690, Kent County, Ontario Crown Attorney, Prosecution Case Files

RG 22-2990, Leeds and Grenville Counties, Prosecution Case Files

RG 22-3390, Middlesex County, Prosecution Case Files

RG 22-3833, Ontario County, Juvenile and Family Court, Domestic Case Files

RG 22-3941, Oxford County Court, Farmers' Creditors Arrangement Act Files

RG 22-4490, Prescott and Russell Counties, Ontario Crown Attorney, Prosecution Case Files

RG 22-4890, Simcoe County, Prosecution Case Files

RG 22-5690, Wellington County, Prosecution Case Files

RG 22-5751, Wentworth County, Official Receiver's Farmers' Creditors Arrangement Files

RG 22-5790, Wentworth County, Prosecution Case Files

RG 22-5835, York County, Metropolitan Toronto Juvenile and Family Court, Children of Unmarried Parents Act Files

RG 22-5836, York County Juvenile and Family Court, Occurrence Files

RG 29 Ontario Department of Public Welfare

RG 29-1, Deputy Minister's Correspondence

RG 29-31, Child Welfare Branch, Former Directors' Files

RG 29-33, Children's Aid Society Permanent Files

RG 29-35, Mothers' Allowance Case Files

RG 29-65, Soldiers' Aid Commission

RG 29-74, James S. Band Files

RG 29-135, General Welfare Branch Statistics and Correspondence

RG 49-63, Press Clippings, Legislative Assembly, MS 755

National Archives of Canada

RG 27, Strikes and Lockout Files

City of Thunder Bay Archives

Series 4, City Clerk's Files, Fort William
Series 17, 77, Port Arthur City Council Minutes
Series 72, 4095, Licences, Police, Relief and Welfare Committee Minutes, Fort
    William
Series 73, 4097, Fort William Public Welfare Board Minutes
Series 76, 4101, Fort William Council and Committee Minutes

Thunder Bay Historical Museum Society

Oral History Project, 1977

Bruce County

Bruce County Archives, B-R, 15, 87, Relief records, memorandum
Brice County Historical Society, Bruce County Museum and Archives, Oral
    Histories of Bruce County

Reports and Government Documents

Advisory Committee on Direct Relief, Wallace Campbell, chair. *Report on
    Provincial Policy in Administrative Methods in the Province of Ontario*. Toronto:
    Kings's Printer, 1932.
Canada. *Census of Canada*, 1931.
– *Report of the Royal Commission on Price Spreads*. Ottawa: J.O. Patenaude,
    1937.
– *Royal Commission on the Textile Industry*. Ottawa: J.O. Patenaude, 1938.
Canada, Department of Labour, National Employment Commission. *Final
    Report*. Ottawa: King's Printer, 1938.
Canadian Youth Commission. *Youth and Jobs in Canada*. Toronto: Ryerson
    Press, 1945.
– *Youth, Marriage and the Family*. Toronto: Ryerson Press, 1947.
Matatall, F.A., and Hector Menard. *Report on the Cost of Relief and Its Adminis-
    tration in the City of Ottawa*. 1934.
Ontario Bureau of Statistics. *A Conspectus of the Province of Ontario*. Toronto:
    King's Printer, 1947.
Royal Canadian Legion. *Report of the Ontario Provincial Command, Annual
    Convention*, 1931–1938.

Newspapers and Magazines

Canadian Congress Journal
Child and Family Welfare
Farmer's Advocate
Globe and Mail
Home and Country Magazine
Legionary
North Bay Nugget
Northern News
Oshawa Daily Times
Peterborough Evening Examiner
Porcupine Advance
Toronto Star

Interviews

Aho, Ruth, Thunder Bay, 14 June 1997
Blood, Borden, Timmins, 19 June 1997
Campbell, Agnes, Rawdon, QC, 25 October 2001
Cleeson, Mary (pseudonym), North Bay, 3 June 1997
Clements, Gladys, Timmins, 18 June 1997
Craig, Earl, North Bay, 5 June 1997
Libby, Basil, Timmins, 19 June 1997
McGeragle, Myrtle, Southampton, 14 August 1997
O'Brien, Hilda, Thunder Bay, 14 June 1997
Osmars, Dorothy, Timmins, 18 June 1997

Published Books, Documents, and Memoirs

Angell, Robert Colley. *The Family Encounters the Depression*. Gloucester: Peter
    Smith, 1965.
Angus, Charlie, and Brit Griffin. *'We Lived a Life and Then Some': The Life, Death,
    and Life of a Mining Town*. Toronto: Between the Lines, 1996.
Bakke, E. Wight. *Citizens without Work: A Study of the Effects of Unemployment
    and upon the Workers' Social Relations and Practices*. New Haven: Yale
    University Press, 1940.
− *The Unemployed Worker: A Study of the Task of Making a Living without a Job*.
    New Haven: Yale University Press, 1940.

Beales, H.L., and R.S. Lambert. *Memoirs of the Unemployed*. East Ardsley: E.P Publishing, 1973. First published in 1934 by Victor Gollancz.

Cassidy, Harry. *Unemployment and Relief in Ontario, 1929–1932*. Toronto: Dent, 1932.

Cavan, Ruth Shonle, and Katherine Howland Ranck. *The Family and the Depression: A Study of One Hundred Chicago Families*. Freeport: Books for Libraries Press, 1969.

Dennis, Lloyd. *Marching Orders: A Memoir, Growing Up in Rural Ontario during the Depression*. Toronto: Umbrella Press, 1997.

Dublin, Louis I. *Suicide: A Sociological and Statistical Study*. New York: Ronald Press, 1963.

Dublin, Louis I., and Bessie Bunzel. *To Be or Not to Be*. New York: Harrison Smith and Robert Haas, 1933.

Elder Jr, Glen H. *Children of the Great Depression: Social Change in Life Experience*. Chicago: University of Chicago Press, 1974.

Ferris, John. *Sault Ste Marie in the Depression, Response: The City and Its Citizens*. Sault Ste Marie: John Ferris, 1982.

Hunter, Peter. *Which Side Are You On Boys? Canadian Life on the Left*. Toronto: Lugus, 1988.

Jackson, Florence. *North Wind Blowing Backwards*. Cobalt: Highway Bookshop, 1977.

Jameson, Hazel. *$10 And A Dream*. Winlaw, BC: Polestar Press, 1988.

Komarovsky, Mirra. *The Unemployed Man and His Family: The Effect of Unemployment upon the Status of the Man in Fifty-Nine Families*. New York: Octagon, 1971.

Lynd, Robert S., and Helen Merrell Lynd. *Middletown in Transition*. New York: Harcourt, Brace, 1937.

Marsh, Leonard. *Employment Research*. Toronto: Oxford University Press, 1935.

– *Canadians In and Out of Work*. Toronto: Oxford University Press, 1940.

Newton White, Muriel E. *The Sunset and the Morning*. Cobalt: Highway Bookshop, n.d.

Ontario Bureau of Statisitics and Research. *Conspectus of the Province of Ontario*. Toronto: King's Printer, 1947.

Phillips, Donna, ed. *Voices of Discord: Canadian Short Stories from the 1930s*. Toronto: New Hogtown Press, 1979.

Richtar, Lothar, ed. *Canada's Employment Problem*. Toronto: Macmillan, 1939.

Smith, Charles F. *I Remember, I Remember: An Autobiography*. North Bay: Author.

Stafford, Ellen. *Always and After: A Memoir*. Toronto: Viking, 1999.

Stortroen, Magne. *An Immigrant's Journal*. Cobalt: Highway Bookshop, 1982.

Sturgeon, Donald R. *For Better, For Worse: A Family in Algoma in the 1930s.* Algoma: Donald Sturgeon, 1996.

Wilken, Lulu Beatrice. *The Way It Was*. Regina: Banting, n.d.

Wright, Richard, and Robin Endres, eds. *Eight Men Speak and Other Plays from the Canadian Workers' Theatre*. Toronto: New Hogtown Press, 1976.

Secondary Sources

Abramovitz, Mimi. *Regulating the Lives of Women: Social Welfare Policy from Colonial Times to the Present*. Boston: South End Press, 1988.

Adamowski, Robert, Dorothy E. Chunn, and Robert Menzies, eds. *Contesting Canadian Citizenship: Historical Readings*. Peterborough: Broadview, 2002.

Ahmed, Sara. *The Cultural Politics of Emotion*. New York: Routledge, 2004.

Alexander, Sally. 'Men's Fears and Women's Work: Responses to Unemployment in London between the Wars.' *Gender and History* 12/2 (2000): 401–24.

Anderson, Benedict. *Imagined Communities: Reflections on the Origins and Spread of Nationalism*. London: Verso, 1983.

Archibald, Peter. 'Distress, Dissent and Alienation: Hamilton Workers in the Great Depression.' *Urban History Review* 21/1 (1992): 2–32.

Arnup, Katherine. 'Educating Mothers: Government Advice for Women in the Inter-War Years.' In K. Arnup, Andree Levesque, and Ruth Roach Pierson, eds., *Delivering Motherhood: Maternal Ideologies and Practices in the Nineteenth and Twentieth Centuries*, 190–210. London and New York: Routledge, 1990.

Avery, Donald. *'Dangerous Foreigners:' European Immigrant Workers and Labour Radicalism in Canada, 1896–1932*. Toronto: McClelland and Stewart, 1979.

Baillargeon, Denyse. *Making Do: Women, Family and Home in Montreal during the Great Depression*. Translated by Yvonne Klein. Waterloo: Wilfrid Laurier University Press, 1999.

Barber, Marilyn. 'Introduction.' In J.S. Woodsworth, *Strangers at Our Gates*, 2nd ed. Toronto: University of Toronto Press, 1972 [1909].

Barman, Jean. 'Taming Aboriginal Sexuality: Gender, Power and Race in British Columbia, 1850–1900.' *BC Studies* nos. 115–16 (1997): 237–66.

Barnes, Michael. *Kirkland Lake: On the Mile of Gold*. Kirkland Lake: Economic Development and Tourism Department. 1994.

Baron, Ava. 'On Looking at Men: Masculinity and the Making of a Gendered Working-Class History.' In Ann-Louise Shapiro, ed., *Feminists Revision History*. New Brunswick, NJ: Rutgers University Press, 1994.

Baron, Ava, ed. *Work Engendered: Toward a New History of American Labor*. Ithaca: Cornell University Press, 1991.

Baskerville, Peter. 'Familiar Strangers: Urban Families with Boarders, Canada, 1901.' *Social Science History* 25/3 (2001): 321–46.

Baskerville, Peter, and Eric Sager. *Unwilling Idlers: The Urban Unemployed and Their Families in Late Victorian Canada.* Toronto: University of Toronto Press, 1988.

Bederman, Gail. *Manliness and Civilization: A Cultural History of Gender and Race in the United States, 1880–1917.* Chicago and London: University of Chicago Press, 1995.

Beeching, William, and Phylis Clarke. *Yours in the Struggle: Reminiscences of Tim Buck.* Toronto: NC Press, 1977.

Belisle, Doncia. 'Toward a Canadian Consumer History.' *Labour / Le Travail* no. 52 (2003): 181–206.

Bellingham, Bruce. 'The History of Childhood since the Invention of Childhood: Some Issues in the Eighties.' *Journal of Family History* 13/2 (1988): 347–58.

Berger, Carl. *The Sense of Power: Studies in the Ideas of Canadian Imperialism.* Toronto: University of Toronto Press, 1970.

– *The Writing of Canadian History: Aspects of English Canadian Historical Writing since 1900.* Toronto: University of Toronto Press, 1986.

Berton, Pierre. *The Great Depression, 1929–1939.* Toronto: Penguin, 1990.

Betcherman, Lita-Rose. *The Little Band: The Clashes between the Communists and the Political and Legal Establishment in Canada, 1928–32.* Ottawa: Deneau, 1980.

Bird, Patricia. 'Hamilton Working Women in the Period of the Great Depression.' *Atlantis* 18/2 (1983): 125–36.

Bitterman, Rusty. 'Women and the Escheat Movement: The Politics of Everyday Life on Prince Edward Island.' In Veronica Strong-Boag, Mona, Gleason, and Adele Perry, eds., *Rethinking Canada: The Promise of Women's History*, 4th ed., 47–58. Don Mills: Oxford University Press, 2002.

Bliss, Michael, and L.M. Grayson, eds. *The Wretched of Canada: Letters to R.B. Bennett, 1930–35.* Toronto: University of Toronto Press, 1971.

Boydston, Jeanne. *Home and Work: Housework, Wages, and the Ideology of Labor in the Early Republic.* New York: Oxford University Press, 1990.

Bradbury, Bettina. *Working Families: Age, Gender and Daily Survival in Industrializing Montreal.* Toronto: McClelland and Stewart, 1993.

– 'Gender at Work at Home: Family Decisions, the Labour Market, and Girls' Contributions to the Family Economy.' In R. Douglas Francis and Donald B. Smith, eds., *Readings in Canadian History: Post-Confederation*, 7th ed., 210–26. Toronto: Nelson, 2007.

Brand, Dionne. '"We Weren't Allowed to Go into Factory Work until Hitler Started the War": The 1920s to the 1940s.' In Peggy Bristow, Dionne Brand, Linda Carter, Afua P. Cooper, Sylvia Hamilton, Adrienne Shadd, 'We're

Rooted Here and They Can't Pull Us Up': Essays in African Canadian Women's History, 171–91. Toronto: University of Toronto Press, 1994.

Brinkley, Alan. *The End of Reform: New Deal Liberalism in Recession and War.* New York: Vintage, 1995.

Broadfoot, Barry. *Ten Lost Years, 1929–1939: Memories of Canadians Who Survived the Depression.* Toronto: Doubleday, 1973.

Brodie, Janine. 'Three Stories of Canadian Citizenship.' In Robert Adamoski, Dorothy E. Chunn, and Robert Menzies, eds., *Contesting Canadian Citizenship: Historical Readings*, 43–66. Peterborough: Broadview, 2002.

Brown, Lorne. *When Freedom Was Lost: The Unemployed, the Agitator and the State.* Montreal and Buffalo: Black Rose, 1987.

– 'Unemployed Struggles in Saskatchewan and Canada, 1930–35.' *Prairie Forum* 31/2 (2006): 193–216.

Brownlie, Robin Jarvis. *A Fatherly Eye: Indian Agents, Government Power and Aboriginal Resistance in Ontario, 1918–1939.* Don Mills: Oxford University Press, 2003.

– 'A Better Citizen Than lots of White Men: First Nations Enfranchisement – An Ontario Case Study, 1918–1940.' *Canadian Historical Review* 87/1 (2006): 29–52.

Bullen, John. 'Hidden Workers: Child Labour and the Family Economy in Late Nineteenth-Century Urban Ontario.' In Bettina Bradbury, ed., *Canadian Family History: Selected Readings*, 199–219. Toronto: Copp Clark Pitman, 1992.

Burton, Antoinette. *Burdens of History: British Feminists, Indian Women, and Imperial Culture, 1865–1915.* Chapel Hill: University of North Carolina Press, 1994.

Bye, Cristine. 'I Like to Toe My Own Row: A Saskatchewan Farm Worker's Notion about Work and Womanhood during the Great Depression.' *Frontiers* 26/3 (2005): 135–67.

Cameron, Ardis. *Radicals of the Worst Sort: Laboring Women in Lawrence, Massachusetts, 1860–1912.* Urbana: University of Illinois Press, 1993.

Campbell, Lara. 'The Strong Ones Were Women: Women in the Great Depression.' Unpublished M.A. project, University of Toronto, 1993.

– '"We Who Have Wallowed in the Mud of Flanders": First World War Veterans, Unemployment, and the Development of Social Welfare in Canada, 1929–1939.' *Journal of the Canadian Historical Association* 11 (2000): 125–50.

Campbell, Robert. *Grand Illusions: The Politics of the Keynesian Experience in Canada 1945–75.* Peterborough: Broadview, 1987.

Chambers, Lori. 'Illegitimate Children and the Children of Unmarried Parents Act.' In Lori Chambers and Edgar-André Montigny, eds., *Ontario since Confederation: A Reader*, 235–59. Toronto: University of Toronto Press, 2000.

– *Misconceptions: Unmarried Motherhood and the Ontario Children of Unmarried Parenst Act, 1921 to 1969*. Toronto: Osgood Society for Canadian Legal History, 2007.

Chambers, Lori, and Edgar-André Montigny, eds. *Family Matters: Papers in Post-Confederation Canadian Family History*. Toronto: Canadian Scholars' Press, 1998.

Chauncey, George. *Gay New York: Gender, Urban Culture, and the Making of the Gay Male World, 1890–1940*. New York: Basic Books, 1994.

Christie, Nancy. *Engendering the State: Family, Work and Welfare in Canada*. Toronto: University of Toronto Press, 2000.

– 'By Necessity or by Right: The Language and Experience of Gender at Work.' *Labour / Le Travail* no. 50 (2002): 117–48.

Christie, Nancy, and Michael Gauvreau. *'A Full-Orbed Christianity': The Protestant Churches and Social Welfare in Canada, 1900–1940*. Montreal and Kingston: McGill-Queen's University Press, 1996.

Chunn, Dorothy. *From Punishment to Doing Good: Family courts and Socialized Justice in Ontario, 1880–1940*. Toronto: University of Toronto Press, 1992.

Clark, Anna. 'The New Poor Law and the Breadwinner Wage: Contrasting Assumptions.' *Journal of Social History* 34/2 (2000): 261–81.

Collins, Richard. *Culture, Communication, and National Identity: The Case of Canadian Television*. Toronto: University of Toronto Press, 1990.

Collins, Robert. *You Had to Be There: An Intimate Portrait of the Generation That Survived the Depression, Won the War, and Re-invented Canada*. Toronto: McClelland and Stewart, 1997.

Comacchio, Cynthia R. *Nations Are Built of Babies: Saving Ontario's Mothers and Children, 1900–1940*. Montreal and Kingston: McGill-Queen's University Press, 1992.

– 'Another Brick in the Wall: Toward a History of the Welfare State in Canada.' *left history* 1/1 (1993): 104–8.

– 'Beneath the Sentimental Veil: Families and Family History in Canada.' *Labour / Le Travail* no. 33 (1994): 279–302.

– 'Dancing to Perdition: Adolescence and Leisure in Interwar English Canada.' *Journal of Canadian Studies* 32/3 (1997): 5–35.

– 'A Postscript for Father: Defining a New Fatherhood in Interwar Canada. *Canadian Historical Review* 78/3 (1997): 305–408.

– *The Infinite Bonds of Family: Domesticity in Canada, 1850–1940*. Toronto: University of Toronto Press, 1999.

– *The Dominion of Youth: Adolescence and the Making of Modern Canada, 1920–1950*. Waterloo: Wilfrid Laurier University Press, 2006.

Connell, R.W. 'The Big Picture: Masculinities in Recent World History.' *History and Theory* 22/5 (1993): 597–623.

Cott, Nancy. *The Bonds of Womanhood: 'Woman's Sphere' in New England, 1780–1835*. New Haven: Yale University Press, 1966.

Creese, Gillian. 'The Politics of Dependence: Women, Work and Unemployment in the Vancouver Labour Movement before World War II.' *Canadian Journal of Sociology* 13/1–2 (1988): 136–140.

Crowley, Terry. *Agnes MacPhail and the Politics of Equality*. Toronto: Lorimer, 1990.

Cruikshank, Douglas, and Gregory Kealey. 'Strikes in Canada, 1891–1950.' In Gregory Kealey, ed., *Workers and Canadian History*, 345–418. Montreal and Kingston: McGill-Queen's University Press, 1995.

Curthoys, Ann. 'Identity Crisis: Colonialism, Nation and Gender in Australian History.' *Gender and History* 5/2 (1993): 65–76.

Davin, Anna 'Imperialism and Motherhood.' *History Workshop* 5 (1978): 9–66.

Dickson, Paul, and Thomas B. Allen. *The Bonus Army: An American Epic*. New York: Walker, 2004.

Donzelot, Jacques. *The Policing of Families*. New York: Pantheon, 1979.

Dumas, Evelyn. *The Bitter Thirties in Quebec*. Montreal: Black Rose, 1975.

Dyer, Richard. *White*. London: Routledge, 1997.

Ehrenreich, Barbara. *The Hearts of Men: American Dreams and the Flight from Commitment*. Garden City: Anchor, 1994.

Evans, Patricia. '"Divided Citizenship?" Gender, Income Security and the Welfare State.' In Patricia Evans and Gerda R. Wekerle, eds., *Women and the Canadian Welfare State*, 91–116. Toronto: University of Toronto Press, 1997.

Faderman, Lillian. *Odd Girls and Twilight Lovers: A History of Lesbian Life in Twentieth-Century America*. New York: Penguin, 1991.

Fahrni, Magda. *Household Politics: Montreal Families and Postwar Reconstruction*. Toronto: University of Toronto Press, 2005.

Faludi, Susan. *Backlash: The Undeclared War against American Women*. New York: Crown, 1991.

Faue, Elizabeth. *Community of Suffering and Struggle: Women, Men and the Labor Movement in Minneapolis, 1915–45*. Chapel Hill: University of North Carolina Press, 1991.

Finkel, Alvin. *Business and Social Reform in the Thirties*. Toronto: Lorimer, 1979.

– *The Social Credit Phenomenon in Alberta*. Toronto: University of Toronto Press, 1989.

– 'Welfare for Whom? Class, Gender and Race in Social Policy.' *Labour / Le Travail* no.49 (Spring 2002): 247–61.

– 'The State of Writing on the Canadian Welfare State: What's Class Got to Do with It?' *Labour / Le Travail* no. 54 (2004): 151–74.

Forestall, Nancy. 'The Miner's Wife: Working-Class Femininity in a Masculine Context, 1920–50.' In Kathryn McPherson, Cecilia Morgan, and Nancy Forestall, eds., *Gendered Pasts: Historical Essays in Femininity in Canada*, 139–57. Oxford: Oxford University Press, 1999.

Foucault, Michel. 'Truth and Power.' In *The Chomsky-Foucault Debate on Human Nature*. New York: New Press, 2006.

– 'Omnes et Singulatim.' In *The Chomsky-Foucault Debate on Human Nature*. New York: New Press, 2006.

Frager, Ruth. *Sweatshop Strife: Class, Ethnicity, and Gender in the Jewish Labour Movement of Toronto, 1900–1939*. Toronto: University of Toronto Press, 1992.

Frank, Dana. 'Housewives, Socialists, and the Politics of Food: The 1917 New York Cost-of-Living Protests.' In K. Sklar and T. Dublin, eds., *Women and Power in American History*, vol. 2, 101–13. Englewood Cliffs, NJ: Prentice-Hall 1991.

Fraser, Nancy, and Linda Gordon. 'Contract versus Charity: Why Is There No Social Citizenship in the United States?' *Socialist Review* 22/3 (1992): 52–6.

Fritsch, Michael. *A Shared Authority: Essays on the Craft and Meaning of Oral and Public History*. Albany: State University of New York Press, 1990.

Gaffield, Chad M. 'Canadian Families in Cultural Context: Hypotheses from the Mid-nineteenth Century.' In Bettina Bradbury, ed., *Canadian Family History: Selected Readings*, 135–57. Toronto: Copp Clark Pitman, 1992.

Garcia, Eva. '"Taking Care of One's Own": Gender, Unemployment Relief, and the London Welfare Board, 1930–40.' Master's thesis, University of Guelph, 1997.

Gardiner, Michael. *Critiques of Everyday Life*. New York: Routledge, 2000.

Gender and History. Special Issue: Gender, Nationalism and National Identities. 5/2 (1993).

Gidney, Catherine. 'The Dredger's Daughter: Courtship and Marriage in the Baptist Community of Welland, Ontario, 1934–1944.' *Labour / Le Travail* no. 54 (2004): 121–50.

Glassford, Larry. *Reaction and Reform: The Politics of the Conservative Party under R.B. Bennett, 1927–38*. Toronto: University of Toronto Press, 1992.

Golz, Annalee. 'Family Matters: The Canadian Family and the State in Postwar Canada.' *left history* 1/2 (1993): 9–50.

– 'Uncovering and Reconstructing Family Violence: Ontario Criminal Case Files.' In Franca Iacovetta and Wendy Mitchinson, eds., *On the Case: Explorations in Social History*, 289–307. Toronto: University of Toronto Press, 1998.

Goodwin, Jeff, James M. Jasper, and Francesca Polletta, eds. *Passionate Politics: Emotions and Social Movements*. Chicago: University of Chicago Press, 2001.

Gordon, Linda. *Heroes of Their Own Lives: The Politics and History of Family Violence, 1880–1960*. New York: Penguin, 1988.

– 'What Does Welfare Regulate?' *Social Research* 55/4 (1988): 609–30.

– *Pitied But Not Entitled: Single Mothers and the History of Welfare, 1890–1935*. Cambridge: Harvard University Press, 1994.

Gordon, Linda, ed. *Women, the State, and Welfare*. Madison: University of Wisconsin Press, 1990.

Gould, Deborah. 'Rock the Boat, Don't Rock the Boat, Baby: Ambivalence and the Emergence of Militant AIDS Activism.' In Jeff Goodwin et al., eds., *Passionate Politics: Emotions and Social Movements*, 135–57. Chicago: University of Chicago Press, 2001.

Gray, Brenda Clegg. *Black Female Domestics during the Depression in New York City, 1930–40*. New York and London: Garland, 1995.

Gray, James. *The Winter Years: The Depression on the Prairies*. Toronto: Macmillan, 1966.

Greenhill, Pauline. *Ethnicity in the Mainstream: Three Studies of English Canadian Culture in Ontario*. Montreal, Kingston, and London: McGill-Queen's University Press, 1993.

Griswold, Robert. *Fatherhood in America: A History*. New York: Basic Books, 1993.

Guest, Dennis. *The Emergence of Social Security in Canada*. Vancouver: University of British Columbia Press, 1985.

Gunning, C. *North Bay: The Lean Years, 1929–1939: A Decade of Adversity*. North Bay: Bond Printing, 1996.

Haddow, Rodney. *Poverty Reform in Canada, 1958–78*. Montreal and Kingston: McGill-Queen's University Press, 1993.

Hall, Catherine. *White, Male and Middle Class: Explorations in Feminism and History*. New York: Routledge, 1992.

Harrigan, Patrick J. 'The Schooling of Boys and Girls in Canada.' *Journal of Social History* 23/4 (1990): 803–16.

Harris, Richard. 'Home Ownership and Class in Modern Canada.' *International Journal of Urban and Regional Research* 10/1 (1986): 67–86.

– 'The End Justified the Means: Boarding and Rooming in a City of Homes, 1890–1957.' *Journal of Social History* 26/2 (1992): 331–58.

Hartman, Mary S. *The Household and the Making of History: A Subversive View of the Western Past.* Cambridge: Cambridge University Press, 2005.

Harvey, Kathryn. 'Amazons and Victims: Resisting Wife Abuse in Working-Class Montreal, 1869–79,' *Journal of the Canadian Historical Association* 2 (1991): 133–4.

Helmbold, Lois Rita. 'Beyond the Family Economy: Black and White Working-Class Women during the Great Depression.' *Feminist Studies* 13/3 (1987): 629–48.

Higginbotham, Ann. '"Sin of the Age": Infanticide and Illegitimacy in Victorian London.' *Victorian Studies* 32/3 (1989): 319–38.

Hoar, Victor ed. *The Great Depression: Essays and Memoirs from Canada and the United States.* Canada: Copp Clark, 1969.

Hobbs, Margaret. 'Rethinking Antifeminism in the 1930s: Gender Crisis or Workplace Justice? A Response to Alice Kessler-Harris.' *Gender and History* 5/1 (1993): 4–15.

– 'Equality and Difference: Feminism and the Defense of Women Workers during the Great Depression.' *Labour / Le Travail* no. 32 (1993): 201–23.

– 'Gendering Work and Welfare: Women's Relationship to Wage-Work and Social Policy in Canada during the Great Depression.' Doctoral dissertation, University of Toronto, 1994.

Hobbs, Margaret, and Ruth Roach Pierson. '"A Kitchen That Wastes No Steps": Gender, Class and the Home Improvement Plan, 1936–40.' *Histoire Sociale / Social History* 21/41 (1988): 9–37.

Hollingsworth, Laura, and Vappu Tyyska. 'The Hidden Producers: Women's Household Production during the Great Depression.' *Critical Sociology* 15/3 (1988): 3–27.

Horn, Michiel. *The League for Social Reconstruction: Intellectual Origins of the Democratic Canadian Left in Canada, 1930–1942.* Toronto: University of Toronto Press, 1980.

– *The Great Depression of the 1930s in Canada.* Ottawa: Canadian Historical Association Booklet no. 39, 1984.

– 'The Great Depression: Past and Present.' Journal of Canadian Studies 11/1 (1976): 41–50.

Horn, Michiel, ed., *The Dirty Thirties: Canadians in the Great Depression.* Toronto: Copp Clark, 1972.

– *The Depression in Canada: Responses to Economic Crisis.* Toronto: Copp Clark Pitman, 1988.

Howard, Irene. 'The Mothers' Council of Vancouver: Holding the Fort for the Unemployed, 1935–38.' *BC Studies* nos. 69–70 (1988): 249–87.

Humphries, Jane. 'The Working Class Family, Women's Liberation, and Class Struggle: The Case of Nineteenth-Century British History.' *Review of Radical Political Economics* 9/3 (1997): 25–40.

Iacovetta Franca, and Wendy Mitchinson, eds. *On the Case: Explorations in Social History*. Toronto: University of Toronto Press, 1998.

Ignatiev, Noel, and John Garvey, eds. *Race Traitor*. New York: Routledge, 1996.

Igra, Anna R. 'Likely to Become a Public Charge: Deserted Women and the Family Law of the Poor in New York City, 1910–36.' *Journal of Women's History* 11/4 (2000): 59–81.

Jamieson, Stuart. *Times of Trouble: Labour Unrest and Industrial Conflict in Canada, 1900–66*. Ottawa: Minister of Supply and Services, 1976.

Janeway, Elizabeth. *Powers of the Weak*. New York: Knopf, 1980.

Jean, Dominique. 'Family Allowances and Family Autonomy: Quebec Families Encounter the Welfare State, 1945–1955.' In Bettina Bradbury, ed., *Canadian Family History: Selected Readings*, 401–41. Toronto: Copp Clark, 1992.

Jetter, Alexis, Annelise Orlick, and Diana Taylor, eds. *The Politics of Motherhood: Activist Voices from Left to Right*. Hanover: University Press of New England, 1997.

Johnson, Loretta T. 'Chivaree/Shivaree: A European Folk Ritual on the American Plains.' *Journal of Interdisciplinary History* 20/3 (1990): 371–87.

Johnston, Wendy. 'Keeping Children in School: The Response of the Montreal Catholic School Commission to the Depression of the 1930s.' In Michiel Horn, ed., *The Depression in Canada: Responses to Economic Crisis*, 162–87. Toronto: Copp Clark Pitman, 1988.

Kaplan, Temma. *Crazy for Democracy: Women in Grassroots Movements*. New York: Routledge, 1997.

– *Anarchists of Andalusia, 1868–1903*. Princeton: Princeton University Press, 1977.

Katz, Jonathan Ned. *The Invention of Heterosexuality*. New York: Penguin, 1995.

Kealey, Gregory. *Toronto Workers Respond to Industrial Capitalism, 1867–1892*. Toronto: University of Toronto Press, 1980.

Keene, Jennifer D. *Doughboys, the Great War and the Remaking of America*. Baltimore: Johns Hopkins University Press, 2001.

Keshen, Jeffrey A . *Propaganda and Censorship during Canada's Great War*. Edmonton: University of Alberta Press, 1996.

Kessler-Harris, Alice. 'Gender Ideology in Historical Reconstruction: A Case Study from the 1930s.' *Gender and History* 1/1 (1989): 31–49.

Kimmel, Michael. *Manhood in America: A Cultural History*. New York: Free Press, 1996.

Klee, Marcus. '"Between the Scylla and Charybdis of Anarchy and Despotism": The State, Capital and Working Class in the Great Depression, Toronto, 1929–40.' Doctoral dissertation, Queen's University, 1998.

Koven, Seth, and Sonya Michel, eds. *Mothers of a New World: Maternalist Politics and the Origins of the Welfare State*. New York: Routledge, 1993.

Leacy, F.H. *Historical Statistics of Canada*. Ottawa: Statistics Canada, 1983.

Levine Frader, Laura. *Breadwinners and Citizens: Gender in the Making of the French Social Model*. Durham and London: Duke University Press, 2008.

Leyedesorff, Selma, Luisa Passerini, and Paul Thompson, eds. *Gender and Memory*. Oxford: Oxford University Press, 1996.

Lewis, Jane. 'Gender, the Family and Women's Agency in the Building of "Welfare States": The British Case.' *Social History* 19/1 (1994): 37–55.

Lipsitz, George. *The Possessive Investment in Whiteness: How White People Profit from Identity Politics*. Philadelphia: Temple University Press, 2006.

Little, Margaret. 'Claiming a Unique Place: The Introduction of Mothers' Pensions in British Columbia.' In Veronica Strong-Boag and Anita Clair Fellman, eds., *Rethinking Canada: The Promise of Women's History*, 285–303. Don Mills: Oxford University Press, 1993.

– 'Manhunts and Bingo Blabs: The Moral Regulation of Ontario Single Mothers.' *Canadian Journal of Sociology* 19/2 (1994): 233–47.

– *'No Car, No Radio, No Liquor Permit': The Moral Regulation of Single Mothers in Ontario*. Toronto: Oxford University Press, 1998.

Liversedge, Ronald. *Recollections of the On-to-Ottawa Trek*. Toronto: McClelland and Stewart, 1973.

McCall, Laura. '"Not So Wild a Dream": The Domestic Fantasies of Literary Men and Women, 1820–60.' In Laura McCall and Donald Yacovone, eds., *A Shared Experience: Men, Women and the History of Gender*, 176–94. New York: New York University Press, 1998.

McCallum, Todd. 'Vancouver through the Eyes of a Hobo: Experience, Identity, and Value in the Writing of Canada's Depression-Era Tramps.' *Labour / Le Travail* no. 59 (2007): 43–68.

McClelland-Wierzbicki, Kathy. *The Great Depression in Northern Ontario, 1929–1934*. Sudbury: Laurentian University, 1981.

McClintock, Anne, Aamir Mufti, and Ella Shohat, eds. *Dangerous Liasons: Gender, Nation and Postcolonial Perspectives*. Minneapolis: University of Minnesota Press, 1997.

McDaniel, Susan, and Robert Lewis. 'Did They or Didn't They? Intergenerational Supports in Families Past: A Case Study of Brighs, Nfld., 1920–45.' In Lori Chambers and Edgar-Andre Montigny, eds., *Family Matters: Papers in Post-Confederation Canadian Family History*, 475–98. Toronto: Canadian Scholars' Press, 1998.

McGenty, Neil. 'Mitchell F. Hepburn and the Ontario Election of 1934.' *Canadian Historical Review* 45/4 (1964): 293–313.

McLaren, Angus. 'Illegal Operations: Women, Doctors, and Abortion, 1886–1939.' *Journal of Social History* 26/4 (1993): 797–816.

McLaren, Angus, and Arlene Tiger McLaren. *The Bedroom and the State: The Changing Practices and Politics of Contraception and Abortion in Canada.* Toronto: McClelland and Stewart, 1986.

McNaught, Kenneth. *A Prophet in Politics.* Toronto: University of Toronto Press, 1959.

MacKinnon, Catharine A. 'Feminism, Marxism, Method and the State: Toward Feminist Jurisprudence.' *Signs* 8/4 (1983): 635–58.

Mackinnon, Mary. 'Relief Not Insurance: Canadian Unemployment Relief in the 1930s.' *Explorations in Economic History* 27/1 (1990): 46–8.

Manley, John. 'Communism and the Canadian Working Class during the Great Depression: The Workers' Unity League, 1930–36.' Doctoral dissertation, Dalhousie University, 1984.

– '"Starve, Be Damned!" Communists and Canada's Urban Unemployed, 1929–1939.' *Canadian Historical Review* 79/3 (1998): 466–91.

Markowitz, Gerald, and David Roediger, eds. *'Slaves of the Depression': Workers Letters about Life on the Job.* Ithaca and London: Cornell University Press, 1987.

Marshall, T.H. *Citizenship and Social Class.* London: Pluto Press, 1992. Originally published as *Citizenship and Social Class and Other Essays* (Cambridge: Cambridge University Press, 1950).

Marshall, Dominique. 'The Language of Children's Rights, the Formation of the Welfare State, and the Democratic Experience of Poor Families in Quebec, 1940–1955.' *Canadian Historical Review* 78/3 (1997): 409–39.

– *The Social Origins of the Welfare State: Quebec Families, Compulsory Education, and Family Allowances.* Waterloo: Wilfrid Laurier University Press, 2006.

May, Martha. 'The 'Good Managers': Married Working Class Women and Family Budget Studies, 1895–1915.' *Labor History* 25/3 (1984): 351–72.

– 'Bread before Roses: American Workingmen, Labor Unions, and the Family Wage.' In Ruth Milkman, ed., *Women, Work and Protest: A Century of U.S. Women's Labor History*, 1–21. Boston: Routledge and Kegan Paul, 1985.

Maynard, Steven. 'Queer Musings on Masculinity and History.' *Labour / Le Travail* no. 42 (1998): 183–97.

Meyer, Sybille. 'The Tiresome Work of Conspicuous Leisure: On the Domestic Duties of the Wives of Civil Servants in the German Empire.' In Marilyn

Boxer and Jean Quataert, eds., *Connecting Spheres: Women in the Western World, 1500 to the Present*, 156–65. New York: Oxford University Press, 1987.

Michel, Sonya. 'Introduction.' *Social Politics* 7/1 (2000): 1–4.

Michel, Sonya, and Seth Koven. *Mothers of a New World: Maternalist Politics and the Origins of the Welfare State*. New York: Routledge, Chapman and Hall, 1993.

Milkman, Ruth. 'Women's Work and Economic Crisis: Some Lessons of the Great Depression.' *Review of Radical Economics* 8/1 (1976): 71–97.

Mitchinson, Wendy. 'The Women's Christian Temperance Union: "For God, Home and Native Land" – A Study in Nineteenth-Century Feminism.' In Linda Kealey, ed., *A Not Unreasonable Claim: Women and Reform in Canada, 1880s–1920s*, 151–67. Toronto: Women's Press, 1979.

– *The Nature of Their Bodies: Women and Their Doctors in Victorian Canada*. Toronto: University of Toronto Press, 1991.

Morgan, Cecilia. 'History, Nation and Empire: Gender and Southern Ontario Historical Societies, 1890–1920s.' *Canadian Historical Review* 82/3 (2001): 491–528.

Morton, Desmond. *Working People: An Illustrated History of the Canadian Labour Movement*. Toronto: Summerhill, 1990.

– *When Your Number's Up: The Canadian Soldier in the First World War*. Toronto: Random House, 1993.

– 'The Canadian Veterans' Heritage from the Great War.' In Peter Neary and J.L. Granatstein, eds., *The Veterans Charter and Post-World War II Canada*, 15–31. Montreal and Kingston: McGill-Queen's University Press, 1998.

Morton, Desmond, and Jack Granatstein. *Marching to Armageddon: Canadians and the Great War, 1914–19*. Toronto: Lester and Orpen Dennys, 1989.

Morton, Suzanne. *Ideal Surroundings: Domestic Life in a Working-Class Suburb in the 1920s*. Toronto: University of Toronto Press, 1995.

Moscovitch, Allan, and Glenn Drover. 'Social Expenditures and the Welfare State: The Canadian Experience in Historical Perspective.' In Allen Moscovitch and J. Albert, eds., *The Benevolent State: The Growth of Welfare in Canada*, 13–43. Toronto: Garamond, 1987.

Mosher, Janet. 'Caught in Tangled Webs of Care: Women Abused in Intimate Relationships.' In Carol T. Baines, Patricia M. Evans, and Sheila M. Neysmtih, eds., *Women's Caring: Feminist Perspectives on Social Welfare*, 139–59. Don Mills: Oxford University Press, 1998.

Myers, Tamara. *Caught: Montreal's Modern Girls and the Law, 1869–1945*. Toronto: University of Toronto Press, 2006.

Neatby, H. Blair. *The Politics of Chaos: Canada in the Thirties*. Toronto: Gage, 1972.

Newton, Janice. 'From Wage Slave to White Slave.' In Linda Kealey and Joan Sangster, eds., *Beyond the Vote: Canadian Women and Politics*, 217–39. Toronto: University of Toronto Press, 1989.

Olsen, Frances. 'Statutory Rape: A Feminist Critique of Rights Analysis.' *Texas Law Review* 63/3 (1984).

Orleck, Annelise. '"We Are That Mythical Thing Called the Public": Militant Housewives during the Great Depression.' *Feminist Studies* 1 (1993): 147–72.

Orloff, Ann Shola. 'Gender and the Rights of Social Citizenship: The Comparative Analysis of Gender Relations and Welfare States.' *American Sociological Review* 58 (1993): 303–28.

– *The Politics of Pensions: A Comparative Analysis of Britain, Canada and the United States, 1880–1940*. Madison: University of Wisconsin Press, 1993.

Ortiz, Stephen R. 'Rethinking the Bonus March: Federal Bonus Policy, the Veterans of Foreign Wars, and the Origins of a Protest Movement.' *Journal of Policy History* 18/3 (2006): 275–303.

Ouellet, Fernand. 'L'évolution de la présence francophone en Ontario: une perspective économique et sociale.' In Cornelius J. Jaenen, ed., *Les Franco-Ontariens*, 127–200. Ottawa: Les Presses de l'Université d'Ottawa, 1993.

Owram, Doug. *The Government Generation: Canadian Intellectuals and the State*. Toronto: University of Toronto Press, 1986.

Pahl, R.E. *Divisons of Labor*. Oxford: Basil Blackwell, 1984.

Pal, Leslie. *State, Class and Bureaucracy: Canadian Unemployment Insurance and Public Policy*. Montreal and Kingston: McGill-Queen's University Press, 1988.

Palmer, Howard. 'Reluctant Hosts: Anglo-Canadian Views of Multiculturalism in the Twentieth-Century.' In R. Douglas Francis and Donald B. Smith, eds., *Readings in Canadian History: Post-Confederation*, 2nd ed., 185–201. Toronto: Holt, 1986.

Palmer, Bryan. 'Discordant Music: Charivaris and Whitecapping in Nineteenth-Century North America.' *Labour / Le Travail* no. 3 (1978): 5–62.

– *A Culture in Conflict: Skilled Workers and Industrial Capitalism in Hamilton, Ontario, 1860–1914*. Montreal and Kingston: McGill-Queen's University Press, 1979.

– *Working-Class Experience: Rethinking the History of Canadian Labour, 1800–1991*. Toronto: McClelland and Stewart, 1992.

Parr, Joy. *The Gender of Breadwinners: Women, Men, and Change in Two Industrial Towns, 1880–1950*. Toronto: University of Toronto Press, 1990.

Parsons, Elaine Frantz. 'Risky Business: The Uncertain Boundaries of Manhood in the Midwestern Saloon.' *Journal of Social History* 34/2 (2000): 283–307.

Pateman, Carol. *The Disorder of Women: Democracy, Feminism and Political Theory*. Stanford: Stanford University Press, 1989.

Patrias, Carmela. 'Relief Strike: Immigrant Workers and the Great Depression in Crowland, Ontario, 1930–1935.' In Franca Iacovetta and Robert Ventresca, eds., *A Nation of Immigrants: Women, Workers and Communities in Canadian History, 1840s–1960s*, 322–58. Toronto: University of Toronto Press, 1998.

Patton, Cindy. 'Outlaw Territory: Criminality, Neighborhoods, and the Edward Savitz Case.' *Sexuality Research and Social Policy: Journal of the NSRC* 2/2 (2005): 63–75.

Penfold, Steven. '"Have You No Manhood in You?": Gender and Class in the Cape Breton Coal Towns, 1920–26.' In Joy Parr and Mark Rosenfeld, eds., *Gender and History in Canada*, 270–93. Toronto: Copp Clark, 1996.

Petroff, Lillian. *Sojourners and Settlers: The Macedonian Community in Toronto to 1940*. Toronto: Multicultural History Society of Ontario, 1995.

Pickles, Katie. *Female Imperialism and National Identity: Imperial Order Daughters of the Empire*. Manchester and New York: Manchester University Press, 2002.

Pierson, Ruth Roach. 'Gender and the Unemployment Insurance Debates in Canada, 1934–1940.' *Labour / Le Travail* no. 25 (1990): 77–103.

Piven, Frances Fox, and Richard A. Cloward. 'Welfare Doesn't Shore Up Traditional Family Roles: A Reply to Linda Gordon.' *Social Research* 55/4 (1988): 631–47.

Platt, Anthony. *The Child-Savers: The Invention of Delinquency*. Chicago: University of Chicago Press, 1969.

Pocock, J.G.A. 'The Ideal of Citizenship since Classical Times.' *Queen's Quarterly* 99/1 (1992): 33–55.

Porter, Ann. *Gendered States: Women, Unemployment Insurance, and the Political Economy of the Welfare State in Canada, 1945–1997*. Toronto: University of Toronto Press, 2003.

Porter Benson, Susan. 'Living on the Margin: Working-Class Marriages and Family Survival Strategies in the United States, 1919–1941.' In Victoria de Grazia and Ellen Furlough, eds., *The Sex of Things: Gender and Consumption in Historical Perspective*, 212–43. Berkeley: University of California Press, 1996.

Powell, Mary Patricia. 'A Response to the Depression: The Local Council of Women of Vancouver.' In Michiel Horn, ed., *The Depression in Canada: Responses to Economic Crisis*, 12–29. Toronto: Copp Clark Pitman, 1988.

Prentice, Alison, Paula Bourne, Gail Cuthbert Brandt, Beth Light, Wendy Mitchinson, and Naomi Black, eds. *Canadian Women: A History*. Toronto: Harcourt, Brace Jovanovich, 1988.

Probyn, Elspeth. *blush: faces of shame*. Minneapolis: University of Minnesota Press, 2005.

Raboy, Marc. *Missed Opportunities: The Story of Canada's Broadcasting Policy*. Montreal and Kingston: McGill-Queen's University Press, 1990.

Roberts, Barbara. *Whence They Came: Deportation from Canada, 1900–35*. Ottawa: University of Ottawa Press, 1988.

Roberts, Elizabeth A. 'Women's Strategies, 1890–1940.' In Jane Lewis, ed., *Labour and Love: Women's Experiences of Home and Family, 1850–1940*, 223–47. Oxford: Basil Blackwell, 1986.

Robin, Martin. *Shades of Right: Nativist and Fascist Politics in Canada, 1920–1940*. Toronto: University of Toronto Press, 1991.

Roediger David. *The Wages of Whiteness: Race and the Making of the American Working Class*. London: Verso, 1991.

– *Colored White: Transcending the Racial Past*. Berkeley: University of California Press, 2002.

Roper, Michael, and John Tosh, eds. *Manful Assertions: Masculinities in Britain since 1880*. London: Routledge, 1991.

Rosenfeld, Mark. '"It Was a Hard Life: Class and Gender in the Work and Family Rhythms of a Railway Town.' In Bettina Bradbury, ed., *Canadian Family History: Selected Readings*, 241–80. Toronto: Copp Clark Pitman, 1992.

Ross, Ellen. *Love and Toil: Motherhood in Outcast London, 1870–1918*. New York: Oxford University Press, 1993.

Rotenberg, Lori. 'The Wayward Worker: Toronto's Prostitute at the Turn of the Century.' In Janice Acton, Penny Goldsmith, and Bonnie Shepard, eds., *Women at Work: Ontario 1850–1930*, 33–69. Toronto: Cana dian Women's Educational Press, 1974.

Rothbart, Ron. '"Homes Are What Any Strike Is About": Immigrant Labor and the Family Wage.' *Journal of Social History* 23/2 (1989): 267–84.

Rudé, George. *The Crowd in History: A Study of Popular Disturbances in France and England, 1730–1848*. New York: Wiley, 1964.

Rutherdale, Robert. 'Fatherhood and Masculine Domesticity during the Baby Boom: Consumption and Leisure in Advertising and Life Stories.' In Lori Chambers and Edgar-Andre Montigny, eds., *Family Matters: Papers in Post-Confederation Canadian Family History*, 309–34. Toronto: Canadian Scholars' Press, 1998.

Sandwell, Ruth W. 'The Limits of Liberalism: The Liberal Reconnaissance and the History of the Family in Canada.' *Canadian Historical Review* 84/3 (2003): 423–50.

Sangster, Joan. *Dreams of Equality: Women on the Canadian Left, 1920–1950*. Toronto: McClelland and Stewart, 1989.

- *Earning Respect: The Lives of Working Women in Small-Town Ontario, 1920–1960*. Toronto: University of Toronto, 1995.
- *Regulating Girls and Women: Sexuality, Family and the Law in Ontario, 1920–1960*. Don Mills: Oxford University Press, 2001.
- 'Making a Fur Coat: Women, the Labouring Body, and Working-Class History.' *International Review of Social History* 52/2 (2007): 241–70.

Saywell, John. *'Just Call Me Mitch': The Life of Mitchell F. Hepburn*. Toronto: University of Toronto Press, 1991.

Schneider, Elizabeth. 'The Dialectic of Rights and Politics: Perspectives from the Women's Movement.' In Linda Gordon, ed., *Women, the State, and Welfare*, 226–49. Madison: University of Wisconsin Press, 1990.

Schulz, Patricia. *The East York Workers' Association: A Response to the Great Depression*. Toronto: New Hogtown Press, 1975.

Skocpol, Theda. *Protecting Soldiers and Mothers: The Political Origins of Social Policy in the United States*. Cambridge, Mass.: Belknap Press of Harvard.

Segal, Lynne. *Slow Motion: Changing Masculinities, Changing Men*. New Brunswick, NJ: Rutgers University Press, 1990.

Seidman, Steven. *Romantic Longing: Love in America, 1830–1980*. New York: Routledge, 1991.

Snell, James. 'Maintenance Agreements for the Elderly: Canada, 1900–51.' *Journal of the Canadian Historical Association* 3 (1992): 197–216.
- *The Citizen's Wage: The State and the Elderly in Canada, 1900–1951*. Toronto: University of Toronto Press, 1996.
- 'The Family and the Working-Class Elderly in the First Half of the Twentieth Century.' In Lori Chambers and Edgar-Andre Montigny, eds., *Family Matters: Papers in Post-Confederation Canadian Family History*, 499–510. Toronto: Canadian Scholars' Press, 1998.

Spanner, Don, '"The Straight Furrow": The Life of George S. Henry, Ontario's Unknown Premier.' Doctoral dissertation, University of Western Ontario, 1994.

Srigley, Katrina. 'The Enduring Family.' Paper presented to the Canadian Historical Association, Quebec City, May, 2001.
- 'In Case You Hadn't Noticed!: Race, Ethnicity, and Women's Wage-Earning in a Depression-Era City.' *Labour / Le Travail* no. 55 (2005): 69–105.
- 'Clothing Stories: Consumption, Identity and Desire in Depression-Era Toronto.' *Journal of Women's History* 19/1 (2007): 82–104.

Stadum, Beverly. *Poor Women and Their Families: Hardworking Charity Cases, 1900–30*. New York: State University of New York Press, 1992.

Stearns, Peter N., and Jan Lewis, eds. *An Emotional History of the United States*. New York: New York University Press, 1998.

Stephens, Jennifer A. *Pick One Intelligent Girl: Employability, Domesticity, and the Gendering of Canada's Welfare State, 1939–1947*. Toronto: University of Toronto Press, 2007.

Strange, Carolyn. 'Mothers on the March: Maternalism in Women's Protest for Peace in North America and Western Europe, 1900–85.' In Guida West and Rhoda Lois Blumberg, eds., *Women and Social Protest*, 209–24. New York: Oxford University Press, 1990.

– *Toronto's Girl Problem: The Perils and Pleasures of the City, 1880–1930*. Toronto: University of Toronto Press, 1995.

Strikwerda, Eric. 'Married Men Should, I Feel, Be Treated Differently: Work, Relief, and Unemployed Men on the Urban Canadian Prairie.' *left history* 12/1 (2007): 30–51.

Stromberg Childers, Kristin. 'Paternity and the Politics of Citizenship in Interwar France.' *Journal of Family History* 26/1 (2001): 90–111.

Strong-Boag, Veronica. *A New Day Recalled: Lives of Girls and Women in English Canada, 1919–1939*. Toronto: Penguin, 1988.

Struthers, James. *No Fault of Their Own: Unemployment and the Canadian Welfare State, 1914–1941*. Toronto: University of Toronto Press, 1983.

– '"Lord Give Us Men": Women and Social Work in English Canada, 1918–1953.' In Allen Moscovitch and J. Albert, eds., *The Benevolent State: The Growth of Welfare in Canada*, 126–43. Toronto: Garamond, 1987.

– 'A Profession in Crisis: Charlotte Whitton and Canadian Social Work in the 1930s.' In Michiel Horn, ed., *The Depression in Canada: Responses to Economic Crisis*, 229–44. Toronto: Copp Clark Pitman, 1988.

– *The Limits of Affluence: Welfare in Ontario, 1920–1970*. Toronto: University of Toronto Press, 1994.

Sutherland, Neil. *Growing Up: Childhood in English Canada from the Great War to the Age of Television*. Toronto: University of Toronto Press, 1997.

Swettenham, John. *Canada and the First World War*. Toronto: Ryerson Press, 1969.

Tabili, Laura. *'We Ask for British Justice': Workers and Racial Difference in Late Imperial Britain*. Ithaca: Cornell University Press, 1994.

Taylor, John. 'Relief from Relief.' In Michiel Horn, ed., *The Depression in Canada: Responses to Economic Crisis*, 245–56. Toronto: Copp Clark Pitman, 1988.

Taylor, Lynne. 'Food Riots Revisited.' *Journal of Social History* 30/2 (1996): 483–96.

Thompson John Herd, and Allen Seager. *Canada, 1922–1939: Decades of Discord*. Toronto: McClelland and Stewart, 1985.

Thompson, E.P. 'The Moral Economy of the English Crowd in the Eighteenth Century.' *Past and Present* no. 50 (1971): 76–136.
- '"Rough Music" or English Charivari.' *Annales* 27 (1972): 285–312.
- 'The Crime of Anonymity.' In Douglas Hay, ed., *Albion's Fatal Tree: Crime and Society in Eighteenth-Century England*, 255–308. London: Lane, 1975.
Tillotson, Shirley. 'Citizen Participation in the Welfare State: An Experiment, 1945–57.' *Canadian Historical Review* 75/4 (1994): 511–42.
- 'Charitable Fundraising and the Origins of the Welfare State.' In Raymond Blake, Penny Brydon, and J. Frank Strain, eds., *The Welfare State in Canada: Past, Present and Future*, 138–55. Concord: Irwin, 1997.
Tilly, Charles. *From Mobilization to Revolution*. Reading: Addison-Wesley, 1978.
Tomes, Nancy. 'A Torrent of Abuse: Crimes of Violence between Working-Class Men and Women in London, 1840–75.' *Journal of Social History* 11/3 (1978): 329–45.
Tomkins, Silvan. 'Shame-Humiliation and Contempt-Disgust.' In Eve Kosofsky Sedgwick and Adam Frank, eds., *Shame and Its Sisters: A Silvan Tomkins Reader*, 133–78. Durham: Duke University Press, 1995.
Tosh, John. 'Domesticity and Manliness in the Victorian Middle Class: Edward White Benson.' In Michael Roper and John Tosh, eds., *Manful Assertions: Masculinities in Britain Since 1880*, 44–73. London and New York: Routledge, 1991.
Trussler, Hartley. *Hartley Trussler's The Best of North Bay*, edited by Michael Barnos. North Bay: North Bay and District Chamber of Commerce, 1992.
Tyler, May Elaine. *Homeward Bound: American Families in the Cold War Era*. New York: Basic Books, 1988.
Urquhart, M.C. *Historical Statistics of Canada*. Toronto: Macmillan, 1965.
Ursel, Jane. *Private Lives, Public Policy: 100 Years of State Intervention in the Family*. Toronto: Women's Press, 1992.
Valverde, Mariana. *The Age of Light, Soap and Water: Moral Reform in English Canada, 1885–1925*. Toronto: McClelland and Stewart, 1991.
- 'The Mixed Social Economy as a Canadian Tradition.' *Studies in Political Economy* 47 (1995): 33–60.
- 'On the Case: A Roundtable Discussion.' *Canadian Historical Review* 81 (2000): 266–92.
Vance, Jonathan. *Death So Noble: Memory, Meaning and the First World War*. Vancouver: University of British Columbia Press, 1997.
Viger Jean-Michel, ed. 'Songs of the Canadian Soldier: The Great War, 1914–1918.' Unpublished Manuscript, Dominion Command Library, Ottawa.

Vipond, Mary. 'The Nationalist Network: English-Canada's Intellectuals and Artists and the 1920s.' *Canadian Review of Studies in Nationalism* 7/1 (1980): 32–52.

– 'Nationalism and Nativism: The Native Sons of Canada in the 1930s.' *Canadian Review of Studies in Nationalism* 9/1 (1982): 81–95.

– *Listening In: The First Decade of Canadian Broadcasting*. Kingston and Montreal: McGill-Queen's University Press, 1992.

Ward, Peter. *Courtship, Love and Marriage in Nineteenth-Century English Canada*. Kingston and Montreal: McGill-Queen's University Press, 1990.

Webster, Charles. 'Health, Welfare and Unemployment during the Depression.' *Past and Present* no. 109 (1985): 204–30.

Welter, Barbara. 'The Cult of True Womanhood.' *American Quarterly* 18 (1966): 151–74.

Wheeler, Kenneth. 'Infanticide in Nineteenth-Century Ohio.' *Journal of Social History* 31/2 (1997): 407–18.

Wilbur, J.R.H. *The Bennett New Deal: Fraud or Portent?* Toronto: Copp Clark, 1968.

– *H.H. Stevens*. Toronto: University of Toronto Press, 1977.

Williams, Clifford J. *Decades of Service: A History of the Ontario Ministry of Community and Social Services, 1930–80*. Ontario: Ministry of Community and Social Services, 1984.

Willis, Paul. 'Shop Floor Culture, Masculinity and the Wage Form.' In John Clarke, Chas. Critcher, and Richard Johnson, eds., *Working Class Culture: Studies in History and Theory*, 185–98. New York: St Martin's Press, 1979.

Willrich, Michael. 'Home Slackers: Men, the State, and Welfare in Modern America.' *Journal of American History* 87/4 (2000): 460–89.

Woollacott, Angela. *To Try Her Fortune in London: Australian Women, Colonialism, and Modernity*. New York: Oxford University Press, 2001.

Young, Walter. *Anatomy of a Party: The National CCF, 1932–6*. Toronto: University of Toronto Press, 1969.

Index

abortion, 103–5
activism: CCF, 149–50, 169; communist, 149–50, 169; motherhood and, 12–13, 166–8, 170
agency (individual), 10–11, 17, 18, 20, 117
agitprop, 72
alcohol: and family conflict, 131–2, 143–4; family court, responses to, 17, 20, 117, 134–5; material consequences of, 129, 131–2, 142; and unemployment, 132–4
Alexander, Sally, 64
Anglo-Celtic identity. *See* Britishness
anti-communism, 176, 181
anti-immigrant sentiment, 180–1

bailiffs, 122, 123, 124, 127, 127. *See also* eviction; eviction protest
Baillargeon, Denyse, 8, 25, 35, 37, 132, 233n120
Bakke, E. Wight, 92, 130, 215n30, 231n75
Bennett, R.B., 5, 40, 60, 124, 151, 163, 169, 179
Berton, Pierre, 79
black market economy, 89
Bliss, Michael, and L.M. Grayson, 151

boarders: and children's labour, 94–5; and relief regulations, 68–9; and violence, 38–9; as women's work, 37–9
Brantford, 33, 118
bread, 29, 32, 128, 154, 158
breadwinner. *See* family wage; masculinity; fatherhood; relief; unemployed associations; unemployment; work, and married men's status
Britishness, 8, 13, 152, 187, 199n56, 245n169; and Canadian identity, 13; and maternalism, 166. *See also* eviction protest; respectability
Broadfoot, Barry, 60, 79
Brookner, Bertram, 72
budgeting. *See* domestic labour, budgeting

Campbell Report, 33–4, 206n62, 239n53
Canadian Council on Child and Family Welfare, 15, 52, 142. *See also* Whitton, Charlotte
Canadian Labour Defense League, 157
Canadian Youth Commission, 90, 131, 223n30, 231n72

case files, 101n19. *See also* family
   courts, and case records
Cassidy, Harry, 4–5, 32, 33, 34, 118,
   142, 190n11
Chambers, Lori, 105, 226n109
charivari, 127, 157. *See also* eviction
   protest
Chatelaine, 41, 203n18
children: and coal theft, 85–8;
   eviction, impact on, 123–4;
   institutional care, placement
   in,142–3; and petty theft, 88–9,
   223n16; and schooling, 85, 90,
   223n30, 224n51, 224n52; theories
   of delinquency, 88; and work
   permits, 94. *See also* boarders;
   family economy; Parents'
   Maintenance Act
Children of Unmarried Parents Act,
   15, 47–8, 54, 55, 62, 93, 105, 141;
   and economic support, inadequacy of, 112–15, 226n109; and
   breadwinners, 108–11; and
   women's sexual character, 105–7
Children's Aid Society, 15, 47–8, 54,
   55, 62, 93, 112, 141
children's participation, in unemployed associations, 173–4,
   244n137
Christie, Nancy, 63, 85
Chunn, Dorothy, 81
citizenship, 197n39; and ethnicity,
   13, 179; and gender, 6, 11–13; and
   respectability, 7; and social
   citizenship, 8, 11–12; and social
   welfare, 6, 152, 182–3, 186–7;
   and taxation, 120, 228n12. *See
   also* Britishness
class: family courts and, 16–17, 21;
   relief and, 190n11; struggle, 176–7;
   unemployement and, 4

clothing, lack of, 28, 34, 41, 75, 77, 95,
   132, 138, 152, 154, 155, 166, 168.
   See also domestic labour; shoes
coal theft, 85–8
Comacchio, Cynthia, 11, 21, 85, 101
Communist Party, 13, 69, 74, 79, 80,
   149, 170, 175, 176, 177, 180;
   agitators, seen as, 14, 176, 235n6;
   and Tim Buck, 76; and
   unemployed activism, 149–50, 169
consumerism, 208n105, 208n107,
   227n128; and women, 40–1, 55
Co-operative Commonwealth
   Federation (CCF), 13, 170, 175,
   180; and unemployed activism,
   149–50, 169
Criminal Code (Section 98), 72
Croll, David, 63, 157, 172; and relief
   school, 215n37; and relief strikes
   of 1936, 238n43
Currie, Sir Arthur, 161–2

Dennis, Lloyd, 123, 138
deportation, 14, 71, 179–80, 183
Deserted Wives' and Children's
   Maintenance Act, 15, 135
desertion, 49, 51, 117, 136, 147, 152;
   as male crime, 55; and male unemployment, 80–1. *See also* motherhood, and desertion of family
domestic labour, 25–36, 184–5;
   budgeting, 39–42, 231n72;
   budgeting conflicts, 129–30; and
   children's appreciation of, 26,
   203n10; emotional labour, 26–7, 40;
   food preparation, 27–8, 29–30,
   204n33, 205n54; making do, 19, 25;
   and men, 66, 217n54; sewing, 34–6.
   See also boarders; family economy
domestic relations courts, 15. *See also*
   family courts

domestic violence, 136, 137–8; and
family courts, 143–4, 146–7; and
poverty, 144–5. *See also* alcohol
Dominion Command of the Royal
Canadian Legion. *See* veterans

East York Workers' Association,
126–7, 158, 174–5, 177, 244n137
ethnic background: and citizenship,
13, 179; and family courts, 201n68;
and relief, 69–71; of members of
unemployed associations, 175–6,
244n147. *See also* anti-immigrant
sentiment; Britishness; immigration
effigy, 127. *See also* eviction protest
eligibility: for Mothers' Allowance,
49–50; the principle of less, 4, 9,
34, 190n10, 195n26
emotional labour, 26–7, 40
entitlement: men's, to work, 71–2;
Mothers' Allowance as, 52–3, 54;
veterans and economic, 150; and
the welfare state, 9, 11
Etobicoke, 127, 157
eviction: fears of, 121–2; impact of,
122–4
eviction protest, 126; tactics, 126–7;
and Britishness, 127; and violence,
127–8
extended families: as economic
support, 139–40, 143, 233n120; and
conflict, 140

Fahrni, Magda, 10
family courts: and agency of clients,
17, 20, 117; and case records, 15–17;
children's theft, responses to, 86–
9; and class, 16–17, 21; and
desertion, 80–1; and ethnicity,
201n68; and expert intervention,
16–17, 20, 117; and probation

officers, 15, 17; and social control,
16; social workers, 15; and
unemployment, 7. *See also*
alcohol, and family courts; case
files; domestic labour, budgeting
conflicts; domestic relations
courts; domestic violence, and
family courts; family economy,
conflicts in court
family economy, 19, 20; and
children's labour, 20, 84–5, 90–2,
95–6; and child-parent conflict,
91–2; and family courts, 92–6; and
family strategies debate, 24–5; and
girls' domestic labour, 94–5; and
women's labour, 23–4; and men's
informal labour, 66–7, 217n55. *See
also* children, domestic labour;
domestic labour; Parents'
Maintenance Act
family wage, 21, 43, 76, 210 n142,
236n15, 237n24; as masculine
right, 59, 153; and maternalism,
166–8. *See also* masculinity
farmers, 4; and foreclosure, 123–6
Farmers' Credit Arrangement Act,
191n19, 124
fatherhood: ideals of, 75–6, 219n93,
237n19. *See also* masculinity
Fathers' Association, 156
feminist models, 9–12, 200n65,
212n171
food preparation, 27–8, 29–30, 204n33,
205n54. *See also* malnourishment;
relief diets
foreclosure. *See* eviction; farmers,
and foreclosure
Forestall, Nancy, 129
Fort William, 30, 34, 73, 118, 119, 173
Foucault, Michel, 16
Fraser, Nancy, 11

Garcia, Eva, 67
gardening, 30–1, 37, 205n48
Gardiner, Michael, 19
gender: crisis, 6, 59, 213n9, 247n1; and
    citizenship, 6, 11–13; ideals, 83,
    187–8, 222n140; regulation, 19, 81–3
girls' domestic labour, 94–5
Gordon, Linda, 11, 131, 145, 244n144
gossip, 61. *See also* relief, and public
    surveillance
Gould, Deborah, 152
Great Depression: economic crisis, 3;
    gender crisis, 6, 59, 213n9, 247n1;
    and historiography, 7–8, 184

Hamilton, 15, 62, 93–4, 127, 172
Henry, G.F., 7, 21, 33, 58, 151; and
    farmers, 125–6; and Mortgagers
    and Purchasers Relief Act, 119
Hepburn, M.H., 7, 21, 58, 151, 168
historiography, 7–8, 9–11, 184
Hobbs, Margaret, 8, 43, 59, 191n18,
    215n36
Home Improvement Plan, 41
Horn, Michiel, 195n27
housing: and homeownership,
    118–21, 228n6, 228n18; and
    respectability, 116, 121–2, 129.
    See also citizenship; eviction;
    farmers, and foreclosure; G.F.
    Henry; Mortgagers and
    Purchasers Relief Act
Hyndman Report, 163, 240n66

illegitimacy rates, 102, 226n89.
    See also unemployment, and
    unplanned pregnancies
immigrants: and anti-communist
    rhetoric, 176, 181; and blame
    for unemployment, 76; and

deportation, 14, 71, 179–80, 183;
    as outsiders, 14. *See also* anti-
    immigrant sentiment
Immigration, Department of, 179
Industrial Standards Act, 76
Innis, Mary Quayle, 72, 121
institutional care, placement of
    children in, 142–3

Kessler-Harris, Alice, 43
King, Mackenzie, 41; and
    unemployment policy, 5
Kitchener, 33, 154, 155
Klee, Marcus, 76, 201n68, 242n99

Labour, Department of, 45, 58, 94;
    and Strikes and Lockout files, 154,
    235n7
labour movement, 149, 235n2
Lakeview, 157, 172, 174
letters to politicians, 7, 58, 60, 61,
    124,177, 236n9; as political acts, 10,
    21–2, 151, 159, 166, 168, 175
liberalism, and the welfare state, 9,
    11–12, 22
Little, Margaret, 10, 53, 85
living wage. *See* family wage
lodgers. *See* boarders
London, 67, 77
Longbranch, 155, 157–8, 168
Love, Frank, 72, 160, 169
Loyalist, United Empire, 14, 178

McLaren, Angus, 103
making do, 19, 25
malnourishment, 28, 31, 113
Manley, John, 150, 177, 243n113,
    244n157
marriage: and fears over premarital
    sex, 101–2; and household conflict,

129–39; rates and youth unemployment, 100–1

Marsh, Leonard, 63, 96

Marshall, Dominique, 10, 18

Marshall, T.H., 11, 12. *See also* citizenship, social citizenship

masculinity: and breadwinner protest, 73–4, 76–8, 82–3; breadwinner status, 58, 59–60, 83, 115, 218n83; and citizenship, 57–8, 83; ideals of, 58; and riding the rods, 79; and unemployment, 19–20, 185–6. *See also* family wage; relief, and male shame

maternalism, 198n47. *See also* motherhood; Mothers' Association

May, Elaine Tyler, 218n83

militant mothers. See motherhood, and activism

Mimico, 155, 157

minimum wage legislation: and women, 45–6, 210nn139, 140; and men, 76–7

moral economy, 166

moral regulation: and family courts, 16

Mortgagers and Purchasers Relief Act, 119

Morton, Desmond, and Richard Wright, 162

Morton, Suzanne, 121

motherhood: and activism, 13, 166–8, 170; and desertion of family, 54–5; and glorification of, 41, 56; and single mothers, 49–59, 211n157. *See also* Mothers' Allowance Act; Mothers' Association

Mothers' Allowance Act: and children's contributions to, 50–1;

and desertion, 51; eligibility, 49–50; as entitlement, 52–3, 54; and investigators, 51–2; and respectability, 53–4

Mothers' Association, 156, 170

National Council of Unemployed Committees, 169, 175, 235n4

National Employment Commission, 41, 118, 228n6

National Unemployed Workers' Association, 80, 150

non-support. See Deserted Wives' and Children's Maintenance Act; relief, and female dependence

North Bay, 30–1, 32, 35, 74, 91

Old Age Pensions, 96, 100

Ontario: northern, 7, 66, 81, 221n129; policy on married women's work, 44; relief policy, 33–4; rural, 7, 66, 91, 92

Ontario Command of the Royal Canadian Legion. *See* veterans

Orloff, Ann Shola, 19

Oshawa, 63, 118, 154, 156, 170, 171, 172, 180

Ottawa, 15, 31–2, 33, 51; relief administration, 63

Palmer, Bryan, 150, 227n128

Parents' Maintenance Act, 20; implementation of, 96; and Old Age Pensions, 96, 100; and parent-child conflict, 98–100; and relief regulations, 97–8

Parr, Joy, 213n6, 233n120

petty theft, by children, 88–9, 223n16

pin money, 42–3, 44

poverty, 144–5; and prostitution,
46–8. *See also* eviction; foreclosure;
malnutrition
probation officers. *See* family courts,
and probation officers
Port Arthur, 155, 181
pregnancy. *See* Children of Unmarried
Parents Act; illegitimacy rates;
unemployment, and unplanned
pregnancies
Probyn, Elspeth, 138
prostitution, 219n88; and poverty,
46–8; and vice, 48–9
public works, 5, 153
Public Works, Department of, 74

relief: administration of, 63, 215n31;
and *Campbell Report*, 33–4, 206n62,
239n53; and class, 190n11; diets,
31–4; and direct relief, 5, 153;
and ethnicity, 69–71; and female
dependence, 5, 135–7; fraud,
67–71; and less eligibility, the
principle of, 4, 9, 34, 190n10,
195n26; and male shame, 61–3,
138–9; and public surveillance,
62, 214n23, 215n26, 215n30; and
public works, 5, 153; rates by
region, 190n8; and refusal to apply
for, 137; spending conflicts, 130–1;
and work tests, 154; and violence
towards officials, 69–71
Relief Acts, 5
relief strikes, 154–6. *See also*
unemployed associations
relief worker unions. *See* labour
movement; unemployed
associations
reserves: and relief administration,
70–1

respectability, 9, 21, 147, 151; and
Britishness, 179; and men, 31, 59,
83, 153; and sexual character, 105;
and veterans, 162, 182; and
women, 23, 46, 53, 54, 107, 174. *See
also* housing, and respectability
revolution, 78, 182
Reynolds, Mary, 160
riding the rods, 79
Roediger, David, 177
Ross, Ellen, 131, 203n10, 223n16
Royal Canadian Legion, 7, 22
Rutherdale, Robert, 218n83, 237n19
Ryan, Oscar, 72

Sandwell, Ruth, 90
Sangster, Joan, 13, 16, 31, 36, 106,
185, 201n68, 202n6, 236n16
scavenging, 66
school strike, 174, 244n137
sewing, 34–6
sex, fears over premarital, 101–2;
illegitimacy, 102, 226n89;
prostitution, 46–8, 48–9, 219n88;
unplanned pregnancies, 102–3
sexual assault, 47. *See also* boarders,
and violence
sexual barter, 47
sexual character, women's, 105–7
shame. *See* unemployment, and
male shame; relief, and male
shame
sheriffs. *See* bailiffs
shoes, lack of, 41, 42, 75, 141, 155
single mothers, 49–59, 211n157
Skocpol, Theda, 239n57
Srigley, Katrina, 209n123, 210n142
Stevens, H.H., 40
Struthers, James, 10, 195n26
Sudbury, 34, 61, 173, 176, 181, 190n8

suicide, and unemployment, 65–6, 216n47, 216n49, 216–17n52
surveillance, public, 62, 214n23, 215n26, 215n30
survival strategies: of families, 6–7; and separation of families, 141–2. *See also* extended families
Sutherland, Neil, 84, 231n72

theories of delinquency, 88
Tillotson, Shirley, 10, 228n12
Tilly, Louise, 24
Timmins, 62, 63, 66, 81, 129, 176, 190n8
Tomes, Nancy, 143
Toronto, 15, 32, 33, 37, 68, 76, 78, 102, 124, 142, 155, 156, 170; and suburbs, 157, 172
truancy. *See* children, and schooling

unemployed associations, 235n4; and breadwinner protest, 152–3; 156; Britishness, 177–9; and children's participation, 173–4, 244n137; and class struggle, 176–7; and concessions won, 158, 239n49; East York Workers' Association, 126–7, 158, 174–5, 177, 244n137; and ethnic background of members, 175–6, 244n147; politics of, 175, 244n157; and relief strikes, 154–6; and social welfare policy, 159; and violence, 157–8, 172; and women's participation, 168–73
unemployment: and breadwinner status, 19–20; and class, 4; and farmers, 4; and fear of, 5, 19; and images of men, 57; and the labour movement, 149, 235n2; and male shame, 58, 60–1, 64–6,

152; in Ontario, 4–5; rates, 3–4; and statistics on women, 45; and statistics on youth, 222n6; and suicide, 65–6, 216n47, 216n49, 216–7n52; and unplanned pregnancies, 102–3

veterans: and anti-communism, 181; and anti-immigrant sentiment, 180–1; and compensation for war service, 160–2; and economic entitlement, 159; and homeownership, 120; and *Hyndman Report*, 163, 240n66; and Royal Canadian Legion, 7, 22; and masculinity, 163–5; and relief, 163; social welfare, support for, 150–1, 159–60, 165, 181–2, 186, 239n55, 246n190; and unemployment, 161–2; and war bonus, 161–2, 240n69. *See also* respectability, and veterans; War Veterans' Allowance Act
violence, 38–9, 69–71, 127–8, 136, 137–8, 157–8, 172
Visiting Housewives Association, 32, 34

War Veterans' Allowance Act, 163–4, 165, 241n85
welfare state: and agency, 10–11, 18; and entitlement, 9, 11; and familial needs, 18; and feminist models of, 9–12, 200n65, 212n171; and gender ideals, 83, 187–8, 222n140; and gender regulation, 10, 81–3; historiography, 9–11; less eligibility, principle of, 9; and liberalism, 9, 11–12, 22; and maternal activism, 12–13

Whitton, Charlotte, 15, 52
Wilkinson, Mrs William, 169–70
Windsor, 33, 165, 175, 181
women's paid labour, 42–6, 207n80
women's participation, in unem-
    ployed associations,168–73.
    See also activism
work: children's employment, 37;
    and criticisms of married women,
    43–5, 56; and married men's
    status, 73–5; and men's
    entitlement to, 71–2; women's
    informal labour, 36–9, 207–8n100;

women's paid labour, 42–6,
    207n80. *See also* boarders;
    domestic labour; prostitution
work permits, for children, 94
work tests, and relief, 154
Workers' Economic Conference, 169,
    243n113
Workers' Unity League, 150, 175

Young Men's Christian Association,
    100, 101
youth unemployment, and marriage
    rates, 100–1

STUDIES IN GENDER AND HISTORY

General editors: Franca Iacovetta and Karen Dubinsky

 1 Suzanne Morton, *Ideal Surroundings: Domestic Life in a Working-Class Suburb in the 1920s*
 2 Joan Sangster, *Earning Respect: The Lives of Working Women in Small-Town Ontario, 1920–1960*
 3 Carolyn Strange, *Toronto's Girl Problem: The Perils and Pleasures of the City, 1880–1930*
 4 Sara Z. Burke, *Seeking the Highest Good: Social Service and Gender at the University of Toronto, 1888–1937*
 5 Lynne Marks, *Revivals and Roller Rinks: Religion, Leisure, and Identity in Late-Nineteenth-Century Small-Town Ontario*
 6 Cecilia Morgan, *Public Men and Virtuous Women: The Gendered Languages of Religion and Politics in Upper Canada, 1791–1850*
 7 Mary Louise Adams, *The Trouble with Normal: Postwar Youth and the Making of Heterosexuality*
 8 Linda Kealey, *Enlisting Women for the Cause: Women, Labour, and the Left in Canada, 1890–1920*
 9 Christina Burr, *Spreading the Light: Work and Labour Reform in Late-Nineteenth-Century Toronto*
10 Mona Gleason, *Normalizing the Ideal: Psychology, Schooling, and the Family in Postwar Canada*
11 Deborah Gorham, *Vera Brittain: A Feminist Life*
12 Marlene Epp, *Women without Men: Mennonite Refugees of the Second World War*
13 Shirley Tillotson, *The Public at Play: Gender and the Politics of Recreation in Postwar Ontario*
14 Veronica Strong-Boag and Carole Gerson, *Paddling Her Own Canoe: The Times and Texts of E. Pauline Johnson (Tekahionwake)*
15 Stephen Heathorn, *For Home, Country, and Race: Constructing Gender, Class, and Englishness in the Elementary School, 1880–1914*
16 Valerie J. Korinek, *Roughing It in the Suburbs: Reading Chatelaine Magazine in the Fifties and Sixties*
17 Adele Perry, *On the Edge of Empire: Gender, Race, and the Making of British Columbia, 1849–1871*

18 Robert A. Campbell, *Sit Down and Drink Your Beer: Regulating Vancouver's Beer Parlours, 1925–1954*

19 Wendy Mitchinson, *Giving Birth in Canada, 1900–1950*

20 Roberta Hamilton, *Setting the Agenda: Jean Royce and the Shaping of Queen's University*

21 Donna Gabaccia and Franca Iacovetta, eds., *Women, Gender, and Transnational Lives: Italian Workers of the World*

22 Linda Reeder, *Widows in White: Migration and the Transformation of Rural Women, Sicily, 1880–1920*

23 Terry Crowley, *Marriage of Minds: Isabel and Oscar Skelton Re-inventing Canada*

24 Marlene Epp, Franca Iacovetta, and Frances Swyripa, eds., *Sisters or Strangers? Immigrant, Ethnic, and Racialized Women in Canadian History*

25 John G. Reid, *Viola Florence Barnes, 1885–1979: A Historian's Biography*

26 Catherine Carstairs, *Jailed for Possession: Illegal Drug Use Regulation and Power in Canada, 1920–1961*

27 Magda Fahrni, *Household Politics: Montreal Families and Postwar Reconstruction*

28 Tamara Myers, *Caught: Montreal Girls and the Law, 1869–1945*

29 Jennifer A. Stephen, *Pick One Intelligent Girl: Employability, Domesticity, and the Gendering of Canada's Welfare State, 1939–1947*

30 Lisa Chilton, *Agents of Empire: British Female Migration to Canada and Australia, 1860s–1930*

31 Esyllt W. Jones, *Influenza 1918: Disease, Death, and Struggle in Winnipeg*

32 Elise Chenier, *Strangers in Our Midst: Sexual Deviancy in Postwar Ontario*

33 Lara Campbell, *Respectable Citizens:Gender, Family, and Unemployment in the Great Depression, Ontario, 1929–1939*